This is a highly significant an
American Presbyterian Missic
genuinely independent and sel

weaknesses and limitations of tne approacnes or tne missionaries are laid bare, there is plenty of evidence that solid foundations were laid which have enabled the evangelical church to become a genuinely mission-minded church.

The two extended case studies are particularly timely and relevant. At a time when Christians in the Middle East face such a serious threat from some expressions of radical Islam, the attempt to assess the different approaches of the missionaries to Muslims and Islam and to Muslim evangelism is especially appropriate today. And the case study on the Sudan demonstrates how the national church has resisted the temptation to think only in terms of dependency and survival, and generated its own missionary outreach in a neighbouring country. The foundations laid by generations of American missionaries in the past are being severely tested by all the challenges facing Egyptian and Arab Christians at the present time.

Colin Chapman
Former lecturer in Islamic Studies, Near East School of Theology, Beirut
Visiting lecturer, Arab Baptist Theological Seminary, Beirut, Lebanon

Tharwat Wahba's *The Practice of Mission* is exactly what is needed in the field of missiology. It is a clearly written investigation into the modern history of missions in Egypt and the Sudan, a study firmly grounded in painstaking archival research. The result is an invaluable and illuminating perspective on the modern formation of Arabic-speaking Protestant communities in the Middle East.

Stephen J. Davis
Pierson College, Department of Religious Studies, Yale University, New Haven, USA

Tharwat Wahba's study, *The Practice of Mission in Egypt*, is a significant contribution to the history of nineteenth- and twentieth-century Christian missions in Egypt. It focuses on the work of the American Presbyterian Mission among the Egyptian Copts beginning in 1854, the establishment of the Evangelical Church of Egypt, and subsequent church-mission relations up to the final separation between church and mission in 1970. The author also examines the church's engagement in mission in Sudan in partnership with the American Presbyterian Mission, which led to the founding of the Sudanese Presbyterian Church. Dr Wahba is an Egyptian scholar and this work is based on extensive and thorough research into primary sources. It makes a substantial contribution to our understanding both of western missions in Egypt and Sudan and of the Evangelical Church of Egypt, and deserves to be more widely known.

Keith Ferdinando
Former lecturer in Missiology, London School of Theology
Director of Postgraduate Studies, Shalom University of Bunia, DRC

This is a significant historical critique of both Western mission efforts to Egypt and pioneering Egyptian indigenous mission efforts in the modern era. Dr Wahba provides a timely warning for how the church can be negatively impacted for decades by failing to seize opportunities, but it is also an inspiring call to emulate the faith of Egyptian pioneers who modeled courageous faith in the face of difficulties and opposition. This is a book with lessons to be learned for this current season of change.

Keith Small
Honorary Fellow, Bodleian Libraries, Oxford University, UK

With a special concern for evangelism, Professor Wahba examines the understanding and practice of mission exercised by the Evangelical Church of Egypt between 1854–1970. Foreign missionary contributions to this history receive their due, but the emphasis here is on the development of an indigenous Egyptian perspective on mission as actually practiced in this particular Muslim majority context. Mission initiatives from Egypt to the Sudan and efforts at outreach to Muslims in Egypt are highlighted in the text. No previous study of this mission history has made such extensive use of Evangelical Church of Egypt primary materials. Interview transcripts add to the rich documentation made available in this welcome study of mission theology and practice.

Stanley H. Skreslet
F. S. Royster Professor of Christian Missions,
Union Presbyterian Seminary, Richmond, USA

This work by Dr Wahba is significant for several reasons. First, it contributes to mission history through its tracing of the work of the American Presbyterian Mission in Egypt, leading to the establishment of the Egyptian church. Second, it records a mission multiplication effect, with the American mission laying the groundwork in Sudan, later carried forward by the Egyptian church. Moreover, this study also demonstrates the important principle of handover, with the American Mission withdrawing once the Egyptian church was self-sufficient. Dr Wahba's analysis is rigorous, compelling, and accessible. It represents an important contribution to mission studies and the history of the worldwide church.

Peter G. Riddel
Vice Principal (Academic), Melbourne School of Theology, Australia
Professorial Research Associate, History, SOAS, University of London, UK

The Practice of Mission in Egypt

A Historical Study of the Integration between the
American Mission and the Evangelical Church of Egypt,
1854–1970

Tharwat Wahba

Langham

MONOGRAPHS

Published 2016 by Langham Monographs
an imprint of Langham Creative Projects

Langham Partnership
PO Box 296, Carlisle, Cumbria CA3 9WZ, UK
www.langham.org

ISBNs:
978-1-78368-103-7 Print
978-1-78368-131-0 Mobi
978-1-78368-130-3 ePub
978-1-78368-132-7 PDF

British Library Cataloguing in Publication Data
A catalogue record for this book is available from the British Library

ISBN: 978-1-78368-103-7

Cover & Book Design: projectluz.com

Contents

Abstract...xiii

Acknowledgments xv

Abbreviations xvii

Introduction... 1

Chapter 1 7
The Arrival of the American Mission in Egypt and the
Establishment of the Evangelical Church
   1.1 Introduction 7
   1.2 Egypt in the Mid-Nineteenth Century.......................................8
   1.3 The Origins and Early Work of the American Mission in Egypt 13
      1.3.1 Origins 13
      1.3.2 Reasons for the Coming of the American Presbyterian
            Mission to Egypt..15
      1.3.3 The Pioneer Missionaries of the American Mission
            in Egypt...18
      1.3.4 The Methodologies Used by the Mission in Egypt 20
      1.3.5 Challenges and Difficulties 24
      1.3.6 The Role of the Egyptians in the Ministry of the
            American Mission 27
      1.3.7 Mission after Fifty Years...30
   1.4 The Mission Work in Egypt before the American Mission
      and the Establishment of New Denominations 31
      1.4.1 The Church in Egypt before the Presbyterian Church:
            Major Denominations and Groups 31
      1.4.2 Early Roman Catholic Missions.......................................33
      1.4.3 Western Missions and Establishing an
            Indigenous Church 35
   1.5 The Establishment of the Egyptian Presbyterian Church............39
      1.5.1 Reasons for Establishing an Evangelical Church...............40
      1.5.2 Important Steps in the Establishment and
            Organization of the Church 42
      1.5.3 Different Opinions 44
      1.5.4 The Relationship with the Government 46

1.5.5 Theological Training 47
1.5.6 The Evangelical Church's Early Contributions to
       Egyptian Society 48
1.6 Conclusion 49

Chapter 2 51
The Relationship between the American Mission and the
Evangelical Church in Egypt (1854–1958)
    2.1 Introduction 51
    2.2 The Relationship in the Early Period (1854–1904) 52
        2.2.1 The Mission in Control of Everything until 1871 52
        2.2.2 The Establishment of the Mission Association, 1871 54
        2.2.3 The Development of the Relationship after the
              Establishment of the Mission Association and the
              Egyptian Presbytery..56
        2.2.4 Training of Egyptian Leaders 58
        2.2.5 Finances...60
    2.3 The Relationship in the Second Period: Steps towards
        Independence (1905–1926) 64
        2.3.1 Synod Assumes a Share in Self-Support, 1908 65
        2.3.2 The Seminary..68
        2.3.3 The Synod Declares Itself Self-Governing, 1926 71
    2.4 The Relationship between 1926–1958 74
        2.4.1 Financial Difficulties and Reductions......................74
        2.4.2 Relationships with the Government.........................76
        2.4.3 Synod Representatives in Mission Meetings.................77
        2.4.4 The Mission Evaluates Its Policy 78
        2.4.5 Board of Administration for Synod........................81
        2.4.6 Church Independence, 1958 82
    2.5 Conclusion 84

Chapter 3 87
The Interaction between the American Mission and
Evangelical Church in Muslim Evangelism
    3.1 Introduction 87
    3.2 The American Mission and Its Ministry to Muslims..................88
        3.2.1 The Mission's Methods of Reaching Muslims..................88
        3.2.2 Experiences and Nature of Muslim Evangelism.............99
    3.3 The Evangelical Church and Muslim Evangelism 102
        3.3.1 The Beginning of the Synod Work among Muslims........102
        3.3.2 The Synod's Methods in the Work among Muslims 104

3.3.3 The Role of American Mission with the
    Evangelical Church in Muslim Evangelism.............................108
3.3.4 The Synod Workers among Muslims................................110
3.4 Reasons for the Lack in Converts' Numbers.........................114
    3.4.1 External Reasons...114
    3.4.2 Internal Reasons in the Mission 121
    3.4.3 Internal Reasons in the Church 126
3.5 Conclusion 134

Chapter 4 137
The Beginning of the American Mission and Evangelical
Church Mission Work in Sudan
    4.1 Introduction 137
    4.2 Sudan at the End of the Nineteenth Century.....................138
    4.3 The American Mission Explores the Sudanese Field 141
        4.3.1 Early Efforts...141
        4.3.2 Exploring Northern Sudan 143
        4.3.3 Exploring Southern Sudan...146
    4.4 The Beginning of the American Mission Work in
    Southern Sudan (1901–1912) 148
        4.4.1 The Beginning 148
        4.4.2 Methods of Ministry...150
    4.5 The Beginning of the Work of the Evangelical Church in
    Sudan (1900–1909) 157
        4.5.1 The Evangelical Church Takes Its First Step in
        Mission Work in Sudan..158
        4.5.2 Gabra Hanna and the First Efforts in Khartoum............159
        4.5.3 Gabra Hanna: A Missionary and Pastor 161
    4.6 The Beginning of the American Mission Work in
    Northern Sudan (1903–1912)..166
    4.7 The Evangelical Church in Egypt's Response to the
    Work in Sudan 171
    4.8 Conclusion 174

Chapter 5 175
The Development of the Ministry of the Egyptian Evangelical
Church to Sudan (1909–1964)
    5.1 Introduction 175
    5.2 Abofarag – a Pastor with a Missionary Heart.....................176
    5.3 Organizing the Work in Sudan 179

5.3.1 The Establishment of the Sudan Presbytery:
    Was It a Solution or a New Problem? 179
5.3.2 The Relationship between the Synod and the American
    Mission in Northern Sudan 1900–1956............................182
5.3.3 The Role of the Committee for the Work in Sudan........186
5.4 The Characteristics of the Work in Sudan 1912–1956 189
    5.4.1 Ministers and Ministry Expansions...............................189
    5.4.2 Schools and Women's Ministry 190
    5.4.3 Political Situation 191
    5.4.4 Work among Sudanese..192
    5.4.5 Visitors from Egypt...193
5.5 The Role of Egyptian Laymen and Women in Mission
    Work in Sudan 193
    5.5.1 Farouza Girgis...194
    5.5.2 Garas Khella 196
    5.5.3 Teachers and Workers with the American Mission 197
5.6 Mission-Oriented Pastors...198
    5.6.1 Tobia Abdelmasih 199
    5.6.2 Bolies Ref'at 201
    5.6.3 William Mos'ad 203
5.7 The Characteristics of the Work in Sudan 1956–1964 205
    5.7.1 Ministry to Southerners in Northern Sudan....................206
    5.7.2 The Separation of the Sudan Presbytery from the
    Synod of the Nile 1956–1964 206
5.8 Why Was It Difficult to Have Mission Work in Sudan? 209
5.9 Conclusion 213

Chapter 6 215
The First Egyptian Missionary to Southern Sudan and Kenya:
Swailem Sidhom Hennein (1953–1970)
    6.1 Introduction 215
    6.2 The Church Preparation...216
    6.3 The Missionary Preparation 219
    6.4 First Year in Southern Sudan 223
    6.5 The Role of the American Mission with the Egyptian
    Mission in Southern Sudan 225
    6.6 Swailem's Ministry in Attar 227
    6.6.1 Evangelism and Baptism 227
    6.6.2 Church Planting and Organization................................230
    6.6.3 Schools 231
    6.6.4 Social Work 233

6.7 The Significance of Swailem's Appointment and Work 234
  6.7.1 The Influence of Mission Work in Sudan on the
     Evangelical Church in Egypt 234
  6.7.2 The Establishment of the Egyptian Mission Council 236
6.8 The End of Swailem's Mission to Sudan 236
6.9 Swailem's Mission in Kenya 240
6.10 The End of an Era 244
6.11 Conclusion 245

Chapter 7 249
The Development of the Relationship between the American
Mission and the Egyptian Evangelical Church 1958–1970
  7.1 Introduction 249
  7.2 The Influence of Political Developments upon the
    Relationship between the Evangelical Church and the
    American Mission 250
  7.3 Changes in Theology and Relationships 253
     7.3.1 The Mohonk Consultation 253
     7.3.2 The Asmara Conference 254
     7.3.3 An Advisory Study 255
     7.3.4 Egyptian Response to Theological Changes 256
  7.4 The Integration between the Synod and the Mission 258
     7.4.1 Steps towards Integration 259
     7.4.2 The Dissolution of the American Mission in 1966 261
     7.4.3 The American Mission Departure in 1967 262
  7.5 The Characteristics of the Practice of Mission in the
    Evangelical Church of Egypt 1958–1970 264
     7.5.1 Administration and Finances 264
     7.5.2 Ministry Approaches and Opportunities 266
     7.5.3 Understanding and Practice of Evangelism 271
     7.5.4 Mission Opportunities 274
  7.6 Conclusion 279

Chapter 8 281
Conclusions and Contributions
  8.1 Conclusions 281
     8.1.1 Politics 281
     8.1.2 The Relationship between the Church and the Mission 283
     8.1.3 The American Mission and the Synod Interactions in
      Mission and Evangelism 284

8.1.4 Egyptian Understanding and Practice of Mission and
    Evangelism 286
8.2 Contributions 288
    8.2.1 Egyptian View of the Relationship between the American
        Mission and the Egyptian Church 288
    8.2.2 Egyptian Contribution to Mission Work 288
    8.2.3 The Influence of the American Church's Changing
        Mission Theology as Experienced in Egypt...........................289

Appendix A 291
*Constitution of the Egyptian Association of the Missionaries
of the United Presbyterian Church of North America*

Appendix B 293
*Constitution and By-laws of the American Mission in Egypt,
UAR of the United Presbyterian Church in the USA, 1966*

Appendix C.. 301
An Interview with Swailem Sedhom Hennein, Cairo, 5 March 2004

Appendix D 337
Interview with Bakheet Matta, Alexandria, 3 March 2004

Bibliography... 351
    I. Primary Sources..351
    II. Secondary Sources...354

Abstract

This thesis is a historical study of the interaction between the American Presbyterian Mission and the Evangelical Church in Egypt from its beginning in 1854 until after the departure of the American Mission from the Egyptian field, and the transfer of all its ministries to the Egyptian Church. Chapter 1 examines the coming of the American Presbyterian Mission to Egypt and the circumstances, events and efforts which led to the establishment of the Egyptian Evangelical Church.

Chapter 2 examines the official relationship between the Mission and the Church including the steps taken towards full independence of the Egyptian Church from the American Presbyterian Church. Chapter 3 describes the work of both the Mission and the Egyptian Synod among Muslims in Egypt as a case study exploring their relational interactions while engaged in internal mission work.

Chapter 4 surveys the beginning of mission work in Sudan by the American Mission and the Evangelical Church. Chapter 5 examines the relationships between the Mission and the Church in the Sudanese field, focusing on the Egyptian understanding and practice of mission. Chapter 6 describes and analyzes the first Egyptian missionary to Southern Sudan and Kenya: Swailem Sidhom Hennein. Chapter 7 explores the relationship between the Mission and the Church from 1958, when the Church gained its independence, to 1970, when the Egyptian Synod declared the official end of its relationship with the American Church.

The thesis contributes to the understanding of mission work in Egypt and Sudan. Further, it analyzes the interactions of the Egyptian Church with the American Mission, and the effects this had on the practice and perspective of mission of this recently established indigenous Church in its Majority World setting.

Acknowledgments

My grateful thanks and appreciation are extended to the many people who have helped and guided me through the process of writing this thesis over the past five years.

My supervisors, Dr Keith Ferdinando, Professor Peter Riddell, and my adviser Rev Colin Chapman have given great understanding and support throughout this time.

I am also grateful to the generous contributions of Drs David Grafton, Michel Shelley, Stephen Davis, Mark Swanson, and Stan Skreslet who all served in the Evangelical Theological Seminary in Cairo and read some chapters and gave valuable advice. In addition, I am so thankful for the great help I had from Rev Dr Darren Kennedy in editing and formatting my dissertation.

I am also very grateful to Rev Dr Swailem Hennein and Rev Bakheet Matta for the interviews that they granted. This has supplied valuable original material for this study. Likewise, I am very thankful for Rev Email Zaki, the former General Secretary of the Synod of the Nile and his assistant Dr Vines Bolies for making the Minutes of the Synod available to me.

The librarians of the Presbyterian Historical Society in Philadelphia, and Dr Heather Sharkey also gave invaluable help during my research there. I also wish to thank Mrs Lisbet Diers, the Research Administrator at London School of Theology, for her consistent help. The librarians in the Evangelical Theological Seminary in Cairo (ETSC), the School of Oriental and African Studies in London, and Princeton Seminary were also of great assistance. Thanks also to Dr Jack Lorimer and Dr Scott Sunquist for making their new books available for my study.

I also extend my gratitude and thanks to my proofreaders Dr Helen Shephard, Dr Keith Small, Miss Elaine Pequegnat, and Mrs Jenny Davis.

I am so grateful for the great support I have experienced from my colleagues in ETSC, especially Rev Dr Atef Gendy the President of ETSC. I have also been the recipient of generous financial support from the Outreach Foundation, the Christian International Scholarship Foundation, the Overseas Council International, and the Presbyterian Church of the United States of America, the First Presbyterian Church in Houston, the Eastminster Presbyterian Church, and the Laing Scholarship trustees.

Finally, my grateful thanks go to my family: to my wife Ebtisam, my father and mother, and my children Lushik, Shadi, and Fadi. Their support, encouragement, and love made the completion of this thesis possible.

Abbreviations

AUC	American University in Cairo
CEOSS	Coptic Evangelical Organization of Social Services
COEMAR	Commission on Ecumenical Mission and Relations
CMS	Church Missionary Society
ETSC	Evangelical Theological Seminary in Cairo
IBMR	International Bulletin of Mission Research
NECC	Near East Council of Churches
OBMR	Occasional Bulletin of Missionary Research
PCUSA	Presbyterian Church in the United States of America
PHS	Presbyterian Historical Society
RG	Record Group
UAR	United Arab Republic
UPCUSA	United Presbyterian Church in the United States of America
UPCNA	United Presbyterian Church of North America
WCC	World Council of Churches

Introduction

Research Outline: Main Questions

Since its arrival in Egypt in 1854, the American Presbyterian Mission[1] played a key role in the life of Egyptian society in general and more specifically in the development of many missiological and ecclesiological concepts and practices in the Evangelical Church of Egypt.[2] The American Mission, representing the Presbyterian Church in the United States as the mother church, established the Evangelical Church in Egypt as its daughter church and shaped it in theology, liturgy, administration, mission, and perspective. The American missionaries were involved in every aspect of church life and directly instructed and influenced the Egyptians in the conduct of their ministry.

This research is a historical study concerning the relationship between the American Mission and the Evangelical Church in Egypt from its beginning in 1854 until after the departure of the American Mission from

---

1. The American Presbyterian Mission in Egypt was known as the American Mission. In this research the name American Mission in Egypt will be used. Often the term 'the Mission' will be used, unless other names are cited.

2. The Evangelical Church in Egypt is the popular name of the Presbyterian Church, which sometimes used the name The Coptic Evangelical Church. Synod of the Nile is the name of the administrative body of that Church. The name of the Evangelical Church in Egypt was changed many times. In its early history it had the name Protestant church. In the establishment of the first Egyptian presbytery it was called the United Presbyterian Church in Egypt, then the Presbyterian Church. After 1952 it was called the Coptic Evangelical Church, and then the Evangelical Church. In this research we will use the name Evangelical Church which refers to the church which the American Presbyterian mission established in Egypt and which became the first and the largest Protestant church in Egypt. Often the simple designation 'the Church' is used and the use of 'the Synod' means the Synod of the Nile.

the Egyptian field in 1967 when the work of the Mission was completely handed over to the Egyptian Church. Firstly, it examines the origins of the Mission and its arrival on the Egyptian field by asking the following questions: What was Egyptian society like in the middle of the nineteenth century? What were the methods that the Mission used to reach Egyptians? What were the difficulties that the Mission faced in its ministry? The study also examines the steps leading to the establishment of the Evangelical Church as a completely independent denomination. Questions to be pursued concerning this are as follows: Was there a real need to found a new denomination or were existing structures sufficient? What steps did the Mission take to establish an indigenous church as opposed to a foreign church existing on Egyptian soil? Were the Mission and the Church successful in their joint attempts to establish an independent, indigenous church with its own administration and its own institution?

All of these questions and issues lead to the major focus of this study: the role of the American Mission in initiating the missionary work of the Evangelical Church both inside and outside Egypt; and the development of the Church's view and practice of mission. The study looks at the ecclesiastical and administrative relationship between the Mission and the Evangelical Church and observes how this relationship influenced the Evangelical Church's view of mission. Using two case studies this research then analyses the missiological viewpoint and practice that the American Mission transferred to the Egyptian Church.

The first case study will look at the work of both the American Mission and the Evangelical Church among Muslims within Egypt. It will highlight the different efforts and methods that the American Mission made to evangelize Muslims. We will then explore the reasons for their lack of success and the effect of this experience on the Evangelical Church. Another issue that bears investigation is the fact that the Evangelical Church had its own committee of Muslim evangelism and its own full-time evangelist, yet the spirit and vision for this ministry never spread among its clergy and church members. This was in spite of the explicitly expressed hopes of the American Mission that the Evangelical Church was going to be God's main instrument in this ministry. This leads to another question for analysis: did

the American Mission and the Evangelical Church accomplish the evangelization of all Egypt or does it remain a great-unfinished task?

The second case study explores the interaction between the Mission
and the Evangelical Church in the mission field in Sudan since 1900. The
Mission opened the door for the Church to operate its own mission in
Sudan. This study will cover the early ministry of the American Mission in
both Southern and Northern Sudan, detailing the political and social situation affecting ministry in Sudan, and comparing this with the conditions
within Egypt. It will also examine how the Evangelical Church responded
to the call of the American Mission to work in Sudan. Between 1900 and
1964, many Egyptian ministers went to Sudan and provided crucial help
in the founding and growth of the Evangelical Church in Sudan. How the
Egyptian ministers handled the ministry in Sudan, how they attempted
to reconcile their pastoral role with missionary work, and what difficulties they faced in Sudan, will receive special attention. Further, we will
explore the role of Egyptian laymen and women in the Sudan Mission; the
relationship between the Evangelical Church in Egypt and the Church in
Sudan; and the steps that led to the eventual independence of the Sudanese
Presbyterian Church.

This research also examines the ministry of Rev Swailem Hennein, the
only official Egyptian missionary to Southern Sudan. His preparation for
this ministry, his choice of the Shilluk tribe in Southern Sudan, the methodologies, and the difficulties he faced, and his premature departure to
start another ministry in Kenya, will all be noted. Rev Swailem served an
important role as an Egyptian missionary pioneer and his life strongly influenced the hopes and vision of the Evangelical Church, which saw itself
as entering a new era of mission.

This historical study will be completed by determining the relationship between the American Mission and the Evangelical Church in the
last years of the Mission in Egypt concerning the Church's mission goal
and ministry. After their shared history of over a century, it is important to
determine if the Evangelical Church in fact attained true independence. In
exploring this aspect, we will note how the Synod of the Nile handled the
work of the American Mission after its departure from Egypt; how they
responded to opportunities to be a missionary-sending body; and what

were the administrative, theological, and financial issues which influenced the practice of mission in the Evangelical Church.

Sources

This study draws on both primary and secondary sources. The primary sources include the minutes of the American Mission in Egypt, the minutes of the American Mission in Northern Sudan and the American Mission in Southern Sudan, the minutes of the General Assembly of the United Presbyterian Church of North America, and the minutes of the Synod of the Nile. They also include the writings of American missionaries including personal letters, reports, and the denomination's newspapers both in the United States and in Egypt. Books written by missionaries and nationals in Egypt and Sudan are also considered as primary sources. Lastly, personal interviews conducted with people who participated in key events and played a historic role in the mission's work supplied important information which was unavailable from written sources. The secondary sources include books, dissertations, newspapers, and other materials relevant to the events and the history of the period which the research covers.

Methodology and Originality

This is an analytical, critical, historical study. It includes major narratives and descriptions that emphasize events that have not previously been studied. It is based on the collection of data from primary source documents and eyewitnesses. Analysis of English documents and the translation and analysis of Arabic documents support the originality of this study. The study will examine particular historical, political, missional, and ecclesiastical events and their influence upon mission work.

The research will look especially at the interaction between the American Mission and the Evangelical Church from a critical historical view. Describing and analyzing historical events will dominate the research. Although the official documents of both the Mission and the Church give few indications of criticism for the events and relationships between the two bodies, they include variety of matters that provided critical aspects that help in analyzing the subject.

Nature of the Original Contribution to Knowledge

This research will cover new areas in the study of the history of mission in Egypt that include:

1. The study of the relationship between the American Presbyterian Mission in Egypt and the Evangelical Church of Egypt.
2. The influence of the American Mission on the thinking of the Egyptian evangelicals and their view of mission work.
3. The role of the Evangelical Church of Egypt in mission work in Sudan as one of the first evangelical churches, in modern history, from the non-Western world that sent missionaries to a neighbouring country.
4. The contributions of early Egyptian missionaries at the beginning of the twentieth century and the mission work in Southern Sudan and Kenya in the 1950s and 1960s.
5. The ways that the Church in Egypt found to conduct its ministry in a predominantly Muslim political and cultural environment.
6. The research will be undertaken from an Egyptian point of view with critical analyses of the work of Western missionaries in Egypt.

Previous Relevant Studies

The history of the American Mission in Egypt is the subject of several studies including books, dissertations, and articles. The studies about the American Mission in Egypt specifically, and in the Middle East in general, cover mission history, its work in education, and related subjects, but none of them talks about the Evangelical Church and its relationship with the Mission, and its work in the indigenous and missionary fields. The main dissertations that study the American Mission in the Middle East and Egypt are:

Badr, Habib. "Mission to 'Nominal Christians': The Policy and Practice of the American Board of Commissionaires for Foreign Missions and Its Missionaries Concerning Eastern Churches, Which Led to the Organization of a Protestant Church in Beirut, 1819-1848." PhD diss., Princeton Theological Seminary, 1992.

Burke, Jeffrey Charles. "The Establishment of the American Presbyterian Mission in Egypt, 1854-1940: An Overview." PhD diss., McGill University, 2000.

Dawson, David. "Presbyterian Missionaries in the Middle East." STM thesis, Yale Divinity School, 1987.

Ghabrial, Samy Hanna. "The Growth of the Evangelical Church in Egypt, with Reference to Leadership." PhD diss., Fuller Theological Seminary, 1997.

Lodwick, Robert Clare. "The Impact of Nationalism on the Schools of American Mission in the Southern Region of the United Arab Republic." PhD diss., Columbia University, 1961.

Sproul, Christine. "The American College of Girls, Cairo Egypt: Its History and Influence on Egyptian Women: A Study of Selected Graduates." PhD diss., University of Utah, 1982.

Wahba, Tharwat. "The American Presbyterian Mission: Its Reception by the Egyptians." Unpublished MA thesis, The Evangelical Theological Seminary in Cairo, 2003.

Werff, Lyle L. Vander. *Christian Mission to Muslims: The Record: Anglican and Reformed Approaches in India and the Near East: 1800–1938*. South Pasadena: The William Carey Library, 1977.

Difficulties

The principal difficulty encountered was the lack of resources which described the work of the mission from the Egyptian point of view. Although the Americans produced a sizable number of documents and books and kept their history well documented, the Evangelical Church in Egypt left very few records. The Secretary of the Synod of the Nile made an important contribution to this research with the discovery in 2005 of previously unexamined minutes of the Synod of the Nile. A visit to the extensive collection at the Presbyterian Historical Society in Philadelphia also provided valuable insights. The missionaries' personal evaluations of the work in Egypt helped to clarify their relationships with their Egyptian ministry partners, and provided a detailed picture of the political and economic background of the ministry in Egypt.

A further difficulty was encountered because this study examines Christian efforts to evangelize Muslims in a country where such activity is illegal. For both the researcher and those involved in ministry or being interviewed, this raised issues of security. However, since the research covered historical rather than contemporary events, the potential security risks were minimized.

CHAPTER 1

The Arrival of the American Mission in Egypt and the Establishment of the Evangelical Church

1.1 Introduction

The pioneers of the American Presbyterian Mission to Egypt arrived in Cairo in November 1854.[1] At that time, Egypt was going through a critical period of its history. There were important changes in almost every part of Egyptian life, in the government, within society, and within the Coptic Church. When the missionaries came to Egypt, they found great potential for various kinds of mission work. The hard work and extraordinary skills of particular missionaries provided the Mission with a significant advance at the start of its work. However, in order to meet the various social and spiritual needs of the Egyptians, the missionaries used a number of methods and strategies in the first decades of their ministry which were particular to this situation such as schools, medical ministry, and spiritual meetings. They focused their work among middle class people including students, young people, and women. From the beginning, the Mission encountered internal and external difficulties and challenges. As the American Presbyterian Mission in Egypt met these challenges during the first fifty years of its ministry, it grew into an organization that was very different

---

1. Earl E. Elder, *Vindicating a Vision: The Story of the American Mission in Egypt 1854–1954* (Philadelphia: The United Presbyterian Board of Foreign Missions, 1958), 1.

from what it was at its inception. The main achievement of the American Mission was the establishment of the Egyptian Evangelical Church.[2]

1.2 Egypt in the Mid-Nineteenth Century

The middle decades of the nineteenth century saw many rapid changes in politics, society, and the Coptic Church in Egypt. First, politically, there had previously been tension between Mohammad 'Ali, the ruler who is known as the founder of modern Egypt, and the Ottoman Empire. 'Ali had wanted to work independently in order to develop an Egyptian mini-empire from Sudan in the south to Anatolia, in Turkey, in the north. This ambition was seen as a threat to the Ottoman Empire and to Europe, too. The Ottomans considered Mohammad 'Ali a threat to their power over Egypt and Sudan while the European powers did not want a virtually in-dependent Egyptian state weakening the Ottoman Empire. The European powers, which included France, Great Britain, Austria, and Greece had a good trade relationship with the Ottoman Empire and wanted it to con-tinue without any interference from outside.[3] A joint European-Ottoman action put an end to Mohammad 'Ali's dreams when his troops were forced to withdraw from Syria after they were defeated by an Anglo-Turkish force. As a result, Mohammad 'Ali found himself alone without the support of any European power.[4] In 1841, the Ottoman Sultan 'Abd al-Majid, with the support of the European powers, issued an edict (*firman*) confining Egypt to its ancient boundaries.[5] The loss of the Egyptian mini-empire dream led to a gradual political and economic decline.[6]

After the death of Mohammad 'Ali in 1849, his grandson, 'Abbas, ruled Egypt from 1849 to 1854. 'Abbas' reign was generally peaceful and qui-et. He concentrated his efforts in developing Egypt's infrastructure with

---

2. For more details about the beginning of the work of the American Mission in Egypt see: Tharwat Wahba, "The American Presbyterian Mission: Its Reception by the Egyptians" (Unpublished MA thesis), The Evangelical Theological Seminary in Cairo, 2003.

3. Albert Hourani, *A History of the Arab Peoples* (London: Faber and Faber, 1991), 273.

4. Peter Mansfield, *A History of the Middle East* (New York: Viking, 1991), 59.

5. Ehud R. Toledano, *State and Society in Mid-Nineteenth Century Egypt* (Cambridge: Cambridge University Press, 1990), 1.

6. Ibid., 2.

building projects such as the railway from Alexandria to Cairo.[7] In July 1854, 'Abbas was murdered and Sa'id became the ruler of Egypt, holding power from 1854 to 1863.[8] Sa'id was more open to foreign influence than 'Abbas had been.

Sa'id had been raised in a francophone environment and had received a French education within Egypt. His educational background opened him to Western culture and foreigners whom he encouraged to come and work in Egypt. He had a good reputation among Europeans; however, he was highly resented by Egyptians because he seemed to prefer foreigners to nationals, giving Europeans permission to invest their money in projects and to build schools. During his time, the number of foreigners in Egypt grew to approximately 30,000, most of whom lived in Alexandria.[9] Because of Sa'id's policy, foreigners increased not only in number but also in power. Foreign consuls tried to influence the Egyptian government, directing its policy to benefit their nation's situation in Egypt.[10] Political changes accompanied by social and economical developments, moved Egypt into a new phase in its history. Importantly for the church, these changes meant that missionaries, like all foreigners, were given easy entry to the Egyptian field.

Egyptian society in general had also been highly impacted. Modernization efforts had resulted in a dramatic improvement in transportation and industry; however, these improvements mainly benefited the wealthy. Most Egyptians in Upper Egypt and in the Delta experienced no economic progress. Instead, Egyptian society was divided into two main groups. The rich minority of Ottoman-Egyptian families, including Mohammad 'Ali's family, remained isolated from the majority of Egyptians while controlling the economy and enjoying a modern lifestyle. By contrast, the impoverished Egyptian masses endured very primitive living conditions and had no access to the services and comforts of modernity. There was some development in the areas of public health and education, but progress was slow and

---

7. George Annesley, *The Rise of Modern Egypt: A Century and a Half of Egyptian History 1798–1957* (Edinburgh: The Pentland Press Limited, 1994), 118.

8. D. A. Cameron, *Egypt in the Nineteenth Century or Mehemet 'Ali and his Successors until the British Occupation in 1882* (London: Smith, Elder & Co., 1898), 227.

9. Adib Najib Salama, *Tarikh al-Kanysah al-Injilyah fy Misr 1854–1980* (The History of the Evangelical Church in Egypt 1854–1980) (Cairo: Dar al-Thaqafa, 1982), 43.

10. Elder, *Vindicating a Vision,* 28.

limited.[11] In general, these were years "of bad finance, of foreign swindling and roguery, of a spendthrift court, and of disregard for the lives of the people."[12] When the missionaries arrived in Egypt, they sought to respond to these social realities. Finding a divided society, they worked with both the rich and poor. As foreigners, they gained smooth entry among the rich and influential, while the poor became the main target of their educational and medical mission work.

The last aspect within Egypt that influenced the effectiveness and direction of the mission was the situation within the Coptic Church. In the mid-nineteenth century, the Coptic Church was experiencing a time of great challenge and found it difficult to serve the needs of their people due to the lack in number and quality of Coptic priests.

Patriarch Peter VII, who reigned from 1809 to 1854, had vigorously resisted the Roman Catholic missionaries who wanted to establish their own church. When a number of Egyptian Coptic families converted to Catholicism, the Coptic Church leaders vigorously repudiated the Catholic efforts as a Western threat against the Coptic Church.[13] The Copts became suspicious of Western influence and its mission efforts.[14] Both the Catholic Church and later the American Mission exploited the pastoral inadequacies of the Coptic Church and recruited some priests to work with them.[15]

Cyril IV succeeded Peter VII and led the Coptic Church from 1854 to 1861. Although his reign was only seven years, he inaugurated a movement of reform within the Coptic Church.[16] He is known as the "father of reformation" because of his advanced thinking and creative responses to the needs of the Church and people. He established schools for boys and the first school for girls, imported and set up the first non-governmental

---

11. Toledano, *State and Society,* 19–20.

12. Cameron, *Egypt,* 226.

13. Aziz S. Atiya, *A History of Eastern Christianity* (London: Methuen and Co Ltd, 1968), 112.

14. E. L. Butcher, *The Story of the Church of Egypt: Being an Outline of the History of the Egyptians Under Their Successive Masters from the Roman Conquest Until Now* (London: Smith, Elder, & Co., 1897), 394.

15. Andrew Watson, *The American Mission in Egypt 1854 to 1896,* 2nd ed. (Pittsburgh: United Presbyterian Board of Publication, 1904), 101–103.

16. Butcher, *The Story,* 398.

private printing press in Egypt, and was responsible for the repair of old churches and the reconstruction of St Mark's Cathedral in Azbakiyah. He rigorously followed traditional church practices, but reorganized procedures for the administration of property, and inaugurated a proper church archival system.[17] He realized that the Coptic clergy "had long been a prey to ignorance, and he summoned all priests within reach of the capital to a regular Saturday assembly at the patriarchate for systematic readings and theological discussions, himself participating in their edification."[18] Cyril IV briefly launched the Coptic Church on a path of reformation, but after his death, the Coptic Church again fell into apathy and weakness, due to his successor's lack of involvement.

The American Mission had only begun its work during Cyril IV's reign and Coptic Church leaders at that time were not fully aware of its work, nor did they feel threatened by its activities. Opposition only began after Cyril IV's death in 1861. In contrast to the Copts' initial benign acceptance of the Westerners, European travellers to Egypt viewed the Coptic Church very critically during the nineteenth century. They considered the Copts far worse in their moral state than the Muslims, and considered the Coptic people ignorant and bigoted, and without history or culture.[19] Hoda Jindy, in her recent work on nineteenth-century travellers, records one visitor's comments that the Copt was "neither a Muslim, and, therefore, not a modern Egyptian, nor is he a Western Christian; he is an Eastern Christian of non-European extraction and thus as a heretic he cannot be accepted as belonging to the Universal Church."[20]

Both the Moravian missionaries and the Church Missionary Society's (CMS) early missionaries to Egypt observed the social and spiritual

---

17. Iris Habib El-Masry, *The Story of the Copts* (Cairo: The Middle East Council of Churches, 1978), 506.

18. Atiya, *A History*, 105.

19. Hoda Jindy, "The Copts of Egypt: Neither Christian nor Egyptian," in *Interpreting the Orient: Travellers in Egypt and the Near East*, eds. Paul and Janet Starkey (Reading: Ithaca Press, 2001), 99.

20. Ibid., 108.

situation of the Coptic Orthodox Church.[21] The Moravians found that the Coptic Church was in need of a spiritual and educational awakening.[22]

The Rev William Jowett, a pioneer missionary from CMS to the Middle East, visited Egypt in 1820 and described the Coptic Church sympathetically. Although he recognized the decline in the worship, the poor state of the clergy and the general lack of knowledge or access to the Bible, he hoped and worked towards its revival.[23]

Mrs Mary Louisa Whately (1824–1889), a CMS missionary to Egypt in the 1860s and 1870s, concluded that Copts were similar to their Muslim neighbours in habits, dress, and appearance, but different in their faith. The Copts were, in general, isolated inside Egyptian society but also under great risk of losing their Christian faith.[24] She recorded her observations saying:

> But the poorer Copts, when isolated, as I observed, are sometimes really under great temptation; they have never been taught the true and spiritual part of Christianity; a corrupted letter *without* the spirit was in general all that they knew, and when deprived, by distance from their own places of worship, of the ceremonies of their church, and dependent for society and neighbourly offices only upon Moslems, it is hardly to be wondered at that some give up the little they have – the shell of Christianity.[25]

Other Western travellers to Egypt found the Coptic Church in a poor condition, and through their writings, the Egyptian needs drove Western

---

21. For more study on the Moravian and CMS mission work to Egypt, see later in this chapter.

22. J. E. Hutton, *A History of Moravian Missions* (London: Moravian Publication Office, 1923), 162–164.

23. William Jowett, *Christian Researches on the Mediterranean, from 1815 to 1820, in Furtherance of the Objects of the Church Missionary Society / . . . with an Appendix Containing the Journal of the Rev James Connor Chiefly in Syria and Palestine* (London: published for the Society by L. B. Seeley and J. Hatchard, 1822), 111ff.

24. M. L. Whately, *Among the Huts in Egypt: Scenes from Real Life* (London: Seeley, Jackson, & Halliday, 1871), 147–149.

25. Ibid., 149–150.

interest in sending missionaries to help the Coptic Church to stand and grow in its teachings and its role in the Egyptian society.[26]

Nevertheless, some exceptional people among the Copts were held in esteem by government and society. A famous example was the Gauhari family, who for generations held high positions in the government and helped the Coptic Church in its relationship with the rulers, especially in obtaining *firmans* for church buildings. They also gave generously for the building of the new churches.[27]

We have seen that the political, social, economic, and religious developments in Egypt during the mid-nineteenth century made the country receptive to change. This enabled the American Mission to enter Egypt and find suitable conditions for beginning its work.

1.3 The Origins and Early Work of the American Mission in Egypt

1.3.1 Origins

During the closing years of the eighteenth century, there was a growing passion for overseas mission in the Presbyterian churches in the United States of America. In part, this was a response to the century's many wars and the rise of atheistic philosophy. There was a conviction among Presbyterians that the end of the age was approaching and that, according to biblical prophecies, Jews, and heathen around the world were going to accept Christianity.[28] The Second Great Awakening that took place in the closing years of the eighteenth century affected the life of North American,

---

26. For more study about the Western travellers to Egypt in the 19th century and their observations on the Egyptian society in general and the Coptic Church specifically see, Andrew Paton, *A History of the Egyptian Revolution, from the Period of the Mamelukes to the Death of Mohammed Ali: From Arab and European Memoirs, Oral Tradition, and Local Research*, vol. II (London: Trubner, 1870); Miss Platt, *Journal of a Tour Through Egypt, the Peninsula of Sinai, and the Holy Land in 1838–1839*, vol I (London: Richard Watts, 1841); Lucie Duff Gordon, *Letters from Egypt 1862–1869: Enlarged Centenary Edition* (London: Routledge & Kegan Paul, 1969).

27. Atiya, *A History*, 100, 104. El-Masry, *The Story of the Copts*, 524–526.

28. Oliver Wendell Elsbree, "The Rise of the Missionary Spirit in America, 1790–1815," *The New England Quarterly* 1, no. 3 (July 1928): 295–322, quoted in Stanley Rycroft, *The Ecumenical Witness of the United Presbyterian Church in the U.S.A.* (New York: Board of Christian Education of the United Presbyterian Church in the USA, 1968), 42.

English and European churches, and was a significant factor in the establishment of numerous missionary societies.

There were many branches and associations of Presbyterians in America.[29] It was the Associate Reformed Church in the West's General Synod that took the initiative and sent missionaries to Syria in 1843.[30] The Mission in Syria worked mainly in Beirut and the area around it, especially Mount Lebanon, and their work led to the establishment of the Evangelical Church of Beirut, which was the first organized church in the Arab World.[31] The missionaries of the Syria Mission were the founders of the American Mission in Egypt in 1854.

In 1858, the Associate Reformed Church in the West and the Associate Presbyterian Church united and formed the United Presbyterian Church of North America. This new, united church directed the mission work in Egypt through its Board of Foreign Mission. Throughout its history, the great majority of the members of the American Mission in Egypt came from the Scottish-Irish ancestry that was the mainstay of the UPCNA alongside other reformed and Presbyterian churches.[32] They were a people, as the Egyptians later observed, of conservative theology, pious life, and hard work, who tended towards peace and unity. Kenneth Crag described them, in these words:

> It could be said that America's earliest missionary commitment served it best in terms of personal quality. Its personnel came with a genuine love, which fulfilled itself in long service

---

29. For further study of the Presbyterians in America and their desire for unity see, John Vant Stephens, *The Presbyterian Churches: Divisions and Unions, in Scotland, Ireland, Canada and America* (Philadelphia: Presbyterian Board of Publication, 1910) and Robert E. Thompson, *History of the Presbyterian Churches in the U.S.*, American Church History Series (New York: Lenox Hill Pub., 1995).

30. Rycroft, *The Ecumenical Witness*, 66.

31. For a wide-ranging study of the roots of the American Mission in Syria and the events leading to the establishment of the Evangelical Church of Beirut, see Habib Badr, "Mission to 'Nominal Christians': The Policy and Practice of the American Board of Commissionaires for Foreign Missions and Its Missionaries Concerning Eastern Churches, which Led to the Organization of a Protestant Church in Beirut, 1819–1848" (PhD diss., Princeton Theological Seminary, 1992).

32. Elder, *Vindicating a Vision*, 10.

and inner rapport, paternalistic perhaps but in the best tradition of American warmth, vigour, and integrity.[33]

These originators of the American Mission came from an evangelical background with a missiological vision. They were eager for evangelism and ready to make many sacrifices as necessary to serve the needs of people of Egypt.

1.3.2 Reasons for the Coming of the American Presbyterian Mission to Egypt

There were many reasons why the American Mission decided to start a ministry in Egypt. Some were internal reasons, related to both the Board of Foreign Mission of the American Church and the American Mission itself; but there were other external factors as well. The American missionaries in Syria had had many difficulties in their ministry, especially due to the dangerous situation with the civil war between the Maronites and the Druze in Lebanon.[34] One of the missionaries in Syria, Dr Paulding, visited Egypt in 1853 hoping to recover from ill health. While there, he was impressed with the possibilities for mission. The missionaries in Syria reported to their board in the United States, giving a number of reasons to "open a new station in Cairo."[35] They hoped:

1. To preserve for the benefit of the church the services of Dr Paulding, whose health permitted him to labour in Egypt, but did not permit him to labour in Syria.

2. To provide encouragement, given the limited results that these missionaries were experiencing in their mission field at Damascus.

3. To open a refuge in Egypt for the missionaries in Syria, in view of impending political dangers within the Ottoman Empire.[36]

---

33. Kenneth Cragg, *The Arab Christian: A History in the Middle East* (London: Mowbray, 1992), 222.

34. Charles R. Watson, *In the Valley of the Nile: A Survey of the Missionary Movement in Egypt*, 2nd ed. (New York: Fleming H. Revell Company, 1908), 133.

35. Watson, *The American Mission*, 61.

36. Although Egypt was mainly a part of the Ottoman Empire, it enjoyed a measure of independence under Mohammad 'Ali and his dynasty.

4. To meet the spiritual needs of the land of Egypt.[37]

These reasons reflected the difficulties of the ministry in Syria, but also depicted the anticipated potential of the field in Egypt. Egypt was viewed as more secure and hospitable to the gospel, but it is noteworthy that the spiritual needs of Egypt came at the end of the list.[38] In addition to the openly stated reasons above, other circumstances led the American Mission to establish a ministry in Egypt that lasted for more than a hundred years.

First, there were American Presbyterian missionaries working in other countries in the Muslim world such as Turkey, Iran, Syria, and among Armenians, but nothing had been established in Egypt even though it was an important country in the Middle East.[39] Given that Egypt had become open to foreign influences and change, this new initiative was considered timely.

Second, other mission organizations like the CMS,[40] the British and Foreign Bible Society,[41] and the Scottish Society for the Conversion of the Jews were already working in Egypt.[42] These missions used different strategies than those employed by the American Mission, and their mixed effectiveness suggested that others with different approaches would be able to meet the needs of other segments of the population. The Presbyterian Mission anticipated opening high quality schools, engaging in more intensive evangelism to larger numbers of the Egyptian population, and training native leaders.

---

37. Charles R. Watson, *Egypt and the Christian Crusade*, 1st ed. (Philadelphia: The Board of Foreign Missions of the United Presbyterian Church of N.A., 1907), 153.

38. Charles Watson found listed in the reasons, which the Synod of the Associate Reformed Church of the West gave when they started ministry in Egypt, that this was the will of God. Charles Watson, "Fifty Years of Foreign Missions in Egypt," in UPCNA, *Foreign Missionary Jubilee Convention: Of the United Presbyterian Church of N. A. Celebrating the Fiftieth Anniversary of the Founding of Missions in Egypt and India, December 6–8,1904, Pittsburgh, PA.* (Philadelphia: The Board of Foreign Missions of the United Presbyterian Church of N. A., 1905), 84–85.

39. Lyle L. Vander Werff, *Christian Mission to Muslims: The Record, Anglican and Reformed Approaches in India and the Near East, 1800–1938* (South Pasadena: The William Carey Library, 1977), 105.

40. Butcher, *The Story*, 396. The Church Missionary Society started its mission in Egypt many years before that. For more details see later in this chapter.

41. Montague Fowler, *Christian Egypt: Past, Present, and Future* (London: Church Newspaper Company Limited, 1901), 280.

42. Watson, *In the Valley,* 133.

Third, the presence of the Coptic Church in Egypt encouraged the American Mission to enter the Egyptian field. The reality that there were Christians in Egypt, who for centuries had survived in a land where Muslims were the majority, suggested to the mission board that it would be easier to establish a mission in Egypt than in other countries with few or no Christians.[43]

Fourth, after the French conquered Egypt (1798–1801), interest in Egypt had increased in the West. Many Westerners had visited Egypt and written about its monuments, society, and people. These writings reached many countries in the West and especially the United States where mission societies recognized a spiritual need in Egypt.

Fifth, the newly improved lifestyle in Egypt made it more accessible for foreigners. The modern standards in transportation and education facilitated their welcome. However, more importantly, the relationship between Egypt and Western countries favoured the foreigners. During his time (1854–1863) Sa'id applied the Capitulations in Egypt which remained until 1936.[44] The Capitulations were rules that gave special treatment for foreigners, granting them more privileges than ordinary Egyptians had.[45] For example, Westerners, including the missionaries, were able to influence Egyptian policy in their favour and to have their legal disputes overseen by their own courts, not Egyptian ones.[46]

All this created an atmosphere that was amenable to the American Mission endeavours. The mission itself was ready to send some missionaries from Syria and others from the United States to start the work in Egypt. The coming of the American Presbyterian Mission to Egypt in 1854 is considered by the Presbyterian Church in Egypt as the date of its own

---

43. Vander Werff, *Christian Mission*, 142.

44. Hanna F. Wissa, *Assiout: The Saga of an Egyptian Family* (Sussex: The Book Guild, 1994), 85, 331.

45. The Capitulations were privileges for foreigners resident in the Ottoman Empire which included the following: liberty of residence, inviolability of domicile, liberty to travel by land and sea, freedom of commerce, freedom of religion, immunity from local jurisdiction save under certain safeguards, exclusive extra-territorial jurisdiction over foreigners of the same nationality, and competence of the forum of the defendant in cases in which two foreigners are concerned. http://56.1911encyclopedia.org/C/CA/CAPITULATIONS.htm (accessed on 20 December 2003).

46. Elder, *Vindicating a Vision*, 29.

establishment. As such, it was also the birth of one of the largest Protestant churches in the Arab World.

1.3.3 The Pioneer Missionaries of the American Mission in Egypt

The first team of the American Mission came from both the United States and Syria. Rev Thomas McCague and his wife were sent out from America, arriving in Cairo on 15 November 1854, twenty days before the arrival of Mr Barnett from Syria.[47] Soon after their arrival, they found a place to live in Cairo, and started their mission activities. They engaged in preaching, personal work, and the distribution of religious literature in the first few months.[48] The American Mission "came in the first place not to evangelize the Orthodox Copts but to convert Muslims. When they found it slow and discouraging to convert Muslims they turned to the Coptic Church and converted many Copts."[49] In the first few months, the missionaries began holding Arabic services in their house every Sunday. The attendance ranged from four to eight people in the first year. Most of them were teachers and parents who had developed relationships with the missionaries through a boys' school that they had opened.

A few months after their arrival cholera broke out in Cairo and, as a result, ten thousand people died in one month. The missionaries "continued in their posts, daily visiting the sick, burying the dead, comforting the mourning and bereaved, and giving what aid they could to the needy."[50] In the first few years, the missionaries focused on building good relationships with the Egyptians by avoiding any conflict with local people even in the hard times.[51]

Over the next years, more missionaries joined the work, including some who contributed significantly to the mission in Egypt. Rev Gulian Lansing arrived in 1857 after six years of ministry in Syria. He had a good knowledge of the Arabic language and culture, and is described by the

---

47. Watson, *In the Valley*, 133.

48. Ibid., 134.

49. Butcher, *The Story*, 402. For more details about the Mission and its evangelistic goals towards Muslims see chapter 3.

50. Watson, *The American Mission*, 76–77.

51. Watson, *In the Valley*, 134.

mission historian Julius Richter as a "learned man, deeply interested in the archaeology of Egypt in its relation to Bible history."[52] He led the mission in Egypt for years and started the annual tour up the Nile to Upper Egypt using the Mission boat *Ibis*. This boat became one of the vital links between mission stations and provided a unique way to reach the villages in the area between Cairo and Aswan. In a book giving daily notes about one of these trips that went as far as Aswan, Lansing wrote that he found that the Egyptians of every religious background were hungry to know the Bible and to discuss its teachings.[53] Until his death in 1892, he helped the mission through many difficulties.[54]

John Hogg, a Scot, was one of the most influential missionaries for the American Mission in Egypt. He had worked in Alexandria at a school established by the Scottish Society for the Conversion of the Jews. When the American missionaries opened a station in Alexandria they invited him to join them, and he agreed, as his mission was going to close its work.[55] Hogg then opened a new station for the American Mission in Assiut province, in the heart of the Coptic population in Upper Egypt. Vander Werff describes his importance there: "His ministry of biblical preaching and teaching helped make Assiut a centre of revived Christianity."[56] Through his efforts, many churches and schools were established in Upper Egypt. He also was involved in the Evangelical Theological Seminary as a teacher and administrator.[57] Because of his ministry, many Bible study groups and prayer meetings started in Assiut and in the surrounding cities and villages.[58] His approach to ministry emphasized the establishment and development of the indigenous Evangelical Church as the main tool for evangelizing Egypt.

---

52. Julius Richter, *A History of the Protestant Missions in the Near East* (Edinburgh: Oliphant, Anderson and Ferrier, 1910), 352.

53. Gulian Lansing, *Egypt's Princes: Missionary Labor in the Valley of the Nile* (Philadelphia: William S. Rentoul, 1864), 91–92.

54. Watson, *In the Valley*, 144, 156.

55. Ibid., 135.

56. Vander Werff, *Christian Mission*, 146.

57. John Hogg and Andrew Watson established the Evangelical Theological Seminary in 1863. See later in this chapter.

58. There is a more detailed biography of John Hogg in Rena L. Hogg, *A Master-Builder on the Nile: Being a Record of the Life and Aims of John Hogg* (New York: Fleming H. Revell Company, 1914).

Andrew Watson arrived in Egypt in 1862 and worked in Cairo as a liaison for the Mission in its relationships with various organizations inside and outside Egypt.[59] He was also a teacher at the Evangelical Theological Seminary with Lansing and Hogg. He started the first magazine for the Mission in Egypt in 1872 under the name *Al-Nashrah Al-Injeyiliah* that was later changed to *Al–Murshid* and then finally *Al-Hoda,* which remains the official publication of the Presbyterian Church in Egypt today. He recorded the early history of the American Mission in Egypt in his book *The American Mission in Egypt: 1854–1896.* His son, Charles Watson, became the secretary of the Board of Foreign Missions of the United Presbyterian Church in the United States before he founded the American University in Cairo in 1919 and became its first president.[60]

The number of missionaries increased from three in 1854 to twenty-two in 1879. In 1904, fifty years after the beginning of the Mission, there were ninety missionaries. Among them were ordained ministers and their families, unmarried women, college professors, physicians, and nurses.[61] Missionaries such as Ebenezer Currie, S. C. Ewing, W. Harvey, Dr D. R. Johnston, J. R. Alexander significantly influenced the work in Egypt.[62]

1.3.4 The Methodologies Used by the Mission in Egypt

In its first fifty years, the American Mission used a number of methods in their ministry in Egypt. The 43rd annual report of the Mission gives a summary of these methods.[63]

1.3.4.1 Evangelistic tours on the Nile

The pioneer missionaries used boats owned by the Mission to reach Upper Egypt. For decades, their annual tours linked the missionaries with people

---

59. Vander Werff, *Christian Mission,* 147.

60. Lawrence R. Murphy, *The American University in Cairo 1919-1987* (Cairo: The American University in Cairo Press, 1987), 2.

61. UPCNA, Board of Foreign Missions, *The 50th Annual Report of the American United Presbyterian Mission in Egypt for the Year 1904,* (Philadelphia: Board of Foreign Missions, 1904), 93.

62. Vander Werff, *Christian Mission,* 143.

63. UPCNA, Board of Foreign Missions, *The 43rd Annual Report by the Board of Foreign Missions of the United Presbyterian Church* (Philadelphia: Board of Foreign Missions, 1897), 5.

in many towns and hundreds of small villages in Upper Egypt. They would stop at key villages to sell Bibles and other Christian books, hold discussions, and conduct worship services in schools and Coptic churches.[64]

Among the missionaries who used the Nile boat in their evangelistic work were Lansing and Hogg. *Egypt's Princes* gave a record of Lansing's trip diaries, and Hogg gave hints about his work in Assiut using the Nile boat, in his letter to *Times of Blessing*. Hogg mentions the results of his ministry in Assiut when he urged the evangelicals there to help in building Assiut College. He quoted Dr Ellinwood, the secretary of the Board of Foreign Missions of the Presbyterian Church in North America, who said:

> Ten years ago, while coming down the Nile, I met a little weather stained boat moored under the bank to avoid a cold head wind. Its only passengers were Rev Dr Hogg with his wife and two small children (Miss McKown was with us), on their way to Osiout. They were to establish a mission in a town mostly built of mud, and where no English speaking neighbour would be found, and few at best of the comforts of life. Never before had I felt so deeply the sacrifices involved in carrying the gospel into foreign lands. Never had such a sense of the lonely exile of mission life come over me as when I bade adieu to that little family and hastened toward my native land.[65]

The tours opened the eyes of missionaries to see the needs of the people and to open new stations that became organized churches. From these tours, the American missionaries recognized that the main needs of the Egyptians were education, health services, and spiritual revival.[66]

1.3.4.2 The establishment of schools

Over the years, the missionaries continued to open schools at almost every mission station in Egypt. During the nineteenth century, education was of concern to the rulers in Egypt, since all other schools at that time were

---

64. Vander Werff, *Christian Mission*, 146.
65. *Times of Blessing.* Sept. 14, 1876 Letters on Christian Missions in Egypt.
66. Richter, *A History*, 347.

operated according to the traditional Islamic religious system and did not teach non-religious courses to the students.[67] By contrast, the western education style incorporated many subjects including medicine, engineering, languages, and commerce. Mohammad 'Ali had sent a number of Egyptian students to study in Europe, especially in France. Under his and his successors' leadership, the Coptic Church, missionaries and other foreigners were invited to contribute to the new educational initiatives.[68]

The American Mission expended a huge effort to meet this crucial need. It was in the fall of 1855, only a year after their arrival, that the missionaries opened the first boys' school in Cairo.[69] Schools played an important role in connecting the Mission directly with the people and their needs. By 1904, from Alexandria in the north to Aswan in the south, there were 167 schools scattered throughout the cities and small town and villages of Egypt, with 14,884 pupils.[70]

1.3.4.3 The publication and distribution of Scriptures and other religious books

The missionaries also used religious book distribution as a major evangelistic tool. The new translation of the Bible in Arabic by Van Dyke, known as the Beirut Bible, was the main book.[71] This endeavour was well received, as can be seen from the number of books distributed or sold yearly. In 1864, they distributed 10,258 volumes, but by 1904, this number had increased to 98,355 volumes.[72]

1.3.4.4 Work among women

The arrival of Miss Dales as a missionary was the beginning of the Mission Women's Work.[73] One of the Mission reports describes its effectiveness.

---

67. Hourani, *A History,* 311. The traditional religious school system focused on teaching the people religious texts only. The other subjects such as mathematics, science, languages, and social studies were not among the subjects which the schools in Egypt used to teach.

68. Philip K. Hitti, *History of the Arabs: From the Earlier Times to the Present,* Tenth Edition (London: The Macmillan Press Ltd, 1970), 723–724.

69. Watson, *In the Valley,* 134.

70. UPCNA, Board of Foreign Missions, *The 50th Annual Report,* 93.

71. Elder, *Vindicating a Vision,* 35.

72. Ibid.

73. Watson, "Fifty Years of Foreign Missions," 86.

"The work with women . . . enabled them to attend the school and often church services as well. These women were taught reading, and had the Scriptures read and explained to them in their homes. At the time, they received sympathy and aid in various ways to enable them to bear the burdens and perform the duties, pertaining to their lot in this world."[74] The ministry that had originally been started by the missionaries' wives increased dramatically so that specialized female missionaries were needed. The number of female missionaries grew gradually until by 1895 there were nine women workers.[75] The American Mission also hired Egyptian women to help in this ministry, calling them "Bible Women." Because they were educated women who had graduated from the Mission schools, but also spoke Arabic, they could effectively communicate the gospel and Christian teaching during their visits. The Women's General Missionary Society of the United Presbyterian Church supported this ministry, together with the girls' education and health ministries in Egypt.[76]

Women at this time were not allowed to leave their homes. Using women to reach women within their family settings avoided offending societal restrictions and was a successful method of reaching the people.

1.3.4.5 The Sabbath schools

Secular education was a key component of the Mission ministry. However, in almost every station, the missionaries also held Sabbath meetings in their churches where they taught the Bible and Protestant doctrine to Coptic Christian children. In 1904, the number of pupils at these schools was 11,182 pupils.[77] These Sabbath schools opened the door for the missionaries to contact new generations and influence them with biblical teaching, and played a significant role in building evangelical churches.

1.3.4.6 The training of young local Egyptian men and women for Christian work

The missionaries recognized the importance of training and developing native leaders to take leadership in the work of the Church and the different

---

74. UPCNA, Board of Foreign Missions, *The 43rd Annual report*, 5.

75. Richter, *A History*, 350.

76. Rycroft, *The Ecumenical Witness*, 81.

77. UPCNA, Board of Foreign Missions, *The 50th Annual Report*, 93.

Mission activities. This led them to establish theological classes in 1863 at Cairo and then at Assiut in 1867. The theological training included both the theory of the classroom, and a practical field ministry.[78] Other colleges for girls in Cairo and Assiut were established to train teachers for the schools of the Mission.[79]

1.3.4.7 Medical work

The medical work of the American Mission started in 1868 with the arrival of Dr Johnston who established the first clinic in Assiut. The work increased and then expanded to Tanta, Banha, and Cairo.[80] Through the medical ministry, the Mission was able to reach many Muslims as well as Copts.[81] Dr Henry, who followed Johnston, further raised the quality of medical treatment and provided an important model by training Egyptians for medical service, including nursing.[82]

The medical mission service was very successful. Because it provided a very tangible and practical response to the deep needs of the ordinary people, it contributed greatly to the establishment and growth of the Egyptian Protestant Church.

1.3.5 Challenges and Difficulties

The establishment and growth of the American Mission in Egypt resulted in many challenges and difficulties.

1.3.5.1 Challenges and difficulties from the outside

In the first few years after the arrival of the American Mission in Egypt, relations between the Mission, the government, and the Coptic Church were good. The growth of the American Mission's work touched many spheres of Egyptian life and drew the attention of the government and the Coptic Church. During Sa'id's reign, (1854–1863), the Mission enjoyed freedom and some religious liberty because Sa'id had a liberal mind and gave freedom for foreigners to initiate many activities, including religious

---

78. Vander Werff, *Christian Mission,* 149.

79. Richter, *A History,* 350.

80. Elder, *Vindicating a Vision,* 53.

81. Vander Werff, *Christian Mission,* 150.

82. Anna A. Milligan, *Dr. Henry of Assiut: Pioneer Medical Missionary in Egypt,* Part 1 (Philadelphia: The United Presbyterian Board of Foreign Mission, 1945), 13–14.

programmes. The first resistance and conflict came from local authorities, especially around Assiut where the Mission had found its greatest growth and success. For example in 1861, Faris El-Hakim, a Syrian assistant to the missionaries in Assiut, convinced a lady who had been a Christian but then converted to Islam and married a Muslim man, to come back to her Christian roots. This case became well known throughout Assiut and created a severe disturbance in the town.[83] Faris was arrested and sent to prison. The Muslim judges beat him badly, and the Protestants were understandably upset about his treatment. The American consul in Assiut, Wasef Khayyat, who was a Protestant himself, sent this case to the American Consul General, Mr Thayer, who took it to the Egyptian Minister of Foreign Affairs and then to the Khedive himself.[84] Orders were sent to Assiut to release Faris and to put the people who beat him in prison. News of this case reached even the President of the United States, Abraham Lincoln, who sent a letter to Sa'id Pasha thanking him for closing the case in such a way, and thus demonstrating his wisdom and open-mindedness.[85]

In Isma'il's time, (1863–1879), the work of the American Mission encountered more opposition from the government than during Sa'id's time. The local governors in Upper Egypt, with the support of the central government in Cairo, began to deny the Protestants licenses to build new churches. Andrew Watson said of that time: "In no period in the history of the Mission was the opposition so obstinate and so long continued as during that period."[86] Although the reasons for opposition were very vague, there was an overall lack of religious liberty in Egypt because of Islamic influence within both the government and society. Although Isma'il sought to limit the influence of foreigners in Egypt, the missionaries spent much time fighting to gain equal rights for Christians.[87]

Difficulties did not come only from the local and central government but from the Coptic Orthodox Church as well. As the American Mission

---

83. Watson, *The American Mission*, 112.

84. Gulian Lansing, *Religious Toleration in Egypt: Official Correspondence Relating to the Indemnity Obtained for the Maltreatment of Faris El- Hakim, An Agent of the American Missionaries in Egypt* (London: Privately printed, 1862), 3.

85. Ibid., 2.

86. Watson, *The American Mission*, 328.

87. Vander Werff, *Christian Mission*, 143.

grew in its influence, the Coptic Church saw its growth as a great threat to its own existence. Patriarch Demetrius II, (1861–1873), excommunicated the Protestant believers and their families from the Coptic Church. With the support of Isma'il's government, he went to Upper Egypt to prevent the work of the American Mission. The Patriarch threatened all the Copts with excommunication, forbidding them to read the Protestants' Bibles and books, to send their children to the Protestants' schools, to attend their meetings, or follow their teachings.[88] Because of this warning, many books, including Bibles, were burned; Coptic children were withdrawn from the Protestants' schools; and many people were persecuted because of their faith.[89] The relationship between the Mission and the Coptic Church remained tense. Suffering from this opposition, the missionaries increased their efforts to resolve the conflict by sharing with the Coptic Church in its festivals and feasts.[90]

1.3.5.2 Internal challenges and difficulties of the Mission

Inside the Mission there were some difficulties related to the hard life the missionaries lived in Egypt and from internal disagreement. The hot weather and the lack of health services in Egypt caused some troubles for the missionaries and their families. Many missionaries suffered from different kinds of diseases and were forced into sick leave or retirement.[91] Some missionaries lost members of their families such as John Hogg and Lansing who both lost daughters during their ministry in the field.[92]

The Crimean War and the American Civil War caused hardship for the Mission, especially with their finances.[93] They overcame these financial situations with the help of an Indian Prince who visited Egypt in 1864. He became a friend of the American Mission after he married one of the students from the Mission school in Cairo. He donated $5,000 annually

---

88. Hogg, *A Master-Builder,* 152–156.
89. Watson, *In the Valley,* 153.
90. Ibid., 155.
91. Vander Werff, *Christian Mission,* 143.
92. Elder, *Vindicating a Vision,* 51.
93. Vander Werff, *Christian Mission,* 143.

for twelve years along with some occasional gifts. These donations helped the Mission to continue the work and avoid serious financial difficulties.[94]

One of the greatest difficulties the Mission faced was doctrinal in nature. Rev Pinkerton, one of their missionaries, adopted Plymouth Brethren doctrines concerning the Holy Spirit and began to spread his ideas among the missionaries and members of the Protestant Church.[95] Some of his followers started separate meetings that caused confusion among the Protestants.[96] In 1869, the Mission confronted him and refuted his teachings. He left Egypt for the United States for a few years, but he came back to teach the same teachings not only in Egypt but also in Syria. As a result, a Brethren Church was established disturbing the unity of the Protestant community enterprise for many years.[97]

1.3.6 The Role of the Egyptians in the Ministry of the American Mission

From the time of its arrival in Egypt, the American Mission built strong relationships with the people. The Mission, however, focused on two categories of people, who then became the cornerstone of its ministry. First, were the rich Egyptian families, and second, intelligent laymen of the middle class who showed an interest in religious pursuits. Both groups found new direction and challenge as they joined the work of the American Mission.

The rich Egyptian families enjoyed a modern lifestyle that differed radically from the traditional ways of the majority. As successful merchants and wealthy landowners, they had access to good education, and often sent their sons to study in Europe. This in turn, enabled them to pursue careers in highly respected professions. Because of their powerful position within society, they also established influential relationships with the government and with leading foreigners. Some even gained unique privileges when foreign consuls put them under their protection. There were numerous

---

94. Watson, *In the Valley*, 146.

95. The Plymouth Brethren Church is a dispensational Protestant denomination that was established in the UK by the influence of John Darby and others. For more details about the history of the Brethren Church and their teachings see: http://74.125.77.132/search?q=cache:CaDKxLX6Ct8J:withchrist.org/MJS/pbs.htm+brethren+church+history+darby&hl=en&ct=clnk&cd=5&gl=uk (accessed on 20 March 2008).

96. Richter, *A History*, 350.

97. Elder, *Vindicating a Vision*, 57.

wealthy Coptic families, whose money and power made them influential within the Coptic Church as well as throughout their local regions. The Wissa family, and Khayyat and Girgis Barsoom were prime examples of this class.

The Wissas were the richest family in Assiut. They traded in wheat, corn, cotton, agricultural land, and textiles and also owned and managed a variety of other businesses. Some of their sons studied abroad in the UK and Beirut,[98] and attained prestigious and powerful positions. Wasef Wissa became an agent of the United States consul while his brother became the agent of the consul of Portugal in Assiut. The Wissa family accepted the missionaries' message, and despite censure by the Coptic Church, involved themselves in the work of the mission, especially in Upper Egypt. Both the Wissa and Barsoom families provided support to the American Mission, and were able to open many doors for the ministry. Likewise, these families benefited from the relationship, gaining supportive relationships as well as increased social prestige and influence and challenging spheres of activity. Their prestige was especially enhanced when the government gave official recognition to the Protestant denomination.[99] The chairpersons of the Protestant denomination came from these families.[100]

The rich families were also significant supporters of the educational projects. They built a number of schools in their own towns and villages, donating their land to cover the expenses of these schools and putting the schools under the supervision of the Mission and the Evangelical Church.[101] This kind of relationship was important for both the American missionaries and the rich families and certainly contributed significantly to the establishment of the Egyptian Evangelical Church.

---

98. Wissa, *Assiout*. In this book we can follow the history of Wissa's family and their interaction with the American Mission.

99. See chapter 2 about the establishment of the Protestant denomination which was the name given by the government to the Evangelical Church which was established by the American Mission.

100. Wissa, *Assiout*, 113, 128–136.

101. Adib Najib Salama, *Alengelioon wal 'mal Alkawmy* (The Evangelicals and the National Work), (Cairo: Dar El-thaqafa, 1993), 57–64. Salama recorded lists of Egyptians who established schools in many villages and towns and gave from their properties to cover the expenses of these schools.

The middle classes also provided support for the American Mission from its inception; some became the pastors of the new churches, while others formed the backbone for the church's evangelistic thrust. First, there were the young men from mainly Coptic families who studied at the Mission schools and adopted the new theology. Many of them joined the Evangelical Church where they provided spiritual leadership. Some used their advanced education to pursue better jobs and raise their standard of living. Others joined the Seminary to receive training in ministry from American missionaries and local teachers. Thus equipped, they became pastors in partnership with the missionaries. They obviously played an important role in the life of the Church and in its interaction with the American Mission.[102]

Second, there were the local laymen who helped the Mission in its evangelistic work. These men of local influence including farmers, teachers, accountants, and government employees were leaders in their communities. They had no, or very limited, theological training, but their knowledge of the Bible and their zeal for ministry contributed greatly to the growth of the work of the American Mission and the Evangelical Church. They used to travel from village to village and surrounding neighbourhoods, preaching the gospel and establishing Bible study groups and prayer meetings. Despite the resistance of the Coptic Church, they were able to take the message to their people and were the foundation on which the Mission built the native lay leadership of the established Church.[103]

1.3.7 Mission after Fifty Years

During the first fifty years, the American Mission's work in Egypt had successfully influenced the life of Egyptians in the important fields of education, medicine, and spirituality. The American missionaries lived among

---

102. The young men whom the Mission recruited to join the pastoral ministry came mainly from the Mission schools. As an example of these young men see Salih Hanalla, *Hayat al-Qis Shenuda Hana* (The life of Rev Shenuda Hana), (Cairo: Matba'at al Muhit, 1922), which gives the biography of one of the first Egyptian pastors who was closely linked to the Mission before and after his theological study and pastoral work.

103. The life and ministry of these lay leaders can be found in the missionaries' books and reports. As an example of the Egyptian leaders see the story of Fam Stephanos in Watson, *History of the American Mission*, 213–241, and Elder, *Vindicating a Vision*, 45–47, and Hogg, *A Master-Builder*, 154–160.

the Egyptians, served them faithfully, and made many friends among them. Their work throughout the years provides an excellent example of what such a ministry can achieve religiously, socially, and educationally in the life of a country such as Egypt.

The growth in the work of the American Mission in Egypt can be examined by various means. The following table gives the number of missionaries, churches, and institutions every ten years from 1864 to 1904, and reflects an increase in almost every field of endeavour. This table comes from the 50th Annual Report of the Mission in Egypt, which contained many details about the numerous activities, and the gradual growth of the Mission.[104]

Activities/Year	1864	1874	1884	1894	1904
Missionaries	10	22	29	38	90
Native Workers	—	17	36	58	75
Organized Churches	1	6	19	33	63
Stations	3	18	61	167	213
Church Members	69	596	1,688	4,554	7,757
Protestant Community	207	1,788	5,054	13,662	29,000
Sabbath Schools Pupils	?	733	2,521	5,365	11,182
Schools	5	24	59	119	167
Pupils	423	1,170	5,106	7,975	14,884
Books Sold	10,285	10,176	37,615	49,397	98,355

The establishment of the Evangelical Church in Egypt was the most significant achievement for the American Mission. This major development came after years of hard ministry and helped the Mission to keep growing in many fields. There were many reasons that led to the establishment of the Church and deliberate steps were taken to make this happen.

---

104. UPCNA, Board of Foreign Missions. *The 50th Annual Report*, 93.

1.4 The Mission Work in Egypt before the American Mission and the Establishment of New Denominations

1.4.1 The Church in Egypt before the Presbyterian Church: Major Denominations and Groups

Christianity came to Egypt in the first century AD. The Coptic Church considers Saint Mark as its founder, believing that he preached the gospel in Alexandria in about AD 61. Apart from this, little is known about the Church in the first 150 years of its history in Egypt.[105] However, from the end of the second century, the Theological School of Alexandria played an important role in the early history of the Christian church. Pantaenus, Clement, Athanasius and Origen, were among the leaders who made a significant contribution to Christian thought throughout Christendom.[106] Then at the end of the third and the beginning of the fourth century, the Church in Egypt suffered persecution by the Roman Emperors, especially Diocletian. The great number of Christians who died in his time (284–305 AD) gave the Coptic Church the appellation of "the Church of martyrs."[107] The Coptic Church not only influenced Christianity through its theological scholars, but beginning with "the father of monasticism," St Anthony, (c.251–356), and St Pachomius (c. 292–348) contributed the root ethos and model of monasticism.[108]

The Coptic Church had its history not only in theology and in monasticism, but in mission work as well. As an oriental church, the Coptic Church had its rich history in mission work.[109] Bishop Michael Nazir-Ali summarizes the mission work of the Coptic Church saying:

---

105. Colin H. Roberts, *Manuscript, Society and Belief in Early Christian Egypt* (London: The British Academy, 1979), 49.

106. Salama, *Tarikh al-Kanysa al-Injilya*, 22-3.

107. Alan K. Bowman, *Egypt after the Pharaohs: 332 BC–AD 642, from Alexander to the Arab Conquest* (Oxford: Oxford University Press, 1990), 191–192.

108. Ibid., 194.

109. Both the Coptic Church and the Nestorian Church are known for their mission efforts to different parts of the ancient world in the first six centuries of their history. For more study about the Nestorian Church mission work especially to China see, John M. L. Young, *By Foot to China: Mission of The Church of the East, to 1400.* (Assyrian

Among the Copts, learning and the monastic tradition have always gone hand in hand with missionary ardour. Pantaenus, the first known head of the celebrated Catechetical School of Alexandria and the revered teacher of St Clement himself, is reported by Eusebius to have been a missionary in India. Saint Athanasius spent his time in exile as a missionary in Europe. Numerous other Copts – soldiers, merchants and artisans – carried the faith with them wherever they went. Coptic Christianity spread from Egypt towards the south and all along the Nile, right up to Nubia and the Sudan.[110]

The main mission field for the Coptic Church was in Ethiopia that was supported by the Coptic Church beginning from its establishment in the fourth century until the middle of the twentieth century.[111]

Because of the Chalcedonian controversy in 451, the Church in Egypt divided into two bodies. On the one side were the majority of Egyptians who followed the Monophysite doctrine, and became what is known as the Coptic Orthodox Church.[112] On the other side was a minority that followed the Diophysite doctrine. They gave their loyalty to the Byzantine Church and were known as the "Melkites" or Greeks.[113] Initially, the conflict was not truly about doctrine, but more about national freedom and independence from Hellenistic domination. The Egyptians believed that the decisions of Chalcedon were linked with Hellenism.[114]

International News Agency, Books Online, 1984) http://www.aina.org/books/bftc/bftc. htm (accessed on 12 September 2007). See also: Atiya, *A History*, 257–266.

110. Michael Nazir-Ali, *From Everywhere to Everywhere: A World View of Christian Mission* (London: Harper Collins, 1991), 28. See also Maurice Assad, "Mission in the Coptic Church: Perspective, Doctrine and Practice," *Mission Studies* 4, no. 1 (1987): 31; Atiya, *A History*, 49–68.

111. Ali, *From Everywhere*, 29. For more details about the mission work of the Coptic Church in Ethiopia and in Western Africa see Antonius Markos, *Come Across and Help Us: The Story of the Coptic Orthodox Church in Africa in Our Present Time, Book One in Ethiopia and East Africa* (Cairo: Coptic Bishopric of African Affairs, 1993). See chapter 7.

112. The word Copt is an ancient Greek word means Egyptian, but after the Arab conquest of Egypt the Arabs called Christians "Copts," and this is the name used for Christians in Egypt today including Orthodox, Catholics, and Evangelicals.

113. Barbara Watterson, *Coptic Egypt* (Edinburgh: Scottish Academic Press, 1988), 46.

114. Raymond Etteldorf, *The Catholic Church in the Middle East* (New York: The Macmillan Company, 1959), 56–57.

In addition to this Christian schism, the AD 640 Arab invasion of Egypt led to the isolation of the Coptic Church from the other churches in both the West and the East. Christians suffered under Islamic persecution and pressures that reduced their numbers to less than one-tenth of the population during the Mamluk Dynasties (1250–1517). The number became less in the time of the Ottoman Empire, which began in 1517.[115] By the mid-nineteenth century, the number of Copts ranged from a mere 150,000 up to 217,000, according to various estimates, out of a total population of five million.[116]

In the first five centuries of Arab rule in Egypt, the relations between the Coptic Church and the Greek Church had been tense. Beginning in the thirteenth century, several unsuccessful attempts were made to draw the two churches together.[117] Today the term Melkite is used to refer to the Greek Catholics, whose members formerly belonged to the Greek Orthodox Church but are now a part of the Catholic Church in Egypt.[118]

1.4.2 Early Roman Catholic Missions

Early Catholic missionary efforts in Egypt started in 1219 during the Fifth Crusade when St Francis of Assisi journeyed to Egypt and spoke with Al-Malik Al-Kamil, the Muslim Sultan, at Damietta.[119] Franciscan mission was established and devoted to the care of the Holy Land. It worked to develop links with Eastern Christians who were living in the Muslim world including Egypt.[120] Franciscans ministered to the Europeans who were living in Egypt and the Egyptians. They established monasteries and churches in Upper Egypt, and because of their ministry, some Egyptian Christians embraced Catholicism in the seventeenth century. In 1741 Athanasius, the

---

115. Otto F. A. Meinardus, "The Coptic Church in Egypt," in *Religion in the Middle East: Three Religions in Concord and Conflict*, Vol. 1, ed. A. J. Arberry (Cambridge: Cambridge University Press, 1969), 425–426.

116. Butcher, *The Story*, 393.

117. Fowler, *Christian Egypt*, 222.

118. G. C. Anawati, "The Roman Catholic Church and Churches in Communion with Rome," in *Religion in the Middle East: Three Religions in Concord and Conflict*, Vol. 1, ed. A. J. Arberry (Cambridge: Cambridge University Press, 1969), 349.

119. Cragg, *The Arab Christian*, 106.

120. Hugh Goddard, *A History of Christian-Muslim Relations* (Chicago: New Amsterdam Books, 2000), 117.

Coptic bishop residing in Jerusalem, declared himself a Catholic. He was anointed as the first Apostolic Vicar of the Catholic Copts.[121] The Coptic Church opposed Catholics, and Athanasius was denied entry to Egypt. In 1895, Pope Leo XIII appointed George Makarios the first Catholic Coptic patriarch.[122] This event is considered as the official establishment of the Coptic Catholic Church in Egypt.

There were some other small Catholic denominations in Egypt, most of whose members were non-Egyptians. Most of these churches were for Catholic minorities that included Roman Catholics, Syrian Catholics, Maronites, Chaldean Catholics, and Armenian Catholics.[123] Each of these Catholic churches served an ethnic group of foreigners who lived in Egypt, but none of them could be considered a national Egyptian Church. The same could be said about the Greek Orthodox, the Armenian Orthodox, and the Syrian Orthodox churches.[124]

The Coptic Church, in general, opposed foreign Christian missions, especially if there were any attempts to draw Copts from their national church. Patriarch Peter VII (1809–1854), was suspicious of the Roman Catholic missionaries who managed to establish a church in Egypt by drawing some national Egyptians from the Coptic Church.[125] This was the situation for most Coptic patriarchs except Cyril IV (1854–1863), who wanted to have a closer communion between the Coptic, the Greek, and the English churches.[126]

1.4.3 Western Missions and Establishing an Indigenous Church

It was in 1633 and 1634 that Peter Heyling of Germany came as the first Protestant missionary to Egypt.[127] This short-term mission failed to

---

121. Anawati, "The Roman Catholic Church," 369.

122. Etteldorf, *The Catholic Church*, 57.

123. Salama, *Tarikh al-Kanysa al-Injilya*, 32–36.

124. Christians of these churches have lived in Egypt for years and some of them and their families hold Egyptian nationality. They considered themselves Egyptians and they contributed to many different fields of life in Egypt alongside other Egyptians.

125. Butcher, *The Story*, 394.

126. Ibid., 402.

127. Richter, *A History*, 92.

establish a lasting Lutheran Church in Egypt; and aside from this individual attempt, the Moravians and the Church Missionary Society were the only other significant Western missions to Egypt before the arrival of the American Presbyterian Mission.

1.4.3.1 Moravians

The Moravians,[128] under the leadership of Count Zinzendorf, were aware of the existence of a Christian church in Egypt and in Abyssinia. They believed that the Christians in these lands were ones ". . . to whom the helpful hand of sympathy and fellowship might be extended."[129] In 1752, Dr Fredrick William Hocker arrived in Egypt as the first Moravian missionary. His main goal was to find an opportunity to go to Abyssinia. He spent his first year in Cairo studying Arabic, practising medicine, and gathering information about Abyssinia. After a year, he visited the Coptic Patriarch, giving him a letter from Count Zinzendorf. The Patriarch received him very kindly. After a failed attempt to visit Abyssinia together with another missionary called Pilder, Hocker spent numerous years in Egypt, but left for Europe in 1761.[130]

After seven years of suspended mission activity, John Henry Danke came to Egypt in 1768. He worked among the Copts of Upper Egypt in Behnessa, which is about one hundred kilometres south of Cairo. He answered the Copts' questions, trying to explain his faith with patience and love. Some were influenced by his new teachings, finding in his life and preaching a means for a changed life, and were converted to the Protestant faith.[131]

---

128. "The Moravians were a small group of Christians that originally formed in 1457, prior to the Protestant Reformation. The name Moravian denotes that this historic church had its origin in ancient Bohemia and Moravia in what is the present-day Czech Republic. The Moravian Church, or Unitas Fratrum (Unity of Brethren), as it has officially been known since 1457, arose as followers of Hus gathered on the estate of Lititz, about 100 miles east of Prague, and organized the church. This was 60 years before Luther and 100 years before the establishment of the Anglican Church. By 1467 the Moravian Church had established its own ministry, and in the years that followed three orders of the ministry were defined: deacon, presbyter and bishop." (http://www.mcsp.org/who_history.htm, (accessed 8 March 2004).

129. Watson, In the Valley, 101.

130. Watson, The American Mission, 23.

131. Watson, In the Valley, 105.

The number of Moravian missionaries to Egypt was not large, and they found many difficulties in their ministry including persecution and opposition from the people and the government.[132] The policy of their mission was not to establish a Moravian Church in Egypt, but instead they "attended Coptic churches and called on Coptic Priests, chatted in a friendly manner on religious topics and endeavoured to do good, not by public preaching but by showing the people that man is saved not by good works or ceremonies but by a living faith in the crucified Christ."[133] The Moravians found opportunities to share their faith with the Egyptians, concentrating on teaching the gospel quietly rather than preaching publicly, and utilizing their life and manners as models.

Nevertheless, in 1782, the Moravian Synod decided to close the work in Egypt because of financial difficulties and the mission's limited results. One of the problems the Moravians had faced was that the people refused any overt religious relationship with the Moravians. In contrast, when a number of Copts chose to leave their national Church they preferred to join the Greek or the Roman Church.[134]

Charles Watson said that the Moravians "undertook to establish no ecclesiastical organization; the results of their devoted labours are found in the individual lives they touched and quickened."[135]

1.4.3.2 The Church Missionary Society

The Church Missionary Society (CMS) is a mission organization of the Anglican Church. It is one of the oldest modern missionary societies in existence, having been established in 1799.[136] In 1815, the CMS established its Mediterranean Mission in Malta with an eye towards establishing missions in Egypt, Abyssinia, Greece, Turkey, Asia Minor, and Palestine.[137] William Jowett, one of their most influential missionaries, visited Egypt

---

132. Watson, *Egypt*, 141.

133. Hutton, *A History of Moravian Missions*, 164.

134. Ibid., 165.

135. Watson, *In the Valley*, 117.

136. Brian de Saram, *Nile Harvest: The Anglican Church in Egypt and the Sudan* (Marlborough, Wilts: The author, 1992), 53.

137. Church Missionary Society, *Outline Histories of CMS Missions*, Vol. 1 (London: Church Missionary Society, 1905), 108.

in 1819, 1820, and 1823,[138] distributing many copies of the Scriptures in Arabic.[139] During his visits, he met with the Coptic Patriarch who gave him letters of introduction to the priests and monks in different cities and monasteries.[140] In 1825, because of the report of his visits, the CMS sent five German missionaries from the Basle Seminary, namely Gobat, who later became Anglican Bishop of Jerusalem, and Lieder, Muller, Kruse, and Kugler.[141]

The CMS intended "to propagate the knowledge of the gospel among the Heathen," and their policy towards the Oriental churches was not to establish a new church but to reform the existing one.[142] One of the CMS leaders said, "the Greek, Armenian, Syrian, Coptic, and Abyssinian churches, though in many points far gone from the simplicity and purity of the truth, are not so entangled; and also possess within themselves the principle and the means of reformation."[143]

The CMS hoped to reform the Coptic Church in order that the Copts would reflect the light of the gospel to the Muslims, to be "a mission of help to the Coptic Church."[144] The missionaries of the CMS started two schools in Cairo for Coptic and Muslim children: one for boys and the other for girls. In 1842, the boys' school was changed into a theological seminary for the training of Coptic clergy under the leadership of Mr Lieder. However, there was opposition to the school from the Coptic Church that led to its closing after ten years of ministry. Nevertheless, one of the graduates of that seminary was selected to be *Abuna* (bishop) of Abyssinia.[145]

These missionaries used a number of methods, including the distribution of the Bible and religious books among Copts and Muslims.[146] Mr

---

138. Fowler, *Christian Egypt*, 250.

139. Watson, *In the Valley*, 119.

140. On some occasions the Coptic Patriarch received Christians from other countries without recognizing their denominational backgrounds.

141. Fowler, *Christian Egypt*, 250.

142. Vander Werff, *Christian Mission*, 153.

143. Watson, *Egypt*, 144.

144. Constance E. Padwick, *Temple Gairdner of Cairo* (London: Society for Promoting Christian Knowledge, 1929), 264.

145. Fowler, *Christian Egypt*, 250.

146. Eugene Stock, ed., *The History of the Church Missionary Society: Its Environment, Its Men and Its Work*, Vol. 1 (London: Church Missionary Society, 1899), 351.

Lieder made frequent trips to sell the Scriptures and tracts in the cities and villages in both the Delta and Upper Egypt.[147] By the permission of the Patriarch, weekly meetings were also held among Copts in Cairo for the reading of the Scriptures.

In 1836, the CMS only had two missionaries in Egypt: Kruse who left in 1852 for Palestine, and Mr Lieder who remained alone in the field until his death in 1865. The mission gradually died, and in 1862, the society decided to discontinue the mission in Egypt because "the difficulties which confronted the representatives of the Society, in their efforts to bring about the self-reformation of the Coptic Church were very great."[148] Bishop Gobat of Jerusalem, who himself had been a missionary to Egypt, stated that the failure of the efforts of the CMS to reform the Eastern Churches, including the Coptic Church, was because:

> The missionaries seem to follow almost too strictly the plan on which the mission was begun, to seek the friendship of the clergy, especially the higher clergy, of the Eastern Churches, with a view of influencing them gently, in the hope that by slow degrees they would become convinced of their errors and themselves reform their respective churches. But the system has failed, and I am convinced that it will ever fail with the several Eastern Churches, as well as with the Church of Rome. Individual conversions must be the aim, as the only means of prosecuting reformation.[149]

The CMS policy did not succeeded in Egypt because the Coptic Church itself was closed within its traditions, and their bishops and priests exerted great influence over their congregations. However, the American Mission found it very beneficial to study their mission goals and practices and thus learn from their mistakes.

Although the CMS had left Egypt in 1862, twenty years later, following the British occupation of Egypt, the CMS decided to begin a second

---

147. Watson, *In the Valley,* 121–122.
148. Fowler, *Christian Egypt,* 250.
149. Watson, *The American Mission,* 33.

mission in Egypt with the purpose of evangelizing Muslims.[150] The relationship with the Coptic Church remained friendly. For years, there was no Anglican Church for Egyptians but only for British expatriates who lived in Egypt. Later, due to Temple Gairdner's efforts, the Egyptian Anglican Church was established in 1921.[151] He had realized that the Coptic Church had a heritage of fear from their history of persecution and that they would not accept the Muslim converts.[152] Gairdner's aim in beginning an indigenous Anglican Church was "to raise a truly militant, evangelical and therefore evangelistic Church, however small, a truly Catholic Church with power to absorb and unify the most diverse elements and gifted with historical order and reverent, inspiring and liturgical services."[153]

In conclusion, the mission organizations that came to Egypt before the entrance of the American Presbyterian Mission, mainly wanted to have friendly relationships with the Coptic Church. Their primary goal was to evangelize Muslims and to revitalize the Copts, enabling them to be good examples and win their Muslim neighbours. It was difficult to accomplish that goal. Both the Moravians and the first CMS missions to Egypt were discontinued after only a few years because the number of Muslim converts was very few and the Coptic Church resisted any reformation.

1.5 The Establishment of the Egyptian Presbyterian Church

The goal of the American Presbyterian Mission in Egypt was not clear when the first missionaries came to Egypt from Syria in 1854. Their original intentions were to help their Mission in Syria to find refuge in Egypt, with the secondary goal of meeting the Egyptians' spiritual needs.[154] When the missionaries began their ministry, they wanted to work among Muslims but "they met with an opposition and a fanaticism . . . They

---

150. Gordon Hewitt, *The Problem of Success: A History of the Church Missionary Society 1910–1942*, Vol. I (London: SCM Press Ltd, 1971), 306.

151. Saram, *Nile Harvest*, 61.

152. Padwick, *Temple Gairdner*, 264.

153. Ibid.

154. See chapter 2.

found themselves despised and rejected."[155] The complications came from both the Egyptian government and people.[156] In fact, the results of their work among Muslims were less than they had expected. The Mission then directed its efforts to the Copts where the results were very encouraging. Eventually, they came to realize that they would need to establish an entirely new Church denomination in Egypt.

1.5.1 Reasons for Establishing an Evangelical Church

The work of the American Mission grew remarkably within its first few years. The number of Copts who followed the Protestant teachings increased because of the methods used by the missionaries. The Mission made the Bible more available for Copts to read. The Copts found different teachings to those that they learned in their mother church. The main emphasis of the conflict in doctrine between the American Mission and the Coptic Church was in their view of salvation and justification by faith.

Andrew Watson described the differences between the Coptic Church's teachings and the missionaries when he said:

> They knew little more of true religion than the Muhammadans. Christ is not their Saviour, the Holy Ghost is not their sanctifier, the commandments of God are not their rule of life. Jesus of Nazareth is not their example, and is not now their Mediator. They know nothing of justification by faith in the death and suffering of Christ; nothing of the new birth and divine life in union with Jesus through dwelling Spirit . . . we know that salvation is not by gaudy ritual, nor by an ancient priesthood, nor by the intercessions of saints, nor by worshiping pictures, nor by the confessional and transubstantiations, nor by a hoary antiquity, but by the precious blood of Christ.[157]

---

155. Davida Finney, *Tomorrow's Egypt* (Pittsburgh: Women's General Missionary Society, 1939), 108–109.

156. See chapter 3.

157. Watson, *The American Mission,* 413; Paul Sedra, "Ecclesiastical Warfare: Patriarch, Presbyterian, and Peasant in Nineteenth-Century Asyut" (Yale Center for International and Area Studies, research.yale.edu/ycias/database/files/MESV5-10.pdf. [Accessed on 16 September 2007]).

The missionaries wanted to proclaim the new teachings about justification by faith and they included in their preaching: "the one Sacrifice of Christ, the one Intercessor, the perfect atonement, the true nature of fasting and prayers, the reasonable service, the fullness of gospel revelation, . . . baptism and the Lord's supper."[158] The Coptic Church, not ready to accept these teachings, excommunicated and persecuted those who did. The new believers had no choice but to start a new church.[159]

As noted before, among the converts to the evangelical teachings there were a number of intellectual and influential Copts. Their social and financial situation put them among the most educated and wealthy classes in society. They became the leaders of the evangelical communities in many places. Some examples were "Saleh ʿAwad of Cairo; Makhiel, a monk; Wasif Khayat and Hanna Buktor of Assiut; Butrus of Manfalut, and Fam of Kus."[160] Some of them contributed a great deal to the ministry of the American Mission by building schools and churches in their towns and by giving money to the American Mission activities.[161]

Furthermore, the political situation in the Ottoman Empire, including Egypt, was favourable for the Protestants to establish their churches. In 1850 the Sultan, ʿAbd al-Majid, issued a *firman* (decree) making the Protestant *millet* (denomination) equal to other Christian denominations in the Empire. It allowed Protestants to have their own churches and their own representative to the government, although the Protestants in Egypt did not select their representative until 1878.[162]

The successful establishment of the Protestant Church in Beirut in 1848 as the first Protestant Church in the Arab World led the American Mission to follow the same strategy in Egypt.[163] They also learned from the Moravians' and the CMS's experience that establishing an organized

---

158. Ibid., 140.

159. John G. Lorimer, Lecture "Presbyterians in the Middle East: A Retrospective," The W. Don McClure Lectures on World Mission and Evangelism, Pittsburg Theological Seminary, 1994, 7.

160. Vander Werff, *Christian Mission,* 146.

161. Wissa, *Assiout,* 117–120.

162. Watson, *The American Mission,* 327.

163. Lorimer, *Presbyterians,* 7.

indigenous church was important for the continuance of the ministry and the best way to retain the fruits of their labour.

1.5.2 Important Steps in the Establishment and Organization of the Church

The formal creation of the Evangelical Church took place in stages. In September 1859, the sacrament of the Lord's Supper was administered in the Arabic language for the first time, and four persons were received into the fellowship of the Church and enrolled to be its first members. "These persons were Father Makhiel el-Belyana, a Coptic monk, Menas Jacob, an Armenian, 'Awad Hanna, and a Syrian, by name Nusr."[164]

Then on the 13 April 1860, an official presbytery in Egypt was formed by permission of the UPCNA. The Presbytery met in the Mission house in Cairo, where Mr Barnett, one of the first three missionaries to arrive in Egypt in 1854 and the oldest of the missionaries, was chosen to be moderator. A meeting was held in Alexandria on 23 May for the ordination of John Hogg.[165] In the same month, a group of seven people in Alexandria, including a woman, was received into communion by the missionaries to the Evangelical Church in Egypt.[166]

The number of people who joined the Evangelical Church gradually increased, to the point where there was a need in many cities and villages to institute a formalized organization of these churches. On 5 January 1863, four elders and three deacons were elected in a Cairo church. They were ordained on 15 February 1863 and the Azbakiyah congregation in Cairo became the first organized Evangelical Church in Egypt.[167]

Following the foundation of the church in Cairo, churches were established in Assiut, Alexandria, Mutiah, Kus, and other cities and villages. The church building in Assiut was the first evangelical church building in Egypt to be built by Egyptians, and was financed by their own money and

---

164. Watson, *The American Mission*, 110.

165. Ibid., 112, cited in Elder, *Vindicating a Vision*, 29; and in J. R. Alexander, *A Sketch of the Story of the Evangelical Church of Egypt: Founded by the American Mission 1854–1930* (Alexandria: Whitehead Morris Limited, 1930), 10–11.

166. Alexander, *A Sketch*, 10.

167. Watson, *The American Mission*, 156.

by their own people.[168] The following table from the 50th Report of the
American Mission in Egypt gives a picture of the growth of the Church:[169]

	1864	1874	1884	1894	1904
Native Ordained Workers	0	2	6	19	36
Other Native Workers	?	15	30	39	39
Organized Churches	1	6	19	33	63
Stations-total	3	18	61	167	213
Church Members	69	596	1,688	4,554	7,757
Average Sabbath Morning Attendance	150	986	3,114	8,886	15,916
Protestant Community	207	1,788	5,054	13,662	29,000
Pupils in Sabbath Schools	?	733	2,521	5,365	11,182

A major step forward in the organization of the Church took place in
1895, when the presbytery was organized into six districts. In each district,
there was a local evangelistic committee of five members, three ordained
ministers, and two elders. These districts were Cairo, Minia, Assiut North,
Assiut South, Girga and Kena.[170]

During the five years from 1895 to 1899, there was notable growth in
the ministry of the Church. Because of the increase in the number of congregations and workers, there arose the difficulty of transportation when
all the ordained ministers met together regularly to oversee the ministry.
In February 1898, in a meeting in Kus, the Presbytery of Egypt decided
to ask the General Assembly of the UPCNA that the Presbytery of Egypt
might be organized into four presbyteries and that these presbyteries might
be formed into a Synod.[171] The Assembly granted the request, and the new
organization divided the presbytery into four presbyteries, the Presbyteries

---

168. Alexander, *A Sketch*, 15.
169. UPCNA, Board of Foreign Missions, *The 50th Annual Report*, 93.
170. Alexander, *A Sketch*, 30-1.
171. Ibid.

of the Delta, Middle Egypt, Assiut, and Thebes, the southern boundary of which included the Sudan. This new structure led to the establishment of the Synod of the Nile, and the name of the Church became the Evangelical Church of Egypt.[172] This step of organizing the Synod of the Nile was seen as a major encouraging turning point in the development of the Evangelical Church in Egypt.[173]

1.5.3 Different Opinions

The establishment of a Protestant Church in Egypt as a new denomination beside the national Coptic Church attracted censure from many people, both inside and outside Egypt. The Copts were very critical. They believed that the missionaries came with a new religion and wanted to force Copts to abandon their faith and embrace a new one.[174] Some of the Coptic theologians of the nineteenth and early twentieth centuries wrote against the Protestant theology and liturgical practices that differed from their traditional teaching.[175] One of these theologians, 'Awad, went with the Patriarch Demetrius II on his trip to Upper Egypt and gave many speeches against Protestants and their teachings.[176]

The Muslims also viewed the establishment of the Protestant Church with suspicion. They believed that it was a Western institution that was being forced on Egypt by the colonial powers.[177] Converts from the Coptic to the Evangelical Church were seen as self-seekers who wanted to advance their own interests, attaching themselves to western powers and thus enjoying the benefits given to non-Egyptians.[178] Muslims in Egypt also opposed

---

172. Watson, *Egypt*, 192.

173. Elder, *Vindicating a Vision*, 105; Alexander, *A Sketch*, 32.

174. Wissa, *Assiut*, 106.

175. Otto F. A. Meinardus, *Christian Egypt Faith and Life* (Cairo: The American University in Cairo Press, 1970), 210–211.

176. Jirjis Philotheos 'Awad, *Tarikh al-Highumanus Philotheos* (The History of Hegomenos Philotheos) (Cairo: Matba'at al-Tawfiq, 1906), 90–91.

177. Sohirin Mohammad Solihin, *Copts and Muslims in Egypt: A Study on Harmony and Hostility* (Leicester: The Islamic Foundation, 1991), 39.

178. Antonie Wessels, *Arab and Christian: Christians in the Middle East* (Kampen: Kok Pharos Publishing House, 1995), 147. See chapter 3.

evangelistic work and later organized a number of campaigns against the missionary activities.[179]

The establishment of the Evangelical Church in Egypt was viewed critically not only by Coptic leaders and Muslims, but also by some Western writers. The historian and theological writer, Otto Meinardus, considered the establishment of the Protestant Church by the American Mission as creating a division among the Copts.[180] The Anglican Reverend Montague Fowler, who visited Egypt in 1900, also opposed the establishment of the Protestant Church in Egypt. He believed that this step was very dangerous for the Coptic Church and its witness to Muslims. He thought that the American Mission should concentrate its efforts on converting Muslims, not taking Copts from their national Church. He was supportive of the Anglican approach that at that time only aimed to build up and strengthen the national Coptic Church.[181]

Stephen Neill summarizes the situation: "The United Presbyterians of the USA came in, in 1854, and at once began to attract a number of the more intelligent Copts. Rightly or wrongly, they decided to found a rival Church, and their success has tended rather to the disruption than to the reconstitution of the ancient Church."[182]

Andrew Watson tried to answer this charge in his paper "Islam in Egypt," read at the First Missionary Conference on behalf of the Mohammedan world held at Cairo 1906, when he said:

> The purpose of the mission was not as has been reported in some places, to labour among the various Christian denominations especially, but to preach and teach the pure gospel of our Lord Jesus Christ to Jews, Muslims and nominal Christians where and when opportunity offered. It so happened that God in His providence opened the door to the Copts, who, it would be easy to prove, were at the time in great ignorance of the Word of God. Instead of beating at the bolted and barred doors of Islam, at a time when there was no

179. Vander Werff, *Christian Mission,* 152.

180. Meinardus, *The Coptic Church,* 430.

181. Fowler, *Christian Egypt,* 278.

182. Stephen Neill, *Christian Mission: A History* (Harmondsworth: Penguin, 1964), 303.

religious liberty, the missionaries entered at the open doors of
"the lost sheep of Israel"[183]

The Coptic Church retained its critical view of the work of the American
Mission and the Evangelical Church, seeing them as coming like "wolves to
kill its sheep." This reputation deeply complicated their relationship with
the Coptic Church and with the Egyptian government.

1.5.4 The Relationship with the Government

As stated earlier, the Ottoman Empire recognized the growth of the
Protestants in its countries. In 1850, the Sultan ʿAbd al-Majid issued a *firman* (decree) making the Protestant denomination equal to any other religious denomination. This *firman* required the Protestants of any Ottoman
territory to select one layperson to be their representative to the government, and to oversee the administration of its personal status laws such as
marriage and heritages issues.[184] This *firman* was not enforced in the first
two decades of the American Mission in Egypt, but after the matter was
raised in negotiations with the Egyptian government, the acknowledgment
was formally made in 1878, and the Protestant community was called
upon to elect one person to be its representative. Girgis Bey Barsoum was
elected to occupy this position. He was a rich Protestant from Beni Sweif
who had been accepted by the missionaries as a member of the Protestant
Church, but only after he freed his slaves. On 4 June 1878, the Khedive
Ismaʿil issued a decree and the Egyptian government formally recognized
Girgis Bey Barsoum as the representative of the Protestants in Egypt.[185]

The Evangelical Church had official status from that time. However,
some matters still needed to be worked out in relation to Egyptian law, as
well as rules for how the church itself should be organized. Andrew Watson
worked hard with the official authorities in Egypt to organize the structure
of the Evangelical General Council. On 3 April 1902, the government sent

---

183. Andrew Watson, "Islam in Egypt," in *The Mohammedan World of To-day: Being Papers
Read at the First Missionary Conference on behalf of the Mohammedan World Held at Cairo
April 4th-9th, 1906*, eds. S. M. Zwemer, E. M. Wherry and James L. Barton (New York:
Fleming H. Revell Company, 1906), 34–35.

184. Watson, *The American Mission*, 327.

185. Elder, *Vindicating a Vision*, 71–72.

its agreement to the Evangelical Church in Egypt that arranged new elections in May 1902, and elected Akhnoukh Fanous as its representative.[186]

The name of the Evangelical Church in Egypt was changed many times to reflect the changes in the life of the Church and its relationships with America and Egypt. In the organization of the first congregation, the church was called the United Presbyterian Church in Egypt. It was named after the church which sent the American Mission to Egypt, the United Presbyterian Church of North America.[187] The government and the people however, knew the church as the Protestant Church. After the organization of the Synod of the Nile, the church became known as the Evangelical Church of Egypt. For political reasons, the name was changed to the Coptic Evangelical Church after the revolution of 1952.[188]

1.5.5 Theological Training

In order to train its leaders, the Evangelical Church organized theological training for national Egyptians working with the missionaries. It was in February 1863 that the Egyptian Presbytery decided to give the missionaries in Cairo the responsibility of starting theological classes "for the training of young men for Christian work in Egypt."[189] Theological evening classes were held in Cairo during some evenings in 1863. In 1864, regular theological classes were started in the houseboat of John Hogg with nine students. Only two of them completed the program and they graduated in 1871, to become the first Egyptian pastors of the Evangelical Church. For some years the theological classes moved according to the changing locations of the missionaries until it settled in Assiut with Hogg for the first two years, and then in Cairo with Andrew Watson for the second two.[190] In 1885, the class moved to Cairo and remained there under the name the Evangelical Theological Seminary in Cairo (ETSC).[191] The Seminary was located in the American Mission headquarters in Azbakiyah until it moved to its present location in 'Abbasiyyah in 1926. From its beginning,

---

186. Watson, *The American Mission,* 327.
187. Ibid., 156.
188. John H. Watson, *Among the Copts* (Brighton: Sussex Academic Press, 2000), 8.
189. Watson, *The American Mission,* 156.
190. The study in the Seminary was for four years.
191. Salama, *Tarikh al-Kanysa al-Injilya,* 152.

the Seminary supplied the Evangelical Church with trained and educated national leaders.

1.5.6 The Evangelical Church's Early Contributions to Egyptian Society

The establishment of the Evangelical Church in Egypt was seen as one of the most important achievements of the American Mission in Egypt, besides its educational and medical efforts. The Church played an important role in the life of the Egyptians who were served by the Mission and it influenced many areas of their lives.

Spiritually, it shared the gospel with many Egyptians and brought the message of salvation to the awareness of the Copts after centuries of neglecting it. The Church used the Bible in explaining its beliefs which raised the awareness of the importance of reading and studying the Bible among the Egyptian Christians. The number of Bibles in Arabic which were distributed and the number of Bible study meetings increased dramatically because of the efforts of the missionaries and Church members. It is interesting to note that while this was occurring, "[t]he Coptic Church experienced its greatest revival in the very regions where evangelical churches sprang up,"[192] initiating reforms in many aspects of their Church ministry. They began using the Arabic language in preaching, and opened Sunday schools for children. Realizing the need for more training of their priests, they opened a Coptic Orthodox Seminary.[193]

The Evangelical Church, through the efforts of both missionaries and rich Protestants, established a number of schools in many cities and villages. In 1899, the schools enrolled a significant number of pupils, only slightly less than all government schools.[194] The evangelical communities came to hold the highest number of literate and educated among all Egyptians.[195]

---

192. Vander Werff, *Christian Mission,* 146; Stanley H. Skreslet, "American Presbyterian Mission in Egypt," *American Presbyterians Journal of Presbyterian History* 64, no. 2 (Summer 1986): 86.

193. Wahba, *The American Presbyterian,* 13–14.

194. Watson, *In the Valley,* 183.

195. Ibid., 184. Charles Watson gives the numbers of the Protestant community in 1898, saying that out of 22,500 Protestants, 521 of every 1,000 men and 200 of every 1,000 women could read. The government census showed that among Egyptians generally only 124 out of every 1,000 men and 11 out every 1,000 women could read.

Socially, the Evangelical Church influenced many areas of Egyptian life, including everyday interpersonal relationships. It worked against the slave trade, and against negative funeral practices such as crying loudly and putting dust and mud upon the heads. In 1868, Protestants were able to change the market day in Assiut and many other towns and villages, from Sunday to alternative days.[196] The Church responded to the health needs of the people by opening clinics and hospitals in towns and villages and indeed its work increased the awareness of the people and the government of the importance of health services.[197] The Evangelical Church in Egypt became known as "the Church of three services": the church, the school, and the hospital.

The role of the Evangelical Church in Egyptian society grew through the years, playing an important role in serving all levels of society in both the cities and villages. Its growth, organization, and service to Egypt gave it great respect and credibility within Egyptian society.

1.6 Conclusion

According to tradition, Christianity in Egypt traces its history back to the first century when it is believed that St Mark came to Alexandria, preaching the gospel to the Egyptians. From that early time until the present day, Christianity has had an important presence in Egypt. The Coptic Orthodox Church, which is the national church in Egypt, is perhaps the oldest recognizable Christian group in the world having retained its particular rituals and teachings for many centuries. Throughout history, other Orthodox and Catholic churches were established in Egypt, but the establishment of a distinctly Protestant Church did not take place until the coming of the American Presbyterian Mission. There were some other Protestant missions in the eighteenth and nineteenth centuries, such as the Moravians and the Church Missionary Society, but they did not establish

---

196. UPCNA, Board of Foreign Mission, *Eleventh Annual Report of the Board of Foreign Mission of the United Presbyterian Church of North America: Presented to the General Assembly in May, 1870* (Philadelphia: Young & Ferguson, Printers, 1870), 38. See also: Elder, *Vindicating a Vision,* 64. The day of the market had been on Sunday from the time of the Pharaohs. It was changed to another day and has remained so until today.
197. Vander Werff, *Christian Mission,* 150.

churches or denominations. The American Presbyterian Mission was the first Protestant mission that sought to establish an indigenous evangelical church.

At its commencement, Egypt was at a pivotal time of its history. Politics, society, and the Coptic Church were in a period of critical change. Among other factors, these changes attracted the American Mission to consider expanding their work beyond Syria to Egypt. The work was limited in the first few years, but the efforts of the first missionaries and the encouraging results seized the attention of the Board and others. As a result, many missionaries were encouraged to join the Mission, hoping to reap much fruit.

Learning from their predecessors, the Mission chose to respond to the practical needs of the Egyptians. The schools of the Mission increased not only the number of students but also the quality of education. Additionally, the health clinics and hospitals served both Copts and Muslims who desperately required medical help and information. Likewise, the number of Bibles and Christian literature distributed reflect the spiritual hunger and ignorance that existed at that time.

Although there was opposition to the work from outside the Mission and difficult issues within, the missionaries continued their ministry. By every means possible they tried to solve the problems they faced, even utilizing their home country's political influence to ameliorate resistance and violence.

The work of the American Mission expanded to cover most of Egypt from Alexandria in the north to Aswan in the south, as well as mission endeavours in the Sudan. Fifty years of mission resulted in reaching many people with the gospel and to establish a national indigenous church. In doing so, the Mission and the Evangelical Church made significant contributions to Egypt's educational, medical, and spiritual needs.

CHAPTER 2

The Relationship between the American Mission and the Evangelical Church in Egypt (1854–1958)

2.1 Introduction

The relationship between the American Presbyterian Mission and the Evangelical Church in Egypt went through different phases. From the beginning, the American Mission in Egypt wanted to ensure the self-government of the indigenous Christian church. However, it took more than a century from the start of the Mission and the Evangelical Church in Egypt until final independence was achieved in 1958.

The idea of giving indigenous churches their independence, allowing them to self-propagate and self-support was one of the central theories among missionaries in the nineteenth century and early twentieth centuries. According to Rufus Anderson, Henry Venn, and Roland Allen, the independence of the native church in the mission field was the main aim of mission work.[1] As key mission leaders and theologians Anderson, Venn and Allen analyzed the mission movement in the nineteenth century and coined the term "indigenous churches." Their teaching was that mission

---

1. Rufus Anderson (1796–1880) was the corresponding secretary for the American Board of Commissionaires for foreign mission from 1932 to 1866, while Venn (1796–1873) was honorary secretary of the Church Missionary Society from 1841 to 1873. Allen (1868–1947) was a theologian and a missionary to China and Western Africa. Anderson, Venn, and Allen encouraged the teachings of giving the indigenous churches full independence in finances, propagating the gospel, and governing themselves.

work should include the converting of the lost, organizing a church of the converted, developing a competent indigenous clergy, and preparing them to be independent and self-propagating.[2] Anderson, Venn, and Allen challenged the missionaries not to be involved in education and medical work but to give more emphasis to evangelism. They separately encouraged the mission societies to help the new churches to be self-governing, self-supported, and self-propagating indigenous churches.[3]

This chapter will examine to what extent these theories of mission applied in the relationship between the American Mission and the Evangelical Church. It will analyze how the American Mission in Egypt applied this policy of progressively giving the Church in Egypt its complete independence. It was not an easy task for either the Mission or the Church, but their mutual goal helped the two bodies fulfil their intentions within the framework of their long-established relationship.

2.2 The Relationship in the Early Period (1854–1904)

2.2.1 The Mission in Control of Everything until 1871

During its first few years in Egypt, the American Mission worked by itself. The missionaries moved from place to place freely, motivated by their vision of evangelization and service. They reported the results of their ministry to the Board in America.[4] Their relationship with the Egyptians was that of foreign missionaries coming to help the people to know Christ in a new way, and the local people were the recipients of their work. The missionaries

---

2. For more about their theories, R. Pierce Beaver, ed., *To Advance the Gospel: Selections from the Writings of Rufus Anderson.* (Grand Rapids: William B. Eerdmans Publishing Company, 1967), 24. See also Wilbert R. Shenk, "Rufus Anderson and Henry Venn: A Special Relationship?," *International Bulletin of Missionary Research* 5 (October 1981): 168–172; R. Pierce Beaver, "The Legacy of Rufus Anderson." *Occasional Bulletin of Missionary Research* 3 (1979): 94–97. See also David J. Bosch, *Transforming Mission: Paradigm Shifts in Theology of Mission* (Maryknoll: Orbis Books, 1991), 330–334.

3. Rufus Anderson, *Foreign Missions: Their Relations and Claims* (New York: Charles Scribner and Company, 1869), 92.

4. Kenneth E. Bailey, "Cross-Cultural Mission: A Tale of Three Cities," W. Don McClure lectureship in world missions and evangelism (Three lectures presented at Pittsburgh Theological Seminary, 1984, audiobook), 14.

enjoyed a great deal of independence in the first few years, and they worked according to what they found convenient for the progress of their ministry. They had direct control and responsibility for their work. There was no distinction made between the Mission and the Evangelical Church.

The establishment of the Egyptian Presbytery in 1860 did not change the relationship between the American Mission and the newly born Church. There was only one body, the United Presbyterian Presbytery in Egypt whose only pastors were the ordained American missionaries. The chairman of the Presbytery was an American and the first role of the Presbytery was to ordain John Hogg to be a minister.[5] The missionaries used English in their meetings and in writing the reports for the board in the United States. The missionaries were responsible for both the organization of their missionary society and the development of the Church.

Although there was growth in the number of congregations and in the raising up of Egyptian leaders within the new denomination, the Mission had sole responsibility for selecting workers and appointing them to the ministry in the Presbytery. For sixteen years, the missionaries controlled the administrative and financial affairs of the Evangelical Church. The Mission paid the salaries of the Egyptian workers who joined the ministry as evangelists, pastors, and teachers in the Mission's schools.[6]

During the years of 1869–1870, missionaries and Egyptians raised many questions about the relationship between the Mission and the growing Egyptian Evangelical Church. At issue was the role of the Egyptian pastors, particularly concerning the financial and administrative affairs of the Presbytery and the Mission, and the authority, superintendence and government of the Church.[7] According to the pioneer missionaries, it was their intention to enable the Church that they had started to become self-sustaining. John Hogg wrote:

---

5. Hogg, *A Master-Builder*, 74.

6. Alexander, *A Sketch*, 16.

7. Ibid. These questions were not mentioned in the early Mission records but have come from the analyses of J. R. Alexander who was a missionary in Egypt for a long time. He was the director of Assiut College from 1887 to 1909. These remarks are from his speech before the Missionary Association in 1930.

We believe that the great ultimate aim of the missionary enterprise is not merely the conversion of individual souls, nor
the culture and enlightenment of the body of the people, but
the planting in their midst of an independent, self-sustaining,
self-propagating, Christian Church.[8]

2.2.2 The Establishment of the Mission Association, 1871

The lay missionaries (e.g. doctors, educators, and single women workers)
made it clear that they wished to have a voice in making decisions. They
demanded that the Mission organize its properties, personnel, and finances
under a separate body.[9] Before this, occurred only ordained missionaries
were members of the Presbytery, and only they were given a vote. Wanting
to separate the mission work from the church ministry and organization,
the Board of Foreign Mission proposed to the missionaries in Egypt that
"they form an organization for the transaction of all business that was not
strictly of a presbyterial character."[10] The missionaries began to study the
best way to respond to the Board's request. After many lengthy discussions, they decided in 1871 to establish The Egyptian Association of the
Missionaries of the United Presbyterian Church of North America. In their
report to the Board about organizing this association, they gave the following reasons:

1) There are now, and probably always will be, lay members
   connected with the mission who, not being members of
   Presbytery, are not entitled to a voice in its deliberations nor a
   vote in its decisions, but who, as regularly appointed missionaries
   from the church at home, have an equal right with their clerical
   brethren to a voice in the management of all matters which are
   secular and missionary, as distinguished from ecclesiastical and
   presbyterial, and whose counsels and aid are particularly valuable
   in all such matters.

2) The blessing of the Great Head of the church upon our labors
   has brought us to begin ordaining native pastors and elders.

---

8. Hogg, *A Master-Builder,* 197.

9. Vander Werff, *Christian Mission,* 147.

10. Watson, *The American Mission,* 281.

These have full right to the official exercise of their functions, not only in reference to the churches over which they have been ordained, but also in the higher courts of the Lord's house, and we recognize their full official equality with ourselves and consequent right to a seat with us in all church courts.

3) On the other hand, besides the relations which we bear to the native community as evangelists, and to the partially organized native churches as temporary pastors – relations which make it our duty and right to sit in all church courts in the mission field, and to unite with native presbyters in the administration and management of all purely ecclesiastical and presbyterial matters – we at the same time sustain other well-defined relations to our Church in America, as its representatives and the responsible almoners of its funds – relations from which arise duties and responsibilities which we cannot transfer to native presbyters. The foregoing considerations indicate the necessity of a clear distinction between those functions which belong to foreign missionaries as such, whether lay or clerical, and those which belong to presbyters both native and foreign, and to effect this distinction and secure the rights and facilitate the performance of the duties of all concerned.[11]

It is clear that the missionaries had found some difficulties in clarifying the relationship within the Mission itself between the ordained and lay missionaries on the one hand, and the need to organize the growing Church in Egypt on the other.

The missionaries not only gave their reasons for establishing this new association, but also sent a draft constitution of 14 articles to the Board in America. After the Board's approval, the first meeting of the Missionary Association was held in Cairo on 17 March 1871.[12]

Later, on 31 October 1871, the Presbytery was held in Nakheliah, a village near Assiut, and for the first time Egyptian members took part. The Presbytery was held on the ordination and installation of Tadros Yusif as

11. Ibid., 282; and Elder, *Vindicating a Vision*, 65–66.
12. See Appendix A.

the first Egyptian ordained pastor.[13] In the same meeting, Tadros Yusif was elected to be the Presbytery's secretary, whereupon it became a rule that the secretary should be an Egyptian.[14] Further progress is noted by the fact that the business discussed in this meeting was translated into Arabic.

2.2.3 The Development of the Relationship after the Establishment of the Mission Association and the Egyptian Presbytery

Beginning from 1871 the relationship between the Mission and the Presbytery became more clearly delineated. The Mission was responsible for administering its own properties and the schools that it had established and continued to staff; to determine the location of their missionaries; and to oversee the care and disbursement of funds.[15] The Presbytery controlled all ecclesiastical matters including the Church funds, licensing preachers, ordaining pastors, organizing churches, and selecting students for theological training.[16] Although the missionaries continued to hold the majority in the Presbytery, the inauguration of the association was a major step forward in establishing the official relationship between the Mission and the Church in Egypt.

This step of organizational separation was viewed positively by the American missionaries and by others who wrote about their work. Most American writers considered it an advancement, and proof of early maturation in the relationship between the Mission and its daughter church. They believed that they had successfully sown seeds of self-government and self-support within the Egyptian Church.[17] They saw the American Mission in Egypt as a model for the relationship between missions and national churches in non-Western countries. One of the American missionaries in Egypt, J. R. Alexander, praised the American Mission, saying that he believed that this practice was in accordance with Apostolic practice and New

---

13. Watson, *The American Mission*, 284.

14. J. R. Alexander, "A Historical Word," in *Kitab al-Yubil al-Almasi lil-Kinisa al-Injilia bi Misr wal-Sudan* (The Book of the Diamond Anniversary of the Evangelical Church in Egypt and the Sudan) (Cairo: Matba'at al-Muhit, 1937), 10.

15. Watson, *The American Mission*, 284.

16. Elder, *Vindicating a Vision*, 66; Watson, *The American Mission*, 284.

17. Ibid., Finney, *Tomorrow's Egypt*, 111.

Testament teaching and methods. Further, he believed that the Mission was successfully planning for the future of the Egyptian Church and its potential growth in members and leaders. He also found in this an application of the Presbyterian teachings concerning democracy and the equal rights of all members of the church whether they were American or native.[18]

With the establishment of the Missionary Association, the missionaries were seeking to give the Egyptians an equal role in the leadership of the Church, but in fact, this failed to happen. The missionaries remained in control of the Presbytery and when the Presbytery decided to arrange itself as a Synod in 1899, the chairman of the new Synod was Andrew Watson. At the same time, two out of the four presbyteries were under the leadership of missionaries.[19] During these early years, few qualified Egyptian leaders could obtain these positions. The Egyptian members in the Synod were loyal to the missionaries and their dominant role in the ministry. The missionaries would continue to consider themselves part of the Synod, and would retain a level of authority in this role until the Church's full independence from the General Assembly in 1958.

The Mission maintained its main work of evangelism alongside their other activities such as education and medical work. These activities were organized by an independent Missionary Association and not by the Presbytery, and were not the responsibility of the Evangelical Church. This, unfortunately, led the Egyptian evangelicals to think of the work of evangelism as only for missionaries. Even when the Egyptians became involved in evangelism, they did it under the supervision of the missionaries. This situation negatively affected the Egyptian view of mission and evangelism for many years.[20] This separation of mission and evangelism from pastoral work was an oversight on the part of both the Mission and the Church. Both entities were unaware of the future effect of this development and never discussed it in detail

Despite this omission, the American Mission intentionally worked to train national leaders as they sought to build an independent Egyptian

18. Alexander, *A Sketch,* 16–17.
19. Salama, *Tarikh al-Kanysa al-Injilya,* 131.
20. Lorimer, *Presbyterians,* 14.

church. The missionaries also worked with the Egyptians to develop a financially self-supporting Church.

2.2.4 Training of Egyptian Leaders

Training Egyptian leaders was one of the missionaries' first priorities and strategies. This was accomplished in two ways: by finding existing leaders, and by training young men to become leaders. During the first few years, the number of people connected with the Mission had been limited. The missionaries had gradually enlarged their contacts through their schools and the evening meetings that they held for the teachers and the students' parents. With great foresight, the missionaries considered the future needs of the church, and looked for people who showed leadership potential. Among the members of the first congregation in Cairo, the first to be noticed were people of influence and leadership. These included: Mikha'il, a previous Coptic monk who had converted to the evangelical faith; an Armenian jeweller; and a teacher in the boys' school.[21] In Upper Egypt, evangelism among Copts had also produced a number of converts who were suitable for leadership. They were rich, educated, and already influential among their people, having important roles in their local evangelical churches and already helping in the development of the Mission and the Church.

Besides recruiting existing leaders, the missionaries encouraged young people from their schools and the Church to join the Theological Class that was established nine years after the work began in 1854.[22] For example, Hogg noticed that one young man had the capacity to be a gospel preacher. Shenuda had been a student in the Mission school in Assiut and became one of the first students in the Theological Class. Hogg said that it "is worth living for to train up a dozen young preachers such as this."[23]

Once the Theological Class opened, many local young men joined, hoping to become pastors. In the first year, 1864, there were eleven students, four of whom were Coptic priests. The students were taught by the

---

21. Elder, *Vindicating a Vision*, 30.

22. The Theological Class was the name of the Seminary from its first beginning. The name later changed to be the School of Theology and then the Evangelical Theological Seminary in Cairo.

23. Hogg, *A Master-Builder*, 146.

missionaries.[24] The lessons were in Arabic and the missionaries translated many materials from English so that the students could understand them. During the summer, students were sent to different cities and villages to evangelize and preach under the supervision of their teachers.[25] Many of the students succeeded, though some did not finish their pastoral training, seeming to lack vision and an understanding of the evangelical pastor's role.

It soon became clear that in order to train secular or religious leaders, the standard of basic education needed to be raised. Consequently, John Hogg undertook the task of convincing the Mission and the Board to financially support the Assiout Training College that he then worked hard to establish. He had great expectations for this college: "Assiout Academy will expand into a college in a very few years. We also maintain that a missionary college (i.e. a college for training pastors, teachers, and evangelists) ought to draw its students chiefly from the families of native converts."[26] The establishment of Assiout Training College in 1874 was a major step in the process of developing trained Egyptian leaders. The College was built with the highest standard in its physical construction and in its academic excellence of its time, and its graduates became teachers, ministers, and laymen of marked Christian spirit who made a meaningful contribution to the life of Egypt.[27] John R. Mott, another well-known missionary, wrote:

> After visiting nearly all the missionary colleges and schools of importance in the non-Christian world, and studying their work and opportunities, I have no hesitation in saying that the Assiout Training College, of Egypt, is one of the most strategic in the world. In fact, I know of no other college which has yielded larger practical results for the amount of money expended than this particular institution.[28]

---

24. Watson, *The American Mission,* 456.

25. This training has continued until today in the Evangelical Presbyterian Seminary in Cairo. During the summer the students go to different presbyteries where they help in the ministry of the churches and prepare for future pastoral ministry. Supervision of student training is the responsibility of the presbyteries and the Seminary.

26. Hogg, *A Master-Builder,* 192.

27. *Times of Blessing,* Sept. 14, 1876, 362–363.

28. Watson, *In the Valley,* 184.

Assiout Training College, or Assiout College, gained an excellent reputation and contributed significantly in preparing Egyptian leaders in a pleasant Christian educational environment.

Graduating from Assiout Training College was made a prerequisite for students who wished to join the Theological Class. The Theological Class, which later became the Seminary, together with the Assiout Training College, sought to provide trained young men for the ministry of the Church.[29] These two schools became the major institutions preparing leaders for both the Church and the Mission schools, and were therefore carefully administered and nurtured by the missionaries.

2.2.5 Finances

The Mission worked not only towards the training of Church leaders but also towards helping the Church to achieve financial self-sufficiency. The financial organization of the Church was one of the most significant issues defining the relationship between the Mission and the Church. The ability of the Church to self-support was viewed as a measure of its maturity. It was also a matter of much negotiation and debate for many years between the Mission, the Board, and the Evangelical Church.

In the first few years, the missionaries depended on the contributions of their Board. The growth of the Mission and the vast needs within Egypt inspired many individual Americans and Europeans to give generously, especially for the schools. Andrew Watson created a list of the special friends and helpers of the Mission. In this list, he included both associations and individuals who gave annually for certain works or projects. Among them were people who had a special relationship with Egypt because they had either lived there or visited regularly. One of these friends was the Indian, Maharajah Dhulup Singh, who continued to give the Mission an annual gift of $5,000 on his wedding anniversary. This practice helped the missionaries during the financially lean times of the Civil War in America.[30]

The missionaries travelled to the United States, England, and Scotland to share the news of their ministry and to encourage Christians to give to the ministry. At the same time, the Mission received contributions from

---

29. Salama, *Tarikh al-Kanysa al-Injilya,* 152.
30. Watson, *The American Mission,* 467–470. See chapter 1.

many passing travellers, both evangelicals and those from other Christian denominations.[31]

The income of the Mission did not only come from donors outside Egypt. School fees, medical fees, and book sales also provided financial support, as shown in the missionaries' annual reports. Thus, for example, the income from schools was $596 in 1870, which sum increased due to the growth in the number of the schools. By 1880, the income had reached $3,225; it was $13,872 by 1890; and reached $58,885 in 1906.[32] Similar income growth could be found in the other departments. The book distribution department sold thousands of books including the Scriptures and other religious and educational books, totalling $167,705 from 1854 to 1896.[33] Likewise, the medical ministry in Assiut collected fees from patients during the years 1891–1894 amounting to $4,085.[34]

In the first few decades of its existence, the American Mission encouraged converts from the Coptic Church to also give donations to the ministry. After the establishment of the local congregations, the members contributed generously to their church and to the work of the Mission. In reports and writings, the missionaries sometimes mentioned the contributions that the nationals had given. The following table details the combined contributions from the local churches to cover ministry expenses as mentioned in a variety of reports and letters:[35]

Year	1870	1875	1880	1885	1890	1895	1906
Amount $[36]	566	3,106	4,726	3,911	7,097	11,431	7,106

---

31. Ibid., 470.

32. Watson, *Egypt,* 278.

33. Watson, *The American Mission*, 432.

34. Ibid., 394.

35. These numbers were collected from different books about the work of the American Mission in Egypt. There are more details in Watson, *The American Mission*, 279, 302, 338, 378 and 386. The year 1906 was mentioned in Watson, *Egypt*, 277.

36. The American Dollar was equal to five Egyptian pounds at that time.

The Mission initially financed its own activities in Egypt, including the costs of establishing the first schools, clinics and churches. However, the Mission gradually received increased funding from the local churches and several rich Egyptians.[37]

Although the Egyptians were generally poor, they made an effort to support the ministry. Nevertheless, it took many years before the Egyptian Protestant Church understood the concept of stewardship and provided for the full support of the ministry. The statistics given by the missionaries declared that the amount of money given by Egyptians to the work of the Presbytery and then the Synod did in fact increase. In 1870, the average annual local contribution per member was $3.14. Ten years later, it was $4.80.[38] Congregants gave for the salaries of the pastors and evangelical workers, and for the costs of general expenses, building repairs, and aid in evangelistic and other benevolent works.[39] The following table shows the total contributions given by Egyptians to their church ministries. The contributions in 1890 were significantly higher than other years, due to a successful stewardship campaign held within the church:

Year	1870	1874	1884	1890	1899	1906
Amount $	10,722	10,653	22,779	50,000	22,900	29,006

Thus, from its beginning, the Evangelical Church in Egypt took steady steps towards self-support. The efforts of the Mission in teaching and training the Church members led to a marked progress in this development. It is interesting to note that the contribution from local resources to the Mission's activities grew gradually until it became larger than the income from abroad. By 1905, the total contribution from Egyptian sources was $124,968 while that of the General Assembly in America was $103,066.[40] Most of the Mission's gifts went towards evangelistic work and the costs of building and maintaining church structures.

---

37. Watson, *The American Mission,* 287.

38. Watson, *Egypt,* 172.

39. Watson, *The American Mission,* 390.

40. Watson, *Egypt,* 279.

In 1901, the Mission discussed the matter of church buildings with the Synod. Before this, the Mission had generously supported the building of churches, but as the number of congregations increased, the Mission asked the Synod to encourage local churches to raise and collect the needed money. Instead, the Mission was wishing to redirect its money from America towards the expansion of missionary activities in Egypt. When this was brought before the Synod, some members were opposed to any changes, stating that the church in America was rich while the church in Egypt was poor. The majority, however, voted to release the Mission from this responsibility considering this as a positive step towards full self-support. The Board also supported the decision of the Mission. From that time, any local congregation that needed money for a new building solicited funds from other local churches and individuals, while also collecting money and materials from their own members and even from their Coptic and Muslim neighbours. The missionaries gave individually from their tithes and not from the Mission's budget.[41] Despite these attempts, the Egyptians were too poor to cover all ministry expenses, so they continued to be dependent on money from America.

After the establishment of the Synod of the Nile in 1899, the financial relationship between the Mission and the Church was clarified further. Every year the Mission gave the Synod a specific amount of money to cover current expenses including pastoral salaries, ministerial relief, and support for evangelists and travel. In 1904–1905, for example, the sum from the Mission to the Synod was $8,465.[42]

In the period just surveyed (1854–1904), the Mission and the Church built the framework which was to enable the Church to be self-governing and self-supporting. As we shall continue to explore, it took many negotiations, disagreements, and misunderstandings before a firm foundation was established. However, the result of these efforts led to the next stage in the relationship, that of the Church's complete independence from the American Mission.

---

41. Alexander, *A Sketch*, 36–37.
42. Elder, *Vindicating a Vision*, 107–108.

Positive as these steps were, the effects were not so clear-cut. Kenneth Bailey, a missionary from the American Presbyterian Church for more than thirty years in Egypt, Lebanon, and Palestine, and the son of missionaries who had also served in Egypt and Ethiopia for forty years, said that the money, which came from America in fact, directed the aims of the Egyptian Mission and Church. The Church felt obliged to please the Western donors who, in fact, often directed the monies towards projects they favoured, and not according to the real needs or vision on the field. Bailey further held that missionaries who came to be servants actually became employers of the Egyptians, thus effectively keeping power in the hands of the Americans.[43]

2.3 The Relationship in the Second Period: Steps towards Independence (1905–1926)

Although there was notable progress towards self-support and self-governance, the missionaries continued to hold most of the leadership positions of the Church. While the number of Egyptians in the Presbytery and later in the Synod was greater than the number of American missionaries, the missionaries were in control of the schools, the seminary, the church magazine, and the Synod committees and thus continued to hold considerable power. Furthermore, between 1899 with the establishment of the Synod, and 1926 when the Church proclaimed its administrational independence, the missionaries were elected to be moderators of the Synod every other year. It was a custom that the Synod elected an Egyptian one year and then a missionary the next year.[44]

Most Egyptians did not distinguish between the Mission and the Church, as the two entities cooperated in many spheres. The steps towards the independence of the Church from the Mission were hard for both. The initiative sometimes came from the Mission and at other times from the Church. The missionaries looked at the Church as a growing body, and hoped that the seeds they had planted for self-support, self-governance, and self-propagation would result in an independent mature church.

---

43. Bailey, "Cross-cultural," 16.
44. Salama, *Tarikh al-Kanysa al-Injilya* , 142–146.

Despite tensions in the relationship, the missionaries admired the Church. Charles Watson said:

> This Church is also loyal to the missionaries. On the whole, there has been little friction such as has often appeared in native Churches of other fields, between the native and the foreign missionary. Even those who have deliberately tried to sow dissension and schism have had little success. This is an earnest, for the future, of many years of harmonious and effective cooperation of foreign and native workers for the evangelization of Egypt.[45]

2.3.1 Synod Assumes a Share in Self-Support, 1908

Despite steps towards self-sufficiency, the evangelical churches were still financially dependent on the West. Many local congregations increasingly began to support themselves, but they seldom provided support for weaker churches. Financial support for the general work of the Synod or for churches in need was very limited, and the Synod itself depended on the contributions of the Mission to run its current expenses. Every year the Synod wrote to the Mission giving an estimate of its needs. The Mission in turn would write to the Board that would consider these figures in its annual payment to the Mission in Egypt.

At the Synod meeting of 1907, the American Mission in Egypt sent a letter to the Synod challenging it to increase its financial contribution for its ministry. The letter suggested that the Egyptian Church should increase its giving to local schools, salaries, and pensions for the pastors, the maintenance, and construction of church buildings, and to evangelistic work and the ministry in Sudan. The Mission explained that funds from America were declining because of new areas of ministry within and outside the United States.[46] This request bewildered the Synod and led to a long discussion. The Synod appointed a committee to study the best way to increase

---

45. Watson, *Egypt*, 245.
46. Synod of the Nile, *Minutes of the Year, 1907*, 142–143. Minutes of the Synod of the Nile are written in Arabic handwriting beginning from 1899, when the Synod was established, until 1969 when the Synod printed its reports.

the giving among local churches and their members and to discuss the whole subject of financial independence.[47]

Throughout the following year, the Mission continued advocating that the Synod should shoulder its monetary responsibilities and reduce the sum it expected to receive from the Mission.[48] One of the missionaries spoke to the Synod in the annual meeting of 1908 encouraging its members to take responsibility for supporting the evangelistic work and the new churches. He urged the Church to do more for its self-support in order to be self-governing. The Synod accepted this challenge, and "with much fear and even trepidation the Synod voted to undertake to provide $1,500 of the $10,286 it was asking the association to include in the estimates to the Board of Foreign Missions."[49]

After studying the financial situation, the Synod established a committee for financial independence in 1908. This Committee challenged the Church members to give money towards the general Synod expenses. The goal was to help the Church support itself by covering all fields of ministry, including Sunday school, publications, daily schools, evangelistic ministry, the work in Sudan, and church buildings.[50] The Committee suggested a unique approach. They proposed that the Synod should increase the number of workers in evangelistic and pastoral work, which in turn would help increase the membership of the Church and thus provide a larger base of financial support. The Committee encouraged local churches, schools, parents, and Sunday school teachers to challenge the young men and children to think of giving their lives for church ministry.[51] They also asked churches to encourage each member to have his own ministry and bring more members. This innovative plan helped the Church to concentrate on its evangelistic ministry. Besides this emphasis on evangelism, the Finances Committee suggested that the Synod, the presbyteries, and local churches have their own administrative structure that would help in increasing the

---

47. Ibid., 153.

48. For example, in 1908 the Synod requested $10,286 from the Mission Association to cover its needs.

49. Alexander, *A Sketch,* 39–40.

50. Synod of the Nile, *Minutes of the Year, 1908,* 172.

51. Ibid., 174.

income.[52] In the Synod minutes of the years following 1908, there were lists of contributors towards the Church's financial independence. The lists included churches, members of the churches, pastors, and missionaries.[53]

The Synod devised a definite plan to attain financial independence. The Mission and the Church agreed that the grants in aid from the church in America would decrease at a fixed rate. The agreement set 1916 as the year when the Church in Egypt would no longer receive any money from the church in America. Year after year, the budget of the Synod increased until it reached $30,000 in 1930.[54] Although the Church tried to keep the agreement with the Mission, due to Egypt's difficult financial situation, more years were needed than originally planned and this dream never becomes a reality.[55]

The Committee of Financial Independence continued to report to the Synod the difficulties it faced in collecting the required annual amount. In the year 1924, the Committee declared that its members and the presbyterial committees had failed in their attempts to raise sufficient money because the growth of the ministry and activities of the Synod had increased expenses. Although the Committee published a number of booklets about stewardship and wrote a number of articles in *Al-Hoda*, there was always a shortage in income. The Synod continued to be dependent on the sum of money from the American Mission that was maintained at the same level every year.[56]

Even with these difficulties, the missionaries were encouraged by the initiative of the Church. In 1930, Alexander wrote:

> It has always been a difficulty to persuade the churches to advance rapidly towards self-support. Even when they lack only a pound or even a half pound per month of reaching the goal

---

52. Ibid., 174–175.

53. For example see Synod of the Nile, *Minutes of the Year, 1909*, 121 & 1911, 280, & 1912, 326. The committee of financial independence had its own notebooks which included its budgets. In these notebooks there are detailed lists of the income and the expenses of each year.

54. Alexander, *A Sketch*, 40.

55. See chapter 6.

56. Synod of the Nile, *Minutes of the Year, 1924*, 11–12.

of entire self-support they find excuse for asking that the help may be continued.[57]

Thus, financial self-support did not happen completely. The Church had needed to be pressed into supporting the costs of ministry themselves, but even when they imposed a plan of gradually cutting aid from America, the Church was still unable to achieve complete financial independence.[58]

However, the efforts made towards self-sufficiency were a positive indicator. When the Sabbath School of AssioutCollege undertook to give some of their contributions to help two village churches become completely self-supporting, the two churches refused to accept it and decided to meet all their needs from local resources. Such a situation demonstrated the desire of the Egyptians to help their Church become fully self-supporting.[59]

The money issue continued to dominate discussions between the Mission and the Evangelical Church for decades. On the one hand, the American missionaries wanted to direct the money they received from America towards the projects or activities for which it had been donated. The Mission was particularly interested in supporting evangelistic ministries. On the other hand, the Evangelical Church continued to pressure the Mission to give more money for pastors' salaries and pensions, and the Church's general expenses. This tension over finances continued until the departure of the American Mission from Egypt in 1967. Throughout, the Evangelical Church remained dependent on the money that came from outside and never succeeded in covering its own needs from local sources.

2.3.2 The Seminary

Progress between the Mission and the Church can also be seen in the changing relationship with the Seminary, which had been directed and supported by the Mission from the time of its establishment in 1863. The Seminary itself was located in the Mission headquarters in Cairo, and its

---

57. Ibid., 41.

58. Finney, *Tomorrow's Egypt,* 111.

59. Alexander, *A Sketch,* 42. This action by these two churches was accepted in Egypt. The spirit of giving by Assiout College challenged the people in these demonstrating that if these young people could give from their needs to the ministry of the Lord, surely the Church could do the same.

faculty was mostly composed of missionaries with a few Egyptian pastors sharing in teaching responsibilities.

In March 1919, the Synod discussed the situation of the Seminary with the Mission. The Seminary, after almost sixty years, needed a larger building and the Mission wanted access to more space in its own building. Thus, the Mission suggested that they would hand over the Seminary to the Synod which would be responsible for providing the building, and supporting and directing the school. They also suggested that the Seminary could remain under Mission control until the Synod built its new Seminary. At that point, the students, teachers, and library would move to the new building.[60]

This discussion was a test of power between the Synod and the Mission. Whereas the Mission realized that the Synod could not fully support the costs of the Seminary building and programmes, the Synod recognized that when the Seminary was directed and supported by the Mission, the Mission controlled all decisions. The Mission would pay the students pocket money and with Synod cooperation, send them wherever they wished during the summer months of training. This style of interaction between Mission and Synod often predominated. Both parties wished to prove that they had power and could work independently.

Because of the discussion, the Synod decided to build a new Seminary building in Cairo and to fully support it. At the same meeting in 1919, the Synod appointed two pastors to be faculty members in the existing Seminary.[61] The Synod also appointed a committee to direct the new Seminary building project. The committee's job was to raise the funds and locate a suitable site for the building. The Synod challenged the committee to collect the project expenses from local resources.[62] In 1924, the committee had collected enough money to buy the land that had been found in 'Abbassiyah, Cairo. Unexpectedly, since evangelicals were registered as an Egyptian denomination, the government donated half the price of the land for the Seminary, as it did with other religious groups.[63] The work on the

---

60. Synod of the Nile, *Minutes of the Year, 1919*, 221.
61. Ibid., 241.
62. Synod of the Nile, *Minutes of the Year, 1923*, 397.
63. Synod of the Nile, *Minutes of the Year, 1924*, 18–19; Elder, *Vindicating a Vision*, 203.

building started in November 1925, and finished in October 1926.[64] The total coast of the project was about $35,000 that was raised entirely from Egyptian sources.[65]

In January 1926, the Synod took control of the Seminary, and the Mission transferred all responsibility for conducting the Seminary to the national Church. The Synod appointed one of its members to be chairman of the administrative Seminary board. Three other pastors were appointed teachers. One was hired full time and the other two remained as full-time pastors of Cairo churches while teaching part time. The Synod paid the full-time professor a salary and built him rent-free housing on the Seminary premises.[66] The Mission continued to give monies towards student scholarships, and the Synod promised to give an equal amount from its budget.[67] This marked the first time that the Synod made such statement and worked towards fully supporting one of its institutions.

In November 1926, the Synod opened the new Seminary building. However, the missionaries continued to play a major role with a missionary holding the position of faculty chairman until 1939 when an Egyptian pastor, Ghubrial Al-Dab', was appointed as the first Egyptian chairman of the faculty.[68] The missionaries continued to be teachers alongside their Egyptian colleagues.

This transfer of Seminary control was an important step in the relationship between the Mission and the Church and their shared vision of progressive independence. The transfer indicated that with motivation and planning, the Church was able to support one of its main institutions. As the training of Egyptian leaders became the responsibility of the

---

64. Salama, *Tarikh al-Kanysa al-Injilya*, 153.

65. The Seminary building still remains. At many places within the building are memorials to the individual Egyptians who gave to various projects. Most of them are from the known Protestant families, such as the Wiesa and Khayyatt families, who used to give generously to the Church.

66. Alexander, *A Sketch*, 42.

67. Elder, *Vindicating a Vision*, 203.

68. Ibid. The American missionaries continued to be faculty members in the Seminary because they were academically qualified for that job. The Egyptian faculty did not have the opportunity at this time to pursue further studies abroad. This step came in later years when the American Mission helped a number of Egyptians to study for Masters and Doctorate in the United States.

indigenous Church in cooperation with the Mission, the local church leadership slowly developed a spirit of independence.

2.3.3 The Synod Declares Itself Self-Governing, 1926

Because of the growth in the number of congregations and ordained ministers, the call for independence became more earnest. There were conflicting opinions about how to take such a step. The Board in the USA was insistent that the time had come to turn over all Mission activities and programs to the Evangelical Church; the Mission in Egypt, on the other hand, thought that the Church in Egypt was not yet ready for this step. They agreed with the ultimate goal of autonomy, but argued that the Board was over-estimating the readiness of the Church in Egypt.[69]

The debate between the Mission and the Board led to a visit by Mr Anderson, the chairman of the Board of Foreign Mission of the UPCNA. During his visit to Egypt, the regulations and roles of the relationship between the Mission and the Church were discussed. It became apparent that there was a level of mistrust between the missionaries and the Synod leaders. Anderson criticized the missionaries for their isolation and inability to make friends with the Egyptians when he said:

> The Missionaries seemed in general to mistrust the natives and not to believe that they are possessed with the qualities that would make them a friend on equality with an American. They seemed to take unconsciously the attitude of a superior race. Of course, the reaction of this upon the native mind is disastrous. While they may not be conscious of it, they resent being held as an inferior race and fail to respond to friendly advances which can be formed only upon the plane of equality.[70]

At the same time, he found that the Egyptian leaders lacked spiritual warmth and were wedded too much to tradition. He also noted that while the leaders of the Synod were intellectually of a high calibre, they seemed more concerned with ecclesiastical matters than a passion for souls.[71]

---

69. Lorimer, *Presbyterians*, 27.

70. W. B. Anderson, *Deputation Tour of Egypt: 1923-1924* n.p. report in PHS UPCNA RG 209-21-16.

71. Elder, *Vindicating a Vision*, 205.

The Mission and the Synod created a joint committee to discuss the administrative and financial independence of the Church. After several meetings, the committee delivered its summary of discussions to the Association of the American Mission:

> The thoughts [of the Church] are prepared at present, after what has been ascertained of the amount of gifts and expenditure for religious work, to regard the native Evangelical Church as independent financially, for that which is paid out by the organized congregations to the regular funds of Synod is larger than the financial help needed by these churches by an amount that could fittingly be employed in evangelistic work which is another branch of work to be engaged in.[72]

The Mission thought that the real need of the Evangelical Church was for "education and encouragement in developing plans for more effective stewardship and evangelism."[73] Further, they deemed that the Synod was too involved in merely ecclesiastical business while neglecting important evangelistic work.

In the end, the Synod took steps to gain its own financial and administrative independence: in March 1926, it declared itself an independent Egyptian Church. The Mission declared its support for this decision.[74] The Synod separated its organized churches from the non-organized ones and from the small village groups. It also assumed supervision of both the Mission in Sudan and the Seminary. These decisions were major accomplishments, and brought the Synod closer to achieving full autonomy.[75]

After this major shift, the Synod and the Mission began to work more cooperatively. It was agreed that the Mission would give no financial support to the organized Synod churches, and a joint committee from the Synod and the Mission was designated to care for both the non-organized churches and the preaching stations.[76]

---

72. American Mission in Egypt, *Minutes of the Year, 1926*, 83.
73. Ibid., 87.
74. Ibid., 86.
75. Alexander, *A Sketch*, 43.
76. Synod of the Nile, *Minutes of the Year, 1927*, 163.

Meanwhile, the Mission retained control of the schools, medical work and evangelization programmes, and assorted other ministries. As before, the ordained American missionaries remained members of the presbyteries and of the Synod of the Nile, and the ecclesiastical relationship between the Synod and the church in America continued unchanged.[77] The Synod was still required to send statistics and fraternal delegates with an abstract of its meetings' minutes translated into English to the General Assembly in America, since the Synod of the Nile was still a member of the General Assembly of the United Presbyterian Church of North America.[78] Nevertheless, this partial independence was a step for the Synod towards taking full responsibility in financial support for its ministry and evangelistic ministry.

In reality however, financial independence only developed slowly, and in fact, was never fully achieved. As noted before, the Mission and Synod developed practical plans for "putting this financial independence into effect,"[79] by continually reducing the percentage of financial aid to be donated by the Mission. Unfortunately, this plan was not implemented and the Synod continued receiving money from the Mission.

The Board in America was pleased by the growing administrative and financial independence of the Evangelical Church, and continued to press the Mission in Egypt concerning this issue. The Board wanted the Mission to increase the Egyptian Church's responsibilities. The Mission continued to disagree, believing that the Board overestimated the strength of the Evangelical Church and that the Board did not keep in mind the limitations of the Church as an "organization gathered for the most part from a minority Christian population in a land of Islam."[80] The Mission also reminded the Board that the Church's dependence on foreign funds was due to the limited resources of its people. The Mission also noted that with full independence, the Church would have control over schools and churches that were already in a discouraging condition. According to the

---

77. American Mission in Egypt, *Minutes of the Year, 1926*, 83–84; Elder, *Vindicating a Vision,* 204.

78. Alexander, *A Sketch,* 43.

79. American Mission in Egypt, *Minutes of the Year, 1926,* 84.

80. American Mission in Egypt, *Minutes of the Year, 1928,* 327.

missionaries, the Egyptian leaders displayed limited administrative ability. Given this negative view of local capabilities, the Mission expressed its intention to help the Church overcome these difficulties. At the same time, the Mission praised its relationship with the Egyptian Church in its correspondence, saying that the Mission and the Church enjoyed a friendly, helpful, and effective relationship in the field. They hoped that this relationship would continue in an atmosphere of open, direct, and friendly discussions.[81]

In short, the complete financial and administrative independence of the church was theoretical not actual. The Synod depended on American money for its general budget, schools, Seminary, and evangelistic stations. The Mission saw this reality and wanted the Board to truly appreciate the situation, while they continued to work with the Synod towards true autonomy.

2.4 The Relationship between 1926–1958

After the Church declared its financial and administrative independence in 1926, many circumstances inside and outside the Mission and the Church influenced their changing relationship.

2.4.1 Financial Difficulties and Reductions

The American economic depression in the late 1920s and early 1930s, led to a reduction for money from the Board in America to the Mission in Egypt. In 1929, the Board asked the Mission to cut 10 percent from its budget.[82] These reductions in money affected the ministry in Egypt in many ways. First, the Mission informed the Synod that a reduction of the Mission's grant to the Synod should be expected.[83]

Second, the Mission began a policy of selling some of its properties in Egypt to support its current work.[84] This began in 1929 and continued for

---

81. Ibid., 327–328.

82. American Mission in Egypt, *Minutes of the Year, 1928,* 356.

83. Ibid., 369.

84. American Mission in Egypt, *Minutes of the Year, 1949,* 253. From its beginning, the American Mission bought a number of properties including schools, hospitals, lands, houses, and farms in different cities and villages.

many years. This developed into an awkward and confusing situation. In 1949, the Mission's minutes summed up the situation:

> We find ourselves in a very difficult position. On the one side we are pressed by the representatives of Synod to support their position that no property should be sold to secure funds for current expenses. On the other hand we are instructed by the Board to sell property to the amount of $25,000 this year and perhaps again next year. Yet we are at the same time told to turn over to Synod properties which they can use, either free or at a low price. The Board may feel that some of our properties are not of use to Synod, but Synod's representatives feel that Synod is the heir to all Mission property. We feel that the Board should give us guidance out of this dilemma in which we find ourselves.[85]

When the American Mission sold some of its properties the Synod asked to have them. For years, with permission from the Board, the Mission sold a number of its properties. Some profits were used to cover shortages in its budget. Other properties, including schools, buildings, orphanages, and youth centres were given outright to the Synod.

Third, there was a reduction in personnel, as a number of missionaries were asked to leave the field in Egypt and find other positions at home.[86] In 1949, the Board asked the Mission to reduce the number of missionaries to only twenty families by 1954–1955. The Mission replied that this number would be very inadequate for the ministry tasks before it. The Synod concurred, recognizing that they needed help in preparing to take over Mission responsibilities.[87] As a compromise, numbers were diminished, but not as drastically as first outlined. According to Mission minutes, the number of missionaries dropped from 92 in 1926, to 79 in 1949, and 66 in 1960.[88]

The reduction in numbers necessitated the training of Egyptians to take over all leadership positions of the various ministries. The Mission

---

85. American Mission in Egypt, *Minutes of the Year, 1949*, 253.
86. American Mission in Egypt, *Minutes of the Year, 1929*, 451.
87. Ibid., 258.
88. American Mission in Egypt, *Minutes of the Years, 1926; 1949;1960*; see also chapter 6.

delegated the evangelistic and education work to Egyptians, and sent some of the potential leaders overseas to study to be better qualified upon their return.[89] The minutes of the Mission in the 1950s and 1960s listed the names of Egyptian leaders who were given scholarships to study in social work, publications, development, theology, and Christian education in the United States. Many of those who went abroad to study were then given leading positions in the Evangelical Church in Egypt that they occupied for decades. Some became Synod chairmen, Synod secretaries, Seminary teachers, Board chairmen, and Synod representatives to ecumenical organizations.[90]

Thus, the financial crisis in the United States provided a significant stimulus in preparing for further autonomy. The Mission salvaged the situation by replacing the departing missionaries with Egyptians. This was an important development, helping to effectively equip the Evangelical Church for complete independence.

2.4.2 Relationships with the Government

During 1940s and 1950s, the Mission had increasing difficulty in its relationship with the Egyptian government. Because of the growth of nationalism and the influence of Islamic groups, the government began to limit foreign activities. A law was passed requiring all foreign schools, including the Mission's, to replace their foreign head administrators with Egyptians.[91] The government also required Mission institutions such as schools and hospitals to pay taxes. In addition, there were growing problems with missionaries' visas, work permits, and foreign money transfers.[92] One of the important changes for the Mission and for all foreigners in Egypt was the end of the Mixed Courts on October 1949. This had been the last remnant of the historic Capitulations that the foreigners had enjoyed for a long time in Egypt. From that time on, foreigners were tried in Egyptian courts.[93]

---

89. American Mission in Egypt, *Minutes of the Year,* 1949, 225.

90. The list included Samuel Habib, Fayez Fares, Swailem Sidhom, Labib Mishriki, Abd el Masih Istafanous and others. There were some professionals in education and medicine from the Mission institutions among those who travelled to study.

91. American Mission in Egypt, *Minutes of the Year, 1959,* 251.

92. Ibid., 255–257.

93. American Mission in Egypt, *Minutes of the Year, 1950,* 271–272.

Living under the shadow of shortages in financial support from the Board in America and the difficulties with government policy, the relationship between the Mission and the Church entered a new phase.

2.4.3 Synod Representatives in Mission Meetings

After the financial and administrative independence of 1926, the Synod told the Mission that it should allow Synod representatives to attend the Mission administration meetings:

> The time has now arrived for the attendance of some of the members of Synod at some of the sessions of the American Missionary Association in Egypt, particularly when consideration is given to matters relating to the Synod, in order that they may enable the Association to understand the point of view of Synod.[94]

It was hoped that in this way they could better coordinate the joint work of the Church and the Mission. The Mission rejected this request and took the issue to the Board. Instead, the Mission suggested appointing a committee with members from both the Mission and the Synod to look into relations with the Synod. This committee was established and for decades played an important role in shaping the relationship between the two institutions.[95]

Accordingly, in 1930 the Mission welcomed some committee members to attend meetings when the association discussed any matters related to the work of that particular committee. At the same time, the Mission decided to ask the missionaries, who were members of the Synod and presbyteries, to withdraw from being voting members. The Mission conceded that the Egyptian Church was the agency which must eventually win Egypt for Christ and that the time would come when the presence of the missionaries would no longer be needed.[96] However, this matter of Synod representation at the Mission meetings continued to be a subject of negotiation between the Mission and the Synod. Missionaries remained as non-voting

---

94. American Mission in Egypt, *Minutes of the Year, 1929*, 458.
95. Ibid., 460.
96. American Mission in Egypt, *Minutes of the Year, 1930*, 545.

members of the Synod and the presbyteries, while Synod members were invited to attend some sessions during the meetings of the Mission.[97]

In 1950, two Egyptian members of the Synod's Committee on Relations with the Mission were invited to regularly attend the Mission meetings. The mission also encouraged the Synod to add women as members of the Committee on Relations with the Mission in order to support the increasing role of women in the ministry of the Evangelical Church.[98]

In 1957, the Mission adopted a suggestion made by some missionaries "that the Mission invite one representative of every presbytery to come to our Winter Association as our guest and that they be given a chance to sit with major committees."[99] The Mission also decided to invite one woman leader from every presbytery to be a delegate at the Mission meetings. From that time on, the Mission welcomed two representatives from every presbytery – a pastor and a woman – to attend Mission meetings and to share in the discussions.[100]

At the same time, representatives from the Synod attended the General Assembly meetings in the United States since the Synod of Egypt was one of the Synods of the General Assembly.[101] Some of the representatives were chosen because they were already in the States for study. The Synod sent representatives from 1929 until its independence in 1958.[102]

2.4.4 The Mission Evaluates Its Policy

Because of multiple pressures and changes, the Mission appointed a committee in January 1955 to survey its policy, practice, ministry, and relationships:

> To make an appraisal of our entire Mission program, institutions, activities, etc., and prepare a table of organization, giving emphasis to those enterprises in which cooperation with the Evangelical Church is most easily achieved; . . . to study

97. Ibid., 575.
98. American Mission in Egypt, *Minutes of the Year, 1950*, 275.
99. Ibid., 1957, 134.
100. Ibid., 135.
101. Synod of the Nile, *Minutes of the Year, 1951*, 68.
102. Elder, *Vindicating a Vision*, 329-30. See later in this chapter and chapter 7.

the whole problem of our Mission's future place in the work of the Kingdom in Egypt; . . . to study the Statement of Policy published by the Board of Foreign Missions and the matter of setting up Advisory Boards for our major institutions. It should give guidance and impetus wherever such policies are adopted, and also gather information on progress for annual reports.[103]

This committee invited a few Synod leaders to attend some of its discussions and prepared a questionnaire to ascertain the missionaries' opinions of the Mission and its policy in Egypt. The final report was placed before the Mission at its annual meeting in January 1956. The report emphasized that the link between Mission institutions and the Evangelical Church was weak, and the members of the Evangelical Community in Egypt did not support the role of institutions such as the schools and hospitals. Many missionaries emphasized the need for more cooperation with the Evangelical Church. In order to ensure the Church's long-term witness to the gospel, they suggested that close cooperation with the Church in youth work, audio-visual aids, literature, and literacy should be their priority.[104]

Some of the missionaries held a positive view of the Evangelical Church, believing it capable of great progress now that it was independent and self-governing, and largely self-supporting and self-propagating. They stated that leadership with vision and courage would advance the ministry of the Church, avoid withdrawal from society, and help it grow in its witness. The missionaries believed that the strengthening of the Church would come from inside not outside. They were open to transferring the entire ministry and institutions of the Mission to the Church so that they would be completely under Church-control.[105]

The Egyptian members of this committee, for their part, expressed the appreciation of the Evangelical Church for the Mission and its contributions to the life of the church and society. They praised the role of the Mission institutions in opening doors for Christian witness. When the

---

103. American Mission in Egypt, *Minutes of the Year, 1956*, 4.
104. Ibid., 6–8.
105. Ibid., 8–9.

missionaries asked Egyptian members of the committee if the time had come for the Mission to officially break ties with the United Presbyterian Church of North America and make the independence of the Evangelical Church complete, they did not express any reason to do so at that time.[106]

The committee studied the Statement of Policy of the Board concerning the indigenous churches and the importance of being in close relationship with it. This Statement said:

> The Board believes that the growth and welfare of the indigenous church should be the central objective of every undertaking of the Mission and individual missionaries. The Mission and missionary should be chiefly concerned that the Church be self-propagating and be increasingly the instrument of witnessing for Christ. The Church should increasingly accept responsibility for administration of the Christian program in the area in which the Church and Mission are responsible for witnessing.[107]

This statement was received with appreciation from the Egyptian members. A translation into Arabic was prepared and circulated among numerous other evangelical leaders.

The report of the Survey Committee also detailed the Mission's perception of the primary needs of the Evangelical Church. The Committee saw a need for spiritual revival, greater stewardship, an increased shouldering of responsibility for evangelism, and a more efficient form of organization and finance. Consequently, they suggested a number of actions in spiritual, administrative, and financial spheres. Concretely, it was suggested that the Church be developed by establishing a Board of Administration for the Synod. Both the Mission and the Church clearly expressed at this time their desire to work together towards the improvement of their relationship.[108]

This report shaped the intentions and role of the Mission as it continued its ministry in Egypt, and the preparation for the complete independence of the Evangelical Church.

---

106. Ibid., 17.
107. Ibid., 16.
108. Ibid., 17–18.

2.4.5 Board of Administration for Synod

In 1952, the Mission and Synod Committee on Relations sent the Mission a proposal for setting up a "Board of Administration for Synod." The Mission asked for time to discuss the proposal with its members and with the Board in America.[109] Both the Synod and the Mission studied the proposal with its members in different stages. It took six years before the Board of Administration for the Synod came into being.[110]

In June 1957, the final form of the proposal came from the Synod as an official document to be discussed in the annual Mission meeting. It suggested that the Board of Administration be given the name "The General Board for administrating the work of the Evangelical Coptic Church in the Nile Valley." The Board was to be composed of a chairman and an executive secretary from the Synod, the chairman and the secretary of the Mission, two missionaries; eight representatives from the eight Presbyteries of the Synod, and later two women.[111]

The Board of Administration was to acquire its authority from the Synod. Its duties were to represent the Evangelical Church before all bodies at home and abroad; to direct the affairs of the Church; manage its properties, and carry out and supervise all the programs of the Church. The Board of Administration was to contain four councils:

- The Council on Spiritual Affairs – its jurisdiction would include home missions, foreign mission, spiritual revivals, the laymen's movement, and work among non-Christians.
- The Council on Christian Education – its jurisdiction was to supervize Synod day schools, Mission schools, literature and literacy, audio-visual aids, Sunday schools, youth work, conference camps, publications, and Church papers and magazines.
- The Council on Finance – its role was to oversee the budget, insurance, Church buildings, ministers' retirement relief, and pensions.

---

109. American Mission in Egypt, *Minutes of the Year, 1952*, 103.
110. Synod of the Nile, *Minutes of the Year, 1957*, 199.
111. American Mission in Egypt, *Minutes of the Year, 1957*, 135.

- The Council on Major Institutions – its purview included the Evangelical Seminary, the hospitals, colleges, and institutions formerly directed by the Mission and social service programs.[112]

The proposal detailed the members of each council, the process of election and length of terms, the regulations governing the meetings; and the form of their reports to the Synod. The proposal was adopted and the Synod proposed a budget for the Board of Administration to cover its work, especially during its initial stages.[113]

Gradually, the Board of Administration and it various councils took control of most Mission activities including schools, hospitals, rural ministry, literature, and youth work. After several years of negotiations, the Mission transferred most of its work to the Evangelical Church, including properties. They laid down principles, ensuring that the properties would be used for the right purposes under the supervision of the Evangelical Church bodies.[114] The main concern of the Mission and the Board in America was the fear that the properties could be transferred to individuals not to institutions.[115] The Mission worked hard with the Synod to guarantee that the properties would be under the control of the Synod and its councils. Conditions limiting the use of properties to their original purpose were written into the agreements of transfer.

2.4.6 Church Independence, 1958

While the Mission and the Synod were discussing the Board of Administration's proposal, the Synod's independence from the Presbyterian Church of North America came before the Synod for discussion. The Mission realized the feelings of the Synod while discussing this matter and stated:

> Synod is eager not to hurt the feelings of the Mission or the Church in America by making this request. The Mission

---

112. Ibid., 135.

113. For more details about the new Board of Administration see, Iskander Abiskhairoun Aboklog, "A Profile of and Proposed Program for the Synod of the Nile" (A Master's thesis submitted to the faculty of the Pittsburgh-Xenia Theological Seminary, Pittsburgh, Pennsylvania, May 1957).

114. American Mission in Egypt, *Minutes of the Year, 1959*, 247.

115. Ibid., 298, 323.

wishes to assure Synod of our approval and our conviction that the step forward is desirable and natural.[116]

The Mission assured the Church that the independence of the Synod did not mean the withdrawal of Mission support from the Church and that it would continue working in its regular ministry in Egypt.[117]

On 13 March 1958, the Synod celebrated its independence from the Presbyterian Church of North America and declared itself an independent Synod. The Mission was represented on the occasion and shared by arranging a tea party for the Synod and visitors. The President and Secretary of the Mission were asked to plan the program and to act as Master of Ceremonies.[118]

The Mission and the Synod had entered a new era of working together towards the newly defined goal of "integration." The ordained missionaries remained as non-voting members of the Synod and its presbyteries, while other missionaries remained as Synod council and committee members helping in the continuation of their ministry. The Synod and the Mission gained maturity in their relationship as two separate bodies – "that of each one working through its problems and seeking answers of its questions in *consultation with the other.*"[119] The Mission praised the growing relationship with the officers of the Synod and their spirit of cooperation. There was a new intention to work together based on the unity of their commitment to Christian witness.[120] Although the official relationship between the Synod and the General Assembly in America had ceased to exist, Synod declared in its meeting in March 1958, that the Evangelical Church in Egypt no longer had an official relationship with the Mission, but a relationship of love, friendship, and cooperation.[121]

---

116. American Mission in Egypt, *Minutes of the Year, 1957*, 20.
117. Ibid., 8.
118. American Mission in Egypt, *Minutes of the Year, 1958*, 215.
119. American Mission in Egypt, *Minutes of the Year, 1960*, 341.
120. Ibid., 342.
121. Synod of the Nile, *Minutes of the Year, 1958*, 270. See chapter 7.

2.5 Conclusion

The relationship between the Mission and the Church had undergone many permutations during more than a century of history together. Changes in both the political situations within Egypt and the United States, and the financial situation of the Board and the Mission played important roles in forming the relationship through the years.

Further, although the Mission wanted to grant authority over the Church to Egyptian leaders, they faced a shortage in the number and quality of the Egyptian leaders. The Mission therefore delayed delegating power until the church was ready. This took more than one hundred years to develop, after which the Mission finally allowed most of its work to be under Egyptian leadership. The delay was the joint responsibility of the Mission and the Church. For numerous decades, the Mission did not consider Egyptians capable of taking leadership, and indeed, during the nineteenth and early twentieth century, Egyptian leaders displayed limited interest or preparedness.

Financial affairs also played an important role in shaping the relationship. Money often equals power, with donors often dictating how money will be spent. Throughout the history of the American Mission in Egypt, most funds came from America. This included sums for the Church institutions and personnel such as the Synod, presbyteries, churches, pastors, and for the many different aspects of ministry. The financial contribution of the Egyptians was small compared to that which came from abroad and especially from the United States. The Egyptians gave as much as they could, but because of low incomes and the high costs of the ministry, this contribution covered only a minor portion of costs. Although the American Mission encouraged the Egyptians to take on more responsibilities, the reality was that most of the financial, administrative, and voting power remained in the hands of the missionaries for a long time. For many years, the missionaries continued to hold most of the leadership positions in the Synod, presbyteries, schools, hospitals, and most of the fields of ministry.

The changing political situation was the main impetus that forced the Mission to slowly transfer authority. This was particularly true from the late 1940s with the rise of anti-colonialist and nationalistic movements. The Egyptian government began to institute laws designed to decrease foreign presence and influence in Egypt. The Mission worked with the Evangelical Church to assign Egyptians for leadership roles over such Mission institutions as hospitals and schools. The separation of the Synod in Egypt from the General Assembly in America created true independence and ushered in the final form of relationship. Mission and Church became two separate, independent bodies working together, while sharing a long history. A mature relationship of equals working with mutual respect, love, and cooperation had finally emerged.

The theories of missions that Anderson, Venn, and Allan wanted to see in the relationships between the missionaries and the indigenousness churches were partly applied in the relationships between the American Mission and the Evangelical Church. After a century of relationships, the Egyptian Church had a kind of independence but not as the theories hoped. The Church became self-governing, but never became self-supporting, and only partially self-propagating. The next chapters will examine more specifically how the Egyptian Church worked with the American Mission to fulfil its self-propagation while enjoying self-government and struggling in regard to self-support.

CHAPTER 3

The Interaction between the American Mission and Evangelical Church in Muslim Evangelism

In the previous two chapters, this study described the beginning of the American Presbyterian Mission in Egypt, and their establishment of the Evangelical Church in Egypt as their intended main agent for evangelizing Egypt. We also examined the interactions between the two organizations since the Church's inception until 1958 when the Synod of the Nile gained independence from the General Assembly of the United Presbyterian Church of North America. It was these interactions and evolving roles that gave the shape and direction to the mission work initiated by the Evangelical Church. In this and the following three chapters, we will examine the mission work of Evangelical Church by exploring two case studies: the Church's work among Muslims inside Egypt; and their mission work in Sudan.

3.1 Introduction

The American Mission initiated the first programmes of evangelism, and later the Evangelical Church adopted the same approaches. The first case study will therefore examine the influence of the Mission's Muslim work upon the Church, and discuss the interactions between the two bodies, and the changes in their viewpoints and strategies. After studying key characteristics and methods of evangelizing Muslims, this chapter will investigate the possible reasons for the relatively small number of converts, including the political, social, and religious situation in Egypt.

3.2 The American Mission and Its Ministry to Muslims

The American Mission stated at the beginning of its work in Egypt that evangelizing Muslims was one of its main goals. However, their success in this was limited even though the missionaries used every modern method of evangelism. In the twenty-six years between the arrival of the American Mission to Egypt in 1854, and 1880, only seventy-five Muslims were converted and baptized, most of whom came from the lower strata of society.[1] By 1900, according to Mission records, this total had grown to 140 converts. In the year 1901, there were six new converts; in 1902, there were eight; in 1903, there were fourteen; and in 1904, there were twelve.[2] This slight growth in the number of converts was due to the increase in number of missionaries as well as the more favourable political and social environment at that time. In the early years of the twentieth century, the missionaries enjoyed a greater degree of freedom of speech in a short period. In later years, the number of converts was not published for security reasons, but from what can be discerned, it cannot have been higher than in the earlier period.

3.2.1 The Mission's Methods of Reaching Muslims

The American Mission used a variety of methods to reach Muslims that included printed literature, schools, the women's ministry, medical work, public preaching, personal relationships, and social work. These were popular methods at the time, not only in Egypt, but worldwide as well, and contributed to the ministry among Muslims.[3]

3.2.1.1 Literature

Distributing the Bible and other literature was regarded as the most crucial method for reaching Muslims, according to Charles Watson in his book, *What is this Muslim World?* This emphasis was consciously chosen,

---

1. Watson, *The American Mission,* 360.

2. Watson, *Islam in Egypt,* 36.

3. The methods that the Mission used were mentioned in chapter 1 as general methods to reach the whole of Egyptian society. In this chapter, these methods will be examined in their connections with Muslim evangelism and how the Mission tried to communicate the gospel through these methods.

in accordance with Islam's self-description as "the religion of the Book." Watson quotes from one of the telegraphic greetings to the American Christian Literature Society for Moslems: "No agency can penetrate Islam so deeply, abide so persistently, witness so daringly and influence so irresistibly, as the printed page."[4]

The Van Dyke translation of the Bible was an effective tool for reaching Muslims.[5] It became popular in the Arab World and gained a wide distribution network including most of the Protestant mission agencies.[6] In the early years, the missionaries travelled to different parts of Egypt, visiting the Delta, Alexandria, Cairo, and Upper Egypt to distribute the Bible among both Christians and Muslims.[7] Christians were the main target of this distribution; however, a number of Muslims made purchases from the missionaries or from the bookstores.[8] In the period from 1854 to 1896, there were 248,386 Scriptures dispersed by the Mission.[9]

The American Mission also published and distributed a number of books about Islam and its differences with Christianity, such as *Shahadat El-Qur'an* (*The Witnesses of the Qur'an*) and *El Hadaya* (*The Guidance*). Watson commented that when *El Kindy* and *Mizan ul haqq* (*The Balance of*

---

4. Charles Watson, *What is this Muslim World* (London: Student Christian Movement Press, 1937), 156. Watson wrote extensively about the importance of translation, printing and distributing Christian books in the mission work in Egypt and in the Muslim World. Cf. *What is this Muslim World*, 156–159; *Egypt*, 209–217, and *In the Valley of the Nile*, 186.

5. Although there were some other Arabic Bible translations, Van Dyke's translation was the first one to be translated from the original languages of the Bible (Watson, *What is this Muslim World*, 157). It is still the most popular version in the Arab World and Christians find it hard to accept any new translation for use in their churches. Samuel Zwemer praises Van Dyke's translation of the Bible saying that it "marked an epoch in missions for the Mohammedan world greater than any accession or deposition of Sultans." Samuel M. Zwemer, *The Moslem World* (New York: Eaton and Mains, 1907), 151.

6. The translation was completed by the American Mission in Syria and Lebanon and was printed in Beirut in 1864. A. L. Tibawi, *American Interests in Syria 1800–1901: A Study of Educational Literary and Religious Work* (Oxford: Clarendon Press, 1966), 165.

7. Some of the pioneer missionaries in Egypt rode donkeys with bags on both sides filled with copies of the Bible and called people in the streets to come and buy it. Salama, *Tarikh al-Kanysa al-Injilya*, 56.

8. Watson, *The American Mission*, 429.

9. Ibid., 432. Watson gives detailed statistics of the book department from the beginning of the ministry in 1854 to 1896. The list includes the Scriptures, religious books, and educational and miscellaneous books (Ibid., 432–434).

Truth) were published, the Mission circulated many copies of both books "in an unobtrusive way."[10]

The Mission opened a number of bookstores in some key cities to sell books and give people a chance to discuss the Bible and the Christian faith.[11] Through these bookstores, Muslims came to understand the Christian faith, and some converted because of reading and discussing the Bible with the Christian workers.[12] Most of the workers in these stores were Egyptians whom the Mission had employed to work in sales and to answer the questions of the people who were interested in Christianity.

3.2.1.2 Education

The Mission schools were another major tool for reaching Muslims. It was clear to the missionaries that schools were intended not merely to introduce a higher quality of education but also, by direct and indirect means, to win students to the Christian faith.[13] McGill, a senior American missionary to Egypt, said about the schools that:

> We have found the Mohammedan people responsive to Christian education when it provides them instruction and a school life of a better grade than they can obtain elsewhere. They and their children soon perceive that the basis of such provision is God, his book and the religion of Jesus. We cannot undo the effect of bigotry and misunderstandings and hatred of the past 1300 years in this Muslim land in a decade, or even in a century; but are we not making great progress when

---

10. Watson, *Islam in Egypt,* 35. These books by Christian and Muslim scholars were newly printed and used by the missionaries in the Arab World as tools to reach Muslims. They contained a number of arguments which the missionaries found helpful for opening discussions with Muslims. For example, a Muslim sheikh from Morocco visited the Mission bookstore in Suez on his way to Mecca and converted after reading and discussing the Christian teachings (Watson, *Egypt,* 214–217).

11. The book department played an important role in the mission work. The bookstores, which the Mission established, were the first stores to ever sell books of any kind throughout all of Egypt.

12. Watson, *Egypt,* 214.

13. In an unpublished document written by McGill to defend the role of the Mission schools he gave a description of the schools and their aim. PHS UPCNA RG 209-26-34: Historical Background, Egypt Mission: McGill, *The American Mission in Egyptian: Its Educational Work,* 1957.

Muslim children enter our Christian schools? And when they read the Scriptures and listen to Christian prayer, when they become able, through the work of the schools and the life of the teachers, to perceive the character of Jesus, His holiness, His purity, His love, when they feel the appeal of His Gospel and its power on their souls, do we not know that they are "not far from the Kingdom"? . . . A second purpose in our schools is to win the young men and women of Egypt to Christ and to Christianity. We wish to lead them into the Church of Christ, into the Kingdom of God. It is imperative that the children of the Church should be saved to the Church. It is equally imperative that others should be enlightened and gathered into the Church.[14]

The schools were relatively successful in attracting Muslim students, and the number of Muslim students in these schools increased through the years. In 1905, for example, 3,115 of the 15,451 pupils in the 171 schools of the Mission and the Synod were Muslim.[15] Many Muslim parents wanted to send their children to the Mission schools because of the high standard of education. Along with the normal secular subjects, the missionaries and Christian teachers emphasized values such as truth telling, abstaining from cursing and swearing, and reverence for God. On occasion, all students, including Muslims, had to attend Bible classes, which gave the missionaries the opportunity to talk with them about their faith.[16] Students were a ready audience for the missionaries, and being at their most impressionable

---

14. McGill, *The American Mission*.

15. Watson, *Egypt*, 278. For more details about the growth in the number of the schools in the first fifty years of the Mission work in Egypt see the tables in chapter 1.

16. Elder, *Vindicating a Vision*, 74–75. Although the Muslim parents knew that their children were reading the Bible in the Mission schools they were open to sending them there. Most of them were open-minded and when they found progress in their children's educational level and changes in their behaviour they did not mind sending them to Christian schools.

age some students converted.[17] The missionaries found that the greatest number of conversions took place at the ages of fifteen or sixteen years.[18]

Stories written by the missionaries also tell of the conversions of a number of Mission schoolteachers.[19] Despite the anti-missionary movement, which opposed the Mission's educational and evangelistic work, "many Muslims remained loyal to the missionaries out of long-lasting friendships (in some cases) and gratitude for the care and quality of education received by their children in the American Mission schools."[20]

One of the main purposes for establishing Assiout Training College was to train Egyptian Christians who could evangelize the whole country. John Hogg argued with the American Mission and the Board in America about the importance of this college as an effective way to bring the gospel to every inhabitant of the country.[21] The Christian influence that dominated this college was very strong and many students made a public profession of their Christian faith.[22]

3.2.1.3 Women's work

Work among women was another method for reaching Muslims. Women could only be contacted in the homes, since in the mid-nineteenth and early twentieth centuries, women were not allowed to leave their homes and their lives were quite restricted. As Andrew Watson described it:

---

17. Watson, *Egypt*, 225–226. See also Finney, *Tomorrow's Egypt*, 191. A common element in these conversions in the Christian schools was the student finding something different in the life of the missionaries and the Christian teachers which made them ask questions and read the Bible. Within this general pattern there was great variety as to individual circumstances. As examples, see the story of the girl in Tanta school (Finny, *Tomorrow's Egypt*, 191–192); or the story of Yusef Butros who became a Christian after his marriage to a converted student and became an evangelist with the American Mission, H. E. Philips, *Blessed Be Egypt My People: Life Studies from the Land of the Nile* (Philadelphia: The Judson Press, 1953), 65–86.

18. Watson, *Egypt*, 225.

19. Watson, *The American Mission*, 310.

20. Jeffrey Charles Burke, "The Establishment of the American Presbyterian Mission in Egypt, 1854–1940: An Overview" (PhD diss., McGill University, 2000), 140. Beginning from the late 1930s and 1940s the Egyptian government put pressure on the foreign schools concerning their religious teachings. This created a crisis for the American Mission schools. See chapter 2 section 2.2.5.

21. Hogg, *A Master-Builder*, 198. For the establishment and the role of Assiout Training College see chapter 2.

22. Watson, *Egypt*, 228.

Indeed, the condition of women in the Nile valley is sad in the extreme. And what makes the case worse is the fact that most Egyptian men take no interest in educating or elevating the women. They do not regard the women as equal before the law or before God.[23]

Women from the Mission were able to teach Egyptian women basic literacy skills that enabled them to read the Scripture and opened them to instruction on a variety of important topics. As a result, a number of women joined the churches and this movement of work among women spread in many parts of Egypt.[24] Although Christian women were the focus, a number of Muslim women attended these meetings.[25] The report of 1879, noted that between 55 and 60 Muslim families were visited out of 130 families.[26] In the annual report of 1884, the missionaries among women reported:

We have two women regularly employed to teach the women in their houses. These Bible-workers had thirty-seven regular pupils last year and also visited ten other houses to read with and instruct women, who were not taking lessons, three of these being Mohammedan women and eight of the regular pupils were of the same faith.[27]

Both missionaries and Egyptian women, known as "Bible Women," who had been employed by the Mission, made home visits to Christians and Muslims in Cairo and other cities. However, the work among Muslim women was gradually neglected and the women missionaries increasingly focused their efforts in education, social services, and church ministry.[28]

---

23. Ibid., 437.

24. For more details about the work among women see chapter 1.

25. Watson, *Egypt*, 222, Watson, *The American Mission*, 441.

26. Elder, *Vindicating a Vision*, 76.

27. UPCNA Board of Foreign Missions of the United Presbyterian Church of North America, *30ᵗʰ Annual Report of the Mission in Egypt, 1884*, 27.

28. Salama, *Tarikh*, 241–242. The work among women, in both education and evangelism, helped the Egyptian women in their liberation movement which was led by liberal Egyptian thinkers such as Qasim Amin and Taha Hussein. For the socio-political reasons which led to the change in the women's situation in Egypt, (Burke, *The Establishment*, 149–151; Elder, *Vindicating a Vision*, 281–287).

3.2.1.4 Medical work

Medical work also played an important role in the work of the Mission among Muslims. The clinics and hospitals in Tanta, Assiut, and later Cairo were well equipped, giving the patients a high standard of care. The numbers of patients increased through the years, and most of them were Muslims.[29] At the hospital in Assiut, which occupied a large place in the work of the Mission, there were daily morning prayers, and a Bible reader who went from room to room to read the Bible to the patients.[30]

The work of Dr Henry in Assiut was unique in both its professional and spiritual influence. Through his ministry, from 1891 to 1939, a number of Muslims came to accept the Christian faith. One Muslim patient, for example, was influenced by the treatment he found in the hospital, and by Dr Henry who kept asking him if he knew the Lord Jesus Christ. After he left the hospital:

> He could not forget his great suffering when he was taken to the hospital. He could not forget the cleanliness and comfort he enjoyed there. He could not forget the kindly ministry, the professional skill of doctors and nurses, the healing and heartening cheer every day of his stay there; and he could not forget the lack of any anger or displeasure on Dr Henry's part, because of his angry reply to his question, time after time, "Do you know the Lord Jesus Christ?" How could it be accounted for? What gave Dr Henry such a loving spirit? Why did he come away from his children in America and wear out his life in Egypt, thousands of miles from home and country, to do such kindly service for him and other Egyptians?[31]

This Muslim man, and others, converted to Christ because of this type of ministry. The medical work gave the Muslim community in Egypt the opportunity to see Christianity truly embodied.

---

29. The number of patients was 43,038 in 1927 and reached 47,063 patients by 1930. Because of difficulties in Mission personnel and the campaign against missionaries the number declined to 34,153 in 1931 and 30,158 in 1935. (UPCNA, *Minutes of General Assembly of the United Presbyterian Church of North America, 1935*, 977).

30. Watson, *Egypt*, 234.

31. Milligan, *Dr. Henry*, 66–67.

3.2.1.5 Public preaching

Although public preaching was not officially permitted, there were occasions when missionaries found opportunities to speak publicly to people.
In the early years of the Mission especially, they used their rights as foreigners to propagate the gospel with much freedom.[32] The Capitulations gave
the missionaries the possibility of preaching publicly without threat from
local authorities. This situation, however, was reversed in later years when
the government placed more restrictions on the missionaries' activities.

In the early years, the Nile boat trips played an important role in reaching many parts of Upper Egypt with the Bible. The missionaries not only
distributed thousands of copies but also publicly spoke with people about
biblical teachings. In 1864, Lansing wrote of people's hunger for the gospel
during one of his Nile boat trips to Upper Egypt:

> As we, ourselves, again and again saw, scarcely would the boat
> be tied up at the bank near one of the many hundred villages
> along the Nile, before men would come, and sitting down
> cross-legged on the deck, or on the shore, listen with intense
> interest while the missionary read and expounded in their
> own tongue the wonderful works of God, often interrupting
> him with anxious inquiries and with expressions and nods of
> warm approval and assent.[33]

These opportunities to speak were greatly enhanced when missionaries
such as Lansing mastered the Arabic language and were able to preach and
communicate with people in their own language.

The Mission enjoyed some exceptional times in its history when it had
the opportunity to preach the gospel publicly. During such times, they
held meetings which Muslims could openly attend and hear the Christian
message. Mikha'il Mansour, a graduate from Al-Azhar University who
converted to Christianity, joined the Evangelical Church in 1897.[34] The
Mission discovered his ability to preach the gospel publicly to Muslims,
and therefore arranged a weekly meeting at the Mission building in Cairo.

---

32. See chapter 1.
33. Lansing, *Egypt's Princes*, 424.
34. Philips, *Blessed be Egypt*, 116–136.

Muslim inquirers started to attend, eager to hear the ex-sheikh who was preaching the gospel.[35] The meetings continued for many years from the end of the nineteenth century when Mikha'il, and then his brother Kamiel, spoke and debated with Muslims, until the 1930s. In one meeting, the audience numbered one hundred men, half of whom were Muslims.[36] Because of these public events, the Muslim community in Egypt organized a campaign against the Mission and its efforts to preach to Muslims. In the 1920s and 1930s, this conflict was reported by the newspapers and resulted in government intervention and the termination of such meetings.[37]

3.2.1.6 Personal relationships

In addition to their formal programmes, the missionaries sought to minister by building personal relationships with Muslim people. As noted in reports, autobiographies and letters, these friendships opened the door for sharing the gospel. Because it was difficult and even dangerous for Muslims to publicly confess their faith in Christ, many kept their relationship with the missionaries a secret. Andrew Watson said "I presume every American missionary has a personal acquaintance with Mohammedans who in secret avow their disbelief in Mohammedanism and their belief in Christianity, and are restrained by fear from making a profession."[38]

Davida Finney wrote about her father, a long-time missionary in Egypt, that at the time of his death a list was found in his desk containing the names of fifty Muslims wanting interviews or Bible study. He had talked about the Christian faith to these fifty people and many others as well. The results of this kind of ministry were significant although unseen and unrecognized.[39]

---

35. This exceptional time of liberty of speech came during the British occupation of Egypt. It did not last long as a result of the problems it caused. The activities of the American Mission were then restricted to inside Mission properties and Evangelical Churches.

36. Elder, *Vindicating a Vision,* 231–232.

37. The anti-mission campaign will be the subject of study in this chapter.

38. Watson, *The American Mission,* 360.

39. Finney, *Tomorrow's Egypt,* 190. There were no security concerns from the missionaries because of the protections they had from the capitulations. The most aggressive action the government could do was to ask missionaries to leave the country within a limited period.

The missionaries worked diligently to establish contacts with people, especially during the early years of the Mission. They communicated with people at work, in the market, in homes and through the mission activities. Some missionaries had better access because they spoke Arabic fluently, while others found Arabic a hard language to learn and use. The missionaries who were involved in public ministry in schools and hospitals could minister effectively among Muslims. However, in later years the missionaries found themselves isolated from direct contact, spending more and more time with "Christians" and managing the Evangelical Church and its affairs. Even in their daily life they spent less time with Muslims, and did not talk openly about their faith as before. Instead, the role of the missionaries gradually changed from evangelism to administration and ecclesiastical business.[40] Furthermore, in response to the changing political situation, the missionaries no longer employed direct evangelistic approaches, but preferred to adopt more indirect methods among the Muslims.

3.2.1.7 Work among Copts

The Mission did not believe that it was abandoning its work of evangelizing Muslims when it took a more indirect approach. Instead, the missionaries commonly believed that reforming the Coptic Church was a preliminary step to winning Muslims.[41] John Hogg tried, in the beginning of his ministry, to reach Muslims whenever he found the opportunity, but he had meagre results. Rena Hogg wrote that her father told her that,

> The great stumbling-block in the way of doing much for them (i.e. Muslims) is the Coptic Church. Mohammedans have not the means at present to knowing what true Christianity is.[42]

She added her own comment saying:

> In the light of this fact, all effort for the regeneration of the Copts acquired a unique value. He saw in it the forging of a key that must eventually unlock the closed portal of Islam,

---

40. Bailey, *Cross-Cultural Mission*, 16.

41. For more details about the Coptic Church and its state and relationship with the American Mission see chapter 1.

42. Hogg, *A Master-Builder*, 93.

and prepare the way for a more direct and concentrated effort
to secure the entrance he coveted amongst Egypt's millions . . .
if we are to view the work from this standpoint, . . . the Copts
seemed to him to bear the same relation to the salvation of the
Moslems that the Jews of Christ's day bore to the salvation of
the Gentiles.[43]

Hogg believed that when Copts became good examples of Christlikeness,
it would become easy to convince the Muslims of the truth of the Christian
faith. Thus, hoping that an evangelistically minded Coptic Church would
be the most effective means to reach Muslims, Hogg and the Mission
switched their focus to reaching Copts and drawing them out of the Coptic
Church. The encouraging results in ministry to the Copts further led the
Mission to concentrate its efforts there. Although the missionaries did not
find a welcome from the Coptic Church itself, some individual Copts,
among them were influential members of society, accepted the Protestant
beliefs, and became founders of the Evangelical Church.[44]

After communicating the gospel to the Copts and establishing the
Evangelical Church, the missionaries then challenged the local believers
to reach out to the Muslims.[45] This, according to the missionaries' expectations, would prove to be an effective method for reaching Muslims as
well as Copts. Instead, the Evangelical Church, encountering the same
difficulties and frustrations that the Mission had experienced in reaching
Muslims, also followed its example and concentrated its evangelistic work
among the Copts.[46]

3.2.1.8 Social work

Social work was another tool used by the American Mission to reach
Muslims. Challenging and changing unhealthy or harmful local customs
was an indirect way to proclaim the Christian faith. The Mission set up

---

43. Ibid.

44. For more details of the establishment of the Evangelical Church and the relationship
between the American Mission and the Coptic Church see chapter 2.

45. Watson, *Egypt*, 221.

46. See later in this chapter.

campaigns to stop social "national evils"[47] such as slavery, child abuse, and licensed prostitution, the use of narcotics and alcohol and religious intolerance.[48] In 1869, after a few years of ministry in Assiut, the Mission succeeded in changing the market day from Sunday to Saturday, and thus raising the profile of the "Protestants" in society.[49] Although this kind of ministry was not direct evangelism, it was a step towards changing the life of people "even if it be without ever ringing the changes upon the Christian label."[50]

3.2.2 Experiences and Nature of Muslim Evangelism

In their ministry to the Muslims of Egypt, the American missionaries experienced both success and opposition. The difficult experiences shaped their changing perspectives and plans for evangelism. The political and social situation likewise played an important role in limiting the number of Muslim converts and led the Mission to attempt different approaches.

3.2.2.1 Early converts

The missionaries in their books, reports, and minutes recorded some unique conversions. The earliest occurred at the Mission in Assiut when Faris tried to covert a woman.[51] In addition, a Muslim female student in one of the Mission schools converted.[52] An important story relates to Ahmad Fahmy who became a missionary in China.[53] Another early convert

---

47. Watson, *What is This Muslim World,* 166.

48. Ibid.

49. UPCNA, Board of Foreign Mission of the United Presbyterian Church of North America, *Twentieth Annual Report of the Board of Foreign Mission of the United Presbyterian Church of North America: Presented to the General Assembly in May, 1870* (Philadelphia: Young & Ferguson, Printers, 1870), 38–39; The story of the change in market day shows the growing political, social, and religious influence of Protestants. Its accomplishment required the permission of the governor, the acceptance of Copts and the satisfaction of merchants. The influence of wealthy Protestant families in Assiut was used by the Mission in their interaction with Egyptian society.

50. Watson, *What is This Muslim World,* 166.

51. This story was recounted also in chapter 1 of this study as an example of the difficulties that the Mission found in its early years. For more details see Lansing, *Religious Toleration in Egypt,* 3–16.

52. Finny, *Tomorrow's Egypt,* 191–192.

53. Ahmed Fahmy came to the Christian faith in 1877 through the Mission School in Cairo. He received threats from his family which led the Mission to send him to Scotland. He studied medicine at the University of Edinburgh. The Mission in Egypt attempted

wanted to minister to his own people and became an evangelical pastor.[54] Both Mikha'il and his brother Kamiel, who had been students in Al-Azhar and become evangelists of the American Mission after their conversion, contributed significantly to the ministry among Muslims.[55] Analysis of these different conversion stories reveals common characteristics that were typical of the ministry with Muslims.[56]

3.2.2.2 The Mission care for converts

When the American Mission arrived in Egypt, they were uncertain of their exact goals and methods. However, once the Mission had reaped some fruit among Muslims, the missionaries decided to organize a specific ministry. They established a committee to oversee the ministry among Muslims and to deal with the affairs of the converts. In the minutes of the Mission in 1911, the Mission approved the suggestion to appoint a committee to look into the matter of "the Moslem Converts."[57] The job description for this committee proposed that it,

> . . . keep the mission informed concerning Moslem converts in Egypt as far as known. It should endeavour to discover opportunities for utilizing converted Moslems in Christian evangelization whenever possible or, in case of absolute need, secure for them the means of livelihood.
>
> Furthermore the committee should arrange for an annual conference for Moslem converts and for all who may be interested in them. This conference should be held at such time

---

to bring him back to work in its hospital in Tanta but because of the danger, this plan did not proceed. Ahmad accepted an invitation from the London Missionary Society to work as a doctor-missionary in China. Watson, *The American Mission*, 305–311; Elder, *Vindicating a Vision*, 76–77. For more details about Ahmed Fahmy and his mission efforts in China see, Norman Goodall, *A History of the London Missionary Society, 1895–1945* (London: Oxford University Press, 1954).

54. Philips, *Blessed Be Egypt*, 116–136.

55. Ibid., 17–43; 44–64.

56. In the preface to his book, *Blessed Be Egypt*, Philips, who was a missionary to Egypt, wrote of six case histories to support his three reasons for writing his book. First, he sought to outline the main beliefs of Mohammedans; second, to depict the difficulties faced by converts; and finally, to prove by the example of the ministry in Egypt that evangelism of Muslims was actually possible.

57. American Mission in Egypt, *Minutes of the Year, 1911*, 27.

and place as may best suit the purpose in view, *viz.*, the development of the spiritual life of all who attend, the formation and cementing of the bond between Moslem converts and other Christians, and the quickening of all in the matter of the conversion of Moslems.[58]

The Mission, through the "Committee of Muslim Converts," worked to keep its converts under the influence of the Mission. Specially donated monthly grants were arranged to aid the converts.[59] This aid for former Muslims was not offered in order to attract them to the Christian faith, but rather, to help the converts cope with the difficult situations they faced after conversion.[60] The Committee also helped the converts in their spiritual life, providing a number of Christian publications and arranging Bible study meetings to help them grow in their faith.[61]

In 1929, as a part of its work, the Mission Evangelistic Board reported to the Mission Association:

A complete list of Muslim converts now living has been made showing 94 men and 51 women who have been baptized and made open profession of their faith in Christ. There are 17 women converts in addition who profess their faith in Christ but who have not yet received baptism. There are also 14 men who have been baptized and later have apostatised or fallen into a state of backsliding.[62]

When new converts confessed their faith, it was the beginning of much hardship. Muslim society took seriously the teaching that an individual is not permitted to change their Islamic faith.[63] The converts' families aggres-

---

58. Ibid.

59. American Mission in Egypt, *Minutes of the Year, 1927*, 245.

60. Because of this aid to converts, the Mission was accused of attracting Muslims to convert for financial reasons. Likewise, the genuineness of the converts' faith was also questioned.

61. American Mission in Egypt, *Minutes of the Year, 1927*, 77.

62. American Mission in Egypt, *Minutes of the Year, 1929*, 397.

63. In Islamic Law the penalty for converting from Islam is death. For example in a hadith, the Prophet of Islam said "*Whoever changed his Islamic religion, then kill him*" cited in Muhammad Muhsin Khan, *The Translation of the Meanings of Sahih Al-Bukhari: Arabic-English*, Vol. 9 (Medina Al-Munawwara: Dar Ahya Us-Sunnah, n.d.), 45.

sively opposed their decision to be Christians. Verbal threats, kidnappings, enforced debates and arguments with Muslim sheikhs, and attempts on their lives, were all used to bring the converts back to Islam. Many converts had to leave their families, jobs, spouses, and even their country. When the opposition and persecution against the converts increased due to religious and social pressures, the missionaries became actively involved in the situation. At times, the missionaries took such cases to the Consul General of Britain or of the United States, who then exerted their influence on the Egyptian government to allow the converts the freedom to change their religion. Sometimes, such as with both Faris and Ahmad Fahmy, the government responded positively to the pressure.[64] Unfortunately, these efforts to protect converts also built a wall of suspicion between the missionaries and the Evangelical Church on the one side and the Muslim community on the other.

3.3 The Evangelical Church and Muslim Evangelism

3.3.1 The Beginning of the Synod Work among Muslims

As mentioned above, the American Mission in Egypt entered the Egyptian field in order to evangelize the whole country. Nevertheless, because of difficulties, they focused their attention on the Copts among whom they found greater success. Then, when the American Mission established the Evangelical Church of Egypt in the 1860s, it was hoped that the Church would be the main instrument to reach the whole country for Christ. Consequently, the American Mission on many occasions urged the Egyptians to take responsibility for evangelizing the Muslims.[65] The Evangelical Church, however, did not respond to this counsel until 1900.

---

64. Lansing, *Religious*, 3–16; Watson, *The American Mission*, 305–311; Elder, *Vindicating a Vision*, 76–77.

65. Watson, *Egypt*, 221, Charles R. Watson, *Report of the Visit of the Corresponding Secretary to Egypt and the Levant: With a Discussion of the Missionary Situation and Its Problems* (Philadelphia: The Board of Foreign Missions of the United Presbyterian Church of North America, 1912), 17.

It was at its second meeting in 1900, that the Synod of the Nile formed a committee for work among Muslims.[66] Ricol Naser El-Hemssy[67] had suggested that the Synod organize such a committee for evangelizing Muslims in both Egypt and Sudan. He offered to pay £48 every year for the salary of an evangelist to work among Muslims.[68] The Synod discussed the request and appointed a committee to explore the idea. The committee then gave the Synod suggestions about such an endeavour. They suggested that the Synod should accept the request by Mr El-Hemssy, thank him for his initiative and vision, and accept his annual donation for the work. Further, the Synod was to ask the Theological Seminary to teach students apologetic works such as *Al-Hedaya (The Guidance)*, and other similar books. The Synod was also to appoint a committee that would choose one or more evangelists for work among Muslims. Moreover, this committee was to develop new methods for quietly sharing the salvation message with Muslims in ways that were appropriate within the Egyptian context. They also suggested that the Synod instruct the presbyteries to appoint members who could challenge churches and organizations to support this project and collect money for the work in Egypt as a preparatory step to later working in Sudan. Lastly, it was suggested that the Synod should encourage the pastors, evangelists, and church members to pray for the success of this project and give money for that purpose.[69]

An American missionary, Mr Yawn, headed the new permanent Committee for Work among Muslims. Dr Andrew Watson, two Egyptian pastors, and an elder were also members, and Mikha'il Mansour was appointed the first Egyptian full-time evangelist for the work with Muslims.[70]

---

66. Before 1899, the Evangelical Church was organized into the Egyptian Presbytery that became the Synod of the Nile in 1899.

67. There is no more information about El-Hemssy but from the name we can suggest that he was Syrian and he was a rich man who wanted to donate to the work among Muslims.

68. Synod of the Nile, *Minutes of the Year, 1900*, 9.

69. Ibid., 61.

70. Mikha'il Mansour, who had the name Muhammad before his conversion, was a student at Al-Azhar University where he was taught that Christians are infidels. (Philips, *Blessed be Egypt*, 17). As a sheikh in his home town he asked Copts about their faith. They directed him to speak with the Evangelical pastor. When he went to the Evangelical church in his town he was surprised by the manner of worship and the Biblical teachings. From the pastor he received a copy of the Bible. After several meetings with two

The Committee also reminded the presbyteries and the churches of their role in Muslim evangelism. They gave suggestions of methods the local churches could use, urging them to distribute tracts and Bibles so that the Muslims could know about the Christian faith. They also asked the teachers in the Protestant schools to teach the Muslim students "the Christian principals and morality so they could accept the Christian religion easily."[71]

3.3.2 The Synod's Methods in the Work among Muslims

The Evangelical Church through its "Committee for Work among Muslims" used a number of methods that they developed through the years following the model introduced by the American Mission. The interaction and cooperation between the American Mission and the Evangelical Church can be seen in these shared ideas and methods.

After Mikha'il's appointment to work as full-time evangelist among Muslims, the American Mission asked him to hold apologetic meetings.[72] Later, in 1900, the Evangelical Church also adapted this method when Mikha'il started a weekly meeting in Azbakiyah, in Cairo, since the social and political atmosphere was open to such activity at that time. The audience in these meetings included Muslims, Christians from other churches, and missionaries, with attendance varying from as high as two hundred some weeks, to only one or two Muslims at other times.[73] These meetings especially addressed issues about the person of Jesus, the authenticity of the Bible as the Word of God, and the way of salvation. Mikha'il, and later Kamiel, attracted many Muslims to the meetings to ask questions and debate. Often, people stayed after the meeting for further discussion. In 1912, the Minutes of the Synod mentioned that these meetings opened the

---

Evangelical Pastors, he started to read and study the Bible, comparing its teachings with the teachings of Islam. After a time of thinking and praying he finally converted and confessed his Christian faith. (Philips, *Blessed Be Egypt*, 17–35). He was baptized in the Catholic Church and had the name Mikha'il because the Evangelical Church was afraid to baptize him. In December 1897, he left the Catholic Church to join the Evangelical Church where he was appointed as an evangelist. He encountered much opposition from his family who even sought to kill him. Later he was appointed the first evangelist among Muslims. For a full biography of Mikha'il see: Kamiel Mansour, *Elsheikh Mikha'il Mansour* (The Sheikh Mikha'il Mansour), Cairo: Matbaat Al-Moheet, 1929), 1–40.

71. Synod of the Nile, *Minutes of the Year, 1901*, 65.

72. Elder, *Vindicating a Vision*, 232.

73. Synod of the Nile, *Minutes of the Year, 1916*, 120.

door for Muslims to come during the week for personal discussion that led some of them to convert.[74]

For many years Mikha'il and Kamiel organized meetings where they would speak to Muslims and encourage local Christians to share their faith with them.[75] These open meetings were also held in cities outside of Cairo. In 1941 for example, Kamiel was invited by many churches in Alexandria, Tanta, Mansoura, Minya, and Assiut to speak at public meetings that Muslims attended.[76]

Besides these public meetings, the Church organized other ministries. Pastors and evangelists held teaching meetings where they encouraged Christians to pray for and speak with Muslims and discussed methodology. In the 1950 Committee report, a pastor in a village in Upper Egypt was used as an example because he had organized weekly meetings to teach church members about Islam and the Christian response. He also spoke to them about methods of Muslim evangelism and they prayed together for Muslims.[77]

Because of the public meetings and through the evangelistic efforts of church members, a number of Muslims wished to know more about the Christian faith. The work of both Mikha'il and Kamiel was also crucial. They both devoted specific days each week for visiting Muslims. In the Synod report of 1912, Mikha'il informed the Committee for the Work among Muslims that besides the weekly meetings he had in Cairo, he visited Muslims in their homes and at work, giving them the Bible and talking to them about his faith. He ministered to all levels of society including both the educated and ignorant, the rich and the poor, the employers and employees. He evangelized high-ranking people in society and invited many of them to attend church meetings.[78] Some of them responded to his invitation and attended Azbakiyah. Mikha'il also held respectful debates with Al-Azhar students for long periods day and night. He was highly

74. Synod of the Nile, *Minutes of the Year, 1912*, 330–331.

75. Synod of the Nile, *Minutes of the Year, 1939*, 67.

76. Synod of the Nile, *Minutes of the Year, 1941*, 230.

77. Synod of the Nile, *Minutes of the Year, 1950*, 13.

78. Synod of the Nile, *Minutes of the Year, 1912*, 330–331.

respected by Muslims, and his intimate knowledge of Islam enabled him to successfully contextualize the message.[79]

The ministry of Kamiel Mansour expanded in 1947 when he, with the help of the American Mission and the Synod, opened an office in Old Cairo where he could meet with Muslims desiring to understand Christian faith. People who attended weekly meetings, missionaries, and other Egyptians who came from other Coptic or evangelical churches visited him. In this office, he also held discussions, Bible studies, debates, and catechism instruction for people wishing to be baptized.[80]

The Committee for the Work among Muslims urged the Synod and the members of the church to use personal contacts for reaching Muslims. In difficult times, during the two World Wars and after the church faced government restrictions, personal relationships with Muslims did in fact become the main method of evangelism.[81] The Committee for the Work among Muslims encouraged the pastors to speak with one Muslim every month and to pray for the work. Both the Committee and Kamiel Mansour taught the Church that the example of a morally exemplary life and personal contacts were the best methods for Muslim evangelism.[82]

As previously practised by the Mission, the Committee also distributed the Bible among Muslims. The American missionary doctor Gibson donated a sum of money for this purpose and both the Mission and the Committee for the Work among Muslims used this fund for their ministry. The Committee gave forty-four New Testaments to personal contacts in the first year of this practice in 1950.[83] Gradually, the number of distributed Bibles increased. In 1958, the Committee reported that in the six previous years 1,400 Bibles or parts of the Bible had been given out by pastors, elders, laymen and women, and missionaries. The Committee asked the members of the Church to first give Muslims the Sermon on the Mount, then Matthew's Gospel, followed by the New Testament, and finally the

---

79. Ibid., 330.

80. Synod of the Nile, *Minutes of the Year, 1948*, 53–54.

81. Synod of the Nile, *Minutes of the Year, 1941*, 230.

82. Synod of the Nile, *Minutes of the Year, 1949*, 148–149.

83. Synod of the Nile, *Minutes of the Year, 1950*, 13.

whole Bible. They challenged pastors and Church members to open discussions with those who requested Bibles, and to pray for them.[84]

The Committee published two tracts written especially for Muslims and distributed a large number of them. It asked both Mikha'il and Kamiel to write tracts and articles on subjects often debated by Christians and Muslims: the divinity of Jesus, the cross, and the Trinity.[85]

Like the Mission, the Evangelical Church used many methods for contacting Muslims and communicating the gospel with them. Throughout the country, the Church operated about 150 day schools with a large number of Muslim students. The teachers used to speak to the students about their faith in these schools, organizing Bible study groups and chapel, and observing the Christian celebrations. The Church and the Mission fought with the Egyptian government for years as it sought to maintain its prerogative to teach the Christian religion and the Bible to all their students.[86]

The Committee for the Work among Muslims suggested that the churches should also use literacy education programmes to reach Muslims. In 1950, a literacy campaign was initiated by American missionaries and spread to a number of villages in Upper Egypt where it found great success. Both Christians and Muslims were involved in this project where parts of the Bible were utilized as textbooks.[87]

As methods of media and communication developed, the Committee for the Work among Muslims suggested that the churches could also use movie and slide projectors to expand Muslim exposure to the Christian message. It also suggested that the church hold parties and invite interested Muslims to attend.[88] Most of these suggestions, however, were not adopted because of social, political and security concerns. The Committee had great expectations for a revival in evangelism among church members, but the reality was that the church as an institution contributed much less to this ministry than had been hoped for by the interested pastors and missionaries.

---

84. Synod of the Nile, *Minutes of the Year, 1958*, 19.
85. Synod of the Nile, *Minutes of the Year, 1915*, 64.
86. Synod of the Nile, *Minutes of the Year, 1949*, 86.
87. Synod of the Nile, *Minutes of the Year, 1950*, 13.
88. Synod of the Nile, *Minutes of the Year, 1956*, 164.

3.3.3 The Role of American Mission with the Evangelical Church in Muslim Evangelism

As noted above, the American Mission had called on the Egyptian Church to fulfil the Christian goal of evangelizing the completely Muslim nation, and sought to help the Egyptian Church to fulfil this goal. First, it offered its building in Cairo for the weekly meetings that Mikha'il and Kamiel conducted for Muslims. They helped by organizing the meetings, and attended in order to contribute to the discussions and to help build relationships.[89] The attendance of the missionaries in the meetings also helped to keep order when passions were raised in heated discussions.[90] Second, they used their capitulation rights in times of riots or confrontations in the meetings, and to rescue some individual Muslim converts who were facing severe persecution.[91] Third, an American senior missionary, often the head of the American Mission Committee of Evangelism, gave leadership to the Committee for the Work among Muslims of the Synod of the Nile throughout its history. Moreover, other missionaries shared Committee membership with the Egyptian pastors and elders.[92] Fourth, the American Mission contributed to the costs of the ministry, even taking responsibility for paying half of Mikha'il's and Kamiel's salary. It also covered the gaps in the Committee budget during those years when the Synod could not cover the expenses.[93] Fifth, the American Mission opened the doors of its hospital in Assiut for Kamiel to have meetings for Muslims, and encouraged the patients to attend and hear the Christian message.[94]

Besides the contribution of the American Mission as an organization, there were individual missionaries who were highly involved with the Evangelical Church's ministry to Muslims. Starting in 1913, the Committee for the Work among Muslims invited Samuel Zwemer to speak at meetings

---

89. Elder, *Vindicating a Vision,* 229–230.

90. Philips, *Blessed Be Egypt,* 48–49.

91. See chapter 1.

92. Synod of the Nile, *Minutes of the Years from 1900–1963*; American Mission in Egypt, *Minutes of the Years, 1900–1958.*

93. Synod of the Nile, *Minutes of the Year, 1919,* 251.

94. Synod of the Nile, *Minutes of the Year, 1954,* 43.

in Minya and asked him to start a publication for this work.[95] Wanting to collaborate more closely with him, the Committee asked the Synod to appoint him as one of its members. Zwemer was also invited by the Synod to speak about Muslim evangelism. Nevertheless, he found the Church's efforts to be quite limited, and pressed the Synod to view evangelism as the main duty of the Evangelical Church in Egypt.[96]

Zwemer's role in the ministry of the evangelical church continued to grow throughout the years. He adopted exclusive theological beliefs and sometimes an aggressive approach of missions to Muslims while being in Cairo.[97] He saw in Christianity "the final religion, and its message – Christ incarnate, Crucified, Risen, and Glorified – is the one thing needed to evangelize the world."[98] Although he was working mainly with the American Mission he was also a great help to the Evangelical Church's mission to Muslims. He not only spoke in meetings to encourage evangelicals to share their faith with Muslims, but also wrote a number of tracts and offered them to the workers among Muslims to distribute.[99] He personally contributed to the financial needs of the ministry.[100]

The Synod had asked the Committee to cover Kamiel's salary when he was first appointed for work among Muslims. Dr Zwemer contributed half of Kamiel's salary and rented him a house in a Muslim district in Cairo so that he could meet with Muslims.[101] Kamiel would spend one day a week in this house, leading a Bible study group with twelve Muslims.[102] The Synod also asked Dr Zwemer to teach Islamic subjects to the students of the Seminary. Even after he left the Seminary, he continued teaching

---

95. Samuel Zwemer was invited by the American Mission in Egypt, and the invitation was seconded by the CMS through Temple Gairdner. The Nile Mission Press joined in the call and Zwemer who was missionary with the Reformed Church in Arabia moved to Cairo. He spent from 1912–1928, teaching, writing, debating and leading a movement of mission for Muslims. (J. Christy Wilson, *Apostle to Islam: A Biography of Samuel M. Zwemer* [Grand Rapids: Baker Book House, 1952], 77).

96. Synod of the Nile, *Minutes of the Year, 1913*, 357–359.

97. Vander Werff, *Christian Mission*, 231.

98. Ibid., 252.

99. Synod of the Nile, *Minutes of the Year, 1919*, 251.

100. Synod of the Nile, *Minutes of the Year, 1923*, 381.

101. Synod of the Nile, *Minutes of the Year, 1919*, 251.

102. Synod of the Nile, *Minutes of the Year, 1923*, 381–382.

comparative religions and Muslim-Christian apologetics and methodologies to local church leaders and missionaries.[103] Zwemer's theology of mission, evangelism, and church, and his aggressive methodology for reaching Muslims, influenced the Evangelical Church. He was the key player in Muslim evangelism inside Egypt and worldwide.[104]

3.3.4 The Synod Workers among Muslims

The Evangelical Church tried to have a role in Muslim evangelism and to fulfil the goal of evangelization of the whole country. The level of interest of the church and its involvement in this work varied from one period to another. In the early years of the establishment of the Committee for the Work among Muslims, there were hopes that the churches and the members would take the vision of evangelizing Muslims seriously. On some occasions, the subject was in the mind of the churches as we see in the reports of the first year when the church showed its excitement for this work. As an example, in the Synod meeting of 1903 the Committee for the Work among Muslims thought that the churches were ready and desired to start working among Muslims on a wide scale when it asked them to invite Mikha'il to talk about his ministry in many churches. However, the committee only received a request for him to visit from one church. This led the committee to ask the Synod to remind the churches of their duty towards Muslims and that the pastors, evangelists, and missionaries should raise the awareness of the members of the church in that matter.[105] They asked them to pray in public meetings for the salvation of Muslims, as they were precious souls for God. They also asked them to pray that "the Lord will destroy the power of the Islamic religion and by the power of his Holy Spirit proclaim to the Muslims that the Christ is the real prophet and the only Saviour."[106]

Unfortunately, the Synod did not want to expand its work among Muslims. Even when Sadeq Swaihey, one of the students of the Seminary, requested the Synod to appoint him for the work among Muslims because

---

103. Synod of the Nile, *Minutes of the Year, 1925*, 59.

104. For more study about Zwemer and the development of his approaches see Vander Werff, *Christian Mission*, 184–268.

105. Synod of the Nile, *Minutes of the Year, 1904*, 87.

106. Ibid., 88.

he dedicated himself for that work, the Synod replied that they were satisfied with the work they were doing and that they did not need more evangelists to work among Muslims. The Synod did not want to give from its budget to this ministry since it was focusing on pastoral work and directed its finances to cover the needs of pastors without looking to the wider field.[107]

Fourteen years after its establishment, and after many years of requests, the Committee for the Work among Muslims had its second evangelist appointed to work among Muslims. Rev Sadeq Swaihey obtained his desire and was appointed to work among Muslims in the Delta region. This was seen as a courageous step but it came very late. To dedicate a minister in the Synod for a work other than pastoral work required the Synod to pay for the salary of the minister who chose to have a ministry that was not a pastorate, and as we have seen above the Synod was not committed to this type of work.[108] The Synod was under continuing pressure for years from the interested members in Muslim evangelism and the Committee answered positively when it appointed Swaihey for the work among Muslims.

In 1913, the members of the Committee visited Swaihey in his ministry field and were encouraged by his ministry among Muslims. A report about his ministry was included in the committee report to the Synod. He started by holding meetings in Zaqazik, in the Delta, where about three hundred people attended the first meetings, a third of them being Muslims. The number declined later for security and social reasons; then Swaihey used homes and work visitation as the main method to reach Muslims. After a few months, when the government prohibited the meetings for Muslims in that town, he went to Cairo where he resumed his ministry. He also visited evangelical churches to empower them in their ministry. He organized church committees for the work among Muslims in the churches he

---

107. Synod of the Nile, *Minutes of the Year, 1905,* 93; 106. There must have been discussion on the Synod about this with people for and against the matter but the Synod's records did not keep these discussions in detail. The records give the final decisions, which did not give a clear idea about the different opinions of the members, and the way they came to these conclusions. There are some hints from which the reasons for taking certain decisions can be found in the Synod minutes or in the church papers of the time. In general, the Egyptians were not as good as the Westerners in keeping records.

108. Synod of the Nile, *Minutes of the Year, 1913,* 357–358.

visited. He had great hopes after his successful first year in ministry and he looked to the future with an optimistic view.[109]

In 1916, when there was a time of difficulty in the ministry in Egypt, the Rev Swaihey continued in his ministry of holding meetings but he spent more time studying Islam rather than having direct contacts with Muslims. He found difficulties in his personal evangelism ministry that led him to make his contacts among his Muslim neighbours and friends. The Committee asked the Synod to allow Rev Swaihey to have some work with the Synod and with one of the American Mission orphanages. He accepted the Synod invitation to take a pastoral ministry in one of the Delta Presbytery churches and end his full-time ministry as an evangelist among Muslims because of the difficulties he found in his ministry.[110]

When the Committee for the Work among Muslims asked the Synod to lend him for two months every year for this ministry, the Synod allowed him one month for only one year. There was also the problem of his salary; the Synod asked the Committee to find ways to cover his salary for that month while the Synod through the Delta Presbytery paid for the rest of his salary. Another obstacle in the ministry of Rev Swaihey was his relationship with his church that the presbytery did not allow him to leave. In 1921, when the Committee asked the Synod to have Rev Swaihey visit churches and encourage them for Muslim evangelism, his presbytery refused to let him go and leave his pastoral ministry. These difficulties led Rev Swaihey to leave his ministry among Muslims and in the following years, there was no mention of the relationship between him and the Committee for the Work among Muslims or any link between him and Muslim evangelism. He was involved in his pastoral ministry and the vision to evangelize Muslims was not the centre of his interest any more.[111]

Thus, a minister who had a vision changed that vision because the atmosphere in the Evangelical Church was not open to have a mission ministry from a pastor. The mentality of the Synod was more pastoral than evangelistic. This situation continued in the Church that could not handle ministers who were not pastors and hold them within its organization or

---

109. Ibid., 358.

110. Synod of the Nile, *Minutes of the Year, 1916*, 121.

111. Synod of the Nile, *Minutes of the Year, 1921*, 328.

under its control. This situation led the Church to lose its evangelistic vision and leave the work to its members who found other ways to practise these kinds of ministries.[112]

From 1958, when the Synod became independent of the General Assembly of the United Presbyterian Church of North America, the Committee for the Work among Muslims continued having difficulties in its mission. Although the Committee challenged the Synod to have more work among Muslims and increase its feeling of responsibility towards Muslims, the ministry of the Committee was in its final stages. Kamiel Mansour was now an old man and after the death of his wife in 1957, his ministry decreased significantly.[113] Even before that in 1956, he did not submit his annual report and he did not attend the Committee meeting.[114] In the following year, he sent a written report but again he did not attend the Committee meeting.[115] In 1960, the Committee did not submit its annual report to the Synod, and only a verbal report was presented to the Synod. The Committee then came under the Council of Evangelism and Pastoral Work of the Synod and lost its independence since its reports were included in this council report.[116]

Throughout its history, an American missionary headed the Committee for the Work among Muslims. In 1962, the Committee asked the evangelistic council to appoint an Egyptian chairman rather than an American. The Synod gave no answer for this request that was the end of the Committee.[117] The Committee ended at the 1964 Synod meeting, after Kamiel died in December 1963 and there was no full-time minister for the work among Muslims in the Synod after him.[118] The work among Muslims by the Synod did not continue as part of the Synod's ministry. It turned into the ministry of some individual members of the Evangelical Church.

---

112. See chapter 7.
113. Synod of the Nile, *Minutes of the Year, 1958*, 19.
114. Synod of the Nile, *Minutes of the Year, 1956*, 164.
115. Synod of the Nile, *Minutes of the Year, 1957*, 245.
116. Synod of the Nile, *Minutes of the Year, 1960*, 170.
117. Synod of the Nile, *Minutes of the Year, 1962*, 103.
118. Synod of the Nile, *Minutes of the Year, 1963*, 234.

3.4 Reasons for the Lack in Converts' Numbers

It was a disappointing reality for the missionaries in Egypt and the Evangelical Church that for many reasons their efforts with Muslims ended with such a small number of converts. Some of these reasons were external, related to the political and social situation in Egypt as a mission field. There were also reasons within the American Mission and the Evangelical Church that prevented their ministry to Muslims.

3.4.1 External Reasons

3.4.1.1 Political situation

One of the main obstacles to successful evangelism among Muslims was the political situation in Egypt. Egyptian politics played an indirect yet very important role in Muslim evangelism, since the missionaries adjusted their activities according to the prevailing political situation. The relationship between politics and Muslim evangelism underwent three main periods.

In the early period of the Mission work, 1854–1882, Egypt was part of the Ottoman Empire. Under pressure from the European powers, the Ottomans declared religious freedom in 1844 for all people in the Empire, including Egypt.[119] Christians were given some freedom to build their churches and organize their denominations. This included the Protestants who received the right to be an official church.[120] In Sa'id's time, 1854–1863, the missionaries took advantage of the tolerance of the governor to defend some of the converts. Lansing, the American missionary, entitled his collection of correspondence with officials concerning this problem *Religious Toleration in Egypt.* The missionaries used this indulgent

---

119. Barton, a missionary in Turkey, stated that "Under pressure brought to bear by the before-named ambassadors, led by the British, the Sultan, on March 21st, 1844, gave a written pledge as follows 'The Sublime Porte engages to take effectual measures to prevent, henceforward, the persecution and putting to death of the Christian who is an apostate.' Two days later Abdul Medjid, in a conference with Sir Stratford, gave assurance 'That henceforward neither shall Christianity be insulted in my dominions, nor shall Christians be in any way persecuted for their religion.'" James L. Barton, *Daybreak in Turkey* (Boston: The Pilgrim Press, 1908), 250.

120. See chapter 1.

atmosphere to develop a ministry among Muslims, but had limited conversions due to other social and religious factors.[121]

In general, however, there was a lack of recognition of the principle of religious liberty by local government officials, except when the Consuls of Christian countries such as England and the United States pressured or compelled them.[122] The powerful families and Egyptian judges followed their own religious laws attacking the efforts of the missionaries to convert Muslims. In this period, the number of converts was small compared with the efforts of the missionaries. Up to 1882, only seventy-five Muslims were baptized because of the work of the American Mission in Egypt.[123]

In the second period (1882–1904), Egypt went through a time of instability as it dealt with both economic and political problems. The army under the leadership of the Egyptian Colonel 'Arabi rebelled against the Khedive and the British army occupied Egypt from 1882–1922. The Christians in Egypt received the British with great hope thinking that they would be favoured by a Christian nation. Lord Cromer, the British governor in Egypt, wrote about the Copts and their expectations in his book *Modern Egypt*:

> When the British occupation took place, certain hopes began to dawn in [the Copt's] mind. I, said the Copt to himself, am a Christian; if I had the power to do so, I would favour Christians at the expense of Moslems; the English are Christians; therefore – and it was here that the Copt was guilty of a sad *ignoratio elenchi* – as the English have the power, they will assuredly favour Christians at the expense of Moslems.[124]

The American Mission, especially in its ministry among Muslims, hoped to receive special privileges. Many Muslims wishing to convert to Christianity also hoped they would enjoy religious freedom under the British occupation. They expected that there would be no official pressure

---

121. Lansing, *Religious Toleration in Egypt*, 3.

122. Watson, *The American Mission*, 360.

123. Ibid.

124. Baring, Evelyn *Modern Egypt: By the Earl of Cromer* Vol. 2 (London: Macmillan, 1908), 209.

and less social pressures.[125] Mission reports between 1880 and 1885 list an increase in the number of Muslim enquirers, and the number of converts increased after the British occupation. There was a great hope among missionaries that the time for a "general exit from Islam to Christianity had come."[126] During the period from 1854 to 1906, the number of converts reached one hundred and forty.[127]

Hopes were high that the numbers of conversions would continue to increase under the occupation, but to their great disappointment, this failed to materialize. Lord Cromer commented on the situation of the Copts saying:

> When the Copt found that his process of reasoning was fallacious, and that the conduct of the Englishman was guided by motives which he had left out of account, and which he could not understand, he was disappointed, and his disappointment deepened into resentment. He thought that the Englishman's justice to the Moslem involved injustice to himself, for he was apt, perhaps unconsciously, to hold that injustice and absence of favouritism to Copts were well-nigh synonymous terms.[128]

Andrew Watson commented on the incorrect assumptions about British support of the Christians in Egypt including missionaries and evangelicals in their work among Muslims. He explained the Copts' situation saying:

> They did not know that political ends are of greater importance with the so-called Christian powers than Christianity itself, and that the power occupying the country would take no especial care of the Christian population, nor manifest any especial interest in converts from Islam.[129]

The missionaries within a few years realized that the British were not going to give them freedom or protection in their ministry among Muslims. Political and social stability were the main British priorities. Not only did

---

125. Watson, *American Mission,* 360–361.

126. Ibid, 361.

127. Watson, *Islam in Egypt,* 36.

128. Evelyn, *Modern Egypt,* 209.

129. Watson, *American Mission,* 361.

the British ignore the desires of the Christian population, but their occupation of Egypt in fact led to an increase in Egyptian nationalism which resisted any foreign interference in Egypt. This movement played an important role in the campaigns against the missionaries in the period after World War One.

In the third period between 1905 and 1952, tension between the missionaries and Muslims over the evangelization and conversion of Muslims increased dramatically. In 1905, the American Mission had arranged weekly meetings for Mikha'il Mansour to debate the differences between Christianity and Islam. One of the meetings became violent because of angry Muslims who rejected the Christian view on Islam and there was considerable anxiety for Mikha'il's safety. The Muslim community could not accept that a Muslim convert who had associated himself with foreign missionaries was now preaching the Christian faith and attacking Islam.[130]

The American missionaries' polemical approach in evangelizing Muslims was influenced by Samuel Zwemer whose writings, approach, and leadership dominated the work among Muslims throughout the Middle East. Because of the aggressive nature of their evangelism, the voices against the work of the foreign missionaries grew stronger during the early years of the twentieth century. The situation reached its peak between 1924 and 1934 when the Egyptian newspapers and magazines further inflamed passions by publishing articles that criticized foreign missionaries in Egypt.[131] The nationalistic movement against the British occupation and their interference in Egypt's interior affairs along with public and high profile mission activities created an anti-mission atmosphere.[132] In 1928, the newspapers reported on Samuel Zwemer, who at that time was helping the American Mission teach new missionaries about Muslim evangelism. He was accustomed to visiting Al-Azhar Mosque, and on one visit, he distributed Christian literature to the worshippers. This brought loud criticism against

---

130. Philips, *Blessed Be Egypt*, 48–49.

131. The American missionaries in Egypt kept records of the articles, which the newspapers wrote against their work, and they translated it. The collection of the translations can be found in PHS, UPCNA, RG. 209-26-12; 209-26-13: Anti-Missionary Campaign, Summaries from Egyptian Newspapers: dated 1933.

132. Elder, *Vindicating a Vision*, 229–230.

the government and the missionaries in Egypt.[133] Although Zwemer left Egypt for Cyprus and the government sought to calm the situation by reporting that Zwemer was no longer in the country, the campaign continued for a number of years.[134]

For many months, newspapers such as *Kawkab El Shark*, *Al Balagh*, and *Al Ahram* wrote articles attacking the missionaries and their attempts to convert Muslims. These articles accused the missionaries of being an instrument in the hand of colonialism to destroy Islam and the national roots of the country. This growing antagonism against the missionaries affected their work among Muslims and led them to utilize different evangelistic approaches.[135]

The political and social pressures upon the missionaries and the Church in their ministry among Muslims reduced the number of converts. Although there were some periods when there was no pressure from the government, society in general continued to reject the missionaries' activities.

3.4.1.2 Religious and social reasons

Islam's "law of apostasy" prescribes the death penalty for any Muslim wanting to embrace a religion other than Islam. Though this law was not in Egypt's official penal code, it was a strongly held religious custom within Egyptian society. The Muslim family was permitted to kill any of its members if they converted. As this law was practised in Egypt, a Muslim could kill his relatives, even an only son, in order to keep him from embracing Christianity. Both family and society were united in this outlook. This law, in the opinion of many missionaries and Christian scholars, was the main

---

133. The campaign against missionaries was the subject of study in many books and periodicals. For example see B. L. Carter, "On Spreading of the Gospel to Egyptians Sitting in Darkness: The Political Problem of Missionaries in Egypt in the 1930s," *Middle Eastern Studies* 20, no. 4 (October 1984): 20–21; Burke, *The Establishment*, 163–177.

134. Elder, *Vindicating a Vision*, 230.

135. For more details on the responses of Muslim leaders to the mission activities in converting Muslims see, Umar Ryad, "Muslim Response to Missionary Activities in Egypt: With a Special Reference to the Al-Azhar High Corps of 'Ulama (1925–1935)," in *New Faith in Ancient Lands: Western Mission in the Middle East in the Nineteenth and Early Twentieth Centuries*, Studies in Christian Mission no. 32, ed. Helen Murre-van den Berg (Leiden: Koninklijke Brill NV, 2006), 281–307; Heather J. Sharkey, "Empire and Muslim Conversion: Historical Reflections on Christian Mission in Egypt," *Islam and Christian-Muslim Relations* 16, no. 1, (January 2005): 43–60.

obstacle for Muslims who wished to be Christians. Samuel Zwemer wrote of the danger which Muslim converts faced if they confessed their faith in Christ:

> It is our conviction that among the many reasons for the small number of converts to the Christian faith in Moslem lands there is, perhaps, none so important, and yet concerning which so little is accurately known, as the Moslem law regarding apostates. Every convert to Christianity is an apostate from Islam, and although there have been apostates throughout all the centuries, and we know of cases even during the lifetime of Mohammed the Prophet, the law of apostasy has become fixed in Islam, and for thirteen centuries has exercised its dread, if not its power, under all conditions and in every land. The apostate dies to his faith and is regarded by his family as worse than dead.[136]

Zwemer believed that if the law of apostasy were not applied, many Muslims would convert to Christianity.

The lack of religious liberty in general was an obstacle for the Mission in Egypt. The missionaries spent much time at the beginning seeking to obtain equal rights for Christians to practise their faith, including rights for Muslim converts.[137] They enjoyed some success in the early years of their ministry, but faced increasingly hostile attitudes that were further intensified by the rise of nationalism.

The Islamic orthodoxy prevalent in Egypt taught that Islam is the final revelation and that other religions are corrupted and inferior. This belief provided strong motivation for people to resist the Christian faith. Further, this belief, which was often held fanatically, created hostility between Muslims and other religions, and built a wall between Muslims and Christians. Missionaries found themselves to be a focal point for this hostility. Mr Reid, a missionary who worked for years among Muslims in Iran, concluded that:

---

136. Samuel Zwemer, *The Law of Apostasy in Islam: Answering the Question Why There Are So Few Muslim Converts,aAnd Giving Examples of Their Moral Courage And Martyrdom.* (London: Marshall Brothers Ltd., 1924), 17.
137. Vander Werff, *Christian Mission,* 143.

The great obstacle is what is commonly called "fanaticism," that high wall of suspicion, proud exclusiveness, and hate that Islam has built up round its followers, to keep them in, and to keep the missionaries out – a wall that, alas! too often proves unscalable and impregnable.[138]

This spirit of exclusion and fanaticism made the Muslim suspicious of any new relationship with non-Muslims. Mr Reid continued his argument saying:

When acts of kindness and love are done to him he is sure to suspect that I am doing it, not for his sake and because of simple disinterested love, but for some reason of self-interest known perhaps only to myself . . . He thinks I have come to heap up merit to balance an old account of evil doing. I am well paid for it. At best I am doing it in order to win him from Mohammed to Jesus Christ, and even this is perceived to be an interested motive.[139]

This spirit of suspicion dominated the relationship between Christian activists and Muslims in Egyptian society, and fostered continual misunderstanding of the Christians' activities.

Islam not only has a stronghold in Egypt, but its version has influenced every other Muslim nation. As Charles Watson comments, Egypt holds a significant place in the Muslim world:

No country, perhaps except Arabia itself, has meant so much to the strength and spread of Islam across the past thirteen centuries as Egypt. Its geographical location made it a distributing center southward to the heart of Africa, westward for the conquest of North Africa. Its wealth provided an endless source of income for the maintenance of its armies and the recreating of their personnel . . . Egypt was to Islam what the camel's hump is to the camel in its long journeys over

---

138. W. H. T. Gairdner, *The Reproach of Islam* (London: Church Missionary Society, 1909), 264.
139. Ibid.

waterless wastes a supply of strength and vigour, especially in material resources.[140]

Al-Azhar University and Mosque held an important position as a leading institute and reference point for the Muslim world. It is the oldest Islamic university and had a large number of students, not only from Egypt but also from many other nations.[141] The teachings and writings of its scholars were highly regarded by Muslims everywhere. The scholars of Al-Azhar worked actively to oppose the efforts of the missionaries and many of their sheikhs wrote against the missionaries and their efforts to convert Muslims. On many occasions, they even travelled to meetings such as the ones in the American Mission centre in Cairo, in order to debate with the evangelists. Their efforts, along with other strategies, succeeded in minimizing the results of Muslim evangelism. Although the American Mission targeted the students and ex-students of Al-Azhar in their evangelism, the results were meagre in number of converts gained. However, it is interesting to note that the few converts from Al-Azhar became involved in Muslim evangelism and were very effective in their ministry.[142]

3.4.2 Internal Reasons in the Mission

Although the Mission used many methods in their attempts to reach Muslims during the early years, due to both the disappointing results and the difficult political, social, and religious situation, the missionaries chose to focus their work among the Copts. Here, they found great success. Many Copts converted and became founding members of the Evangelical Church. The missionaries, encouraged to see their efforts resulting in new life for the Copts, became busy organizing the new church and put most of their resources into building it up and dealing with its problems. As a result, their focus shifted from evangelizing Muslims, and this aspect of

---

140. Watson, *Moslem World,* 13.

141. A statistical report about the number of foreign students in Al-Azhar University shows that in 1903 the number was 639 students from 17 different countries. These countries range from Morocco, Sierra Leone, Indonesia, to Turkey and central Asia. A. Chris Eccel, *Egypt, Islam and Social Change: Al-Azhar in Conflict and Accommodation* (Berlin: Klaus Schwarz, 1984), 302–305.

142. Watson, *Egypt,* 241.

their ministry was relegated to a minor role in their agenda.[143] However, as we shall suggest, there were also other internal reasons for the Mission's change in focus.

3.4.2.1 Lack of training

In later years, the missionaries' lack of training in Arabic and Islamic religious issues affected their ability to clearly communicate the Christian message to Muslims. In the early years, the missionaries gave time and effort to learn the language and study Islam although they found both difficult in many aspects.[144]

In his visit to Egypt in 1912, Charles Watson noticed that the missionaries were in need of more training in Arabic and knowledge of Islam, and he argued that the Mission should consider these as requisite in the training of missionaries to Egypt:

> Special training in language and in the religious conceptions and practices of Islam were laid down as a prerequisite of all work for Moslems, and indeed the experience of those who labored among Moslems in the cities seemed to only add emphasis to the necessity for such training . . .
>
> Then it seemed as if a new situation, or rather the real situation, was uncovered. It seemed as if the missionary who had hitherto labored among the educated classes and in the cities, had indeed stood face to face, whichever way he turned, with the learned sheikh who scorned his imperfect Arabic and challenged him with Moslem arguments that he could not fully answer.[145]

---

143. Watson, *Report of the Visit*, 17.

144. Andrew Watson put the ability to learn the language at the top of the qualifications of the missionaries who wanted to come to Egypt. It was difficult for most of the missionaries to master Arabic and use it in their daily communication or in preaching. He said that out of 27 missionaries in Egypt in 1897, there were only three who could preach in Arabic. Then he explained the difficulty of Arabic for missionaries saying "As the Arabic language is very difficult, both in construction and its pronunciation, and is very extensive in its vocabulary, and differs so widely from all Western languages, the number of missionaries who acquired a thorough knowledge of it is very few." Watson, *The American Mission*, 421–422.

145. Watson, *Report of the Visit*, 22.

D. B. MacDonald, the founder of the Islamic Centre at Hartford Seminary, spent one year in Cairo in 1907–1908. In a letter to Constance Padwick he commented on the missionaries who were working there:

> I was profoundly conscious that they did not understand the Muslims because they were not properly trained for the work – were, in fact, as far as Islam was concerned, horribly ignorant . . . The result for me was that I made up my mind if ever I could do anything to train missionaries to Muslims to know Islam, I would put my back into it.[146]

The American Mission and other Protestant missions to Egypt recognized this need. In 1911, they called Samuel Zwemer to Cairo where he contributed to the work among Muslims through writing, publishing, teaching, training missionaries and establishing a school for oriental studies.[147] This school played an important role in training new missionaries and scholars in Islam and other oriental subjects.[148] It covered an essential need for the missionaries in Egypt, equipping many of them for more effective communication with Muslims.

3.4.2.2 Cultural gap

The inability of some missionaries to bridge the language and culture gap with the Egyptians also affected their effectiveness. One of the criticisms of the missionaries to Egypt, and the East in general, came from an Egyptian elder who worked with the American Mission in publication and literature. Elder Metry S. Dewairy said about the Western missionary that:

> If he could consider his Eastern brother on the same level with himself without regard to colour, nationality or social prestige, if he could deny himself some of his old usage and habits and adopt some new ones from the East, then and only then could

---

146. MacDonald to Padwick, 11 October, 1928 (Quoted in Michel Thomas Shelley, "The Life of W. H. T. Gairdner, 1973–1928: A Critical Evaluation of a Scholar-Missionary to Islam" [PhD diss., University of Birmingham, 1988]), 111; Colin Chapman, "Rethinking the Gospel for Moslems," in *Muslims and Christians on the Emmaus Road,* ed. J. Dudley Woodberry (Monrovia: MARC, 1989), 109.

147. Wilson, *Apostle to Islam,* 77.

148. Ibid., 176.

the Western church be successful in her missionary undertaking and fulfil her task of evangelizing the non-Christians of the Near East. Then and only then would Moslems see the spirit of Christ himself – the spirit of sacrifice and service – manifested in the lives of the apostles of the twentieth century.[149]

Although Dewairy was a close friend to the Mission and worked with it in ministry, he criticized the Mission for being isolated from people. He observed that when missionaries crossed the social and cultural gaps, they were more successful in their mission.[150]

3.4.2.3 Limited contribution of the Evangelical Church

Facing the same problems as the American Mission, the Evangelical Church's limitation to take on the task of evangelizing Muslims likewise became one of the main reasons for the lack of converts from Islam. The Mission worked hard to establish, teach, and challenge the Church to reach out to the Muslims and spread the gospel among them, but was largely unsuccessful. Andrew Watson believed that the native Christians should be the main means to evangelize Egypt. In 1897 he said, "Foreign missionaries . . . can never be the chief means of evangelizing and converting the inhabitants of the Nile valley. It must be done by native trained."[151]

In 1906, Charles Watson explained his fear that the Evangelical Church would not carry on its task of evangelization because of the historical hatred between Muslims and Copts in Egypt that had been passed onto the Evangelical Church:

> There is also danger lest prejudice to Islam and converts from Islam, should hinder this Church from exercising her widest influence among Moslems. It would be easy for the hatred of

---

149. Metry S. Dewairy, "The Contribution of the Western Church," in *Voices from the Near East: Chapters by a Group of Nationals Interpreting the Christian Movement*, ed. Milton Stauffer (New York: Missionary Education Movement of the United States and Canada, 1927), 99.

150. Many of the missionaries lived in pleasant houses and enjoyed high living standards. Their lifestyle was that of the rich, and not even that of middle class, Egyptians. Few of the missionaries opened their homes to Egyptians, especially to those who lived in small towns.

151. Watson, *The American Mission*, 421.

Copt for Moslem, born of centuries of suffering from Moslem oppression, to pass over into the Protestant Church with the large accessions which this Church has received from the Coptic body. Against this, missionaries and Church leaders must set their faces as flint, or the Evangelical Church will miss her true calling to become a National Church of Egypt.[152]

It seems that these fears were realized, considering that Kamiel Mansour's ministry to Muslims was the only instance when the evangelical churches chose to support Muslim evangelism.[153] Addison, a mission scholar, analyzed the approach of the American Presbyterian Mission in Egypt:

The difference in missionary spirit between members of the Coptic Church and members of the Egyptian Evangelical Church is discouragingly slight. It had been the hope of the American Mission that the Protestant Christians would become missionaries to Moslems, but that hope has not yet been realized. In spite of their far better training in the Christian faith and its principles, they still share with the other Copts the reluctance to approach the Moslem and the conviction that genuine conversion from Islam is next to impossible. Like their fellow Christians in the ancient Church, they fear the hostility of the great Moslem majority and view with suspicion the sincerity of the few Moslems who seem drawn toward Christianity.[154]

The Evangelical Church thus could not become a major instrument for evangelizing Muslims, due to their hatred of Muslims and their fear of possible reprisals.

3.4.2.4 Changing theological approaches

The missionaries initially utilized an aggressive polemic approach in evangelizing Muslims, but after World War II, the missionaries adopted milder

---

152. Watson, *Egypt*, 243–244.

153. Finney, *Tomorrow's Egypt*, 192.

154. James Thayer Addison, *The Christian Approach to the Muslim: A Historical Study* (New York: Columbia University Press, 1942), 165.

approaches. Jack Lorimer, who served as a Presbyterian missionary in Egypt from 1945 to 1990, commented on this latter period:

> Tutored by Samuel Zwemer the generation who came out after WWI devoted themselves to the study of that faith (i.e. Islam) so that they might find the means by argumentation and example to convert Muslims to Christian faith. After WWII it was hoped that changing conditions in the post-war world could afford new opportunities. Moreover, while not forsaking the original goal it is clear that attitudes had softened and that various indirect approaches were being favored.[155]

The changing approaches to Islam were evident within both the Mission and the Egyptian Evangelical Church. Both stopped holding open meetings to debate with Muslims. Instead, literacy campaigns, social work, media, publications, and dialogue were used to approach Muslims and direct evangelism was neglected.[156]

3.4.3 Internal Reasons in the Church

The Evangelical Church produced few converts throughout its history. The Committee for the Work among Muslims reported very few baptisms even though their totals also included those who had been converted through other mission groups rather than through the Evangelical Church's ministry alone. Even if evangelistic success were to be measured by the number of occasions when the gospel was proclaimed, the Evangelical Church's efforts would still be considered disappointing. The responsibility for this weakness in the programmes and results can be shared by both the Mission and the Church. In its evangelistic endeavours, the Church faced similar problems as the Mission and as we shall observe, struggled with other factors as well.

3.4.3.1 Lack of training

Kamiel and Mikha'il both used to visit the churches to speak about Muslim evangelism. However apart from this, the Evangelical Church had very

---

155. Jack Lorimer, *The Presbyterian Experience in Egypt: 1950–2000,* (Denver: Outskirts Press, 2007), 103.
156. Ibid., 104–110. See chapter 7.

limited training for its members. This was not adequate and the Committee for the Work among Muslims wished to have more thorough training for the Seminary students as well as for the Synod members. When Zwemer came to Egypt, the Seminary asked him to teach the students comparative religion and methods of Muslim evangelism.[157] However, such courses were taught only sporadically, and depended on the individual efforts of people like Mikha'il, Kamiel, and Zwemer.

Recognizing the need to encourage the Egyptian Churches and train its members, in 1911, the Mission Committee for the Work among Muslims asked the Mission Association to consider,

> the holding of a special conference for those of our pastors, licentiates, theological students, and laymen who have evinced a special interest in the Moslem questions in order to interest them further and, by means of them, start among our own people a campaign for evangelizing Mohammedans.[158]

This was finally realized in 1929 when missionaries from different mission organizations arranged for a conference in Helwan, south of Cairo, concerning missions among Muslims. The aim of the conference was to explore the role of the indigenous churches in evangelism. The conference speakers presented evangelism as the most important duty of the church and concentrated on empowering churches by training members, and exposing the attendees to methods of evangelism. This conference raised hopes that the Egyptian church was finally going to take responsibility for evangelizing their own people.[159] However, while it encouraged a small number of people to minister among Muslims, it did not become a wider movement in the Evangelical Church. Only a limited number of people received training and only some of them were involved in Muslim evangelism. Furthermore, the local presbytery and church committees had little

---

157. Synod of the Nile, *Minutes of the Year, 1925*, 59.

158. American Mission in Egypt, *Minutes of the Year, 1911*, 13.

159. Anonymous, *Haya Lelmal: kholasset mobahs wa mohadrat fy nassb al-kanaes al-watanyea men altabsheer* (Come to the Work: Summary of Discussions and Lectures in the Role of the Indigenous Churches in Evangelism) (Cairo: Matb'at Al-Neel Al-Masseheya, 1930), 1.

training, and were incapable of helping their church members start a ministry among Muslims.

3.4.3.2 The heritage of fear

The Evangelical Church was, and still is, a part of the wider Christian church in Egypt that has faced many difficulties throughout its history. Although the Evangelical Church enjoyed recognition by the government as a Christian denomination, and was allowed freedom in its worship, there were many restrictions in Muslim evangelism. In effect, efforts to evangelize Muslims were against both the law and the customs of the country. A 1944 report by the American Mission in Egypt states:

> If every inducement is held out to a Christian to become a Moslem, every obstacle is put in the way of the Moslem who wishes to embrace Christianity. By the law of apostasy in Islam, the pervert should be put to death. Since 1883 this law has not been enforced in Egypt, but the position of the convert from Islam is still most unsatisfactory. Whereas the Government has established a regular procedure for registering the conversion of a person from Christianity to Islam, there is no similar process for registering conversion from Islam to Christianity. The convert is unable to inherit from his Moslem relations. His wife is usually separated from him and his children left in her custody. He almost invariably loses his employment. A woman convert often pays for her change of faith with her life, or is forced into marrying a Moslem. The convert is regarded as a traitor to both his religion and his nation. Freedom of religion in Egypt is officially interpreted as the right of each religious community to worship in its own way, but not the right of conversion, except to Islam.[160]

As previously noted, there were periods when there was a greater degree of freedom of speech and religion. Especially after the First World War, the Evangelical Church hoped that the time had come when a large number of

---

160. PHS UPCNA RG 209-27-5: Religious Situation in Egypt: "Christian minorities in Egypt," unpublished report, dated 1944, 3.

Muslims would come to Christ. Kamiel Mansour articulated these hopes when he found encouraging results in his ministry in the year 1926:

> The number of people going to Christian religious meetings this year is far greater than in former years. Every Sunday morning you will find evangelical churches, whether in town or in country districts, crowded with Moslem attendants. These multitudes who come ask many questions about Christian morality, whereas they used to ask abstract metaphysical questions about the way in which a man can conceive of the divinity of Jesus, his incarnation and his death-beliefs which their religion denies. It has also become easy to preach to Moslems, and a preacher can speak about Christ's salvation in the midst of the most fanatical Moslem district today without being opposed. I myself have visited most of the mosques, have spoken about Jesus in many of them, and have distributed pamphlets and gospels to those who have asked for them. Even to the mosque of Azhar, where I was brought up and where many of its teachers know me, I have often gone, alone or with others, and many a time we have spoken and prayed with the students there.[161]

Unfortunately, these efforts did not continue and in the face of this liberal movement, the Muslim Brotherhood started in 1928. The Brotherhood worked directly against the Mission activities and the evangelistic efforts. These campaigns also attacked the Evangelical Church and its involvement in Muslim evangelism.[162] The church schools, likewise, became a source of conflict with the Egyptian government when the teaching of the Islamic

---

161. Kamiel Mansour, "The Status of Islam," in *Voices from the Near East: Chapters by a Group of Nationals Interpreting the Christian Movement*, ed. Milton Stauffer (New York: Missionary Education Movement of the United States and Canada, 1927), 59.

162. In the Egyptian newspaper, *Kawkab El-Shark*, in August 1933, there was a debate between Taha Hussien, the famous Egyptian writer, and Ibraheem Sa'id, the Presbyterian pastor, concerning the conversion of one of the students in an evangelical school. This kind of debate was not repeated since the Evangelical Church sought to separate itself from conflicts with Muslims or with the government over Muslim evangelism. (*Kawkab Al-Shark*, 12 August 1933; 14 August 1933).

religion to Muslim students was required and evangelistic activities were curtailed.[163]

In 1948, the Evangelical Church discussed the difficulties they were experiencing due to government intervention in their schools and evangelical ministry. Four areas were discussed: the problem of building churches, lack of religious free speech, school curriculum demands, and personal issues. In discussing the issue of religious freedom of speech the Synod stated that the government gave freedom to Muslims to preach using all possible means in the newspapers, radio, books, and public meetings, while at the same time, Christian evangelism of Muslims was considered a crime subject to legal restrictions.[164] Some suggested that the Synod should speak out about the problem through prayers, talking to the churches, writing to the government and as a last resort, approaching the United Nations. The Synod appointed a committee to study these problems and suggested that the Evangelical Church should organize a supreme council to deal with the government, and that the Synod should write to the government explaining its situation.[165]

As a Christian community within a Muslim country, the Evangelical Church had many fears, and these fears influenced its mission to Muslims. Previously, the Coptic Church had suffered from the pressures of living in an Islamic society and had therefore refused to preach the gospel to Muslims because of these fears. The American missionary Alexander talked about these fears:

> The Evangelical Church naturally has inherited the fears and alienations and aloofness of its ancestral Church towards Islam and it has been unable to escape the impact of its environment.
>
> Is it to be wondered at that they are timorous, fearful, and distrustful of the Muslims? How can they forget the atrocious events of their own experience and observation that occurred in 1882, 1919, and 1929 when occurred the unjust arrest and

---

163. Synod of the Nile, *Minutes of the Year, 1949*, 165.

164. Ibid., 86–87.

165. Ibid., 119. See chapter 7.

trying imprisonment of Sheikh Kamiel, for weeks without trial, and the wicked murderous mobs of 1932–33?

Is not the Egyptian excusable if he fears when he sees the mighty power of the State arrayed, not to protect him but against him to destroy him and his? He fears Islam's venomous press and its cruel, deadly mobs.

So greatly did these things affect them that even during the British regime they would not in an official way, not even privately, ask the British Residency to intervene to secure for the Christians of Egypt, as has been done in Palestine, the freedom of the Lord's day, lest it might be known and they become marked men!

They know their Muslim neighbours. They have heard their "breathings of threatenings and slaughter." In 1928 these "threatenings" became so strong that even Dr Zwemer was forced for a time to leave the country, although he could claim the protection of his Consul.[166]

Because of these fears, most evangelicals spoke to Muslims only when the Muslims attended church meetings. With the exception of some American missionaries and the appointed evangelists, the church members did not go to speak to Muslims in their houses or offices. Further, they kept in mind that they could face legal consequences if they distributed the Bible to any Muslim who had not expressly requested one.[167]

3.4.3.3 Financial difficulties

The financial problems that the Evangelical Church faced in its history were significant and influenced the direction of its ministry. Most money came from the American Mission as well as the donations of church members. As previously discussed, the American Mission and Evangelical Church had a long-running conflict over the financial independence of the Church. On many occasions, the Synod took steps towards its independence but

---

166. D. J. Alexander, *Should the American Mission Dissolve Its Organization and Merge Itself into the Evangelistic Church of Egypt and Its Organizations?* (Assiout: non-published document, 1939), 12.

167. Synod of the Nile, *Minutes of the Year, 1950*, 13, and Synod of the Nile, *Minutes of the Year, 1957*, 245.

the problem continued until the departure of the American Mission in 1967. This issue not only affected the pastoral and educational ministry of the Church, but also ensured that the work among Muslims would be limited, since the Synod gave priority to the pastors' needs and current ministry expenses, and budgeted little for mission and evangelistic work among Muslims.[168]

The financial support for the Church's evangelism came from outside sources and was insufficient to promote its growth. In the early years of its work, Mr El-Hemssey who had initiated the idea and supported the ministry for two years financially supported the Committee for the Work among Muslims. He hoped that the Church would take further steps, but when he found that ministry among Muslims was stagnating he withdrew his support. The Committee asked the presbyteries to help cover ministry expenses, but they only covered half of Kamiel's salary. The other half came from the American Mission. In those years when the Synod found itself in financial difficulty, some voices called for the end of this ministry and of Kamiel's position. Alexander explained this problem saying:

> Twenty years and more, however, have passed and synod has not increased its share of the salary of its Muslim Evangelist. On the contrary, in the years of the financial depression, a number of the members of the synod urged that the work be stopped, that there had been no converts and that the effort was a failure.
>
> But notwithstanding every effort to persuade them to continue and to persevere they reduced their share of the evangelist's salary to the extent of $60.00 per year.
>
> Although members of the Synod enjoyed the presence of Sheikh Kamiel in their pulpits and in their congregations they have not restored the decrease to their share of his salary although they are aware of his financial needs. They appear never to have even dreamed of undertaking his entire salary.[169]

---

168. See chapter 2.
169. Alexander, *Should the American Mission,* 11–12.

The only expenses that the Committee for the Work among Muslims covered were half of Mikha'il's and Kamiel's salaries and the Committee's travel expenses for its annual meetings. For many years, the Committee had its own budget, and during most of these, they operated at a deficit while urging the Synod to make up the difference. In the 1950s and 1960s, Kamiel's salary came from the Synod general budget.[170]

When there were hopes in the 1910s that the work among Muslims could be extended by adding another evangelist, the Synod replied that there was no money for this. The Synod expected the Committee for the Work among Muslims to find ways to support its second evangelist financially. This proved impossible, and even when Rev Swaihey wanted to undertake a part-time ministry of evangelism, there were insufficient funds to cover his salary. The Synod also failed to support Mikha'il and Kamiel, expecting the churches that invited them to speak about Muslim evangelism to cover their travel and living expenses during their visits to these churches.

3.4.3.4 The political and theological changes

The Evangelical Church could not fulfil the goals of the Committee for the Work among Muslims, and the Synod, as an organization, did not support the efforts of Muslim evangelism. In the 1950s and 1960s, Egypt underwent a revolution, the nationalist movement, and Arabism and decolonization, all of which affected the policy of the Egyptian government towards Western organizations including missionaries and their institutions. Likewise, the Evangelical Church reviewed its mission and relationships during this time. The transformation of Egyptian society influenced all mission organizations including the American Mission, and the Evangelical Church of Egypt.[171]

These developments led to the neglect of evangelistic and mission work. The members of the Synod were active personally in direct evangelistic work only in so far as their compelling pastoral duties would permit. The pastoral needs of their congregations were first in their minds and their

---

170. Synod of the Nile, *Minutes of the Year, 1962*, 141.
171. Lorimer, *The Presbyterian Experience*, 104–110. For more study about the political and theological developments in the 1950s and 1960s see chapter 7.

hearts.[172] The efforts of evangelization for both Muslims and nominal Christians disappeared from the programmes of the Synod, although some Church laymen grasped the vision of evangelism and in turn enabled other parachurch mission organizations to engage in ministry.[173]

3.5 Conclusion

The great expectations of the American Mission to convert Muslims ended in a relatively disappointing reality. In the early years, the Mission used every possible direct and indirect method to reach Muslims. They built bridges within Egyptian society and achieved good access to people, but this did not result in a significant number of converts. Although the American Mission's ministry among Copts resulted in a great number of converts to evangelical beliefs, it failed to give any great impetus to a ministry among Muslims.

The establishment of the Evangelical Church did not advance the work of Muslim evangelism. The evangelicals shared the same heritage as the Copts, and shared their great fear of evangelizing Muslims. The Evangelical Church tried to have its own ministry among Muslims but achieved little progress. The Synod was involved in administration business more than actual ministry, and the efforts of individuals and a small number of congregations could not develop a strong mission movement. The death of Kamiel Mansour in 1963 put an end to the Committee of the Work among Muslims. Then, in the 1960s and afterwards, the Synod tried to please the Egyptian government which was against any kind of evangelism. The work among Muslims turned into a secret work by a few Church people without real support from the Synod.

Muslim evangelism continued to be the major unfulfilled goal of the missionaries with the number of converts very small in proportion to the missionaries' hopes and efforts. This was not only the problem of the American Mission, but also of all Protestant missions working in Egypt

---

172. Alexander, *Should the American Mission*, 25.

173. Scott W. Sunquist, "An Epilogue and Prologue: 'Wisdom Gained for the Future'," in *A History of Presbyterian Missions, 1944–2007*, eds. Scott W. Sunquist and Caroline N. Becker (Louisville: Geneva Press, 2008), 303.

and the Muslim world. Samuel Zwemer summarized the problem when he quoted the report of *Missionary Survey* 1924, which said:

> Although there are 438 missionaries in Egypt, and although some of the mission bodies are working almost exclusively for the Moslems, and although there are about 19,000 Evangelical Christians in Egypt with good church organizations and a well-educated ministry, and although there are in the various mission schools approximately 2,500 Muslim students continuously receiving instruction in Bible study, the visible result of the missionary work for Moslems is not very great. At the present time we probably could not point to more than 150 living converts from Islam in Egypt. If the Moslem converts were distributed among the missionary workers there would be about one convert for every three missionaries. If the comparison is made with the Evangelical Church, there would be about one for every congregation in Egypt. Every missionary method known to man has been tried and is being tried, but until the present neither the missions nor the Evangelical Church have whereof to boast in the face of this great and baffling problem.[174]

Although the Mission and the Church contributed significantly to Egyptian society, especially in education, they did not achieve the conversions among Muslims for which they had hoped. More effective methods needed to be developed and different approaches adopted in order to effectively share the Christian message with the Muslim Egyptians. The task of evangelizing Muslims remained for both the Mission and the Church "the unfinished task."[175]

---

174. Zwemer, *The Law of Apostasy*, 16.
175. Watson, *Report of the Visit*, 15–19.

CHAPTER 4

The Beginning of the American Mission and Evangelical Church Mission Work in Sudan

4.1 Introduction

The interaction between the American Mission and the Evangelical Church influenced their practice of mission. Besides their interaction in Muslim evangelism, as mentioned in the previous chapter, the mission work in Sudan emphasizes another example in the development of their relationship regarding mission practices.

In the early years of the twentieth century, the American Mission in Egypt considered mission work in Sudan as a natural expansion of its ministry. After initiating their work in Sudan, they invited the Egyptian Church to become involved. This chapter will examine the American Mission's exploration and commencement of ministry within Sudan, as well as the beginning of the Evangelical Church's involvement in Northern Sudan. We will also explore the methods used by both the American Mission and the Evangelical Church in light of the political, cultural, and social situation that they encountered in Sudan. This chapter will also examine the relationship between the American Mission and the Evangelical Church in their work together in Sudan, as well as the Egyptian Evangelical Church's response to this specific mission endeavour.

4.2 Sudan at the End of the Nineteenth Century

The relationship between Sudan and Egypt dates back to ancient history when Northern Sudan was part of the Egyptian Empire. Cultural, political and trade connections have existed between the two countries until recent times, undergoing numerous developments and changes throughout the centuries.

Under Mohamed ʾAli and his family, the Egyptian-Ottoman government ruled Sudan after 1820. Egyptian involvement and cultural and religious influence in Sudan increased during the nineteenth century including campaigns against the slave trade. However, the situation began to change when Mohammed Ahmed appeared in Sudan as a religious leader. He gathered a large following of Sudanese and in 1881 proclaimed himself as the Mahdi or "divinely guided one." He began to unify the central and northern Sudanese tribes, exploiting their growing discontent with the ruling Turks and their unjust, defective administration, and their resentment against the Egyptians' exploitation of Sudanese resources.[1] The Mahdi, in effect, instigated both a national revolution and an Islamic revival, in opposition to Turkish, Egyptian, and British interests. Following the example of the Prophet Mohammed, he established an Islamic state, which was organized according to the early Islamic model including control of the army, the government, the national treasury, taxes, and the legal system.[2]

Turkish-Egyptian rule ended with the fall of Khartoum and the death of British General Gordon Pasha who had been sent to lead the Anglo-Egyptian troops in quelling the rebellion.[3] The assassination of Gordon, who was considered a committed Christian, brought Sudan to the centre of

---

1. Ried F. Shields, *Behind the Garden of Allah* (Philadelphia: United Presbyterian Board of Foreign Missions, 1937), 52–62.

2. I. M. Lewis, "Introduction," in *Islam in Tropical Africa,* ed. I. M. Lewis (London: Oxford University Press, 1966), 42–43.

3. The story of the conflict in Sudan and the death of Gordon is noted in many missionary books as a key event which raised their interest in Sudan. These books included: Watson, *The American Mission,* 368–371; Charles R. Watson, *The Sorrow and Hope of the Egyptian Sudan: A Survey of Missionary Conditions and Methods of Work in the Egyptian Sudan* (Philadelphia: The Board of Foreign Mission of the United Presbyterian Church of North America, 1913); J. Kelly Giffen, *The Egyptian Sudan,* 2nd. Edition (New York: Fleming H. Revell Company, 1905), 21–29.

British attention and inspired many Westerners in England and the United States to serve in Sudan.[4]

In 1885, the Mahdi died and his son succeeded him. Then in September 1898, the British-Egyptian army, led by Major Kitchener, defeated the Mahdiyya troops and put an end to their movement. Beginning from March 1899, Sudan entered a new era, and was titled Anglo-Egyptian Sudan. Under the combined government of Britain and Egypt, Sudan experienced many changes not only as a political entity, but also in its social, religious, and economic life.

After the defeat of the Mahdi's movement, the Anglo-Egyptian government gained political control of the whole country. They instituted developmental changes that affected every aspect of Sudanese life. As the Egyptians became more involved in Sudanese administration, the links between Egypt and Sudan became stronger, and many Egyptians moved to work in the Sudanese government.[5]

Sudan remained a Sunni Muslim country, particularly in the north. The south and west however, continued almost untouched by Islamic influence or modernization and preserved their traditional African religions.[6] Recognizing this situation, the Anglo-Egyptian government refused permission for missionary activity in the north among the Muslims, but allowed mission organizations to work in the south among the non-Muslim tribes.[7] Under British leadership, the government sought to maintain political stability in the north by protecting the interests of the Muslim majority. In later years when the political situation calmed down, the government allowed missionaries to have limited access in the north through schools and orphanages.

The Anglo-Egyptian authorities built a railway from Halfa in the north to Khartoum and beyond. This modern transportation link connected the

---

4. J. Spencer Trimingham, *Islam in the Sudan* (London: Frank Cass & Co. Ltd., 1965), 95.

5. Giovanni Vantini, *Christianity in the Sudan* (Bologna: EMI, 1981), 259.

6. Trimingham, *Islam,* 151–153.

7. Harold Macmichael, *The Sudan,* (London: Ernest Benn Limited, 1954) 138; Hassan Makki Mohamed Ahmed, *Sudan: The Christian Design: A Study of the Missionary Factor in Sudan's Cultural and Political Integration, 1843–1986* (Leicester: Islamic Foundation, 1989), 38–41.

different parts of Sudan and contributed dramatically to its social and economic life, opening the way for more Egyptian involvement in Sudan. The trip from Cairo to Khartoum now took a few days rather than weeks, thus permitting Egyptians to live and work in Sudan more easily. Many schools were also built, leading to significant developments in the education system within Sudan. Egyptian teachers moved to Sudan, finding jobs while ensuring a good education for Egyptian and Sudanese children.

The end of the nineteenth and the early twentieth century also saw a time of great economic growth. Significant effort was put into modernizing Sudan. Khartoum and Umdorman were rebuilt as centres of government, which encouraged people to buy land and build homes. Merchants from different countries were attracted to the opportunities in Sudan and their new businesses likewise stimulated further economic growth.[8]

Such developments forged stronger links between Sudan and Egypt, with Egypt the gateway to Sudan: the religious, cultural, economic, and social changes in Sudan entered via that gate. Many Christian mission organizations started to send their missionaries to Sudan either through or from Egypt. The Church Missionary Society, Daniel Comboni's mission work, the Sudan Pioneer Mission, and Catholic missionaries all utilized a base in Egypt as they extended their efforts into Sudan. They trained their missionaries there and found safe refuge for them in times of illness and political troubles.[9] The American Presbyterian Mission and the Evangelical Church of Egypt were among the first Christian organizations that went to Sudan to begin mission and ecclesiastical work after the defeat of the Mahdi's movement in 1898.

---

8. Elder, *Vindicating a Vision*, 101.

9. Andrew Wheeler, "Gateway to the Heart of African: Sudan's Missionary Story," in *Gateway to the Heart of Africa: Missionary Pioneers in Sudan*, eds. Francesco Pierli, Maria Teresa Ratti, and Andrew C. Wheeler (Nairobi: Paulines Publication Africa, 1998), 183–185; 215; 229–230.

4.3 The American Mission Explores the Sudanese Field

4.3.1 Early Efforts

The history of modern missions in Sudan goes back to the 1840s when Catholic missionaries covered a wide area of the Nile valley in both Northern and Southern Sudan. Daniel Comboni (1831–1881) was one of the pioneers who inspired many other missionaries to work in Sudan.

The American Mission in Egypt began to consider Sudan as a possible mission field when the Mission sent one of its workers to distribute Bibles in Sudan. In its 1881 report, the Mission said:

> Khartoom has long been a place of some importance, as it is the centre of trade for the Governor General of the Provinces in Soodan and Darfoor, that are now held by the Egyptian government, and which extend almost to the equator. The importance of this place will increase as the Provinces in the interior develop, and we trust that the time is not far distant when it will be one of our mission stations. The agent sent there gives encouraging report of his work. He has instructions to visit, as he returns to Egypt, all the towns located between Khartoom and Aswan.[10]

In 1882, an Egyptian book salesman working with the Mission visited Sudan to distribute Bibles. His visit to Sudan opened the eyes of the American Mission and the Egyptian Church to the needs of Sudan and the growing missionary opportunities. In 1882, the Mission reported that:

> The Colporteur who was on his way to Khartoom when the last report was prepared, reached the distant place in safety, and found many willing to purchase the Scriptures and he disposed of his stock of 462 copies and returned to Egypt. It will hardly be possible for any one to go again to Khartoom or

---

10. UPCNA, *United Presbyterian Mission in Egypt for Year Ending Dec. 31, 1881* (Philadelphia: Edward Patteson, 1882), 24.

to any place in the Soudan, until the Mahdi or new Prophet and his followers are suppressed [*sic.*].[11]

The missionaries in Egypt considered the political developments in Sudan important, and included these details in their reports and minutes. In the Mission report of 1885, Mr Giffen, who was to become the first American missionary to Sudan, wrote:

> The field in its most limited measurement extends from the Mediterranean on the north, to Wadi Halfa on the south. From thence one looks out on the Sudan and Central African provenances. He sees what is morally a wild unbroken prairie towards which we may look and for which we may pray; but there is ample room for our little blowing, and sowing and watering in Egypt proper.[12]

One of the main factors encouraging the American Mission and then the Evangelical Church to start work in Sudan was that there were already evangelicals living in Sudan. At the end of the nineteenth and beginning of the twentieth century, great numbers of Egyptians moved to Sudan, being enticed by the Egyptian government with high salaries and luxurious accommodations upon their transfer to Sudan. A number of Christian families seized this opportunity. Most were Copts, but there were also numerous members of the Evangelical Church in Egypt. These families wished to practice their faith in their new home and began holding meetings in their homes as they waited the time when they could establish places for public worship. In the 1900 report of the American Mission in Egypt, it was estimated that there were 50–100 evangelicals out of about 600 Egyptian Christians in the Khartoum and Umdorman area.[13] This number encouraged both the American Mission and the Evangelical Church to find ways to both serve their needs, and use them as a nucleus for mission work and development of the Evangelical Church in Sudan.

---

11. UPCNA, *The Annual Report of the Mission in Egypt for the Year 1882*, 23.

12. UPCNA, *Annual Report of the Mission in Egypt, Thirty-second Year, 1886* (Philadelphia: Patteson Printing House, 1886), 4.

13. UPCNA, *The Forty-First Annual Report of the United Presbyterian Church of North America 1899–1900* (Philadelphia: Patterson Printing House, 1900), 105.

4.3.2 Exploring Northern Sudan

Although the Mission wanted to start a work in Sudan, there were financial objections. The Board in America was $20,000 in debt and the Mission had insufficient funds for its Egyptian expenses. In 1898, the Board in America discussed the possibilities of finding the necessary financial resources to start a ministry in Sudan. By 1899, the Board of Foreign Mission had found a solution. The Freedmen's Missions Aid Society of London offered the Board $5,000 for the Sudan Mission, and individuals in Great Britain contributed another $5,200 privately. The Presbyterians in America were only able to give an additional $800 for the beginning of the Mission in Sudan.[14] After solving the financial problem, the American Mission looked for the right people and methods to open its mission to Sudan.

On 16 November 1899, the Board of Foreign Missions asked the missionaries in Egypt to send two of them to visit Khartoum and write to the Board and the Mission giving their recommendations for the best methods to begin operations in Sudan. On 28 December 1899, Dr Andrew Watson and J. Kelly Giffen[15] left Cairo for Khartoum and spent a month exploring the areas of Nubia, Khartoum and Umdorman, and the Blue and White Nile districts.[16] They reported to the Mission in Egypt and the Board in America suggesting that Sudan could be divided into three geographical areas.

The first territory was the land of Nubia, which ran from the south of Egypt and across Southern Sudan to the Ethiopian border. It was suggested that the Mission could start working immediately in Nubia because of its connections with Egypt. They felt that one American missionary and a few native Egyptian helpers would be sufficient for the work. They also

---

14. Michael Parker and J. Kelly Giffen, "Launching the American Mission to Sudan 1898–1903," in *Gateway to the Heart of Africa: Missionary Pioneers in Sudan*, eds. Francesco Pierli, Maria Teresa Ratti, and Andrew C. Wheeler (Nairobi: Paulines Publication Africa, 1998), 89.

15. Kelly Giffen worked in the Egyptian field for some years before his trip to Sudan. He worked mainly in evangelistic and school ministries during his years in Assiut, on the Nile boats, and in Tanta. When he started his trip to Sudan, he and his wife were living and working in Tanta teaching at the girls' school. He is considered by many to be the pioneer missionary to Sudan and the establisher of the American Mission work in both Northern and Southern Sudan.

16. Extension of Mission Work on the Nile. In UPCNA, *The Forty-five Annual Report of the American United Presbyterian Mission in Egypt for the Year 1899*, 72.

suggested that the best method to reach the people would be to establish English language schools for children, since the local language had no written form and they reasoned that this would be easier than committing themselves to the arduous task of recording and creating a written language. They hoped that young people who had been taught English would easily become receptive to the gospel. However, this plan was never followed due to the mass migrations that took place.[17]

The second region considered by the American missionaries was the area from Wadi Halfa to Halfaiyah, which is opposite Khartoum on the Blue Nile. It was 560 miles in length and had a number of cities and villages. However, the Mission quickly discovered that this area had limited potential since it was almost all desert with few cities. Further, it was difficult communicating with the people, since only a few knew Arabic, speaking only the Berber language. There were also very few Christians in this area, which would make mission work more difficult.[18] The American missionaries chose instead to concentrate on the third area – Khartoum and Umdorman. Watson and Giffen explained their reasoning:

> This is by far the most fertile, most populous and most capable of being developed of all the regions of our investigation. It was also the most interesting and from a missionary's point of view the most hopeful . . . We were fortunate in having abundant facility in this regard from the government officials, but more especially from our Protestant young men, of whom there are from 50 to 100 in this region, serving in government offices and the army or in trading.[19]

The report suggested that the Mission could start its work in Umdorman as a temporary centre, buying properties there and in Khartoum in order to secure places for missionaries who would follow. The Mission also hoped that the government would supply them with the land they needed. They

---

17. Ibid., 73–74. The Nubians left their homes for other regions in Egypt when the government built the Aswan Dam in 1902. Then after the building of the High Dam in the 1950s, the land of the Nubians was covered by the Nile and they again migrated to other parts of Egypt, especially around Aswan and Cairo.

18. Ibid., 74–75.

19. Ibid., 75.

further proposed that the staff of the Mission in Egypt should be increased in number to cover for the anticipated needs within the new field in Sudan.

The missionaries also anticipated involving the Egyptian Evangelical Church in their expansion into Sudan. They recommended that the Synod of the Nile could undertake work in Umdorman by sending one of its evangelists as soon as possible to act as a pastor among the evangelicals who were already there. They expected that such a step would form "a nucleus for more extended operations in the future, and that an appeal should be made to the Egyptian Evangelical Church to sustain this work."[20]

Both the American Mission in Egypt and the Board in America welcomed the report of the two missionaries, and their correspondence indicates that they were excited about the possibilities of the Mission and the Evangelical Church working together, hoping that this joint mission would stimulate the growth and development of the Evangelical Church in Egypt. The Mission praised the eager desire of the Evangelical Church to cooperate with the Mission in work in Sudan,[21] and asked the Board to provide it with money and missionaries to start working in Sudan.[22] The Board gave its approval and directed the Mission to open their first station in the Blue Nile area in Khartoum and Umdorman as soon as they received permission from the Anglo-Egyptian government.[23]

The Evangelical Church had been excluded from all processes during the exploratory stage. Only American missionaries investigated Sudan, even though there were a number of evangelicals in Sudan who could have provided assistance. It was only after the American Mission had made its decision to inaugurate this new Mission in Sudan, that the Evangelical Church was invited to participate by sending one of their ministers. The Mission even assigned the task their minister would fulfil, confining his role to that of pastor to the Evangelical Egyptians living in Northern Sudan. Although his role and position was pastoral, he was to be called a missionary. This

---

20. Ibid., 78.

21. J. K. Giffen, "Our Sudan Mission," in *Foreign Missionary Jubilee Convention of the United Presbyterian Church of N. A. Celebrating the Fiftieth Anniversary of the Founding of Missions in Egypt and India, December 6–8, 1904, Pittsburgh, PA.* (Philadelphia: The Board of Foreign Missions of the United Presbyterian Church of N. A., 1905), 120.

22. UPCNA, *Extension of Mission Work on the Nile*, 79.

23. Giffen, *The Egyptian Sudan*, 65–66.

indicated to the Evangelical Church that its missionaries should be licensed or ordained clerics, and neither the Mission nor the Church ever considered sending laymen or women as missionaries to minister to the many differing needs of the region. This limiting concept affected the Evangelical Church to such an extent that it has never sent an unordained missionary to any part of the world.

The Mission requested permission in 1900 to start its work in Khartoum, but the answer was delayed. After a few months, two missionaries met with Lord Cromer, the British Governor General of Egypt and Sudan, and told him about the Mission's plan to start work in Sudan. Their main request was for permission to hold meetings for the Protestants who lived in Khartoum and Umdorman. They also asked the government to grant them property in Khartoum. Lord Cromer offered little encouragement and rejected any mission work among Muslims in the Blue Nile area. At the same time, he was open to grant them great liberty to do whatever they desired among the non-Muslim people of the White Nile in the south. After further formal negotiations, the government allowed the Mission to hold meetings for the Protestants in Khartoum and Umdorman, but did not permit them to procure land in Khartoum.[24]

4.3.3 Exploring Southern Sudan

After the government prevented the Mission from working among Muslims in the north, the Mission decided to direct its efforts among the non-Muslim tribes of Southern Sudan. At the suggestion of Lord Cromer, the missionaries went on a trip to explore the field along the White Nile.[25] In January 1901, both Mr Giffen and Dr McLaughlin, an American missionary doctor, began their trip, reporting to both the Board in America and the Mission in Egypt upon their return:

> It was the Twentieth of January before we were able to leave Umderman. We took with us four donkeys, two servants, provisions for three months and two tents. We took passage on a gunboat, and, by special order from the Sirdar, we were allowed to travel at half the usual rates. We took passage direct

---

24. Ibid., 60.
25. Giffen, *The Egyptian Sudan*, 64.

to Tawfikiah, which is on the east bank of the White Nile about ten miles north of the mouth of the Sobat River. The journey occupied thirteen days. Here we made our camp, and from this explored the surrounding country. We made a trip north of Tawfikiah to east of the White Nile for about twenty-five miles, and for about sixty miles on the Sobat, on its north bank. We left Tawfikiah March 3rd, and returned to Umderman, where we arrived March 10th, having been absent just forty-nine days.[26]

The missionaries' report described the country, industries, products, climate, population, and religion. They suggested a location for their station in the South, and even noted the possible materials they would need to start their mission there.[27] The Mission selected a site called Doleib Hill on the Sobat River about 560 miles south of Khartoum. It was a pleasant location with a healthy climate and near to the river, which was the waterway to the north. Located at the centre of the population in the south and between numbers of villages, Doleib Hill was close to Tawfikiah, the government station in Southern Sudan, which made communication and transportation much easier.[28]

In April 1901, the Mission sought permission from the government to begin its mission in Doleib Hill and requested a piece of land. The government granted them permission to start and to occupy 200 acres of government land at the mouth of the Sobat River.[29]

However, while the missionaries were preparing themselves to go to Doleib Hill, they received a letter from the government telling them that it had withdrawn its agreement. This was because an Austrian Catholic Mission had been established about sixty miles from Doleib Hill, and government policy prohibited different mission organizations to be located in the same region. The government asked the American missionaries to

---

26. Report of the Soudan Mission to the Board of Foreign Missions, January to June, 1901. In UPCNA, *The Forty-Seventh Annual Report of the American United Presbyterian Mission in Egypt for the year 1901*, 63.

27. Ibid., 63–68.

28. Charles Watson, *Sorrow and Hope,* 140–141.

29. Report of the Sudan Mission for 1901, in UPCNA, *The 47th Annual Report of the Mission in Egypt,* 70.

find another site at least 150 miles away from the mouth of the Sobat. In July 1901, the missionaries presented a formal protest, but the government delayed replying to this protest until October 1901 after the return of Lord Cromer from England. Meanwhile, the missionaries started their journey from Egypt to Sudan, reaching Umdorman in September 1901. The government's positive answer to their protest was delayed until February 1902. During that time, the missionaries worked with the Egyptian minister to Sudan, Mr Gabra Hanna, in the establishment of the Egyptian Evangelical Church work in Sudan.[30] The delay also gave them opportunity to learn more about the country and the people around Umdorman, which later helped them when they started their mission work in the North some years after this.[31]

As we previously observed, the American Mission in Egypt did not involve the Evangelical Church in its decision to work in Sudan. The relationship between the Mission and the Church was not one of cooperation between two equal parties. Rather, the Mission saw itself as pioneering leaders, and expected the Evangelical Church to follow its plans and directives.

4.4 The Beginning of the American Mission Work in Southern Sudan (1901–1912)

4.4.1 The Beginning

After months of waiting for the government's answer and after much preparation in Khartoum and Umdorman, the missionaries were ready to leave for Doleib Hill. On 4 March 1902, they left Umdorman using two boats to ferry them and their supplies. This included building materials for the homes they would build on the land granted by the government.

The journey was a difficult one for Mr Giffen and Dr McLaughlin and their families, spending twenty-three days on two small boats. It was made worse since the boat crew did not have the training or the experience to

---

30. Ibid., 73.

31. Kelly Giffen, "Letter from the Soudan," in *Blessed be Egypt* (April 1902): 308. In his letter, Giffen explained the situation in 1902 when he was waiting in Khartoum for permission to start his mission in the South. He gave a picture of the political, social, and economical developments in Sudan and the opportunities for mission work in the north.

take responsibility for the whole trip. In his book, *The Egyptian Sudan*, Giffen described the trip and his first three years of mission in Doleib Hill and his feelings about the climate, people and landscape. As they soon discovered, the American missionaries were about to experience a more difficult and challenging situation than in Egypt, due to the differences in the climate, the nature of the people, the customs, the language, the religion, and the different culture of Southern Sudan.[32]

The Shilluk were the main tribe in the surrounding area.[33] They initially received the missionaries with much curiosity because many had never seen white people before. The missionaries took a long time to establish any kind of communication with the people, who were suspicious that the missionaries were like other white people who had taken their children as slaves. Their experiences with foreigners, either Arabs or Europeans, discouraged any trust. Even after many months, the people continued to treat the missionaries with suspicion. In a meeting with the chief of the villages surrounding their station, the missionaries told him of their desire to serve his people and of their expectations from the new government. He replied:

> Master, you speak well. We had here the Turks (old Egyptian government) and they said "Be submissive to us; we will protect you, we will fight your battles for you, we will teach you of God." But they took our cattle, they destroyed our villages, and carried away our women and children into slavery, and they are gone. Then came the Ansar (the Mahdists) and they said: "Come with us, we have a great army; we will care for you and protect you; we will give you plenty to eat, and a good place to live; we have The Book and we will teach you the truth and teach you of God." But they slew our men, and right here where these missionaries built their houses many of our men fell fighting for their women and children. They took away our cattle, destroyed our villages, carried off our women and children, and they too have gone. Now you come and say:

---

32. Giffen, *The Egyptian Sudan*, 77–91.

33. In the reports and books of the early missionaries the name of the tribe was "Shulla" as used by the tribe itself. But because of the Arab influence, the common pronunciation of the name later became "Shilluk," which will be used in this study.

"We will care for you; we will protect you, we will fight for you, we have *The Book*; we will teach you." Master, you speak well; but we will see.[34]

This was a major hurdle to overcome, trying to both ensure and prove that they were not serving a colonial government, but seeking to help the Shilluk in their spiritual and material needs. This took much time, which they used to determine the real needs of the people and to explore the appropriate methods to respond.

4.4.2 Methods of Ministry

The missionaries started by building their own houses on the land that had been given them by the government. At first, they received no help, but after weeks of working on their own some Shilluk started to help them. This gave an opportunity for their first positive interactions and allowed them to learn about each other. Through this contact, the missionaries gained their first foothold. The missionaries discovered that the needs of the people were different from those in Egypt. They found that the people were in need of learning many basic skills in the spheres of agriculture, trade, and language. The Shilluk were not used to cultivating their lands; their language had no written form; and they totally lacked medical and educational services. The missionaries aimed to address the basic needs of the people, hoping to respond to their medical, educational, financial, and spiritual needs.

After building their houses, the missionaries began to prepare their land for cultivation. Their goal was to provide their own food since the Shilluk planted very little fruit or vegetables and there was very limited clean or fresh food available. Second, they intended to teach agricultural methods to the Shilluk who merely depended on naturally growing crops. The missionaries hired some of the people to help them clear the grass, and introduced a number of new fruits and vegetables. In helping the missionaries, the Shilluk began to learn rudimentary agricultural skills.[35]

The missionaries had also brought many goods to sell, hoping to develop close contacts through daily trade. The Shilluk did not have a monetary

---

34. Giffen, *The Egyptian Sudan*, 120–121.
35. Watson, *The Sorrow and Hope*, 164–165.

system, instead exchanging goods through bartering goods or services. Nevertheless, when the missionaries employed the Shilluk to build houses or work the fields, they paid them with money. They taught them to receive weekly rather than daily salaries, and encouraged them to buy from the shop that they had opened at their station. In 1903, the missionaries in Doleib Hill reported:

> We began paying in money those who labored for us, or brought us materials for building, or supplies for our table, and we opened a store where they could buy such things as they needed. We arranged our prices so there might be a reasonable profit, and yet the people secure what they required at a smaller price than anywhere else. In fact, we placed it on a business basis, allowing such profits as would be necessary to an honest man doing business among this people. We were agreeably surprised at how well this method worked, and how quickly the people learned to do their little trading.[36]

The missionaries used these trade and agriculture practices for many years, considering this "Business Department" as a ministry like that of the medical and the evangelism departments.

Besides teaching the people primary life skills, the missionaries responded to overwhelming medical needs. Dr McLaughlin, who was one of the first two missionaries in Sudan, used his skills as a doctor to help many of them with various ailments. He reported that during the first nine months, "in the midst of building, clearing, gardening, etc., I have prescribed for 831 and made 34 visits."[37] Limited in time and by other responsibilities, Dr McLaughlin was unable to meet all the medical needs he encountered. As a result, the missionaries asked other medical missionaries to join them. In 1905, Dr Magill joined the team in Doleib Hill, visiting many villages around the mission station. Both Dr McLaughlin and Dr Magill worked together in the dry season of that year visiting the surrounding villages and

---

36. "Report of the Sudan," in *The 49ᵗʰ Annual Report of the American United Presbyterian Mission in Egypt and the Sudan for the Year 1903*, 75.
37. Ibid., 74.

treating a large number of people. They also found opportunities to speak to people about sin, salvation, and eternal punishment.[38]

After his arrival, Dr Magill wanted to establish a hospital in the area to better treat the many needs. He made his proposal to the American Mission in Egypt and the Board of Foreign Mission, asking for a hospital to be built in Doleib Hill as the centre for medical work; and secondly suggesting that a boat hospital could be used to travel the Nile between the villages of the Dinka and Nuer tribes. In his proposal, Dr Magill also asked for a trained nurse who could learn the local language and help the doctors in their work.[39] The medical ministry met a dire need and the missionaries were eager to respond.

The medical work of the American Mission in Sudan gained recognition in America. In his visit to Sudan in 1910, Theodore Roosevelt visited Doleib Hill where he viewed their medical mission work. In a public address in Khartoum, he said:

> I stopped a few days ago at the little Mission Station on the Sobat. One of the things that struck me there was what was being done by the medical side of that mission. There were about thirty patients who were under the charge of the mission doctor. Patients had come in to be treated by the mission doctors from places 125 miles distant. I do not know a better type of missionary than the doctor who comes out here and gives his whole heart to the work and does his work well. He is doing practical work of the most valuable type of civilization and for bringing the people up to the standards you are trying to set. If you make it evident to a man that you are sincerely trying to better his body, he will be much more ready to believe that you are trying to better his soul.[40]

Roosevelt's comments greatly encouraged the Board and the missionaries and helped enhance their reputation. The medical work was a successful

---

38. Shields, *Behind the Garden*, 138–139; Sudan Mission Association, *The American United Presbyterian Mission in the Sudan, the 5th Annual Report, 1905*, 24.

39. Sudan Mission Association, *The American United Presbyterian Mission in the Sudan, the 5th Annual Report, 1905*, 21–26.

40. Watson, *The Sorrow and Hope*, 169.

bridge, enabling the missionaries to build relationships with the people, and opening them to hear the gospel.

The Shilluk did not have schools, nor did they recognize the importance of having their children educated. Shortly after their arrival at Doleib Hill, the American missionaries began classes for Shilluk children, thus establishing the educational arm of their ministry. They began with a small class for boys with two to sixteen pupils each day in the first month. During that first year of 1903, classes did not meet regularly due to missionaries' illness and the parents' lack of interest. Parents needed their children to help with the work, sending them out with the cattle to find better grazing. In order to encourage better attendance, the missionaries offered prizes for the children who came regularly. This ministry continued to grow, and within a few years, a school was built in Doleib Hill.[41] The mission used education as a means to reach the children and their families with the gospel, concentrating its work among the children by providing not only a secular education but by establishing Sunday schools as well.[42] These Sunday schools were highly effective, and were primarily the result of the work of the missionary wives.[43]

Explaining the gospel proved to be a challenge. The Shilluk had their own traditional faith that made the Christian message difficult for them to accept. In their report of 1903, the missionaries summarized the beliefs of the Shilluks:

> They believe in a great God, Creator of all things, and a demi-god or prophet, who, under the great Creator, controls every event for good or evil. Directly, they do not seem to offer worship to the Great Creator, or have any responsibility to him,

---

41. The educational work in Dolieb Hill progressed greatly in 1924 when the Mission opened a boarding school. Shields, *Behind the Garden*, 134.

42. Shields, *Behind the Garden*, 136.

43. In 1917, three Sunday classes were established in Doleib Hill with 15 children. In 1925, Mrs Oyler, the wife of Dr D. S. Oyler, established a Sunday school teachers' class to train teachers in children's ministry. She challenged the young teachers to invite 100 children to come to the Sunday school. The young teachers worked hard to visit the villages around continuing to invite children until the number reached 167. The Mission established many other Sunday classes in the villages around their station. In that year the number of the children in the villages' Sunday schools reached 1,350 children. This movement led to the growth in the number of converts. *Al Hoda*, 1926, 203.

but rather to the demi-god, or prophet, who is called Nik-kanga. There is a house, or temple, sacred to this prophet, where the people assemble once each year and sacrifice an animal. There is a line of priests, descendants of the Nik-kanga, who sacrifice the victim. The people do not all assemble at one time, but village by village in turn, at the beginning of the rain season.

This sacrifice, in their belief, has some influence on the amount of rain, the growth of their crops and the prosperity of their flocks and herds . . . They have no belief in a devil and have no word for such a being; neither have they properly a heaven or a hell.[44]

The missionaries analyzed the Shilluk beliefs and came to the conclusion that these people had no concept of sin or guilt, which made the gospel almost incomprehensible to them. It was a long time before the missionaries found a way to communicate the gospel concepts initially using an interpreter who knew both Arabic and the local language. The limited results during the first few years were to be expected given the newness of their contact, and the disparity in worldviews. The missionaries organized weekly Sunday services for themselves, hoping also that in this way they could also teach the Shilluk the importance of the Sabbath and of worship.

In their report for 1906, the missionaries described the early efforts of evangelism. They had held their first meetings for the Shilluk in a newly constructed church building at their station in Doleib Hill; a number of Shilluk had attended these meetings to see what the missionaries were doing in their prayers; and the gospel had been explained through an interpreter. The missionaries had also visited neighbouring villages in order to evangelize the people there. Gradually the missionaries were learning the language and communicating the gospel in the people's tongue.[45]

In the sixth annual report of the Mission in Sudan, the missionaries explained the reasons for the lack of the results in their evangelism:

---

44. "Report of the Sudan," in *The 49th Annual Report of the American United Presbyterian Mission in Egypt and the Sudan for the Year 1903*, 72.

45. Sudan Mission Association, *The Sixth Annual Report of the American United Presbyterian Mission in the Sudan, for the Year 1906*, 92.

No converts or inquirers can be reported as yet. The time of
seed growing is yet at hand, but will it not soon give place to
the harvest? It must be said that the people generally listen
with respect to the Word of God, and as it is the pure Gospel
only that is preached to them (the ten commandments, the
nature and viciousness of sin, the need of atonement, the love
of God, the life and deeds, the death and resurrection of the
wondrous Christ and the judgement to come), have we not a
right to believe that ere long the living Word will bring forth
its predestined fruit, even repentance unto life, in the hearts
of this people?[46]

In their attempts to evangelize the Shilluk, the missionaries faced an
enormous barrier in communicating the gospel, lacking any translation of
the Bible into the Shilluk language. In order to rectify this, the missionaries needed to create a method for reducing the language to written form.
This meant developing an alphabet and determining the rules of grammar.
The missionaries spent eight years observing and studying the language and
then started the task of Bible translation in 1908. In the report of 1908,
one of the missionaries wrote:

In connection with the language work, considerable time was
spent in collecting material for a Shilluk grammar. A fairly
good working vocabulary of between 1,700 and 2,000 Shulla
words has been gathered together, comprising the words collected by all the missionaries during the past years; a much
clearer insight has been obtained into the Shilluk grammar
and some translation have been made. Much work yet remains
to be done, chiefly in acquiring those peculiar idiomatic expressions which are at once the distinguishing features and
genius of any language, and then translating the Scripture.[47]

---

46. Ibid.
47. "The Sudan Mission Report" quoted in Watson, *The Sorrow and Hope*, 158.

The Board of Foreign Mission invited Professor Diedrich Westermann, a German missionary and linguist to help the missionaries.[48] He came to Doleib Hills for a few months in 1910 to write a grammar book and a dictionary of the Shilluk language, which then enabled other missionaries to assist in Bible translation.[49] The gospel according to John was the first book of Scripture to be translated and printed by the American missionaries in Doleib Hills.[50]

The work of the American Mission in the Southern Sudan field was completely different to the work in Egypt. It also was different from the field in Northern Sudan "in almost every respect – language, climate, dominant religion, state of civilization, and methods of missionary work."[51] During the early years of the twentieth century, they lacked all comforts and tools of civilization: communication with the outside world was very limited, and there was no running water. Before the missionaries, there were no schools or medical help. The experience in Southern Sudan was unique among the various ministries and programmes of the Board of the Foreign Mission of the United Presbyterian Church of North America.

The American Mission found the work in Sudan to be slow and difficult. However, there were results. In 1912, the Mission opened another station to work among other tribes, going first to the Nuer tribe situated towards Nasser. Finally, after fourteen years of ministry in Doleib Hill, they

---

48. Diedrich Hermann Westermann (1875–1956) was a German missionary and linguist. He is viewed as one of the founders of modern African linguistics. In 1927 he published a *Practical Orthography of African Languages*, which later became known as the *Westermann Script*. Westermann carried out extensive linguistic and anthropological research from Senegal eastwards to the Upper Nile. His linguistic publications cover a wide range of African languages, including the Gbe languages (notably Ewe, Nuer, Kpelle, Shilluk, Hausa, and Guang). http://encyclopedia.thefreedictionary.com/Diedrich+Westermann. Accessed on 22 May 2005.

49. Roland Warner, William Anderson, and Andrew Wheeler, eds., *Day of Devastation Day of Contentment: The History of the Sudanese Church across 2000 years,* Faith in Sudan no. 10 (Nairobi: Paulines, 2000), 238.

50. Watson, *The Sorrow and Hope,* 160. For more details about the Bible translation into the different languages in Sudan see: Janet Persson, *In Our Own Language: The Story of Bible Translation in Sudan,* Faith in Sudan no. 3 (Nairobi: Paulines Publication Africa, 1997).

51. Watson, *The Sorrow and Hope,* 142.

rejoiced at the baptism of their first convert.[52] Moreover, in 1939, they opened another station among the Anuak at Akobo.[53]

4.5 The Beginning of the Work of the Evangelical Church in Sudan (1900–1909)

When the American Mission came to Egypt its success had been mainly among the Copts, some of whom were men of influence and education. Some of these converts had then accepted the challenge to carry the gospel to their fellow Egyptians in the cities and the villages throughout Egypt. The licentiates and evangelists, as well as the ordained ministers, had gone to places where there was no other missionary work. These activities, together with the efforts of the missionaries, had led to the growth of the Evangelical Church not only in members, but also in the opening of new locations within Egypt for evangelical work.[54] In 1908, fifty-four years after the coming of the American Mission to Egypt, Charles Watson praised the missionary spirit and the achievements of the evangelicals when he said:

> There is in the Church also a fine missionary or evangelistic spirit. Here lies the secret of the rapid growth of the Church during the past half century. Every member was a worker. The obligation to extend the kingdom by personal work was accepted as an inevitable corollary to the enjoyment of the privileges of salvation.[55]

In those early years of the twentieth century, the American Mission expected that the Evangelical Church would become an agency for sending missionaries. These hopes were shared among some church members who believed that they had both the responsibility and capability to carry the gospel to people inside and outside Egypt. This spirit of mission and evangelism increased within the evangelical churches, resulting in endeavours within Egypt, and then expanding to include Sudan as a mission field.

---

52. *The United Presbyterian*, February 22, 1934, 12.
53. Macmichael, *The Sudan*, 139.
54. Watson, *American Mission*, 318; Watson, *Egypt*, 195–196.
55. Watson, *Egypt*, 245–246.

These ideas were recorded during the Synod discussions at its first meeting of 1899 when the invitation came from the American Mission to consider Sudan as mission field.[56]

4.5.1 The Evangelical Church Takes Its First Step in Mission Work in Sudan

Sudan was the first place considered by the Evangelical Church and the American Mission as their joint mission field. Although the American Mission had excluded the Church from the beginning stages, the interactions between the American Mission and the Evangelical Church in sharing the task pointed to the possibility of cooperation. In fact, the missionaries who first explored the idea of opening a mission in Sudan had envisioned a joint operation. Their report to the American Mission in Egypt and to the Board of the Foreign Mission recommended that the Evangelical Church should send a pastor for the work in Sudan:

> That we recommended to the Synod of the Nile to under-
> take work in Umderman, by appointing a native evangelist as
> soon as possible, to act as pastor among young men already
> there, and thus form a nucleus for more extended operations
> in the future, and that an appeal be made to the Egyptian
> Evangelical Church to sustain this work.[57]

There were great expectations from the outset that both the Mission and the Church would have the opportunity to cooperate in this new mission field. The Mission found in the Synod and in the members of the Church "an eager desire to cooperate with the Mission in work in Sudan."[58] When the Evangelical Church recognized the need for pastoral work among the evangelical community in Sudan, the Synod decided to send its first worker. This project was enthusiastically promoted by the Assiout College that offered twenty-five pounds to start the work, and asked the Synod and churches to send money and men to share in the task of evangelizing Sudan.[59]

---

56. Synod of the Nile, *Minutes of the Year, 1899*, 9.

57. Extension of Mission Work on the Nile. In *The Forty-Fifth Annual Report of the American United Presbyterian Mission in Egypt for the year 1899*, 78.

58. Ibid., 79.

59. Synod of the Nile, *Minutes of the Year, 1899*, 9

The ministry of the Egyptian Evangelical Church in Sudan began in the early years of the twentieth century and continues until now. The Mission had the expectation that the Egyptian Church would eventually act as a sending body for missionaries to Sudan. Many pastors and ministers who went there contributed to the building of the Sudanese Evangelical Church and to the evangelization of the country. But at the outset, the American Mission requested men to primarily do pastoral work among the expatriate Egyptian community. Missionary work among the Sudanese was not therefore really seen to be part of the Church's original mandate. This vision never evolved, and the American Mission was unable to transfer this task to the Egyptian Church. The Evangelical Church understood mission work in its own limited fashion, making pastoral work its central focus. The Church left mission work and evangelism either to the Americans or to the efforts of individual pastors and lay men and women, without giving its support as an institution.

4.5.2 Gabra Hanna and the First Efforts in Khartoum

The first American missionary group reached Umdorman in 1900, in preparation for entering Southern Sudan. The Egyptian minister, Gabra Hanna who came a few days after them, joined the Giffen and McLaughlin families. Gabra Hanna was a licentiate minister from the Delta Presbytery who had been ministering in the Middle Egypt Presbytery before his move to Sudan.[60]

On his way to Umdorman, Gabra Hanna stopped at Halfa and Berber, two cites in Northern Sudan, where he arranged a number of meetings for young Egyptian Coptic and evangelical men working there. In these meetings, he "preached the Gospel of salvation."[61] Once in Umdorman, Gabra Hanna worked with the American missionaries to find a place to hold meetings for evangelicals. At first, the work was discouraging, with very

---

60. Ibid., 6.

61. Gabra Hanna, "Second Annual Report of the Work in the Soudan in the Report of the Soudan Mission for 1901," in *The 47th Annual Report of the Mission in Egypt*, 73. In this report the American missionaries to Sudan included the report of Gabra Hanna to the Synod of the Nile. This report is also in the Synod of the Nile, *Minutes of the Year, 1900*, 15–20.

few attending; however, the numbers gradually increased. Gabra Hanna reported his experiences:

> The history of the work for the past year is something like that of a small child. Sometimes it would show growth and strength, and at other times weakness and ceasing to grow, or a dwarfing away. Sometimes there would be a strengthening of the members of the body and an effort to walk; and again a deep sleep. There would be an attendance of 20, 30, 40, or 45; then again 4 or 5; and more than once we came to the hour of meeting and not one present, and at the end of the time only a few.[62]

Most of Hanna's ministry in Umdorman and Khartoum focused on pastoring the evangelicals from Egypt and other Arab countries such as Syria and Lebanon. He concentrated on holding meetings, visiting families, and evangelism among the non-Sudanese populations. He visited other cities in Northern Sudan, such as Berber and Halfa, to encourage the evangelicals. He also communicated with Copts and served their spiritual and pastoral needs.

Hanna encountered many difficulties, suffering from the weather, the Islamic influence and from the British governor who supported the Muslim leaders by giving them financial privileges. He also experienced many encouragements at the growing attendance at meetings and the eagerness of some people to serve and care for others. In March 1901, he arranged for the first Lord's Supper in Umdorman, and in the presence of Rev Giffen he received new members. Ten men and two women participated.[63] In the same year, two people from a Muslim background accepted the Christian faith and confessed their faith in front of others.[64]

Although Hanna found growth to be slow, he continued in his ministry and requested that the Synod send more workers to meet the needs of those in the cities that he was not able to visit regularly. He worked alone for some years, but his persistent work prepared the way for many other

---

62. Hanna, "Second Annual Report," 74.

63. Ibid., 75–77.

64. Synod of the Nile, *Minutes of the Year, 1901,* 16.

ministers from the Evangelical Church and additional missionaries from the American Mission.

Rev Giffen praised Gabra Hanna and his work in Sudan in his report of 1906. At that time, Giffen was working with the Mission in Khartoum and was cooperating with the Evangelical Church and its workers there.[65] He reported that:

> In presenting our report for Northern Sudan, many things, of value in the aggregate of influences, are still as the seed sown from which a harvest is expected, but the time for reaping is not yet.
>
> Of all the services rendered, from which there are tangible results, the greater part has been done by the missionary representing the Synod of the Nile and the Egyptian Church. The Rev Gabra Hanna needs no introduction here. He has been labouring in the Sudan for more than five years and very successfully. Some of the difficulties that he had to meet at first are gradually disappearing, and by faithfully teaching a pure Gospel, and by an earnest, consistent life he has gained the confidence of all who know him.[66]

The American missionaries had opened the door for the Evangelical Church to send its first missionary pastor to Sudan. They followed his work and encouraged him despite their different focuses, with Hanna concentrating on pastoral work among the Egyptians and the American missionaries seeking to influence the lives of the Sudanese and introduce them to Christ.

4.5.3 Gabra Hanna: A Missionary and Pastor

Gabra Hanna saw himself as both a missionary and a pastor. In 1900 and 1901, he joined the American missionaries in their ministry at Khartoum before they went to the South. Since he had not yet been ordained and

---

65. As mentioned above, the American Mission found it could use education as a means to access to Northern Sudan field, since the government allowed the American Mission to establish schools. The Mission included a spiritual dimension by holding prayer and worship meetings for evangelicals in cooperation with Gabra Hanna.

66. J. K. Giffen, *The Fifth Report of the Sudan Mission of the year 1905*, 11.

there were no church buildings, he concentrated on evangelizing and preaching among the Egyptians in Sudan. He visited many cities and established a number of meetings for the evangelicals who were working in the government.[67]

Gabra Hanna was an educated person who studied Sudan and its history. On one visit to Egypt in 1904, he made a presentation to the Synod about the work in Sudan, summarizing the history of Sudan from the Roman period through the spread of Christianity, to the establishment and growth of Islam. He spoke of the sufferings of the Sudanese under the Islamic influence, and of the defeat of Christianity. He reminded the Synod that together with the American Mission, they were at the dawn of a new beginning for Christianity in Sudan.[68]

His early reports to the Synod described the potential and needs of Sudan as a mission field. He outlined the religious situation, explaining about the Muslim and Coptic communities and their spiritual needs. In each of the first four annual reports he sent to the Synod, he mentioned the relationships between the Copts and evangelicals. He preached in many Coptic meetings in Halfa, Khartoum North, and Umdorman, using the same methods to reach nominal Christians from the Coptic Church that he had learned in Egypt.[69] He approached, with the gospel message, Muslims who had converted from Christianity during the Mahdi's time and wanted to embrace Christianity again. He mentioned a few cases of returnees who were attending the meetings and showing definite growth in their faith and Christian behaviour.[70]

As a missionary, he encouraged the Evangelical Church to establish an evangelical school since other churches had their own schools. He recognized the importance of having an evangelical school for the ministry and for the growing church. He used the American Mission as his model, and hoped that the Synod would also act as a missionary agent with similar foci and methods. He sent a description of the other missionary

---

67. Synod of the Nile, *Minutes of the Year, 1901*, 15–20.

68. Gabra Hanna, "The Work in Sudan," *Al Murshed* (1904): 89.

69. The American Mission in Egypt and the Evangelical Church used this approach as their method for evangelism in Egypt.

70. Synod of the Nile, *Minutes of the Years, 1901*, 17; *1903*, 62–63; *1904*, 77.

and government schools, including their student numbers and conditions, and argued that the Synod should build such a school. Unfortunately, his call was not positively received, and his dreams remained unfulfilled until the American Mission came to the North in 1903 and began to establish many schools.[71] The Synod was unwilling or unable to view Sudan as its mission field, considering only its obligation to pastor the Egyptian emigrant population.

As a missionary, Hanna explained the geographical, political, social, and economic conditions of his field. He talked about the facilities and benefits that the Anglo-Egyptian government gave to the Muslim leaders in their schools, mosques, and salaries. He had a burden for recording the historical information of the field and its situation and ministry events, telling the Synod that he was recording the history of the evangelistic work in Sudan.[72] In this, he followed the example of the American Mission, whose field and ministry reports included extensive details for posterity's sake.

As a missionary, in his reports he focused on the work of the American Mission in Southern Sudan. He visited the Sobat River area, where the American Mission was stationed in Doleib Hill, and through an interpreter, preached in the local villages. When the American Mission started its work in Northern Sudan in 1903 he worked with them in women's ministry, and before his ordination, the missionaries administered the sacraments at his meetings for the evangelicals.[73] Seeing the great need, Hanna appealed to the Synod to send missionaries to the South and to open new stations in other Sudanese cities.[74] He asked the Synod to send a Bible woman to work among the families in Khartoum and Umdorman. Regrettably, the Synod did not respond to his call. The mission work in the South and with women was left solely in the hands of the American missionaries.

As a missionary, Hanna had a vision of evangelical families spreading throughout Sudan and thus carrying the Christian message to all. He told stories of families and individuals living in remote cities of Sudan who had established spiritual meetings at their homes and preached the gospel to

71. Synod of the Nile, *Minutes of the Year, 1906*, 116.

72. Synod of the Nile, *Minutes of the Years, 1901*, 16–17; *1902*, 35; *1904*, 78.

73. Synod of the Nile, *Minutes of the Year, 1903*, 63.

74. Ibid., 64.

others. He praised the graduates of Assiout College and their missionary practices as good examples to their communities and a great help in the ministry. Likewise, in more than one report to the Synod, the Committee of the Work in Sudan[75] praised these graduates for their missionary role and their influence in Sudanese life.[76]

Gabra Hanna went to Sudan as a missionary having in mind the American Mission model. He hoped to see the Synod develop into a sending organization that would dispatch its missionaries throughout Sudan, build schools, send women to work among the families, and commission families to be witnesses for the gospel. Hanna and a few other Egyptian Church leaders shared the hopes and perspective of the American Mission that the Synod could become a sending agent for mission work. When his missionary vision found little response from the Synod, Gabra Hanna changed his own focus and vision, and came to believe that the Synod was only responsible for, or capable of, pastoral work. There was a confusing lack of clarity in the expectations of the role of Egyptian ministers to Sudan, and Hanna was the first Egyptian missionary to face this contradiction.

Gabra Hanna was ordained in 1903 as the first Egyptian pastor in Sudan during a visit to Egypt. His ordination came under the supervision of the Upper Egypt Presbytery that had responsibility for the pastoral work in Sudan.[77] His ordination gave him new responsibilities that directed him to concentrate on the pastoral task of strengthening and organizing the church. The Synod did not ask him to undertake any missionary work among the Sudanese but only to care for the Egyptians.

One of Hanna's main achievements was the establishment of the Evangelical Church in Khartoum. On 30 December 1907, the Evangelical Church in Khartoum celebrated its inauguration when a church board was elected and Gabra Hanna was ordained as its first pastor.[78] The Upper

---

75. The Committee of the Work in Sudan was the body which the Synod established to follow and support the work in Sudan. It was the link between the Synod and the ministries of the Evangelical Church in Sudan. There will be more explanation about this committee and its role in the coming chapter.

76. Synod of the Nile, *Minutes of the Years, 1906*, 144; Synod of the Nile, *Minutes of the Years, 1907*, 187.

77. Synod of the Nile, *Minutes of the Year, 1904*, 77–78.

78. Watson, *The Sorrow and Hope*, 172.

Egypt Presbytery sent some of its leaders to ordain elders and deacons and to celebrate with the new church. These leaders also preached in a number of meetings during their visit.[79] This step of organizing the Khartoum Church demonstrated the Synod's true goal in sending a minister to Sudan. The Synod understood mission work as pastoring the Egyptians living in Sudan, organizing them in churches, and maintaining a link with their parent Egyptian Evangelical Church.

After his ordination, Hanna was able to administer the sacrament and be involved in church government. The project that took most of his energy during this time was the construction of the Khartoum Church building. He worked with the Synod, the evangelicals in Sudan and the American Mission, and he wrote to the Synod for support for the project and encouraged the members of the Egyptian Church to give towards the building.[80] He collected money for the project from churches in Egypt and from evangelicals at the different mission stations throughout Sudan.[81] The American missionaries helped him find the property, develop the building plans, and organize the construction. The Synod however caused him many difficulties, not only expecting him to get their approval for the budget, but interfering in the construction details.[82] Because of these problems, he had already left the field before the building was completed.

In his last years in Sudan, Hanna's interest in mission work and the activities of the American Mission waned. He visited fewer places for evangelism, leaving this task to the American Mission. He became increasingly dissatisfied, and argued with the Synod asking them to send evangelists to work in Sudan and using critical language that the Synod did not accept.[83] He asked the Synod to approve his vacations, and demanded that they cover his and his wife's travel expenses. The Synod responded by giving

---

79. Synod of the Nile, *Minutes of the Year, 1908*, 164.

80. Synod of the Nile, *Minutes of the Year, 1903*, 77.

81. Synod of the Nile, *Minutes of the Year, 1907*, 164.

82. Synod of the Nile, *Minutes of the Year, 1908*, 202.

83. Synod of the Nile, *Minutes of the Year, 1906*, 126.

him notice to leave the field within a few months.[84] In February 1909, he left Sudan, moving back to Egypt where he served as a pastor in Fayoum.[85]

Gabra Hanna's original vision of being a missionary to Sudan was not achieved because he became occupied with pastoral work. Nevertheless, Hanna is honoured as the first pioneer missionary to Sudan, and as the founder of the Khartoum Evangelical Church. Many other ministers followed his example and served as pastors in numerous cities throughout Sudan.

4.6 The Beginning of the American Mission Work in Northern Sudan (1903–1912)

In 1901, when the American missionaries were waiting for permission to start their work in Sudan, they bought a property in Umdorman. This became the place where the Egyptian Protestants would meet, and where the American missionaries participated in the ministry with Gabra Hanna before they moved to Doleib Hill. The American missionaries never lost hope that their major work in Sudan would be located in the tripartite capital, which included Khartoum, Umdorman, and Khartoum North, among the Arabs in the north. This happened two years later. When they left to start their permanent mission work in Southern Sudan, the Egyptians continued to use this place in their worship and kept the ministry alive during the absence of the American missionaries.

In 1902, the missionaries in Doleib Hill wrote to the Mission in Egypt requesting that an additional missionary be sent to help them in the South and another to work in Khartoum. They felt that Hanna could not carry on the work alone in Khartoum:

> At Khartoum and Umderman the work is growing and becoming more permanent. No doubt the work there has suffered because there was no missionary to lend its influence with the evangelist of Synod, and give precedence by his presence, which is so much expected and appreciated by this people. But Mr Gebera [*sic.*] Hanna has unflaggingly labored

---

84. Synod of the Nile, *Minutes of the Year, 1908*, 202.
85. Ibid., 209.

on, single handed, and often without much encouragement from any one. The Lord has acknowledged his faithfulness in giving him blessing . . . We wish to emphasize the request we made a year ago, viz.: that at least two missionaries be sent to the Sudan at once: One for Khartoum and Umderman, and one for this station . . . We sincerely hope that this call will not be lightly regarded.[86]

The American Mission in Egypt answered by sending two American families, one for the work in Doleib Hill, and Rev G. A. Sowash and his wife who worked closely with Hanna in the meetings for the evangelicals in Khartoum and Umdorman.[87]

The Anglo-Egyptian government continued to discourage evangelism of Muslims but allowed the Mission to cooperate with the evangelicals living in Northern Sudan to establish worship meetings and Bible study groups. The American Mission thus worked side by side with the Evangelical Church of Egypt in their joint mission to Northern Sudan. Together, they utilized all opportunities offered within the restrictive political and social circumstances.

Rev Sowash and his wife lived in Khartoum, working with the Egyptians, holding meetings, and seeking possible opportunities for mission work. They soon discerned that the best way to increase their effectiveness would be to begin an educational ministry.[88]

In its 1904 report to the General Assembly of the United Presbyterian Church of North America, the Board of Foreign Mission reported about the Sudan Mission that:

> Missionary work at Khartum and vicinity, which was hampered last year by a government prohibition against all missionary work, has found, with the partial removal of that prohibition, so many opportunities opening up that this year's embarrassment is to follow up these opportunities effectively.

---

86. "The Second Annual Report of the Sudan Mission, 1902" in *the Annual Report of the American United Presbyterian Mission in Egypt and the Sudan for the year 1902*, 78.
87. Elder, *Vindicating a Vision*, 103.
88. Shields, *Behind the Garden*, 86.

We now have missionary work either in the form of school, regular preaching or prayer meetings in Khartoum, Umdorman, Halfaya, and Halfa. The presence at these points of many who were trained in our mission schools in Egypt, or who were even members of our Egyptian Evangelical Church, gives rise to a responsibility which we have to assume and an opportunity which we cannot neglect.[89]

Within two years, four schools had been started at Umdorman, Khartoum, Khartoum North, and Wadi Halfa with an aggregate enrolment of two hundred students.[90] Since the government did not allow Sudanese children to attend Christian schools, these mission schools attracted their students from families with a Coptic, Evangelical, or Abyssinian Christian background. A few years later, Lord Cromer who was the British High Commissioner in Egypt, permitted Muslim children to attend Christian schools, with the provision that the schools must first inform the parents that Bible study and Christian teaching were a requirement for all students, including Muslims.[91] Unexpectedly, many Muslim parents sent their children to the mission schools, raising the number of schools to seven by 1912 with six hundred students.[92]

Only boys were eligible to attend the American Mission schools until 1908 when Miss Hannah McLean[93] started a joint daytime and boarding school for girls in Khartoum North.[94] This school was the first in Sudan to

---

89. UPCNA, *Minutes of the Forty-Sixth General Assembly of the United Presbyterian Church of North America, Greenville, PA. May 25th to June 1st 1904*, Vol. XI–No. 1. (Pittsburgh: United Presbyterian Board of Publication, 1904), 51.

90. UPCNA, *Minutes of the Forty-Eighth General Assembly of the United Presbyterian Church of North America, Richmond, Indiana, May 23rd to May 30th 1906*, Vol. XI–Number 3. (Pittsburgh: United Presbyterian Board of Publication, 1906), 611.

91. Shields, *Behind the Garden*, 89.

92. UPCNA, *Minutes of the Fifty-Fourth General Assembly of the United Presbyterian Church of North America, Seattle, Wash. May 22 to 29, 1912*, Volume Thirteen–Number one (Pittsburgh: United Presbyterian Board of Publication, 1912), 60.

93. Miss Hannah McLean was a missionary sent by the Women's Board of the United Presbyterian Church of North America to start mission work among the Sudanese women.

94. Khartoum North is the name which was given to Halfaya which developed from a village to a town and joined both Khartoum and Umdorman to make the triplet capital of Sudan.

educate Sudanese girls. The number of girls increased from ten to two hundred fifty in a few short years. A result of the ministry of the girls' school was that there were a number of conversions and baptisms.[95]

The ministry of the girls' school grew to become a women's ministry. Since women were not permitted to leave their homes, the American Mission in Sudan followed the strategy, which had previously proved successful in Egypt, and concentrated its work within the Sudanese homes.[96] The Women's Board of the United Presbyterian Church of North America sponsored this work, and a number of women missionaries were sent and worked to improve the Sudanese women's situation in education, health, and social life.[97] The women missionaries and the missionary wives ministered from home to home, teaching women and sharing the gospel as they found opportunity. All this produced a number of converts. The American Mission also trained the native Christian women (most of whom were local Egyptians) to help them in this ministry. The women's ministries grew and expanded to other cities such as Khartoum North, Umdorman, Wad Meadni, Port Sudan, and Atbara.[98]

Rev Giffen and his wife had been working in Southern Sudan, but in 1905, after their furlough in the United States, they moved to Khartoum in Northern Sudan. They realized that there was a need for a boys' orphanage, with many children having been separated from their families during the war years, or having parents who could not meet their basic needs. This ministry began with one boy under their care.[99] However, the work grew gradually until by 1911 the Board of Foreign Mission recognized it as one of its own projects and offered it a budget.[100] This home met a real need in the lives of the boys and many of them became active Christians. This was

---

95. UPCNA, *Minutes of the Fifty-Second General Assembly of the United Presbyterian Church of North America, Philadelphia, Penna. May 25 June 1, 1910*, Volume Twelve-Number Three (Pittsburgh: United Presbyterian Board of Publication, 1910), 675.

96. Watson, *The Sorrow and Hope*, 174.

97. UPCNA, *Minutes of the Fifty-Second General Assembly*, 675.

98. Shields, *Behind the Garden*, 103–104.

99. Ibid., 93.

100. Ibid., 96.

a new method for the Board of Foreign Mission but they agreed to fund it because of Rev Giffen's influence and because of the promising results.[101]

Medical work was another tool that the American Mission used in the beginning of its ministry in Northern Sudan. The Church Missionary Society had its own medical ministry in Khartoum, but this ended with the death of the pioneer medical doctor, Dr Hill. The CMS then asked the American Mission to take the medical work under its responsibility.[102] In 1907, Dr McLaughlin and his wife moved from Doleib Hill to start a clinic in Khartoum. During the next few years, Dr McLaughlin provided 9,752 clinic treatments, visits and operations, but due to the lack of suitable equipment and his own illness, he could not continue in his ministry.[103] In 1910, Dr Magill, who had also served as a medical missionary in Doleib Hill, came to Khartoum. In 1911 alone, he provided 2,565 medical treatments. Nevertheless, providing modern medical help to uneducated people who naturally depended on harmful traditional treatments was a difficult ministry.[104] By 1915, the medical work in Northern Sudan ceased due to the lack of staff and funds.[105]

Apparently, there were few spiritual results from the medical ministry in Northern Sudan. The CMS had a more advanced medical ministry than the American Mission, so in 1910 the two missions agreed to place the medical work of Northern Sudan under the CMS, while the American Mission would concentrate on educational work.[106]

The beginning of the American Mission work in Northern Sudan had been difficult, and had brought only limited results. However, the few missionaries involved had planted good seeds. The schools had proven to be most successful, and they flourished in the following years to become the

101. The Boys' Home continued until the death of Rev Giffen in 1932 when it turned into a boys' boarding school and moved to Umdorman. (Werner, *Day of Devastation*, 322).

102. Watson, *The Sorrow and Hope*, 175.

103. UPCNA, *Minutes of the Fiftieth General Assembly of the United Presbyterian Church of North America, Pittsburgh, PA, May 27 to June 1908*, Volume XII–No. 1. (Pittsburgh: United Presbyterian Board of Publication, 1908), 70.

104. UPCNA, *Minutes of the Fifty-Fourth General Assembly*, 59–60.

105. Werner, *Day of Devastation*, 234.

106. Ibid.; Watson, *The Sorrow and Hope*, 178.

main ministry of the Mission in Sudan. Until 1904, the work in Sudan was considered an expansion of the American Mission work in Egypt, and depended on the American missionaries who were already serving in Egypt.[107] Later, the missionaries in Sudan asked the Board to allow them to have their own mission association and from 1905, the Sudan Mission had its own meetings, reports, and budget that helped in the expansion of the ministry and gave the missionaries the opportunity to make their decisions more rapidly and independently.[108]

4.7 The Evangelical Church in Egypt's Response to the Work in Sudan

The mission work in Sudan left its mark upon the whole Evangelical Church in Egypt. Many people were interested in knowing about and supporting the work in Sudan. The Church paper, *Al-Murshed*, raised awareness of the mission, reporting on the growth and needs of the new initiative. In 1902 and 1904, many issues of *Al-Murshed* contained articles and poems challenging the Evangelical Church in Egypt to meet the needs of Sudan, and especially those of the Sudanese women. One poem described the hard conditions of the Sudanese women and asked Evangelical Egyptians to go to their aid, to educate and guide them from sin and ignorance to find the Saviour.[109] Another writer described the poverty, diseases, and hard life of Sudanese women. He appealed to the Evangelical Church in Egypt to give from the spiritual and material gifts it had received from God, and suggested that all 6,400 members of the Evangelical Church in Egypt should give a small sum of money to support the ministry in Sudan.[110]

In 1902, Hanna asked the members of the Evangelical Church to send more ministers to help in the women's work and in ministry to the various cities around Sudan. He described the difficulties but also stated that the standard of living in Sudan had improved and that one day it would match

---

107. Werner, *Day of Devastation*, 238.

108. UPCNA, *Minutes of the Forty-Sixth General Assembly*, 1905, 51.

109. *Al-Murshed* (1902): 172–174.

110. The piaster is 1/100 of the Egyptian pound. In the early years of the twentieth century the Egyptian pound equalled 5 American Dollars. Eid Tadros, "The Sudanese Young Woman," *Al-Murshed* (1902): 153–154.

that of Egypt. Some of his descriptions seem exaggerated, comparing the weather to that of a Swiss winter or a Lebanese summer, and encouraging rich evangelicals to visit Sudan for their winter vacations. He invited all trades and workers to consider moving to Sudan in order to help evangelize Sudan through good example and reputation. He urged them to hurry because other minorities had already arrived and he wanted the evangelicals to reap the potential blessings of the land. He believed that evangelical families could be an important instrument in evangelizing Sudan.[111]

These reports challenged the Evangelical Church in Egypt, and gave it the opportunity to contribute to the ministry in Sudan financially, in prayer, and by sending other ministers to work in the new field. During the early stages, there was great interest among the Evangelicals in Egypt concerning the work in Sudan.

The American missionaries who later served in Northern Sudan realized the uniqueness of the mission work of the Egyptian Evangelical Church in Sudan. In their report of 1906, they said:

> The work upon which we have expended the most energy is the direct preaching of the Word. Regular services have been maintained in each of the towns mentioned above.[112] It is only due to the Rev Gebera [sic.] Hanna for me to state here that he has done the greater part of his work, the missionaries cooperating with him in all. As the representative of the Egyptian Church, this is his legitimate field, and all the more so because these congregations are formed, very largely, from Egyptians and Syrians who were in some way connected with the Evangelical Churches of Egypt and Syria.[113]

One of the big challenges faced by the mission of the Evangelical Church in Sudan was the lack of financial resources. The funding for Hanna and his ministry, including rent for meeting places, salary and travel expenses

---

111. Gabra Hanna, "The Evangelical Church in Sudan," *Al-Murshed* (1902): 273–274.

112. His reference was to Khartoum, Khartoum North, Halfaya, and Umdorman, which were centres of trade and wealth and a large number of government operations. The bulk of Evangelicals lived in these cities.

113. J. K. Giffen, "the sixth Annual Report of the Mission in the Sudan for the Year 1906," 87.

came from the Evangelical Church in Egypt. When a church building was needed in Khartoum, both the evangelicals in Sudan and in Egypt contributed to the purchase of the land and the building costs. Hanna led a movement among the evangelicals in both Sudan and Egypt to collect the money. In asking the Egyptian Church to contribute, he told stories of the sacrificial giving of those in Sudan who gave more than their finances would realistically allow. He reminded the Church in Egypt that the church in Khartoum was their church too, and that it would become a great work when all members contributed.[114]

Al-Murshed published lists of individuals and churches who gave to the building of the Evangelical Church in Khartoum.[115] Hanna told the readers that such giving meant that the church in Sudan was part of the Church in Egypt and was a "part of its life, blood, and nature."[116] It was not an easy task to raise sufficient money for such a project. The Egyptian church raised about $5,000, and in doing so increased awareness of the needs of the mission field. The remaining $3,000 came from Egyptians in Sudan and from individual American missionaries. Financial involvement helped promote a spiritual revival and encouraged giving for the work of the Church.[117] From 1900 to 1908, the Synod was able to greatly increase financial support for its spiritual ministries. In 1901, the Synod's budget was 1,918 EGP (Egyptian Pounds)[118] to cover the expenses for evangelistic work and the pastors' salaries. By 1908, the budget had increased to 7,328 EGP.[119] At the same time, the number of communicants grew from 6,580[120] in 1901 to 10,341 in 1908.[121] Beside these numerical increases, there was a growing eagerness among laymen and young people in the churches, which

---

114. *Al Murshed* (1904): 100.

115. Ibid., 100–101.

116. Ibid., 144.

117. The call to raise money for the work in Sudan came at the same time as the call for the Synod to have full financial independence from the American Church. This call led to the establishment of a committee for financial independence that worked for many years to help the Synod in that direction. See chapter 2 and the Minutes of the Synod of the Nile from 1907 and after.

118. Synod of the Nile, *Minutes of the Year, 1901*, 23.

119. Synod of the Nile, *Minutes of the Year, 1908*, 167.

120. UPCNA, *Minutes of the Forty-Fourth General Assembly, 1902*, 770.

121. UPCNA, *Minutes of the Fifty-First General Assembly, 1909*, 550.

led to the establishment of youth meetings and a laymen's organization.[122] These two initiatives played an important role in the life of the Church and its ministry. All these developments happened during the beginning of the work in Sudan and suggested that the Church was indeed maturing and ready to become a financially independent institution. Likewise, it increased hopes that the Church would one day operate as a mission-minded sending body.[123]

4.8 Conclusion

When the American Mission explored the possibility of expanding its work into Sudan, it hoped that the Evangelical Church of Egypt would become a partner in this enterprise and eventually become an independent missionary body. They sought to nurture a vision for mission and evangelism.

Initially, the American Mission did not regard the Evangelical Church as an equal partner, but moved alone. It explored the potential mission field and decided how it would minister in Sudan without consulting the Synod. It then requested that the Synod send a minister to pastor the Egyptian evangelicals who lived in Sudan. In doing this, the Mission limited the Church's missionary vision. On the other hand, the Evangelical Church followed the Mission's proposal with no intention of making further missionary efforts to reach the Sudanese either in the North or in the South.

The Synod appointed Gabra Hanna as its pioneer Egyptian missionary to pastor the Egyptians in Sudan. This title led to great confusion. Although he himself initially engaged in true missionary and evangelistic endeavours, he soon limited himself to the pastoral role that the Synod expected. In the first few years of the work in Sudan, the Evangelicals in Egypt generously supplied his salary and ministry expenses, and seemed excited about the call to work in Sudan. Hopes were raised that a great mission spirit would spread throughout the Egyptian Church. However, Synod decisions and the conflicting visions of their mission reduced the Evangelical Church's work in Sudan to a pastoral rather than missionary role.

---

122. Synod of the Nile, *Minutes of the Year, 1908*, 157.

123. In 1900 when the Synod sent its first minister to Sudan it also established the Committee of the Work among Muslims and appointed and supported another full-time minister to work among the Muslims. See chapter 3.

CHAPTER 5

The Development of the Ministry of the Egyptian Evangelical Church to Sudan (1909–1964)

5.1 Introduction

The work of the American Mission and the Evangelical Church of Egypt continued in Sudan until 1964 when the political situation forced all foreign ministries to leave. This chapter will study the progress of the work during this era, and the Egyptian contribution to the Christian ministry in Sudan.

After Gabra Hanna had left Sudan, many factors influenced the direction of the ministry in Sudan. The Synod took steps to organize the work under one body, to direct the ministers, to provide for their succession, and to deal with the growing needs of the ministry. Hanna was followed by other pastors who came with similar hopes of engaging in mission work, but were likewise confined to pastoral work. Only in a few exceptional cases did mission work replace the core pastoral tasks. This chapter will examine the work of the official pastors, and of the laymen and women who were engaged in mission endeavours even though they had not been called by the Synod to be missionaries. These unofficial missionaries had a different perspective to that of the Synod that needs to be explored. This chapter will also examine the role of the American Mission in the work that the Evangelical Church undertook in Sudan. We will also seek to understand the reasons for the Synod's decisions and vision, and in doing so, will concentrate on the work of the Evangelical Church, with less attention to the work of the American Mission.

5.2 Abofarag – a Pastor with a Missionary Heart

In 1909, Abofarag Sa'd, a minister in Assiut Presbytery, was sent to pastor the church in Khartoum.[1] In his first report to the Synod, Abofarag commented positively on the work of his predecessor Gabra Hanna. In his role as a pastor, Abofarag visited the Egyptian evangelical communities around Sudan, and reported to the Church in Egypt about the growing ministry. He could see the spiritual and social needs of the people and wanted to involve the Synod in providing as much care as possible.[2] On the other hand, his main concern as a pastor of the Khartoum Church was to complete the church building that Hanna started.[3]

Abofarag was based in Khartoum but also travelled to other cities. In his travels, he was encouraged by the number of evangelicals he found and by their desire to receive spiritual care. In Port Sudan, eighteen Christians of Egyptian origin had managed to buy a piece of land for a church building, despite their limited finances. He reported stories of sacrificial donations by members of the churches in Khartoum, Umdorman, and Khartoum North[4] to the costs of ministry in Sudan, and the completion of the church building in Khartoum. Evangelicals in Sudan also gave money for the medical ministry of the American Mission, to buy medicines for poor Sudanese people.[5] Abofarag organized and participated in all these tasks, while trying

---

1. Synod of the Nile, *Minutes of the Year, 1910*, 184. It is interesting to notice that the first two ministers to Sudan, Hanna and Abofarag were called "missionaries" by the Synod. Those who went after them were called "pastors" if they were ordained or "evangelists" if they were seminary graduates and not yet ordained.

2. Synod of the Nile, *Minutes of the Year, 1910*, 220.

3. Synod of the Nile, *Minutes of the Year, 1911*, 264.

4. During the first decades of the twentieth century a number of Egyptian families immigrated to Sudan where they found jobs, bought property, integrated into Sudanese society, and became Sudanese nationals. Many of these families were from the Evangelical Church and became the nucleus upon which the Evangelical Church in Sudan built its membership. The native Sudanese were not considered in the membership of the Evangelical Church in Northern Sudan.

5. Synod of the Nile, *Minutes of the Year 1911*, 264.

to fulfil the job, which the Synod had assigned him: to serve as a pastor for the Khartoum Church.

His missionary trips were very time consuming, and left him little time for his pastoral work. He had a missionary's heart, and was called by the spiritual and social needs of the country. He noticed that many graduates of the American Mission schools in Egypt were scattered all over the main cities in Northern Sudan. These Christians were the nucleus upon which the churches in Sudan were built during the first half of the twentieth century. Although he targeted Egyptians with his ministry, he shared his faith whenever he had an opportunity with the Sudanese. Following Hanna's example, he contacted some Muslims who had converted to Islam during the Mahdi's movement but wanted to come back to the Christian faith.[6]

His reports were full of details about his trips to many cities in the North, South, and East of Sudan, where he found Christians who needed pastoral care, Christian education for their families, and the opportunity to worship with other believers. He noted that in many cities for months at a time, no pastors visited them, or preached God's Word or offered the sacraments.[7]

Abofarag's attempts to work as both a pastor and a missionary at the same time caused troubles with his church in Khartoum, which led the Synod to interfere in the situation. After negotiations between Khartoum Church, the Committee for the Work in Sudan and the Synod, he left his ministry as pastor in Khartoum and in 1910 moved to Atbara.[8]

After this move, Abofarag continued his missionary and pastoral activities. He reported to the Committee for the Work in Sudan concerning his missionary trips. On one occasion, he spent sixty-four days riding camels and visiting Eastern Sudanese cities such as Khadarief, Sabkha, Seenar and Wad Madani. His purpose was to encourage the evangelicals who lived in these remote areas. At the same time, he contacted native Sudanese and shared the message of salvation. He was accompanied by a Bible distributor and preached the gospel to many people while also collecting money

---

6. Ibid., 266.

7. Ibid.

8. Synod of the Nile, *Minutes of the Year, 1910*, 220. Atbara is a small city located north east of Khartoum on the Atbara River.

to build a church in Atbara. Another time, he travelled to Western Sudan. He was encouraged by the results of these evangelistic trips and planned to undertake more. Once again, he demonstrated his heart for mission, and neglected many of his pastoral responsibilities. This eventually led to difficulties with his church in Atbara.[9]

Abofarag valued his partnership with the American Mission in Sudan.[10] In his reports to the Synod, Abofarag praised the educational work of the American Mission and noted the number of students in their schools. He also took note of all mission efforts either by American missionaries or by Egyptians who shared in the Mission's work.[11]

He sought to help meet the ministry needs, giving a passionate presentation about the need for new workers, and trying to convince the Synod to appoint more missionaries. Anticipating their negative response, he suggested solutions to the difficulties, which the potential workers might encounter in their ministry, such as severe weather conditions and ill health.[12]

The Committee for the Work in Sudan also argued that more people were needed in Sudan and suggested ways to cover the costs of the work.[13] In 1910, the Synod replied positively to the requests of the Committee and approved the idea of sending two additional ministers to Umdorman and Atbara. However, there were no applicants. The Committee announced the need for workers to Sudan in the church paper, *Al-Hoda,* but there were no responses.[14] The Committee asked Dr Andrew Watson, who was in charge of the Seminary, to recruit students. Eventually, two applicants applied but they were not qualified for this ministry.[15] Despite the encouraging news

9. Synod of the Nile, *Minutes of the Year, 1911,* 295.

10. Synod of the Nile, *Minutes of the Years, 1909 to 1914* contained Abofarag's reports with many details about his ministry and Sudanese conditions. The reports were too long to be included in the Synod minutes which led the leaders of the Synod to ask him to summarize the main achievements and needs of his ministry (Synod of the Nile, *Minutes of the Year, 1911,* 266).

11. Synod of the Nile, *Minutes of the Year, 1911,* 260. For example, he reported that there was a school in Wad Madani which was run by an Egyptian teacher who spent most of his time in evangelism and Bible study for the people there.

12. Synod of the Nile, *Minutes of the Year, 1911,* 273–274.

13. Synod of the Nile, *Minutes of the Year, 1910,* 239.

14. *Al-Hoda* (1913): 274.

15. Synod of the Nile, *Minutes of the Year, 1910,* 239.

of the growth in the Sudanese ministries, the Synod was unable to recruit more ministers for service in Sudan, and had no recruiting or training programs to encourage people to take up this challenge.[16] Despite this lack of response, the Synod refused to consider anyone who was not a seminary graduate, because they were looking for pastors only, and not missionaries or evangelists.

When another complaint came from some members of the church in Atbara to the Committee for the Work in Sudan, the Committee delegated the matter to the Synod, asking them to decide whether to give Abofarag another term or to end his ministry.[17] After spending five years in Sudan trying to reconcile his mission vision with his actual job as a pastor, Abofarag resigned from his post in 1914. The contradictions between his missionary vision and the Synod expectations were too large to bridge. He returned to Egypt where he served as a pastor in Manfalut in Upper Egypt until he died in May 1958.[18]

5.3 Organizing the Work in Sudan

American Mission in Egypt originally directed the work in Sudan, but after the American Mission in Sudan was formed in 1905, it took over the responsibility. The Synod also established a committee for the work in Sudan in 1900. After the growth of the work among Egyptians in the North, there was a need to organize the evangelical churches in Northern Sudan under one body. This decision shaped the work in Sudan considerably since the Synod, Committee, Mission, and Presbytery seldom worked together in harmony.

5.3.1 The Establishment of the Sudan Presbytery: Was It a Solution or a New Problem?

The news of the problems in Khartoum Church and the need to organize the work in Sudan pressured the Synod to become more involved.[19] In 1911, the Synod sent two pastors to visit Sudan to investigate the

---

16. Synod of the Nile, *Minutes of the Year, 1911*, 273.
17. Synod of the Nile, *Minutes of the Year, 1914*, 19–20.
18. Synod of the Nile, *Minutes of the Year, 1959*, 48.
19. Synod of the Nile, *Minutes of the Year, 1911*, 273–274.

situation. They spent a month there and met with the members of the church, while also visiting evangelicals in other places on their way to and from Khartoum. They realized that there was a need for more workers to respond to many ministry opportunities in other parts of Sudan. Because of their visit they suggested that the Synod ask its minister in Sudan, the ordained American missionaries, and the elders in the Khartoum Church to join together to establish a new presbytery called the Sudan Presbytery. This new presbytery would take responsibility for directing the evangelistic work in Sudan by appointing ordained and lay workers to address the ministry needs. They also suggested that the presbytery should meet its own financial needs through collections from the Khartoum Church and other churches at Atbara and Port Sudan. The financial needs of other workers and evangelistic work could then be supplied through the Synod and the American Mission in Sudan. The Synod members concluded with the suggestion that the appointment of ordained workers should be done through the Committee for the Work in Sudan but that other lay workers could be appointed by the new presbytery.[20]

At its annual meeting of 1912, the Synod appointed a committee to study these suggestions and then give the Synod details of the formation of the new presbytery. The Synod accepted the report of that committee and decided,

> That this presbytery contains cities and provinces which exist in the Upper Egypt Presbytery and that under it come the churches and meetings of the United Presbyterian Church in these cities . . . This means that this presbytery consists of the churches and evangelistic centres in all the provinces and governates of which now known as Anglo-Egyptian Sudan. That the members of this presbytery come from the American ordained missionaries sent by the United Presbyterian Church of North America, the Egyptian pastors, and the elders who live in Sudan. That the first meeting of this presbytery be held at the Evangelical Church in Khartoum on 21st March 1912. The head of the presbytery in its first meeting will be Dr Kelly

20. Synod of the Nile, *Minutes of the Year, 1912*, 312–313.

Giffen following the United Presbyterian procedures in forming presbyteries. That this presbytery is going to be the fifth
presbytery of the Synod of the Nile enjoying all rights and
advantages of other presbyteries.[21]

This step established an official relationship between the Synod and the
church in Sudan and laid out the main characteristics of its future work.
As one of the Synod of the Nile presbyteries, the Sudan Presbytery would
send delegates and an annual report to the Synod meetings. This decision
also clearly established that the role of the Synod and its workers was to
take care of the churches and pastor the Protestant community. The Synod
through the Sudan Presbytery was allowed to build new churches and send
pastors, but the mission work was in the hands of the American Mission.
No mention was made of the native Sudanese or ministry among them,
all the focus was on the Protestants of other nationalities, most of whom
were Egyptian and Syrian. The Synod was also concerned to secure the
financial support for the ministry in Sudan from the local churches and the
American Mission.[22]

The General Assembly of the United Presbyterian Church of North
America was informed of the new presbytery, and the problems of the
church in Khartoum were reported. In their minutes of a 1912 session, the
Board of Foreign Mission noted:

> In Northern Sudan, great damage resulted to the cause through
> a serious church dissension which occurred in the Khartoum
> congregation. Happily, the causes of that dissension now seem
> to be removed and harmony is being restored. Prayer should
> be offered on behalf of the troubled work, that its losses may
> now be speedily retrieved by more earnest effortc [sic] in the
> days to come.[23]

---

21. Ibid., 324–325.

22. Warner, *Day of Devastation*, 233.

23. UPCNA, *Minutes of the Fifty-Fourth General Assembly of the United Presbyterian Church of North America, Seattle Wash. May 22 to 29, 1912*, Vol. 13, no. 1 (Pittsburgh: United Presbyterian Board of Publication, 1912), 59.

The General Assembly also added the new presbytery to the list of Presbyteries of the Synod of the Nile.[24]

The establishment of the Sudan Presbytery was a declaration that the Synod wished to only undertake church work in Sudan. Church policies and management interested the Synod more than the mission work, and they preferred to focus on forms of ministry with which they were comfortable. The Synod was already struggling financially, and did not want to cover the financial costs of the work in Sudan or lessen its resources of labours.[25]

The establishment of the Sudan Presbytery, which added another governing body to the ministry in Sudan, was an occasion to review and re-form the relationships between all wings of the ministry that included the Synod, the Sudan Presbytery, and the American Mission. However, the different bodies had different agendas, and their relationships were often marked by conflict and miscommunication.

5.3.2 The Relationship between the Synod and the American Mission in Northern Sudan 1900–1956

The American Mission in Sudan played an important role in the formation of the Egyptian ministry in Northern Sudan. The relationship between the Mission in Sudan and the Synod of the Nile between 1900 and 1956 underwent many changes. These can be divided into three different phases, each of which needs to be examined.

5.3.2.1 The beginning (1900–1912)

From the beginning of the work in Sudan in 1900, the Mission had hoped that the Evangelical Church of Egypt would eventually take primary responsibility for the Sudanese fields. The Mission explored the field, established the strategies, and created opportunities for Egyptian ministers to assist them in beginning a ministry among the Egyptians in Sudan. However, the American Mission in Sudan was dissatisfied with the Synod's work in Sudan, stating in 1911:

---

24. Ibid., 276.
25. Warner, *Day of Devastation*, 233.

We urge upon the Synod of the Nile the necessity of more rigorously prosecuting the Evangelistic work in the Sudan, which we consider is theirs to be done, and that the responsibility rests with them to do it, and that we regret the Synod has not been going forward, but rather back, in their work in the Sudan. And further, that the Secretary be instructed to furnish the representative from Egypt with a copy of the above resolution, and to elaborate the thought that prevailed, "that the Egyptian Church should overtake the evangelistic work of the Sudan."[26]

During this period from 1900 to 1912, both the Mission and the Synod were just beginning to work together in Sudan. Each side had great expectations of the other. On the one hand, the Mission hoped that the Synod would become a sending body and give priority to evangelizing Sudan. On the other hand, the Synod hoped that the American Mission would support the financial needs of the work in Sudan and help the Synod as ministry partner.

5.3.2.2 Time of tension (1912–1938)

After the establishment of the new presbytery in Sudan, relationships changed. The Mission recognized that the Egyptian ministers intended to concentrate on their work among Egyptian evangelicals rather than reaching out to the Sudanese. The Mission wanted to help the Synod to change its focus to evangelistic work, while the Synod wanted the Mission to take greater accountability for the financial costs.

The period from 1912 to 1938 was thus a time of tension since there was no clear agreement on how to work together. On many occasions, the American Mission in Sudan criticized the Synod and its ministry in Sudan while it was quick to praise any instances of greater involvement. For example in 1913 when the Synod sent more ministers the American Mission in Sudan supported and encouraged the ministers:

The Secretary was directed to write to the Synod of the Nile, first of all to thank them for the three most excellent men sent

---

26. Sudan Mission Association, *Minutes of the Year, 1911*, 12–13.

to the Sudan during the past year, and to assure them of the splendid work they are all doing. We are proud of such men, for they are powers in the propagation of the Gospel. The Secretary was also directed to present the need to the Synod and the opportunity now afforded for doing effective work both among Egyptians and Sudanese; to set before Synod the almost hopeless inadequacy of the workers on the field, and to assure it, that contrary to the popular belief in Egypt, the Sudanese are ready to listen to the Gospel if presented to them in a kindly spirit.[27]

Understanding the great mission potential of Sudan, the Mission asked the Synod to cooperate with it in evangelistic work.[28] The negotiations between the Mission in Sudan and the Synod took more than three years after the establishment of the Sudan Presbytery before the Synod agreed to cooperate in any evangelistic endeavours.[29]

In 1915, the Mission in Sudan had proposed that all the organized churches in Sudan should come under the authority of the Sudan Presbytery and that the non-organized churches and evangelistic stations should be put under a joint committee that would represent both the Sudan Presbytery and the American Mission. After discussions, the American Mission in Sudan informed the Synod of the proposal they had made with the approval of the General Assembly of the United Presbyterian Church of North America. However, the joint committee proposal was postponed for twenty-six years because both the Mission and the Synod managed their ministries without forming such a committee.[30]

During the years between 1912 and 1938, there were signs of cooperation in some aspects of ministry. When the Synod could not cover the salaries of its ministers, the American Mission helped provide financial

---

27. Sudan Missionary Association, *Minutes of the Year, 1915*, 12. Also the American Mission praised the work of the Egyptian pastors in its reports of *1929*, 192; *1931*, 276; *1938*, 10; *1939*, 21; *1943*, 6. In other years the Mission regretted that the Evangelical Church neglected the work in Sudan as exampled in the minutes of the American Mission in Sudan of the years *1911*, 13; *1919*, 23; *1944*, 5.

28. Synod of the Nile, *Minutes of the Year, 1914*, 2–3.

29. Ibid., 42.

30. Sudan Missionary Association, *Minutes of the Year, 1938*, 10.

support for the Egyptian pastors.[31] On another occasion, the American Mission provided the annual salary of Rev Tobia Abdelmasih, pastor of the Khartoum Church, because he was a Muslim convert and active in Muslim evangelism.[32]

The Evangelical Church in Egypt also helped the American Mission by providing it with members to work in the schools and evangelistic stations.[33] In 1932, the American Mission closed the school in Khartoum because of the lack of finances. The Khartoum Church rented the building from the Mission and reopened the school.[34] After extensive negotiations between the Mission in Sudan, the Board of Foreign Mission, and the Sudan Presbytery concerning the issue of paying rent for the building, the Board finally gave the school to the church in Khartoum.[35]

5.3.2.3 Time of cooperation (1938–1956)

In 1938, the joint committee to supervise the relationship between the Sudan Presbytery and the Mission in Sudan was finally formed. This committee contained four members from the Presbytery and four from the Mission, and allowed members of the Presbytery to attend the Mission Association meetings to have better explore ways of working together.[36] It especially sought to facilitate cooperation in educational and evangelistic work.

The period from 1938 to 1956 was a time of cooperation, with the two bodies working closely together. The Mission and the Synod, represented in the Sudan Presbytery, worked in different areas. The Sudan Presbytery had its own evangelistic committee that oversaw the evangelistic work in new stations and the work among non-Christians. The Mission offered to pay all the financial costs of the work among non-Christians that included the salary of a minister to work among Muslims.[37] They also cooperated in

---

31. Sudan Missionary Association, *Minutes of the Year, 1921*, 44.

32. UPCNA RG 209-14-5: Shields, Ried F. Papers: Reed to Mr. Shields, dated 7 July 1931.

33. Sudan Missionary Association, *Minutes of the Year, 1919*, 8.

34. Warner, *Day of Devastation*, 328.

35. Synod of the Nile, *Minutes of the Year, 1940*, 103.

36. Sudan Missionary Association, *Minutes of the Year, 1938*, 10.

37. Sudan Missionary Association, *Minutes of the Year, 1943*, 13–14.

many other fields, working together in schools, Bible Women's ministry, adult literacy classes, and social services.[38] There were joint subcommittees from the Mission and the Presbytery to handle these ministry activities.[39] This cooperation resulted in an increased number of evangelistic centres and ministry among natives. This close relationship united the Mission and the Presbytery in their dealing with the government and the Sudanese community. They finally came to an agreement concerning strategies and methods of ministry. The tone of criticism and recrimination became softer and cooperation dominated the relationship.

5.3.3 The Role of the Committee for the Work in Sudan

In 1900, the Synod had established a committee of pastors, elders, and American missionaries to oversee the work in Sudan.[40] They reviewed the work in Sudan, and discussed its problems. The Synod wanted the Committee to take the responsibility of collecting donations from Egyptian churches and individuals for the work in Sudan. In response, the Committee on one occasion visited local churches in Egypt to raise the needed financial support.[41] The Committee for the Work in Sudan had an important role during the early years, but after the Khartoum Church was established, and the Sudan Presbytery recognized, the role of the Committee was questioned. From 1912, the annual Synod minutes record two reports; one from the Sudan Presbytery and the other concerning the Committee for the Work in Sudan. The Synod was unwilling to deal with the relationship between the two. Meanwhile, the Sudan Presbytery could not act as an independent body like other presbyteries in Egypt but needed the approval of the Committee. No longer involved in recruiting and sending new members, the Committee tried to interfere in other spheres of the ministry.

The Sudan Presbytery recognized the duplication between its role and that of the Committee. They therefore asked the Synod to let it take the evangelistic work under its own supervision. In the Synod meetings of

---

38. Adult classes were held to help in teaching adults literacy through Bible stories.
39. Sudan Missionary Association, *Minutes of the Year, 1943*, 14–15.
40. Synod of the Nile, *Minutes of the Year, 1901*, 9.
41. Synod of the Nile, *Minutes of the Year, 1903*, 63.

1913 and 1919, the role of the Committee was questioned, but nothing was done.[42] At a Synod meeting in 1920, one of the ministers in Sudan explained the situation as experienced by the Sudan Presbytery. He asked the Synod to give the Presbytery full authority over its evangelistic work, including the recruitment of ministers and their appointment to either churches or stations as needed. He also said that the Sudan Presbytery should be responsible for their salaries, vacations, and ministry.[43] This request meant that the Committee could be annulled. At the same meeting, the Committee for the Work in Sudan also asked the Synod to take steps to resolve the relationship between the Presbytery and the Committee.[44]

In 1921, the Synod decided to dissolve the Committee for the Work in Sudan and delegate its work to the General Evangelistic Committee.[45] This step meant that the Synod began to treat the Sudan Presbytery as any other presbytery in the Synod. This also meant that the Synod no longer considered Sudan as a foreign missionary field. Instead, ministry in Sudan was viewed as normal pastoral and evangelistic work and the missionary vision of work in Sudan was disregarded.

The work in Sudan was placed under the supervision of the General Evangelistic Committee until 1933. The ministry in Sudan, however, was experiencing severe disruption and difficulty during the early 1930s because government restrictions forced a great number of Egyptians to leave Sudan. The American Mission also withdrew some of its personnel and reduced their financial contributions including some of their support for the Presbytery's evangelistic ministry.[46] In response, the Sudan Presbytery asked the Synod to reappoint a committee for the work in Sudan,

---

42. Synod of the Nile, *Minutes of the Year, 1913*, 345; Synod of the Nile, *Minutes of the Year, 1919*, 253.

43. Synod of the Nile, *Minutes of the Year, 1920*, 260.

44. Ibid., 270.

45. Synod of the Nile, *Minutes of the Year, 1912*, 330. The General Evangelistic Committee was established in 1920 to oversee the evangelistic work in the Synod. It had the responsibility of placing pastors in churches, licensing new ministers, and recruiting new students for the seminary. It organized sub-committees in every presbytery including the Sudan.

46. Synod of the Nile, *Minutes of the Year, 1933*, 459.

to be in direct contact with the Sudan Presbytery to share with it the responsibility in choosing and hiring the workers who have a special tendency and a real desire for work; those who have spiritual gifts and body strength to be suitable for the conditions of the ministry which are different than the conditions in Egypt.[47]

The Synod refused to reappoint the Committee for the Work in Sudan saying that the General Evangelistic Committee should continue to be responsible for the ministry in Sudan.[48] In 1934, the Sudan Presbytery repeated its request to the Synod and sent a letter explaining the needs of the work in Sudan. They asked the Synod to give more attention to the work in Sudan especially among Muslims. They also asked the Synod to increase its financial contribution towards the salaries of the ministers and their travel expenses. The Synod responded to the request and appointed a new committee for the work in Sudan. Gabra Hanna was appointed as the head of this committee.[49]

The relationships between the new Committee for the Work in Sudan and the Sudan Presbytery remained unclear, with each side unsure about the role of the other. The Committee wanted to be consulted by the Presbytery before they appointed pastors or moved them from one church to another; while the Presbytery wished that the Committee would allow them to carry out its work as any other Synod presbytery, believing that there was no need for a second body to manage the actual work in Sudan.[50] This conflict again demonstrated the Synod's indifference to the real needs in Sudan, and again raised the issue of whether the Synod's role in Sudan was pastoral or missional. If it was merely pastoral then there was no need for a committee to follow the work. However, if the Synod wished to be engaged in mission, then they needed to organize a mission board. If the Synod considered Sudan to be a mission field then they needed to direct more work among native Sudanese and Muslims. Rather, the Synod remained unclear about its role and its vision for Sudan.

---

47. Ibid.
48. Ibid.
49. Synod of the Nile, *Minutes of the Year, 1934,* 504.
50. Synod of the Nile, *Minutes of the Year, 1941,* 209.

The new Committee for the Work in Sudan continued its routine work, and conflict with the Sudan Presbytery continued until 1953, when a new door was opened to send an Egyptian missionary to Southern Sudan. At this point, the Committee named itself the Egyptian Mission Council, expecting that they should be responsible for this new initiative.[51] Meanwhile, they asked the Synod to place the work in Northern Sudan completely under the jurisdiction of the Sudan Presbytery.[52]

5.4 The Characteristics of the Work in Sudan 1912–1956

The character and methods of ministry in Sudan underwent numerous changes in the years after the establishment of the Sudan Presbytery in 1912, until 1956 when the country of Sudan announced its independence. During this period, political changes in Sudan also directly and indirectly influenced the ministry.

5.4.1 Ministers and Ministry Expansions

The number of ministers sent from the Synod of the Nile to Sudan did not increase as hoped. There was only one minister in Khartoum until 1914 when the Synod sent three other ministers: one ordained pastor and two evangelists.[53] The number of ministers rose gradually until 1920 when there were four ministers working with the Synod, two of whom were pastors.[54] By 1923, there were three pastors,[55] in 1932, there were five,[56] and from 1935 until 1956, six pastors were ministering in Sudan.[57] At the same time, other Egyptian evangelists were working with the American Mission

---

51. Synod of the Nile, *Minutes of the Year, 1955*, 67.

52. Synod of the Nile, *Minutes of the Year, 1957*, 277. See next chapter for more details of the work in Southern Sudan and the development of the Egyptian Mission Council role.

53. Synod of the Nile, *Minutes of the Year, 1915*, 47.

54. Synod of the Nile, *Minutes of the Year, 1920*, 284.

55. Synod of the Nile, *Minutes of the Year, 1923*, 379.

56. Synod of the Nile, *Minutes of the Year, 1932*, 405.

57. Synod of the Nile, *Minutes of the Year, 1935*, 267; Synod of the Nile, *Minutes of the Year, 1956*, 106.

in different stations.[58] For decades, the work focused mainly on ministering to Egyptians and Syrians. The Sudan Presbytery Report of 1939 listed three elders in the Khartoum Church: one Egyptian, one Syrian, and one American.[59]

The ministers of the Evangelical Church targeted Egyptians who were living in the northern cities. Some of these stations grew through the years and started churches with their own pastors, such as at Wad Madani, Port Sudan, Khadaref, Halfa, Atbara, Obaied and Khartoum North. At the same time, there were other stations such as Kostey, Shendy, and Kewey, which also hoped to become churches, but because there were few Egyptians living there, the work was suspended.[60]

In 1940, the Presbytery reported that special emphasis was being given to work in very remote areas such as Shendy, Khadaref, Kareema, and Malakal. Some of the pastors undertook evangelistic trips of two to three weeks' duration,[61] travelling from place to place under very difficult circumstances.[62] Money and Christian publications were sent from Egypt to help.[63] On these trips, which were considered evangelistic endeavours, the pastors shared the gospel with both Egyptians and Sudanese; however, with few exceptions, the Egyptian Protestant expatriates remained the major focus of their ministry.[64]

5.4.2 Schools and Women's Ministry

As noted above, the Khartoum Church had a large school on its property that it directed in cooperation with the American Mission.[65] Other churches, such as those in Port Sudan, Shendy and Kareema, also operated schools. Most of these schools were meant to serve the needs of the Egyptian

---

58. Synod of the Nile, *Minutes of the Year, 1929*, 247; Synod of the Nile, *Minutes of the Year, 1933*, 459.

59. Synod of the Nile, *Minutes of the Year, 1940*, 101.

60. For more details of the progress of the ministry in these stations see the Synod of the Nile minutes and *Al-Hoda*, where one can often find news of the mission work there.

61. For example, in 1950 four pastors went for evangelistic trips visiting Khadaref, Kostey, Port Sudan, Shendy, and Kareema, Synod of the Nile, *Minutes of the Year, 1950*, 16.

62. At this time transportation depended on camels and some trains and steamers.

63. Synod of the Nile, *Minutes of the Year, 1940*, 101.

64. Synod of the Nile, *Minutes of the Year, 1945*, 142.

65. Synod of the Nile, *Minutes of the Year, 1934*, 502.

evangelical community while others were opened to native Sudanese from all backgrounds.[66] Although these schools were used by the churches to help the local communities, they did not flourish as the American Mission schools did. The Sudan Presbytery therefore requested that the Mission support these schools financially.[67]

The local churches also had women's societies that sponsored missionary activities among the Sudanese. The Synod minutes of 1943 listed three schools that had been opened due to women's initiatives among the Shilluk of the Upper Nile. In Nasser, the teachers were supported by the women's societies while they were teaching in the mornings and evangelizing in the evenings.[68] These activities had much potential but were often limited by neglect. These efforts were short-lived and never became widespread. The Synod did not support these initiatives financially, nor did they list them as active programmes in Sudan.

5.4.3 Political Situation

The Evangelical Church ministry in Sudan was further affected by the political, social, and economic developments within the country. Under the Anglo-Egyptian government, the church in Sudan had enjoyed stability. However, in 1924 the British quelled the beginnings of a Sudanese rebellion, and forced most Egyptians to withdraw from Sudan. This drastically reduced the membership of the evangelical churches in Sudan, and meant that many churches were no longer able to pay their pastors' salaries.[69] At the same time, the American Mission in Sudan was facing financial difficulties and could not afford to pay the salaries of the Egyptian Evangelists working in different stations.[70] These financial difficulties dominated the work in Sudan for many years. Every year during 1920s to 1940s, the Sudan presbytery would ask the Synod to raise its contributions for the work in Sudan. Generally, the Synod was unable to comply and would direct the presbytery to cover its own needs. In 1936 the relationship between

---

66. Synod of the Nile, *Minutes of the Year, 1940*, 101.
67. Synod of the Nile, *Minutes of the Year, 1942*, 58.
68. Synod of the Nile, *Minutes of the Year, 1943*, 57.
69. Synod of the Nile, *Minutes of the Year, 1933*, 419.
70. Ibid., 456.

Egypt and Britain was restored, Egyptian officials were allowed to return to Sudan, and church membership again increased.[71]

5.4.4 Work among Sudanese

Despite the lack of attention by the Synod, the work among Muslims increased from year to year in Sudan. The Synod minutes reveal that more Muslims were baptized in Sudan than in Egypt. This was because of the work of the American Mission in Sudan that sent their converts to the church for baptism.[72] In the 1940 report of the Committee of the Work among Muslims, the number of converts totalled thirty-nine, nine of whom were from Egypt and thirty from Sudan.[73]

Most of the Egyptian pastors did little to preach the gospel to Muslims. Tobia Abdelmasih and Bolies Refat were major exceptions, working together with the Sudan Presbytery and the American Mission to actively evangelize Muslims.[74] In the 1940s and 1950s however, some of the Egyptian pastors used the radio, literature, and education work to evangelize Muslims.[75]

On a few occasions, the Sudan Presbytery reported its desire to reach out to the native Sudanese. Awareness was increased during the 1930s and 1940s when the Sudan Presbytery asked its churches to establish evangelistic stations. In 1934 the Presbytery confessed its past neglect and failure to do mission and evangelism among the Sudanese. Suggestions were made to rectify this: personal work, clubs, women's ministry, and book distribution.[76] In 1942, the Presbytery report to the Synod again admitted to its failure and made suggestions for mission work. In response, individual churches were allocated specific geographical areas to manage as their

---

71. Warner, *Day of Devastation*, 328. In the 1950s, the political situation influenced the work of both missionaries and churches in Sudan. For more details about how the American Mission and the Synod were affected, see later in this chapter.

72. Synod of the Nile, *Minutes of the Year, 1944*, 102. In 1942, the Sudan Presbytery reported 150 baptisms by the American Mission in Sudan most of them from Southern Sudan but some were Muslim converts. Synod of the Nile, *Minutes of the Year, 1942*, 58.

73. Synod of the Nile, *Minutes of the Year, 1940*, 181.

74. See later in this chapter.

75. Synod of the Nile, *Minutes of the Year, 1956*, 106.

76. Synod of the Nile, *Minutes of the Year, 1934*, 502.

missionary fields. Some individuals visited these areas but this initiative did not develop into any organized programmes.[77]

5.4.5 Visitors from Egypt

Through the years, pastors from Egypt would visit Sudan for a variety of reasons. On many occasions, the Synod sent pastors to solve problems in churches.[78] On other occasions, ministers went to preach the gospel and to visit the churches to encourage and support them.[79] The time that these pastors and leaders of the Church in Egypt spent in Sudan strengthened the connections between the Church in Egypt and in Sudan. Reports in church papers or church presentations also helped to increase the Egyptian churches' interest in the work in Sudan among Egyptians.[80]

5.5 The Role of Egyptian Laymen and Women in Mission Work in Sudan

Some laypersons and pastors had a missional vision and continued to contribute to the mission work in Sudan, despite the general lack of missionary vision among most of the pastors who went to Sudan, and despite deficiencies within the system. The Synod and Sudan Presbytery were involved with numerous ecclesiastical issues which prevented them from meeting real needs; finances and administrative problems took the time and effort of the Synod; and unfortunately, mission work occupied only a minor place in the mind of the churches in Egypt and Sudan. Thus, the missionary endeavours of Egyptian lay people were separate from the organized church. However, individual churches became connected to the various mission efforts of some of their lay people; and some pastors persisted in

---

77. Synod of the Nile, *Minutes of the Year, 1942*, 28.

78. Synod of the Nile, *Minutes of the Year, 1941*, 17–19.

79. Synod of the Nile, *Minutes of the Year, 1936*, 13. Synod of the Nile, *Minutes of the Year, 1950*, 16.

80. One of these trips was by elder Metry Eldwairy who had many jobs in both the Synod and the American Mission, including being editor of *Al-Hoda*, founder of elders' and laymen's organizations, and secretary of the Sunday Schools in Egypt and Sudan. He wrote a series of articles for *Al-Hoda* in 1918, telling the story of his trip, describing the conditions and activities of the local churches and the varied ministries of the American Mission, and sharing his dreams for the work in Sudan.

reminding the Synod of its missionary call, in the midst of the administrative details that consumed them. Hanna, Abofarag, Tobia Abdelmasih and others had caught the missionary vision, but because of this faced difficult times as pastors and laymen.

5.5.1 Farouza Girgis

Farouza was a Bible teacher who had been sent from Egypt to work with the American Mission in Sudan. This was a work that suited Muslim communities, and could generally be undertaken by older women, often widows. Since this ministry had proved useful in Egypt, the Mission used the same strategy in Sudan. In Sudan, the Mission women, with the help of full-time workers from Egypt and a few from Ethiopia and Sudan, visited from home to home teaching literacy, personal and family health, sewing and cooking. Bible stories were included in the topics covered, in hopes of gaining an opportunity to present the gospel.[81]

The work among women in Sudan was very difficult. The American Mission proudly noted Farouza's role in teaching women and converting Muslims in the face of many barriers:

> For this purpose a Christian woman named Faruza Girgis was secured from Egypt. She came to the Sudan in 1917, the first Egyptian woman missionary to the Sudan. The woman missionaries had done a great deal of visiting in the homes, of course, but this was the first attempt at definite work in the harems. Mrs Giffen undertook to inaugurate it with Sitt Faruza [*sic*.]. They were welcomed by some Coptic and Abyssinian women whom they visited. The Sudanese who knew this white-haired woman that had so long walked among them were glad to have her come in for a visit. Many curious ones were pleased to have a visit from a foreigner . . . to see her close up . . . finger her clothes . . . ask about her strange customs . . . her freedom . . . her marriage . . . her husband's regard for her . . . her children. But to listen to her book . . . that was another matter. And to learn to read it? Allah forbid! How many days

---

81. Warner, *Day of Devastation*, 323–324.

they tramped through the streets, the burning sand, the grill-
ing heat, to one door after another . . . the women had gone
to a mourning . . . or to the river to wash . . . or on a journey
. . . or their husbands needed them. And so the missionaries
returned often to the Mission house without having gained
entrance to a single Sudanese home.[82]

Farouza had worked with the American Mission in Egypt. Later, when
the Mission in Sudan started a Bible Women's ministry, it recruited her to
join the work in Sudan. She was effective in her ministry and made good
progress in sharing the gospel and mentoring disciples who continued to
carry the same message. In one of the reports about the work in Sudan, the
United Presbyterian Magazine wrote about the influence of her ministry:

We are rejoicing in a letter received from Hafiz Effendi, a former Mohammedan who has become a Christian. He formerly
lived in Khartoum North, but a few months ago was transferred to Wad Medani. It was while he was living in Khartoum
North that he became interested in reading the Bible through
Sitt Firooza [sic.], our Bible woman, who was at that time
giving lessons to his wife. She directed him to Dr Giffen for
further instruction, and he read the Bible, together with other
books given him, taking it with him when he went to work
to read when he had spare time. He reports that he is meeting opposition at Wad Medani among his Mohammedan ac-
quaintances, but he rejoices that he has an opportunity to bear
witness before them to the power of Christ, and that he is
being kept in a wonderful way.[83]

This focus on evangelism was the main goal of the American Mission
in its early years in Sudan. Although the Egyptian pastors to Sudan at
the time were being torn in two directions by contradictory expectations,
and churches were struggling to meet financial needs, lay people such as
Farouza kept the vision and mission alive.

---

82. Shields, *Behind the Garden,* 103–104.
83. *The United Presbyterian,* June 9, 1921, 2.

5.5.2 Garas Khella

Garas Khella, who was ordained as an elder in the Khartoum Church in 1929, was another unofficial missionary.[84] When the Synod sent Swailem Sidehom as its first missionary pastor to Southern Sudan in 1953, Khella wrote to the church paper *Al-Hoda* supporting this mission initiative.[85] While there is no information about his work in Sudan, there are some hints in his articles that suggest his missionary activities. By sharing his own experience, he challenged the church to support and help the mission work in Sudan:

> I was so happy to know that the Synod has started its first mission steps by sending pastor Swailem to Malakal to preach among the Shilluk tribe. May the Lord continue his work and help you to send more missionaries. I want to write to you about me and the ministry here in south Malakal, blaming the Synod for not helping me but by prayer. I came here to "Yambio" in the "Niam Niam" region where they eat human flesh, and as I arrived, I called the Anglican pastor and started to learn the Zandy language, I met the Bishop at Khartoum who welcomed me. They invited me to preach in the church in English and to visit the Christian and the pagan families to preach to them the Gospel and to strengthen them. Finally, I want to remind you to pray for us and I promise to send you reports about God's work here [*sic.*].[86]

In another article, Khella urged the Synod and members of the Church in Egypt to donate as much as they could to the mission work that the Synod had initiated in Southern Sudan. He gave examples of what Swailem would need for his ministry – a fridge, a steamer, and a car – and was critical of the Synod for not making mission work a priority. He reminded the Synod that the schools, hospitals and orphanages of which they were so proud were not their own. They belonged to the American Mission, and if

---

84. Synod of the Nile, *Minutes of the Year, 1929*, 123.

85. The ministry of Rev Swailem Sidhom Hennein in Southern Sudan will be the subject of study in the next chapter.

86. *Al-Hoda* (1955): 152.

they were proud of them, they were like the slave who is proud of his master's children. He argued that the church needed to have its own children by giving to the mission work in Sudan.[87]

Khella was not a missionary sent by the Synod but an elder who happened to live in Sudan where he practised mission work. We do not know if he joined a known missionary organization, only that he was a Presbyterian Egyptian who considered himself a missionary of the church in Sudan. He also took upon himself the responsibility of encouraging the church to continue supporting and developing mission work in Sudan, while urging the church to give more care to its evangelistic work inside Egypt as well. In his articles, he further challenged the church to pray and fast for spiritual revival.[88]

5.5.3 Teachers and Workers with the American Mission

There were a number of workers in the mission field beside Farouza and Khella who had no official connection to the Synod. This included workers with the American Mission in Sudan and teachers in the Mission, government, and Church schools. The minutes of the American Mission in Sudan mention Egyptian workers who helped the Mission in its educational and evangelistic ministry. In 1919, the American Mission in Sudan reported on Egyptian workers in Southern Sudan:

> It is a very real pleasure to report that all of these men[89] have made good. The sending of one to Nasser was with considerable misgiving, as it was an experiment. The language was not his own and there would be no one of his kind there. The Egyptian dislikes being anywhere that he cannot have his own to associate with, and possibly that is human. But the missionaries at Nasser are unstinting in their praise of Daniel. He has shown an excellent spirit and readiness in the work.
>
> Scander, who was sent to Merowe has also an entirely new field. Dongola is a large province and around the old town of

---

87. *Al-Hoda* (1956): 316–318.

88. Ibid., 316.

89. He meant the Egyptian evangelists who were working with the American Mission in Sudan.

Dongola there are a good many Copts; but it was thought that at first, at least, to have him make his center at Merowe, as that is nearer a railroad and also the place of greatest commercial and political activity. He has from this point visited many other towns in the province and has been astonished with his reception from all the people, and their readiness to listen to the Word of God. Often he had to meet with the people in the streets or in the open, which is contrary to regulations here in the Sudan.[90]

These missionaries were working with the American Mission because they had a heart for missionary work. They represented a number of Egyptians who had a vision for mission work but could not exercise it within the official ministry of the Evangelical Church. Such people performed well when they were given a chance to act on their missionary vision.

The 1958 minutes of the American Mission in Sudan mentioned people who made a notable contribution to their work. Nasif Mansour, an elder of the Khartoum Church, was one such person. He worked in the government and travelled to different parts of Sudan. He established a new evangelistic centre in Shendy and the Christians there asked the Presbytery to send them a minister, offering to share in paying his salary.[91] Mansour also tried to recruit much-needed Christian teachers for the American Mission schools. He also contributed to the evangelistic and administration work of the churches.[92]

5.6 Mission-Oriented Pastors

Hanna and Abofarag were the pioneers in their ministry who tried to blaze a missionary path for the work of the Egyptian Evangelical Church in Sudan. The Synod however, emphasized pastoral work. Thereafter, most of the evangelical pastors from Egypt were involved in serving the pastoral needs of the Egyptian evangelicals and neglected the missionary needs of Sudan. The American Mission criticized this strongly, viewing it as an

---

90. Sudan Missionary Association, *Minutes of the Year, 1919*, 9.
91. Synod of the Nile, *Minutes of the Year, 1940*, 101.
92. Sudan Missionary Association, *Minutes of the Year, 1958*, 11.

un-Christian attitude and hoping to change it. A letter by an American missionary in Sudan explained his doubts whether a new pastor would undertake ministry among the Sudanese:

> The evangelist in Port Sudan, Hilmi Eff. Riskalla, is to be ordained soon. Opinions as to his fitness vary greatly but a majority of his brethren voted for his ordination. I think he has not done badly among the Christian community there but doubt his effectiveness – or even his desire – for work among the Sudanese. The Church there will not likely become a strong congregation but it has a wonderful opportunity as a missionary center. We ought to have a missionary located there.[93]

There were however, a few Egyptian pastors sent by the Synod who were mission-oriented. Few historical records of their ministries remain. However, since the American Mission made full reports, some records are available concerning those who had an association with the Mission and its programmes. This section will mention a few.

5.6.1 Tobia Abdelmasih

Tobia[94] had a Muslim Sudanese father and an Egyptian mother. As a young man, he encountered the American Mission and converted from Islam to Christianity.[95] He was sent to Egypt where he studied at Assiout College and then at the Evangelical Theological Seminary in Cairo.[96] In 1917, he was sent to Sudan where he worked with the Sudan Presbytery as a pastor in Umdorman, Wad Medani and Khartoum North. While in Umdorman, he would visit and talk with Muslims about his faith.[97]

One of the Egyptian evangelists who were working with the American Mission in Sudan reported the early efforts of Tobia's work among Muslims

---

93. PHS UPCNA RG 209-14-9: Shields, Ried F. Papers: Reid F. Shields to Rev Glenn Reed, dated March 14, 1950.

94. In some resources his name was written *Tubia* while in others it was *Toobia*. In this thesis we will refer to him as *Tobia*.

95. *Al-Hoda*, 1920, 85.

96. Charles Partee, *Adventure in Africa: The Story of Don McClure* (Grand Rapids: Ministry Resources Library, Zondervan Publishing House, 1990), 106–107.

97. Reid F. Shields to Milligan.

in *Al-Hoda*. He spoke about Tobia's evangelistic efforts, and of how he encouraged the converts to hold on to their faith during difficult times.[98] He remained constant in his work among Muslims, so that the American Mission in Sudan included his evangelistic ministry in its 1930 annual report:

> The Umdorman congregation is under the direction of the Rev Tubia Abd el Masih who is the only college and seminary trained black man in charge of a congregation in Africa north of Uganda. He is doing good work and is known and highly respected by the people of Umdorman – Mohammedan, Jew and Christian.[99]

Tobia also helped the American Mission in its work in Southern Sudan. In 1936, the Mission praised his work in Malakal where he was attending a meeting for Shilluk and Dinka, seeing it to be a great encouragement and inspiration to the growing church in the South.[100] They reported that his ministry inspired the Southerners when they realized that Christianity "belong[ed] to more than the white man."[101] The American Mission considered his ministry as an indirect contribution by the Evangelical Church of Egypt to the mission work of evangelizing Sudan, and of a pastor taking seriously his evangelistic responsibility.[102]

Tobia's devotion to the work among Muslims in Sudan did not arise from the vision of the Evangelical Church but from his personal background and his link with the American Mission. The Synod dealt with him as any other pastor when he was assigned to churches or received his salary. On one occasion, the Synod refused to pay some extra costs for his travelling saying that there was no money for things the Synod did not approve.[103] The Synod did not try to capitalize on his special skills and opportunities as a Muslim convert from a Sudanese background. They merely appointed him to their one paid position – that of church pastor.

---

98. *Al-Hoda*, 1917, 234.

99. Sudan Mission Association, *Minutes of the year, 1930*, 238.

100. Partee, *Adventure*, 107.

101. Sudan Mission Association, *Minutes of the year, 1936*, 5.

102. Ibid., 6.

103. Synod of the Nile, *Minutes of the Year, 1925*, 34.

Tobia linked himself with the evangelistic work of the American Mission, which helped him financially.[104] The Mission admired his contribution to the work among Muslims in Sudan. Although he pastored his people, he emphasized his role as evangelist among Muslims of Northern Sudan. Some years he was hired by the American Mission in Sudan to work as an evangelist and they paid his salary. The Synod permitted this because they did not have enough money to cover their financial responsibilities for the work in Sudan.[105]

In 1942, the Synod received a request from Bishop Gwynne of the Anglican Church in Egypt and Sudan asking them to release Tobia to serve with the CMS among native Sudanese. Tobia himself asked the Synod to grant him this opportunity.[106] He left his pastoral position in Khartoum North, and worked with CMS among the Sudanese people until 1952 when he returned to Egypt and worked as a pastor in El-Kanatyer north of Cairo.[107]

5.6.2 Bolies Ref'at

Bolies Ref`at was another Muslim who joined the American Mission school in Umdorman as a student and then as a teacher. In 1926, Tobia, who was pastor of the Evangelical Church in Umdorman at the time, sent news of Bolies' conversion to the Evangelical Church paper *Al-Hoda*. He reported that Bolies, who had the name Kamel before his conversion, had been baptized in February 1926. Three leaders of the American Mission had attended, including two missionaries in Sudan – Rev Giffen and Dr Sowash – and Samuel Zwemer who was on a visit to Sudan at that time.[108] Bolies then went on to study at the Evangelical Theological Seminary in Cairo and graduated in 1929. He joined the ministry as an evangelist in Sudan

---

104. Reed comments on Tobia's salary saying: "This salary for the Rev Tubia is on the way again from East McKeesport. They are sending $150 this time but as usual it is coming through the Board of Administration. I do not know whether you need to be informed of this, but I am doing it anyway just to be on the safe side." (Reed to Mr. Shields, dated 7 July 1931).

105. Synod of the Nile, *Minutes of the Year, 1920*, 284.

106. Synod of the Nile, *Minutes of the Year, 1942*, 19–20.

107. Synod of the Nile, *Minutes of the Year, 1953, 71*; Synod of the Nile, *Minutes of the Year, 1959*, 46.

108. *Al-Hoda* (1926): 228.

where he moved to different places such as Madany, Blue Nile region, and Al-Fing, sending news of his travel and ministry to *Al-Hoda*.[109]

Rev Bolies would go out into outlying villages around Umdorman and talk to people about his faith. He made his ministry mainly with Muslims "although" as he said, "this kind of work cannot be organized and shows up very slowly in statistics."[110] He made his contacts through distributing the Scriptures and was active in Bible teaching. He visited hundreds of men, talking to them about the Christian faith, and many others came to him as inquirers.[111]

Bolies started his ministry with the Sudan Presbytery and then worked full time with the American Mission.[112] The Mission viewed him as a unique minister:

> Rev. Boalos' [*sic.*] work is considered the most significant piece of work now being done in the area. The number of houses or groups where he makes regular visits is continually growing in number and in variety of class and character. His aptitude for finding and making opportunities for religious discussions and carrying it on without giving offence or provoking oppositions, enables him to naturally give a Christian message and he usually reads or relates a portion of Scripture.[113]

The Mission employed him as its worker among Muslims in Sudan for many years. In 1950, he asked the Sudan Presbytery to allow him to go back to his work as an evangelist among Muslims in Umdorman.[114] The Synod agreed that he could return to work under the Sudan Presbytery but that his position would be the same as any other pastor. The Synod further required that he accept work in any place the Sudan Presbytery demanded,

---

109. *Al-Hoda* (1932): 105, 112–113.

110. Reid F. Shields to Milligan dated November 7, 1931.

111. PHS UPCNA RG 209-21-53: Field Committee Handbook: Young Church Comes Forward: Foreign Missions Handbook 1947.

112. This move from the Sudan Presbytery to the work with the American Mission caused confusion in his relationship with the Presbytery. The conflict was about his salary, vacation, and to which authority he should submit. Synod of the Nile, *Minutes of the Year, 1944*, 125.

113. Sudan Missionary Association, *Minutes of the Year, 1943*, 19.

114. Synod of the Nile, *Minutes of the Year, 1950*, 16.

doing the proper work of a pastor. The Synod did not intend to use him as a full-time worker among Muslims. Instead, they asked him to give himself to the pastoral ministry and give some of his time to work among Muslims.[115] After discussions between the Synod, the Sudan Presbytery, and the Committee for the Work in Sudan, Bolies was finally appointed to work among Muslims in Umdorman while also giving time for pastoral work among Christians in the region.[116] He served in this capacity until his retirement and returned to Egypt in 1959.[117] Bolies is another example of a mission-minded pastor who faced a conflict between his calling, and the pastoral role available within the Synod.

5.6.3 William Mos'ad

William Mos'ad was a pastor of the Synod of the Nile that in 1956 sent him to the church in Umdorman.[118] During his ministry, he was committed to mission work especially among the Southern Sudanese. This was a rarity, since Egyptian pastors seldom ministered to the Sudanese, especially since most Christians in the North were of a foreign background even if they held a Sudanese nationality. Because of the political situation and the conflict in Southern Sudan, a large number of Southerners had emigrated to the North and lived in Khartoum, Umdorman, and other northern cities looking for safety and work.[119] A small number of evangelical churches in Northern Sudan ministered to these newcomers. William Mos'ad helped Southerners, establishing a night school in his church to teach them Arabic and the Christian religion.[120] He also welcomed them at worship, and his church helped support a Sudanese pastor to work among them.[121]

Mos'ad sent an article to *Al-Hoda* summarizing the conditions and needs of the Southern Sudanese who had immigrated to the northern cities. He described those living in Khartoum as friendly people who were

---

115. Ibid., 33.

116. Synod of the Nile, *Minutes of the Year, 1951*, 48.

117. Synod of the Nile, *Minutes of the Year, 1959*, 41.

118. Synod of the Nile, *Minutes of the Year, 1957*, 267.

119. The political situation in Sudan in the 1950s and 1960s will be the subject of study later in this chapter.

120. Salama, *Tarikh al-Kanysa al-Injilya*, 101.

121. *Al-Hoda*, 1957, 82–83.

always willing to help others, and who always called anyone, even strangers, "brother." However, he explained that they did not know whom they belonged to since they had suffered a loss of identity due to the war and displacement, and that this was the reason that the mission and churches were helping them regain their identity and learn how to serve society. There were immature believers among them, and alcohol addiction was widespread. Mos'ad reported that the churches were working to form an association to help these refugees whether they were Christian or Muslim. Mos'ad reminded the church of its responsibility towards them. He said that Christians should not blame them for what they did but rather help them to know Christ the Saviour. He reported that the Evangelical Church, the American Mission and the Anglican Church had started an evening school to teach them Arabic. He also suggested training new Southern leaders so that they could continue the ministry and help teach in their churches.[122]

Although most of the leaders of the Evangelical Church in Sudan were not involved in this ministry to the Southerners, and many churches did not welcome them, Mos'ad was a pioneer in helping and supporting them. Some missionaries noted his ministry among Southerners, reporting that he had encouraged Nuer and other young people from Upper Nile by gathering them together and organizing programs to serve their spiritual and social needs.[123]

As part of his work as a missionary to the Sudanese, Mos'ad helped in the translation of the Gospel of John into Northern Sudanese Arabic. This was one of several translations made into the various Sudanese languages. The few Egyptians who could help in such projects were mainly lay people or interested pastors.[124] Mos'ad also made many visits to the Nuba Mountains and Kordofan to minister to the Sudanese, and was one of the ministers who established the Evangelical Church in Obied. He reported on the celebration at which the Sudan Presbytery dedicated the new church, stressing that out of thirty-seven church members, three young men were ready to go to the Theological Seminary that the American

---

122. *Al-Hoda*, 1956, 449–450.

123. Warner, *Day of Devastation*, 464.

124. Persson, *In our Own Languages*, 18.

Mission had started in the Southern city of Mandary.[125] He persevered in his work despite many difficulties.

Mos'ad was passionate about his ministry, even though the Synod did not approve of his work. He blamed the Church in Egypt for not having a wider vision and plan for evangelistic and missionary work, saying that the Church involved itself in many activities but neglected the most important tasks of evangelism and planning to develop the field for this kind of spiritual work. He ended an article explaining his experience by praying that God would open the eyes of the church to recognize the needs and that a revival would come.[126]

After many years in the field, he came back to Egypt to pastor a church in the Minya Presbytery in 1981.[127] His work and ministry as a missionary pastor is a model of what an Egyptian pastor with a missionary vision could do, in spite of grave difficulties.

5.7 The Characteristics of the Work in Sudan 1956–1964

After World War II, the call for independence was heard clearly in Majority World countries. In 1953, the Anglo-Egyptian government agreed that Sudan could become self-governing in 1956. On 1 January 1956, Sudan became a completely independent country and a Sudanese government took control. The new government made rapid changes towards nationalizing every aspect of Sudanese life. At this time, the government took control of the schools and asked the missions to hand their property to the Sudanese.[128]

5.7.1 Ministry to Southerners in Northern Sudan

Prior to independence, one of the important political developments that had previously influenced the ministry of the Evangelical Church in Sudan was the immigration of the Southerners to Northern Sudan. The

---

125. *Al Hoda* (1961): 208.
126. *Al Hoda* (1966): 260–261.
127. Synod of the Nile, *Minutes of the Year, 1982*, 13.
128. Synod of the Nile, *Minutes of the Year, 1955*, 21.

hard economic and political situation in the South had led to waves of Southerners fleeing as refugees to northern cities such as Khartoum and Umdorman. In the 1950 report of the Sudan Presbytery to the Synod, the Presbytery informed the Synod of this migration. Some leaders of the Evangelical Church welcomed these people and established a number of activities, such as clubs, night schools to teach them the Arabic language, Sunday schools, Bible studies groups, and catechism classes. The church asked the Synod to increase its support to the Sudan Presbytery to cover the dire needs of the Southerners. Because of the ministry among these displaced Southerners, a number were baptized and they joined the churches.[129]

The Evangelical Church in Sudan thought that their limited resources were only enough to cover the needs of its original members, so some leaders did not encourage a growing ministry to Southerners. On the other hand, a small number of Egyptian pastors considered this new situation as an opportunity for the Church to fulfil its original vision to serve the Sudanese people. The American Mission in Sudan encouraged the Church to welcome the Southerners and helped in many aspects of ministry.[130] Because of the growing number of Southerners and the decline in the numbers of Egyptians, the churches underwent a transition period before including the Southerners in their membership and leadership.[131] This transition however, was a helpful preparation for the changes which national independence would bring.

5.7.2 The Separation of the Sudan Presbytery from the Synod of the Nile 1956–1964

Prior to Sudan's independence, the American Mission realized that nationalism would play a dominant role in the future of Sudan, and they prepared to hand over the Mission properties to the Sudanese. The Sudan Presbytery, however, was part of the Synod of the Nile and all its properties were in the name of the Synod. Before granting the properties to the Sudan Presbytery, the American Mission stipulated one prior condition: the Sudan Presbytery was to first attain full independence from the Synod of the Nile. It was

---

129. Synod of the Nile, *Minutes of the Year, 1950*, 16.
130. Synod of the Nile, *Minutes of the Year, 1957*, 267.
131. Warner, *Day of Devastation*, 464.

because once Sudan was nationalized, it was important that the Sudan Presbytery's relationship with Egypt be clarified. This also indicates that a lack of trust had developed between the Mission and the Synod, with the American Mission distrusting the Synod's priorities.[132]

The relationship between the Synod and the Sudan Presbytery came to an official end in 1964. With Sudan's declaration of independence all missionaries were evacuated from Southern Sudan and it became critical to give the Sudanese Evangelical Church complete independence from what was considered an Egyptian organization. The Sudanese government required that the Evangelical Church in Sudan be independent from both the Egyptian Church and the American Mission.[133] Although the Synod wanted the properties to be under its own name, the American Mission and the Sudan Presbytery insisted that the properties should be under the Sudan Presbytery only.[134]

After a long discussion in the Sudan Presbytery and after a request from the Evangelical Community Council in Sudan, which represented the Evangelical Presbyterian Church before the Sudanese government, the Sudan Presbytery requested full independence from the Synod. The Sudan Presbytery relayed the request to the Synod and in an emergency meeting in January 1964 attended by two of the Synod leaders, the Presbytery discussed the advice of the Evangelical Community Council in Sudan which read:

> The Evangelical Community Council in Sudan advises and has become completely convinced of the need and necessity of the independence of the Evangelical Presbyterian Church in Sudan from all the organizations which come under it from the Synod of the Nile in view of the independence of Sudan as an independent nation which has its own authority. So we advise the Sudan Presbytery to announce its independence at the nearest possible opportunity, and if possible in an emergency meeting of the Presbytery, and to announce the

132. Sudan Missionary Association, *Minutes of the Year, 1944*, 5.
133. Synod of the Nile, *Minutes of the Year, 1964*, 243–245.
134. Ibid., 244.

independence of the Evangelical Church in Sudan completely and consider the Presbytery as the highest religious authority for Presbyterian Evangelicals in Sudan without reporting to any other authority. The Presbytery should announce its openness to keep the friendly spiritual relationship with all Presbyterian churches all over the World and especially with the Synod of the Nile particularly in the spiritual cooperation and ministers' exchange and the ministry in all the fields of the spiritual ministry. All the members of the Council agreed on this advice. God leads you to the good of the Evangelical Church in Sudan.[135]

The Synod granted the Sudan Presbytery the right to accept the properties from the American Mission and to be the highest authority for the Presbyterian Evangelicals in Sudan. After the formation of the Evangelical Community Council in Sudan, the Sudan Presbytery decided that,

According to the desire of the Sudan Presbytery and the Evangelical Community Council and referring to the previous discussions which considered the Sudan Presbytery to be the highest religious authority for the Evangelical Presbyterians in Sudan with the rights to direct all the business and affairs with all freedom but at the same time to keep the friendly relationships between the presbytery and the Synod.[136]

The Synod then referred its future relationship with the Sudan Presbytery and this request to an ad hoc committee to discuss. The Committee decided to accept the request of the Sudan Presbytery and give full independence to the Sudanese Church. The Committee also transferred all churches, schools, and any other buildings that were under the authority of the Synod to the Sudan Presbytery. Financial support for the Sudan Presbytery was to continue for one year only, without any further support after 1964. The Committee agreed to maintain friendly and spiritual relationships with the Sudanese Church.[137]

---

135. Ibid.
136. Ibid., 245.
137. Synod of the Nile, *Minutes of the Year, 1965*, 30.

After 1964, the Synod no longer received official reports from Sudan and maintained contact only through the ministry of the Egyptian pastors who remained in Sudan. At the same time, the Synod opened the door for Sudanese students to study at the Evangelical Theological Seminary in Cairo in preparation for serving their people in Sudan.[138]

The Egyptian contribution to the ministry did not immediately cease with the official separation between the Synod and the Sudan Presbytery. They continued to provide leadership to the church in Sudan, with many Egyptian pastors continuing in their ministry for many years, while the Sudanese leaders slowly developed the skills to take over the full responsibility for leadership.[139] The relationship developed into a mature exchange between two equal bodies.[140]

5.8 Why Was It Difficult to Have Mission Work in Sudan?

The Egyptian Evangelical Church had been given an excellent opportunity to develop an extensive mission work in Sudan, which it failed to grasp. The role of the official church was minor, although some individual members contributed significantly on their own initiative. There were numerous reasons that led to this result. At the beginning, the Synod had been pressured by the American Mission to send workers to the field in Sudan.

---

138. The Evangelical Theological Seminary in Cairo has played an important role in teaching Sudanese students. Most of the native pastors in Sudan had their theological training in Cairo. The number grew in the 1980s and 1990s because of the increase in the number of Sudanese living in Egypt.

139. Warner, *Day of Devastation*, 508.

140. In recent years, Egypt received a great number of Sudanese refugees because of the civil war between Northern and Southern Sudan. The Egyptian Churches made a significant contribution towards the ministry to these refugees. Both the Anglican and the Presbyterian Church in Egypt organized different ministries to cover the physical and spiritual needs of the Sudanese in Egypt. A refugee organization was established by the Anglican Church and helped them concerning their legal matters, medical treatment, and employment. The Presbyterian Church started spiritual meetings for the Sudanese in many churches in Cairo, Alexandria, and other large cities. The Evangelical Theological Seminary in Cairo also opened its doors to train leaders for the Church in Sudan. For more details about the efforts towards Sudanese refuges in Egypt see Elizabeth Ferris, *Churches Reach Out to Refugees in Egypt*, World Council of Churches Office of Communication. http://www.wcc-coe.org/wcc/news/press/00/18feat-e.html (accessed on 2 April 2007).

The Church in Egypt had not planned to work in Sudan and therefore had not made any plans to continue sending its ministers to work as missionaries. Instead of having a clear missionary vision, the Synod considered the work in Sudan as a drain upon its financial and personnel resources. On many occasions, there were requests for people to go but very few ministers responded. The number of pastors could not cover the actual needs and many of them stayed for only a short time.[141]

The physical demands of life in Sudan also limited the number of pastors and evangelists. In the early years of the work, transportation from Egypt to Sudan and within Sudan was arduous and complicated. The trip from Egypt to Sudan took many days by train, river, and camel. In later years transportation improved from Egypt to Khartoum but inside Sudan there were very few navigable roads connecting Sudanese cities. Hot weather, wild animals, snakes, and insects also presented challenges. The prevalence of numerous diseases and the lack of electricity, running water and health care facilities also made life difficult. The pastors and workers could find some services in the large cities but in small towns and villages, conditions were quite primitive. In many articles in *Al-Hoda*, workers in Sudan and church leaders who had visited tried to give a better picture of the life in Sudan, hoping to encourage others to go and serve.

The monetary shortage that the Church in Egypt habitually experienced throughout its history was another major reason for the unenthusiastic response of the Synod to the mission in Sudan. In its early years, the church was struggling to gain its own financial independence from the American Mission. Most of its resources were directed to cover the costs of the organized churches, the Synod schools, and the pastors' salaries and pensions. They were already unable to support the evangelistic work and the non-organized churches within Egypt, meaning that these ministries had to be supported by the American Mission. There were thus only very limited funds available to support the work in Sudan. Although the Committee for the Work in Sudan received annual contributions from the Egyptian presbyteries, it was directed to cover just the Synod's share of the salaries of the pastors in Sudan. When there was a need to build a church or to

---

141. After Hanna and Abofarag there were a number of ministers who went to Sudan but they only stayed for few months and then returned to Egypt.

support a school in Sudan, the Committee for the Work in Sudan and the pastors of the Sudan Presbytery urged the churches to give for these projects. The Egyptians gave as much as they could, but the costs were beyond their abilities. The entire support came from wealthy individuals and local churches, but not from the institutional Church body. The Synod was not ready to support the mission work from its general budget and did not have a special budget for its work in Sudan.

Although the Mission wanted the Synod to eventually consider the Sudan as its own foreign mission field, the Mission initially took responsibility for evangelizing the Sudanese while leaving the Synod to minister only among the Egyptians. The Synod was content to limit their Egyptian ministers to a pastoral role in Sudan. Both the Synod and the Mission misunderstood each other's roles and intentions, which led them to criticize each other rather than cooperate. This tension reached its peak in 1964 when the Mission asked the Sudan Presbytery to request its independence from the Synod in order that the Mission properties could be transferred to the Presbytery.

The Synod did not handle the administrative work in Sudan well. The Committee for the Work in Sudan suffered from its unclear mandate, especially after the establishment of the Sudan Presbytery in 1912. The Synod had established the Sudan Presbytery because it viewed the task in Sudan as pastoral; however, the Committee's task of raising funds and recruiting ministers shows that the Sudan Presbytery had special needs and differed from other presbyteries. Thus, the position of both the Committee and the Presbytery were ambiguous. The conflicts between the two bodies led to the dissolution of the Committee in 1921, but after the departure of many Egyptians from Sudan in the 1920s and 1930s caused financial hardships, the Presbytery asked for the Committee to be re-established. Even then, conflicts continued between the two bodies because the Synod did not have a clear missionary strategy.

The majority of Egyptian pastors concentrated their work among the Evangelical Egyptians who had emigrated from Egypt as well as the Sudanese of Egyptian origin. It was not until the 1950s and 1960s when a large number of Southerners fled to the North, that their ministry began to target the needs of the Sudanese. Churches struggled with the impact, finding it difficult to welcome the newcomers among its numbers. Pastors who wanted to minister to them organized night classes and meetings that were held separately from regular church meetings. These problems affected the church for many years and built a wall of separation between the Sudanese Christians and the Egyptian or Egyptian-Sudanese within the Presbyterian churches:

> The Evangelical Church was an Egyptian dominated Church, but its Presbyterian Church order made it familiar to those connected to the American Mission and the Presbyterian Church of Upper Nile. In the late 1960s and early 1970s William Mussad and Wesley Istassy, Egyptian pastors of the Evangelical Church, were encouraging Nuer and other young people from Upper Nile to gather at the central church in Khartoum North. This relationship was not an easy one. Many of the Egyptian members of the Evangelical Church disliked the influx of black African Southerners. They recognized that they could easily be outnumbered and lose control of their Church. Many Southerners, therefore, felt frustrated, and considered that they were being discriminated against on racial grounds.[142]

The lack of mission training for the Egyptian pastors who went to Sudan also made the field experience very difficult for them. Most of them were either new graduates of the Seminary or pastors with experience only in pastoral ministry. Specialized training for mission work was not available through either the Seminary or the Synod. Because of this, most workers approached their ministry according to their pastoral experience and not as missionaries. Only a very few pastors had a true understanding of mission principles and practices.

5.9 Conclusion

The work in Sudan was an important opportunity for the Synod to develop an understanding of missions. The American Mission and a few other

---

142. Warner, *Day of Devastation*, 464.

individuals hoped that this new initiative could be the beginning of a mission movement and that the Evangelical Church would establish its own mission board. However, because this vision was held by individuals and not by the whole Synod, this hope remained unfulfilled. The Egyptian evangelicals were unable to find a way to take advantage of the mission opportunities before them. Mission-minded pastors and laymen and women made their own contribution to the mission work but with much pain in their relationship with the Synod, finding no room inside the official construct of the Church to practise their vision of mission ministry. Instead, they found other channels for service, joining either the American Mission or other mission organizations in order to fulfil their call.

The Committee for the Work in Sudan could have developed into a board for foreign mission. However, the Synod simply created the same kind of church structures that were in place in Egypt. In this way, the Synod lost its chance to have its own independent mission work.

Although the Evangelical Church in Egypt did not consider Sudan as a mission field, an exceptional change in practice occurred in 1953 when the Synod sent its first fully supported missionary to Southern Sudan. This remarkable action opened the possibility for the Synod to become a sending missionary organization.

CHAPTER 6

The First Egyptian Missionary to Southern Sudan and Kenya: Swailem Sidhom Hennein (1953–1970)

6.1 Introduction

The previous chapter examined the difficulties encountered by the Evangelical Church in developing a clear vision for mission work in Sudan, which resulted in a focus on pastoral work among Egyptians. In spite of these policies, a few exceptional individuals found a way to do mission work. The mission-minded pastors and laymen made significant contributions among the Sudanese, but it was not organized under the Synod. Although this was the case in Northern Sudan, important progress occurred when the Synod sent its first missionary to Southern Sudan in 1953.

In the 1950s and 1960s, the Evangelical Church experienced remarkable growth in its leadership and missions through a domestic spiritual revival and the use of new methods for reaching Egyptian society. The establishment of the Egyptian Mission to Southern Sudan was one of the great achievements of the Evangelical Church during this era. For the first time in its history, the Evangelical Church in Egypt sent and fully supported one of its ordained pastors as a missionary in Southern Sudan. The Church took financial, spiritual, and administrative responsibility and its work in Southern Sudan became an example of what a church in the Middle East could accomplish in cooperation with Christians around the world. This effort was closely coordinated with the American Mission of Egypt and Sudan, and displayed a productive and vital relationship.

The sending of Swailem S. Hennein stands as one of the most important actions in the history of the Egyptian evangelical mission because his ministry in Southern Sudan and Kenya influenced the Evangelical Church in Egypt and abroad. The Evangelical Church was inspired by this ministry and was consequently spurred to a revival of evangelistic effort.

Swailem was a model missionary who adapted to two very different cultures and to changes in mission practice; who served continually without complaint; and did so in a spirit of simplicity and integrity. He spent ten years, from 1953–1964, in the Upper Nile Province, mostly in Attar on the White Nile. This was followed by seven years in Kenya, where he was in charge of a major mission area. During this time, he also served as director of Limuru Conference and Training Centre.

6.2 The Church Preparation

After more than fifty years of sending pastors to Sudan to serve among the evangelicals who lived there, the Evangelical Church started to look at its mission in Sudan differently. The growth in theological teaching and their long-standing relationship with the American Mission in Egypt had slowly produced a different perspective and vision. The prior efforts of the American Mission in the South of Sudan had led to the establishment of the Upper Nile Presbytery in 1948.[1] The chairman of the presbytery of Northern Sudan, who himself was an Egyptian, went to share in the official celebration of the new Presbytery which was comprised of American missionaries as well as local leaders who had converted from tribal backgrounds to Christianity. While in Southern Sudan, the Rev Faried Manquarious recognized that the potential for missions was great among these tribes, and this inspired him to encourage the Church in Egypt to take the initiative in sending a missionary.[2]

In 1948, Donald McClure, the American missionary in Southern Sudan, visited Egypt and he invited the Synod to send missionaries to the South. In September 1948, the same invitation came from the Upper Nile Presbytery to the Synod. In March 1949, Rev Lawry Anderson, the American Mission

---

1. Synod of the Nile, *Minutes of the Year, 1948*, 60.
2. Ibid., 61.

chairman in Southern Sudan, visited Egypt with one of the local Sudanese elders, Adwok Mayoum, and they spoke to the Synod asking for Egyptian missionaries to work in the South. They left written requests asking the Synod to consider sending missionaries to Southern Sudan:

> We are encouraged by the interest members of the Evangelical Church in Egypt have shown in the evangelization of the South Sudan, and the desire of certain ministerial students to work here as missionaries.
>
> We would welcome all qualified Christian workers to serve with us as equal members in our mission.
>
> We invite the Synod of the Nile to take steps immediately to prepare and send such workers and to support them with money and prayers.[3]

The Synod of the Nile's Committee for the Work in Sudan asked the Synod to accept the invitation of the American Mission in Sudan to send a missionary, explaining that the time was ripe for such a venture. This was the first time that the American Mission in Sudan had asked for an Egyptian missionary to work in the Upper Nile region. Further, it was the first time for the Sudanese government to give permission for Egyptians to work and live in the South; and finally, the American Mission had offered to provide housing and other ministry benefits for the Egyptian missionary.

The American Mission at that time realized that the political situation in Southern Sudan was moving towards nationalization that would probably hamper future missionary work. They wanted to quickly open as many new stations as possible that could then be given over to Sudanese leadership. Realizing that the prevalence of the Arabic language was increasing, they wished to have more Arabic-speaking people to preach and teach. This led them to look to their Egyptian partners to cover this need.[4]

---

3. Synod of the Nile, *Minutes of the Year, 1949*, 116. This statement was delivered in front of the Synod in 1949 and was written in the Synod minutes in English. The minutes of the Synod usually were written in Arabic but the speech of Anderson was written and delivered in English at the Synod meeting.

4. Minutes and report of the American Mission Southern Sudan, First Annual Meeting, Doleib Hill, January 1949, 3.

A further reason given by the Committee for the Work in Sudan for the Church to start a new mission work in Sudan was that the Evangelical Church membership in Northern Sudan was declining. The number of members who were retiring from their jobs and returning to Egypt was higher than the number of newcomers moving to Sudan, which meant that action was needed to maintain the presence of their church in Sudan. The Committee suggested that the bulk of the financial costs for the new missionary work could be covered from the Committee budget, as well as donations from pastors and from the large churches that had a Sunday collection for missionary work. The remainder could come from the Synod budget.[5]

The Synod took four years to take action on this request. In 1952, Rev Iskander Abaskhairoun, who was the head of the Evangelistic Committee of the Synod, paid a visit to Southern Sudan to explore the field. Struck by the expansion of Islam and the spread of Arabic among the tribes, he realized the urgency of the situation.[6]

There were two obstacles facing the Synod: raising financial support and recruiting suitable personnel. The annual Conference of Ministers of the Evangelical Church held in Tanta in July 1953 chose the theme "The Missionary Task of the Church," and considered what should be done. The needs in Southern Sudan were presented, and when the issue of finances was raised, some local churches volunteered to give annually for this work. Many of these were small village churches who could give little; however, their example inspired many other churches and enough money was raised to send a missionary to Southern Sudan.[7] The American Mission in Egypt reported:

> The 1953 conference was unique in that it gave a new impetus to the missionary task of the church. The Rev Iskandar Abiskhairoun who visited the South Sudan the past year gave a stirring report and an earnest plea that the Synod of the Nile should send a lifetime missionary to the tribes of the South.

---

5. Synod of the Nile, *Minutes of the Year, 1950*, 23.

6. Elder, *Vindicating a Vision*, 334.

7. *Al-Hoda* (1954): 142.

Pledges were voluntarily offered by many pastors for their churches amounting to L.E. 264 annually in support of this new missionary enterprise. Following the conference the Rev Swailem Sidhom offered and was accepted to go as first missionary from the Evangelical Church of Egypt. He arrived on his new field of service the middle of November.[8]

Because of this new initiative in mission work, the Synod decided to establish a Council of Mission to follow the work in Sudan. This council had two main jobs: to raise money for the needs of the mission in Southern Sudan, and to look after the ministry of the missionaries there. By 1953, the Evangelical Church was ready to send its first missionary to Southern Sudan.[9]

6.3 The Missionary Preparation

Swailem Sidhom Hennein was born in a village in Upper Egypt in 1927 to an evangelical family. He attended a school at the nearest town, Dairmawas, where there was an evangelical primary school. This school had been established by a rich evangelical man, Asaad Abd-ul-Mutajalli, and was under the supervision of the evangelical church.

After finishing his primary education, he studied at Assiout College.[10] During this time, he would travel with his college friends to minister in the surrounding villages. This ministry, along with his rural background, created in him a love of simple village people, which helped prepare him for his future career as a missionary.[11] He came to know American missionaries in Assiout, including Davida Finney whose vision was to serve rural areas in Egypt. Her ministry influenced Swailem and his colleagues and many of them decided to join the Seminary in Cairo, recognizing their need for training to meet the spiritual, social, and developmental needs of Egyptian

---

8. American Mission in Egypt, *Minutes of the Year, 1954*, 213.

9. Synod of the Nile, *Minutes of the Year, 1953*, 124.

10. Assiout College was for secondary education.

11. Most of the information in this chapter came from an interview with Rev Swailem Hennein in Cairo in 2004. There is little information about his ministry in the Church papers, Synod minutes or American Mission resources.

villages. This was a time of preparation in communicating with villagers and learning how to serve their needs.[12]

After finishing his high school studies at Assiout College, he joined the Evangelical Theological Seminary in Cairo in 1949, planning to become a pastor in the Evangelical Church. During his three years as a seminary student, Swailem was appointed to serve in a village church in Upper Egypt on the weekends and during the summer break. After finishing his studies in the Seminary, he continued studying while ministering in the same small village, and completed a BA degree in Social Sciences at the American University in Cairo. This curriculum exposed him to basic sociological research methods, which he applied in his study of the village where he was serving. Remembering this period, he said:

> So I concentrated my work on rural people: their agriculture, their cottage industries, and their family life. The focus of my work was dealing, and being involved with how to improve life in the village. At that time, it was clear to me that sanitation was very important, so also was hygiene and nutrition. It was not basically medical, but it was rather uplifting their own physical condition and helping it, while thinking more about how to improve their income.[13]

This study and research was a cornerstone in his preparation for the coming mission work. It opened his eyes to the impact of spiritual and social needs upon people. With his academic qualifications and practical background, Swailem attracted the attention of the Evangelical Church and the American Mission. In 1951, the Synod of the Nile and the American Mission jointly created a Committee of Applied Christianity, which Swailem was asked to join. The task of this committee was "to develop Community Centre work in connection with the churches."[14] He served for a short time on this Committee. That summer at the meeting of the American Mission Davida Finney suggested that Swailem should be

---

12. Synod of the Nile, *Minutes of the Year, 1953*, 124–125.

13. Swailem Hennein, interview by researcher, 5 March 2004, Cairo. See Appendix C.

14. American Mission in Egypt, *Minutes of the Year, 1952*, 81.

given the opportunity to study in India. The minutes record the decision of the Mission:

> We approve of the suggestion of Miss Finney that the Rev Suwailim Sidhom be given the opportunity of studying social work in India for three months in connection with his visit to that land as a delegate to the World Council of Churches Youth Conference in Travancore in December 1952, if adequate provision is made to cover his expenses, and if the Synod of the Nile approves. The Executive Committee will send its recommendation directly to the Board.[15]

The Board of Foreign Missions in America granted $600 for Swailem's study in India and to cover his travel expenses.[16] While travelling to India by steamer, Swailem stopped at Port Sudan where he sent a letter to Davida Finney describing the very needy, poor people he saw there. He was moved with compassion at their hard situation, but never thought that after only one year he was going to serve these people and be the first Egyptian missionary to Southern Sudan.[17]

During his time in India, Swailem received more experience in rural development. He found many similarities between the villages in South India with those back home in Egypt, which gave him practical insights that he would later apply. His time there was extended to one year of further study and research, in programmes organized by the YMCA Rural Training Centre in Martandam.[18] During the same period, he visited and attended programmes of the Dutch Reformed Church, Disciples of Mahatma Gandhi, and the Indian Government.[19] Swailem received cross-cultural training through his experience among other missionaries and students, and from living with the local Indian families. While studying in India, Swailem also found opportunities to minister among the Indians. He travelled to villages, preaching the gospel in English to communicate. During

---

15. Ibid., 112.

16. American Mission in Egypt, *Minutes of the Year, 1953*, 119.

17. PHS UPCNA RG 209-2-54: Davida Finney Papers: Sawilem Sidhom to Davida Finney dated 20 November 1952.

18. American Mission in Egypt, *Minutes of the Year, 1953*, 153.

19. Hennein, interview.

his years of study and service, he had improved his language, research, evangelism, and cross-cultural skills. His preparation was now complete and he was well equipped for the task ahead of him in Southern Sudan.[20]

The American Mission in Egypt had hoped that after his return from India Swailem would work with them on social service projects while also ministering to his local church in Qalandul.[21] The Minutes of the American Mission of the year 1953 reported:

> Rev Suwailim used the time before and after the Youth Conference in visiting work in Central India and in Travancore. He is due to return to Egypt the first of April. He is to remain with his church at Qalandul, and there experiment along the lines of his study in India. There is no thought in the present of asking Synod for release of Rev Suwailim from his Church. His own church and community furnish him with an ideal opportunity in carrying out Social Services projects. The Joint Committee is prepared to encourage and help him in whatever way it finds possible after he returns to Qalandul.[22]

Nevertheless, the American Mission was pleased when the Evangelical Church appointed Swailem to be its first missionary to the Southern Sudan. Although this appointment caused some delay in the social work projects of the American Mission, they appointed an Egyptian layman to take over this task as a full-time job. In order to relieve the Synod and Swailem from the costs of his study in India, the Mission requested the Board to pay these expenses, since his time of study in India would aid the new mission work in Southern Sudan.[23]

When Swailem had finished his studies in India in 1953, he returned to Cairo where he found that the Synod had already decided to send him to Southern Sudan. He asked the Synod for permission to travel to his

---

20. Ibid.

21. Qalandul is a small village near Mallawy in Upper Egypt, about 300 km. south of Cairo.

22. American Mission in Egypt, *Minutes of the Year, 1953*, 150.

23. American Mission in Egypt, *Minutes of the Year, 1954*, 229.

placement by steamer rather than by airplane in order to spend the time thinking and preparing himself for this new task.[24]

6.4 First Year in Southern Sudan

After spending about eight days travelling to Southern Sudan, Swailem reached the American Mission headquarters in Malakal, Southern Sudan. He spent a year in Malakal and Doleib Hill, learning the Shilluk language and a little Dinka, two of the local languages that he was going to use in his ministry. The American Mission in Southern Sudan appointed a local Christian, Paul Adiang Adholjok, to teach Swailem the language and to help him in his early mission tasks. Fortunately, Swailem learned the Shilluk language rapidly.[25]

During his first year in Southern Sudan, Swailem familiarized himself with the culture and tribal lifestyle. He found opportunities to do evangelism in the villages around and beyond Attar, the station where he stayed after the training year.

Rev Faried Manquarious, the chairman of the Egyptian Mission Council, wrote an article in *Al-Hoda* to tell the Evangelical Church about Swailem's first year of mission. He reported that Swailem had visited many places in Southern Sudan, learning about the cultures and traditions of five different tribes. He had learned the Shilluk language and made 350 village visits.[26] Moreover, he had visited the hospital and the prison, and had a ministry among the youth. Rev Faried Manquarious also noted Swailem's pastoral and evangelistic work that had included leading and preaching at a local church in Abwong, and the baptism of twenty-two members of the Dinka tribe. He had also helped people to improve their lives by teaching them agriculture and fishing skills. In addition, Swailem had taught the Bible and occasionally, geography, in the local school where he also trained a group of Christian leaders.[27]

---

24. Travailing by steamer was common in these years since there were limited airlines between Egypt and Sudan. (Hennein, interview)

25. Hennein, interview.

26. *Al-Hoda* (1954): 142–143.

27. *Al-Hoda* (1955): 26.

The chairman of the Egyptian Mission Council noted the difficulties that Swailem had faced, including the dangers of torrential rains and wild animals, such as snakes and scorpions. He praised the missionary and the quality of his work. He found in Swailem all the qualifications needed in a missionary, namely a sportsman's body, an open mind, an eager heart, a humble spirit, a good educational background, and even a dark skin close in colour to that of the Sudanese.[28]

After the one year of orientation in language, culture, and cross-cultural evangelism, Swailem went back to Egypt to marry Samira Shehata Rizk, to whom he had been engaged since before leaving Egypt for Sudan. While he was in Egypt, the Evangelical Church expressed pride in its missionary. The Church held several meetings to hear the news of his work in Southern Sudan. A number of articles were written in Church papers that encouraged the young missionary and challenged the Church to give prayers and money to help the mission in Sudan.

After their marriage, Swailem and his wife left for South Sudan. They had to remain in Khartoum for a while as they waited for government visas to travel to the South. While in Khartoum, they received the news that Samira's father in Cairo had died. Because of this, Samira found it difficult to continue their trip to the South. Many of their friends suggested that they should return to Egypt, especially since the visa was being delayed. This was a difficult choice, but they remained strong in their desire to serve the great needs of the Southern Sudanese, and with encouragement from the Church in Wad Medani they persisted in their plans. Once the visa arrived, they proceeded to the South to Attar, where the American Mission had a station. They were the only missionaries there.[29] Both Swailem and his wife were looking forward to working in the field assigned them.[30]

---

28. Ibid., 25–26.

29. *Al-Hoda* (1956): 447.

30. In his reports to the Synod, Swailem mentioned the ministry of his wife saying that she was their missionary. She also used to send ministry news to the church paper. See *Al-Hoda* (1956): 446–449.

6.5 The Role of the American Mission with the Egyptian Mission in Southern Sudan

As ministry partner of the Synod, the American Mission made its resources available to the Egyptian missionary, offering him a house and inviting him to join their team. The Mission also provided Swailem with training and orientation to the field in Southern Sudan. They knew the difficulties he would encounter at Attar. They also recognized the limited role that the Synod could play in supporting his work and sending other specialized missionaries.[31] The Americans realized that the Synod was still learning what part it could play, and what resources it would be able to supply.

In 1955, steps were made to clarify the relationship between the Synod and the American Mission and the Egyptian missionary. The Egyptian Mission Council, EMC, proposed that the Synod accept the suggestions of the American Mission in Sudan as to how to organize the work. The proposed items included:

1) At the end of the first two or three years of the missionary work, the American Mission takes the decision and advice if the missionary could come back to his field or not. The Committee gives its opinion in the ministry of the missionary, the weak and strong points and gives its report to the EMC which should decide according to the report if the missionary continue in the field or go back to Egypt.

2) The missionary will be under the supervision of the American Mission in Southern Sudan. If the missionary feels uncomfortable with his ministry assignments which he receives from the American Mission he can ask the Synod to intervene and the Synod has the final word.

3) If the Mission found a reason which demonstrates that the Egyptian missionary is not accomplishing the work, the

---

31. Alex C. Wilson, who was a missionary in Southern Sudan, reported to Donald Black, Chairman of the Board of Foreign Mission, that Swailem said the Synod could not send another missionary to work as a printer on the press of the American Mission. He said that this qualification was far beyond the ability of the Synod and they want the Egyptian missionaries to work among people not with machines. PHS UPCNA RG 209-14-29: Alex C. Wilson Papers: Wilson to Donald Black dated October 18, 1954.

American Mission can at any time ask the Synod to withdraw the missionary and the Synod has the final decision.[32]

This agreement formalized the relationship between the Mission and the Synod not only for Swailem's ministry but also for any other missionary who might come to Southern Sudan. Although this agreement was only applied to Swailem, it proves that the American Mission had the upper hand in deciding if the missionary should serve for another term. The Synod depended on the Mission's direct involvement in the field and authorized it to evaluate and advise the Synod concerning their missionary. This agreement would also help ensure that any Egyptian missionary who proved to be qualified and faithful would be enabled to continue in his ministry.

The Board of Foreign Mission of the United Presbyterian Church in North America had received the news that an Egyptian missionary was to be sent to Southern Sudan with joy and excitement. They found this step an "important event in the Nile Valley."[33] Ralph McLaughlin, a missionary in Egypt, commenting on the meeting at which Swailem had been blessed by the Synod, reported that: "It was indeed, an impressive service of dedication and an auspicious beginning of the new foreign missionary enterprise of our Church in Egypt."[34]

During his ministry, Swailem worked as a member of the American Mission in Southern Sudan. He attended the Mission administrative meetings and participated as a full member. The only difference was that he received his salary from Egypt while his fellow American missionaries received theirs from America.[35] The relationship between the Church in Egypt and the American Mission in the field in Sudan serves as an early model of the partnerships that can be established between a foreign mission and a Majority World church.

---

32. Synod of the Nile, *Minutes of the Year, 1955*, 67.

33. Ralph McLaughlin, "Important Event in the Nile Valley," *United Presbyterian* (1953). The article was reprinted by "NILE" National Youth Project in a flyer PHS UPCNA RG 209-6-22: Watkins, Bradley Papers: "Important Event in the Nile Valley" dated 1953.

34. Ibid.

35. American Mission in Southern Sudan, *Minutes of the years from 1954–1958*.

6.6 Swailem's Ministry in Attar

Swailem and his wife had spent a short time in Malakal before moving to Attar, where they worked for about nine years. The American Mission provided them with their field needs such as a boat and a projector. The Evangelical Church was committed to providing the salary for Swailem and some other mission expenses such as the travelling costs, and the salary of a Sudanese assistant.[36] During his time in Attar, Swailem and his wife were involved in a number of mission activities including evangelism, teaching at the school, pastoral care to the students, church planting, translating the New Testament into Shilluk, and relief work.

6.6.1 Evangelism and Baptism

Swailem and his wife considered that their most important task was to evangelize the local people. They visited many villages, building relationships with local tribal leaders and people in order to gain their trust and then speak to them about the Christian faith.

The Shilluk followed a traditional African religion that believed in Jwok Atang, a supreme deity and creator of all that we see. Under Jwok Atang came levels of divine beings, mostly composed of the souls of the parents and ancestors, who continued to inhabit the residential quarters of the family. These beings watched over the families, and provided their basic needs of rain and health. The Shilluk believed that there were also evil spirits that brought about illness, bad crops, starvation, and other harmful events. The people sought to appease the spirits by offering them libations of food, blood, and sacrifices.[37]

The people lived a simple life, but many customs contradicted Christian teaching, such as polygamy, divorce, idol worship, and excessive drinking. Swailem and his wife found it difficult to convey the gospel. The people listened well to the good news of one God, who loved them and sent his Son. Nevertheless, it was hard for them to accept the message of the cross, to confess their sins and to see their need for the Saviour. Samira asked the

---

36. Hennein, interview.

37. "Report of the Sudan" in the *49th Annual Report of the American United Presbyterian Mission in Egypt and the Sudan for the Year 1903*, 72; Watson, *Sorrow and Hope*, 160.

Church in Egypt to pray for the opening of the hearts of the people by the power of Holy Spirit to see this need.[38]

Swailem went with an assistant from village to village to evangelize people using a slide projector which worked by kerosene, and a cassette recorder machine that used a manual spring. These simple means drew people to hear Bible stories.[39] He reported:

> We went to villages carrying those machines which were interesting and attracted the people. We would have a crowd of 200–300. We run those machines and the people listened and at night they would see the pictures. Then we invite them to accept the Lord, if they were willing and raise their hands. We would meet those who made the decision for themselves and make follow up classes for them.[40]

During his ministry in Southern Sudan, Swailem won a sizable number of people to the Christian faith. In *Al-Hoda,* there was news of the work in the South that included the numbers of the new believers and the numbers of baptisms. In the 1958 issue of *Al-Hoda,* it mentioned that fifteen people had been baptized in one month.[41] In one of Swailem's reports to the Church in Egypt, which *Al-Hoda* reproduced in 1961, he stated that the number of baptized was ninety-nine people in four months.[42] He also said that the number of the people he baptized from the beginning of his ministry in 1953 until he left Sudan in 1964 had reached 3,000 people including women and children.[43] The most exciting baptisms to him were when he baptized a whole family together. This made him happy because he believed that this meant there was a new church in one home.[44]

---

38. *Al-Hoda* (1955): 447.

39. Hennein, interview.

40. Ibid.

41. *Al-Hoda* (1958): 22.

42. *Al-Hoda* (1961): 209.

43. This number of baptized converts was not only because of Swailem's direct evangelism. Swailem was an ordained pastor and the missionaries in the South delegated to him the responsibility of baptizing new converts who came as a result of the missionaries' work among the tribes. Swailem needed to visit different stations in the South to help missionaries in tasks like baptism and the Lord's Supper.

44. Hennein, interview.

Besides evangelizing small groups in villages, the missionaries in Attar would organize an annual public meeting in their centre. They used the Christmas season to gather people from different villages, including the tribal leaders. They would tell the Christmas story, and then invite people to adopt the Christian faith. This event also provided a good opportunity for building stronger relationships with local and tribal leaders. On one such occasion, they developed a friendship with Kuur, the young king of the Shilluk.[45]

Swailem visited many other areas in the South to evangelize in villages. In 1954, he visited Abwong, which was located on the Sobat River. After nine days of preaching the gospel, Swailem baptized seventeen converts by immersion in the river.[46] Such conversions raised new questions, concerning the amount of time that the converts should wait between conversion and baptism. Some missionaries believed that they should wait and mature through follow up and Bible study groups. On the other hand, Swailem and his wife wanted to baptize the new converts shortly after their confession of faith and then disciple and train them for a year or more after baptism. Although Samira asked the Church in Egypt for their opinion in that matter, she received no answer.[47]

Swailem and his wife faced another theological dilemma in their ministry. This related to the new convert who had more than one wife before being a Christian. Should the man keep only one wife, leaving the others free to return to their parents' village? Alternatively, should he keep all of them, which would present a deficient idea of Christian ideals and values? Other missionaries also sought answers to this and other complex questions.[48] The Evangelical Church had no solution and was not prepared to give an opinion since they did not face such problems among its own members. They were not theologically or missiologically equipped to explore these pressing concerns.

These challenges were new for the Egyptian missionary. Swailem needed to change his methods to help the Sudanese grow in their ability to learn

---

45. Ibid.
46. Salama, *Tarikh al-Kanysa al-Injilya*, 106.
47. *Al-Hoda* (1955): 391–392.
48. Hennein, interview.

new things and to change some customs and viewpoints. Understanding this led him to consider starting a school.

6.6.2 Church Planting and Organization

The Swailems worked together to evangelize and build the church in Southern Sudan. Swailem was concerned not just for the immediate future, but took many steps to prepare leaders. Samira was involved in the church in Attar. She held meetings for women, telling them about the Christian faith. The women enjoyed hearing and learning the gospel, but it was difficult to enable them to see their need of a Saviour.[49]

Swailem served at the major church in Attar but also ministered throughout the district. There were six sizable church congregations in the surrounding area, and he saw potential for more churches in some other small villages where one or more families had converted. He would visit these villages to preach, baptize, and celebrate communion. Some of these churches had been established because of Swailem's ministry.[50] For example, after a visit to Abowng in 1954, and his continuing ministry there, a church was organized. Four elders and two evangelists were then appointed to serve it and the villages around it.[51]

As a part of his administrative role in the Church of Southern Sudan, Swailem was elected to be chairman of the Church of Christ in the Upper Nile from 1955–1957.[52] He also contributed to the future of the church in Southern Sudan by training new local leaders. He organized numerous training conferences in evangelism and leadership for local believers, and appointed a number of evangelists to help him preach in the villages. In his report to the Synod in 1961 he informed them that he had five evangelists who had worked with him for some time in areas around and beyond Attar.

---

49. Synod of the Nile, *Minutes of the Year, 1956*, 120.

50. Some of these village churches were results of the American Mission evangelistic ministry.

51. Salama, *Tarikh al-Kanysa al-Injilya*, 106.

52. The Church of Christ in Upper Nile was established as a united church of the Presbyterians and the Reformed Churches of Holland in North America who were working together in the field of Southern Sudan. The American Mission requested from the Synod of the Nile that the Church of Christ be an independent church but with strong ties to the mother Churches. The Synod permitted this Church which replaced the Southern Sudan Presbytery. See chapter 4; Salama, *Tarikh al-Kanysa al-Injilya*, 108; Vantini, *Christianity in the Sudan*, 267.

They were members of the Presbytery of the Church of Christ in Southern Sudan. Swailem met with them weekly for Bible study and to discuss the difficulties they faced in their ministry among the villages. He linked them to the Presbytery to make sure that they would have direct supervision and financial support for their salaries. Although he had problems with one who was dishonest and subsequently expelled from the Presbytery, the rest were known for their integrity in ministry.[53]

Through the Presbytery of Southern Sudan, Swailem also established links between the local pastors and evangelists and the Evangelical Church in Egypt. He organized trips so that they could visit the Church in Egypt, attending conferences and visiting churches to observe methods of ministry and of administration. He challenged the Church in Egypt to contribute to the cost of such a visit.[54] He also recruited some of the local young leaders to join the Evangelical Theological Seminary in Cairo. In 1961, he informed the Church in Egypt that the Presbytery was going to send one student to study in Cairo, in order to come back and join the ministry as a pastor in Southern Sudan.[55] Swailem recognized the importance of training local leaders, and he made it one of his priorities. He believed that eventually local leaders should lead the church in Sudan and so he worked to equip them for this future task.[56]

6.6.3 Schools

In the early 1950s, schools in Southern Sudan were few in number because under the British occupation primary, intermediate and secondary education had chiefly been left to the various missions. The Roman Catholics were responsible for the Bahr-il-Ghazal area; the Episcopalians, for the Equatorial area; and the Presbyterians, for the Upper Nile region. In Attar, there was an Intermediary School which recruited its students from the three provinces, and of which the government was very proud. This school assumed the responsibility for transporting pupils from their home areas,

---

53. *Al-Hoda* (1961): 209–210.
54. Ibid., 210.
55. Ibid.
56. *Al-Hoda* (1961): 209.

and for offering free board, clothing, and education.[57] Attar Intermediary School had one of the best-equipped laboratories in Southern Sudan.[58] The school was also unique in that, here, the three main denominations in Southern Sudan worked together in an ecumenical spirit.[59]

Attar was special in many ways. It was built on an extension of land between a branch of the Nile, the Chord Attar, and the White Nile. Swailem's house was at the very end of the Intermediary School campus, next to the forest. Many of the Attar pupils who came from all three provinces had already been baptized. Swailem provided pastoral and evangelistic care to the students while also teaching such subjects as Bible and geography.

An extension service brought education across the Nile and Attar area into villages, forming small churches and bush schools. Building and staffing these bush schools was one of Swailem's main methods for ministering in Southern Sudan. The bush schools around Attar began with twenty to twenty-five students each, bringing in children from the villages around. They would meet in one-room buildings, preparing boys for joining primary school whenever possible. Swailem and his assistant, Paul Adiang Adholjok, put much effort into convincing the village chiefs to help start bush schools that were then used as centres for worship and literacy campaigns as well. In some cases, village chiefs cooperated in building those centres.[60]

At that time, recruiting girls for a girls' school was virtually impossible. The parents wanted their children to stay home to work with them, and the girls to marry. The families received wealth in the form of cows as a dowry from the husbands when the daughters married. This meant that villagers saw little value in postponing the marriages while their daughters were educated.

57. Lilian Passmore Sanderson and Neville Sanderson, *Education, Religion &Politics in Southern Sudan 1899-1964* (London: Ithaca Press, 1981), 387.
58. Synod of the Nile, *Minutes of the Year, 1958*, 66–67; Hennein, interview.
59. Hennein, interview.
60. Ibid.

6.6.4 Social Work

In his ministry among the Shilluk and Dinka, Swailem worked to develop basic skills in agriculture and health care and to change harmful customs. He also helped the people to access social services in times of emergency

Swailem grew crops to cover his family's food needs, and hired one of the locals to help tend the vegetables and fruits. The local people had little agricultural knowledge and came to learn how to grow their own crops. Swailem supplied them with seeds and advice, which proved especially helpful during the yearly dry season.[61] Since life in the South depends on the rains, years of drought are disastrous. During such times, when the people were starving, Swailem sought aid from abroad, and was able to distribute both food and money to buy seeds. He encouraged the people to share and was amazed by their unstinting generosity and communal solidarity, even though the majority of them were, in his opinion, not Christians.[62]

Samira gave aid to the women, which included providing clothes and food for the poor families. The Swailems also made the mission equipment available for the use of local people including the mission steamer that was the main transportation for the villages and was a great boon during emergencies. The Swailems also hosted and welcomed people in their home, and supplied food, water and shelter in times of crisis.

Swailem sought to address some of the local practices and beliefs. Polygamy, excessive drinking, and sorcery were especially difficult issues, taking great effort and time to convince people that such practices were harmful. Most difficult was the custom of polygamy, because the people believed that it was their right to have more than one wife, and to be free to divorce her at any time. Swailem encouraged people, especially those who converted to Christianity, to have one wife.[63]

Another dangerous social custom that Swailem tried to address was the practice of holding duels that had resulted in many injuries. But medical needs went far beyond such incidents. There were no doctors or medical facilities in the villages, and so Swailem and the American Mission established a clinic in Attar station that was equipped to deal with emergencies

---

61. Hennein, interview.
62. Ibid.
63. Ibid.

and give primary health care. The American Mission hired a worker to take care of the clinic, and paid his salary.[64]

In his second visit to Southern Sudan in 1957, Rev Faried Manquarious, who was chairman of the Egyptian Mission Council, noticed the differences in the lives of the converts. He found that they had given up alcohol and sorcery, and were now well-dressed, married to one spouse and living in peace with others. He also noted that all the local people looked to Swailem as their friend, counsellor, teacher, and father.[65] Swailem had established good relationships that had then enabled him to teach and inspire change.

6.7 The Significance of Swailem's Appointment and Work

6.7.1 The Influence of Mission Work in Sudan on the Evangelical Church in Egypt

For the first time in its history, the Evangelical Church had sent a missionary, not to be a pastor for Egyptians living outside their country, but to start a missionary ministry among non-Christians. The Swailems' service in Sudan had a considerable impact not only in Sudan, but upon the Evangelical Church in Egypt. The Synod, local churches, and individuals welcomed this missionary endeavour. Many articles were written explaining the importance of sending missionaries and their task of spreading the gospel and serving people's needs. The Church papers challenged local churches and members to pray and give financially to the new mission to Sudan.

Some local churches committed themselves to pay an annual contribution to the Mission in Sudan.[66] The 'Attareen Church in Alexandria, for example, took responsibility for the salary of one of the native Sudanese evangelists, whom Swailem had recruited to help in his work among the villages.[67] The chairman of the Egyptian Mission Council challenged the

---

64. Ibid.
65. *Al-Hoda* (1957): 229–230.
66. Salama, *Tarikh al-Kanysa al-Injilya*, 107–108.
67. *Al-Hoda* (1959): 378.

evangelicals not only to give financially but also to donate needed materials, such as a camera and a refrigerator.[68] Many church members gave generously to the work in Sudan and the Church paper published lists of contributors and their donations.[69]

From 1954–1960 many Synod organizations held conferences focusing on missions. Many young people were inspired by Swailem's ministry and wished to follow his example. Bakheet Matta was one of these. When he graduated from the Evangelical Seminary in Cairo in 1954, he was chosen to give the students' address and spoke about missionary awareness within the Evangelical Church.[70] Later Matta followed his dream, starting a pastoral work in Sudan where he also conducted remarkable mission work among the Sudanese.[71]

The Church in Egypt was also experiencing a revival in in-country mission and service. There was a noticeable growth in youth ministries, social work, and mass-evangelistic events. The Synod envisioned the possibility of future evangelistic work in new regions. In 1954, the Synod discussed expanding the ministry to the oases of the western desert.[72] In 1958 and 1959 the Synod's Spiritual Revival Committee organized evangelistic campaigns all over Egypt. Evangelistic meetings in the cities and villages brought remarkable growth to the local churches.[73] There were calls to train seminary students in mission and evangelism work through courses and seminars.[74] In 1960, some Church leaders challenged the Synod to focus on evangelistic work, using all of the Church resources for that purpose.[75] News about spiritual revival around Egypt began to be one of the main topics in *Al-Hoda*, the Church paper.

---

68. *Al-Hoda* (1954): 144.

69. *Al-Hoda* (1955): 402.

70. *Al-Hoda* (1954): 259–260.

71. Rev Bakheet Matta, interview by the researcher, 3 March, 2004, Alexandria. See Appendix D.

72. *Al-Hoda* (1954): 338.

73. Such calls came to the attention of the Synod numerous times. The Synod discussed the issue but for administrative and financial reasons the work would stop until another call came. There was no long-term plan for mission and evangelistic work, because it was the visions and effort of only a few leaders and not the majority of the Synod.

74. Synod of the Nile, *Minutes of the Year, 1959*, 60.

75. *Al-Hoda* (1960): 347–351.

6.7.2 The Establishment of the Egyptian Mission Council

As a result of the mission in Southern Sudan, the Committee for the Work in Sudan proposed to the Synod that the work in Northern Sudan be put under the jurisdiction of the Northern Sudan Presbytery, and no longer be a concern of the Committee.[76] Moreover, they suggested that the Committee should change its name to the Egyptian Mission Council. Whereas before, the Committee had been a sub-committee under the Board of Spiritual Affairs, they now wished to establish an independent council for mission. Their vision was to have an Egyptian mission work with more than one missionary in Southern Sudan.[77] The establishment of such a council indicated the importance and interest in missions within the Egyptian church. The council worked for many years to build a strong mission movement, organizing and establishing the rules and principles to facilitate this.[78]

Monetary contributions for Southern Sudan were sent and dispersed by this new council, and Swailem now sent his annual reports to them. The council had hoped to send more than one missionary to Sudan and to other countries as well. Unfortunately, for a variety of reasons, this never materialized.[79]

6.8 The End of Swailem's Mission to Sudan

In 1961, Swailem left the field in Southern Sudan for one year in order to obtain a Masters in Education in Pittsburgh in the United States. In his report of the year 1960, Swailem gave it as his opinion that the work should be transferred to the local leaders in the near future. He felt that the church in Attar would benefit by his absence because some people had become too dependent on the missionaries to provide their financial and leadership needs. He considered that upon his return his task would be to train the

---

76. Synod of the Nile, *Minutes of the Year, 1954*, 124. For more details about the relationship between the Sudan Presbytery and the Committee for the Work in Sudan see chapter 5.

77. Matta, interview.

78. Synod of the Nile, *Minutes of the Year, 1960*, 163; *1961*, 280–286.

79. In Synod meetings from 1954 to 1960, the Egyptian Mission Council reported to the Synod of its efforts to raise money for Sudan mission and urged the Synod to raise its support. See minutes of the Synod from years 1954–1960.

local leaders and thus planned to teach at the Seminary of Mundri in the Equatorial area.[80] His wife also planned to change the focus of her ministry after their time in America, expecting to train the national pastors' wives.[81]

On his way to the United States, Swailem visited Egypt where he shared his experiences and expectations with the Church. He had previously written to the Synod in Egypt asking another missionary to replace him while he was away, with the hope that he would also remain after towards to work together. The Church was not able to find a replacement, nor did they have the finances to support an additional person, so the American Mission in Southern Sudan appointed one of its own missionaries to help the station in Attar.[82]

In 1962, Swailem finished his masters degree and returned to Attar for about two years, after which Sudan's political changes forced him and many other foreigners to leave. The Sudanese government decided to expel all missionaries from Southern Sudan, in order to spread its authority over the whole country.[83] After ten years of difficult but effective service in Southern Sudan, the Swailems' mission had ended.

---

80. This seminary was established by the CMS as a Divinity school in 1945 to train Sudanese church leaders, without sending them abroad. In 1947 it was moved to Mundri, close to Juba in Southern Sudan. It was named Bishop Gwynne College. In 1950s other Protestant Churches in Sudan including the Presbyterian Mission and Church sent teaching staff and students to Mundari. (Werner, *Day of Devastation,* 360).

81. *Al-Hoda,* 1961, 211.

82. Ibid.

83. On 27 February 1964, the Sudanese Council of Ministers agreed to:
 1. Repatriate all foreign priests and missionaries in the three Southern provinces.
 2. Take measures to ensure the Sudanization of the Church, giving financial assistance to Sudanese priests and qualifying them for their various religious posts.
The reasons which were later given for the expulsion were that foreign missionaries were:
 1. working inside and outside the Sudan, against the stability and the internal security of the country, by spreading false information against the government, abetting citizens to leave Sudan to join the resistance movement, abetting students to strike and assault their Northern teachers and by giving shelter and provision to mutineers.
 2. Interfering in the internal affairs of the country and their participation in local politics, such as: inciting for the separation of the South, preaching against the changes of weekly holiday, preaching against the settlement of Northerners in the South and trying to influence the electorate during elections.
 3. Breaking the laws by a massive trade in drugs without licence, teaching Christianity to Muslim children and baptizing them without the consent of their families, prompting citizens to pray for the victory of the mutineers, and building churches without permission. (Ahmed, *Sudan,* 102–103).

The local governor in Southern Sudan, who had been appointed by the Northern government, was a friend of the Swailems. When he told them that they must leave, he said that they could leave everything as it was, thinking that it would be but a brief time before they could return.[84] Many efforts were made to have the government reverse its decision, including an attempt by the Egyptian pastors in the North who begged that Swailem be allowed to stay. The government insisted that as a missionary he must leave.[85] Swailem left Southern Sudan in 1964, and went to Khartoum for a short time before returning to Egypt, where he reported on the situation:

> It was a drama, not just for me, but for all the missionaries.
> We did not want to leave because we all thought that if we left
> the church would be dead. We knew how vicious the motives
> in the North could be and they could destroy all the churches.
> The Southerners had no weapons at all, how could they resist
> these kinds of stupid power. We were sad. Before we left, I had
> a meeting with the missionaries and they were crying.[86]

This was not the end of Swailem's efforts to serve Sudan. Later he was appointed to join an African committee for peace between Northern and Southern Sudanese. The All Africa Conference of Churches was invited by the Sudan Government to mediate in Sudan's case, and to help make peace between the Northern Sudanese Government and the Southerners. In 1967 Swailem was appointed to join a peace-making committee that visited many countries – Russia, France, England, Switzerland, and several African countries – in order to build international support for its efforts. In negotiations with the Sudanese, Swailem used his communication skills, experiences, and relationships as a former missionary to the Southern Sudanese region. He met with the Southern Sudanese leaders, including John Garang who had been one of Swailem's students while he was in the mission school in Attar. The committee came to an agreed peace proposal about which Swailem said:

---

84. Hennein, interview.
85. Ibid.
86. Ibid.

We agreed on a peace agreement and it was written. In this agreement, the South would be autonomous, not independent but it would have its autonomous government. The Southerners would share together the police, the army, and any economical income. The Southerners would have their own Parliament and government and there will be Northern representation in the South and southern representation in the North. There was a great celebration and the embassies were involved. Then they respected the agreement and the war stopped completely. There was peace until 1970, when Jaafar Nimeiry destroyed it all.[87]

The efforts of this committee did not succeed in bringing permanent peace to Sudan but while there, Swailem had the opportunity to contact leaders in Sudan and see where he had served for so many years. Swailem was greatly encouraged when he met with the Christians in Southern Sudan. After his four-year absence, he discovered that the churches were full of people, with meetings held in the open air because the buildings were too small to hold all those attending. Although Swailem also saw where church and mission buildings had been destroyed, he was amazed by the revival and growth that had occurred under the leadership of the local Sudanese Christians. He recalled:

The amazing thing that even after all the missionaries left, the Church and the usual Christians started to carry the Gospel. There were no previous arrangements. Although the war made them very defiant and stubborn, many villages endorsed the religion and they became Christians. The majority now in Southern Sudan are Christians. The Church in Malakal could not accommodate the people. They were standing in the back yard, eight acres of grass, 3-4 thousand people were there, from where and how did they come? I had no idea.[88]

He visited Attar, but the station had been destroyed by the Sudanese troops from Northern Sudan. Swailem had left Sudan in 1964 with deep

---

87. Ibid.
88. Ibid.

sadness, but he discovered that in the end, God had used it for the good of the Church; that the indigenous church, with its enforced independence, had matured wonderfully.[89]

When the Swailems had been forced to leave Sudan, they had not known what they would do next. However, the Synod received a new request for a missionary to help in Kenya, and they decided that Swailem was the right person for this challenging position.

6.9 Swailem's Mission in Kenya

The Presbyterian Church of East Africa, with its headquarters in Nairobi, had become autonomous in 1956: the first African church to become independent. John Gatu became the first General Secretary of this Presbyterian Church, and it was he who visited Egypt asking for a missionary to come to teach at St Paul's United Theological College in Limuru outside of Nairobi. The churches in Africa were at an important stage of their history. First, the spirit of independence was spreading, and many were breaking loose from the foreign mission organizations and forming indigenous African churches. Second, these African churches were looking for ways to work together and organized various mutually cooperative systems.[90] The Synod in Egypt joined the African Conference of Churches in 1963 that then opened the way for communication and collaboration between the Church in Egypt and other African churches.[91]

When the request from the Kenyan Church first came to the Synod, they thought to send one of the pastors to this new mission. Later, they changed their minds, realizing Swailem's experiences in mission work that included good English language ability and good cross-culture communication skills.[92] Swailem's move to Kenya was one step of cooperation, with

---

89. Ibid., Matta, interview.

90. Zablon Nthamburi, "The Beginning and Development of Christianity in Kenya," in *From Mission to Church: A Handbook of Christianity in East Africa*, ed. Zablon Nthamburi (Nairobi: Uzima Press, 1991), 23–24.

91. Synod of the Nile, *Minutes of the Year, 1963*, 151.

92. Synod of the Nile, *Minutes of the Year, 1964*, 280.

an older African leader helping to equip younger African leaders for the leadership of newly independent churches in Africa.[93]

Swailem left his family and visited Kenya to explore the field there. He met with the leaders of the Presbyterian Church in Kenya, who explained the needs of the Seminary of St Paul.[94] He was asked to teach courses on the new subject area of "The Work and Mission of the Church in Contemporary Society."[95] Later, the Seminary asked him to establish a new department by that name. Christians staffed this department from three denominations: Presbyterians, Methodists, and Anglicans. Swailem also worked to prepare the curricula and develop the structure of a new lay training program, called the Conference and Training Centre. His vision was to train lay people including teachers and nurses to become good examples for others to make the gospel message known through their good example in their society.[96]

This was a new task for Swailem, enabling him to use his experience to assist the Christian church in Kenya in training its members and leaders. During his time at the Seminary, Swailem witnessed the hiring of the first Kenyan leaders to become teachers in the Seminary. As faculty professor, Swailem along with other foreign missionaries, had an effective role in training local Christians for positions of leadership and authority. One of the leaders of the Seminary wrote to the chairman of the Egyptian Mission Council summarizing Swailem's ministry saying:

> We consider Rev Swailem as a gift from God for us in Limuru, as he is the only Presbyterian teacher in St Paul College. He has great experience in the theological Christian education and it is great that he is an African from Egypt. He is working with us in the Seminary and in the administration board. He

---

93. Salama, *Tarikh al-Kanysa al-Injilya*, 297.

94. Hennein, interview.

95. *Al-Hoda* (1965): 269. In this article of Al-Hoda the head of the Egyptian Mission Council wrote about the ministry of Swailem in Kenya according to the letter he had received from one of the leaders in the Kenyan Church who praised Swailem and his ministry.

96. Hennein, interview.

gave us new ideas and perspectives which helped us a lot. It was hard to have these perspectives from another person.[97]

Besides his work at St Paul's College, Swailem had two other ministries. First, he collected information to understand the evangelistic opportunities around him. In 1966, he began work among the Maasai tribe. He would often visit the Maasai taking seminary students every Sunday with him to help in the ministry.[98] He spoke about the Christian faith and gave them Bibles in their own language. After only a few months, thirty-five men and women were ready for baptism, and many others were greatly interested in the gospel. Swailem helped establish a school for the children, which was also used as a place for Sunday morning meetings.

Second, Swailem chose to minister to another marginalized group in a slum area called Pumwani. This area on the outskirts of Nairobi was very poor and had many social, economic, and spiritual needs. In response to a request from the Presbyterian Church in Kenya, he studied the area, looking for the best means of building a ministry of evangelism and social development. After months of study, Swailem and the seminary students started to visit Pumwani once a week. There already was a Christian presence in the area, but there were still great needs and issues to be addressed. As he had in Southern Sudan, Swailem used the projector and tape recorder to present the Bible stories. Because of their ministry in Pumwani, a number of people were baptized. After this, Swailem organized Bible study groups to help them grow in their faith.[99] Because of his ministry among the people of Pumwani, the Kenyan government asked Swailem to study the area in more detail and propose methods for developing the area and solving its social and economic problems. His work there became an example of slum regeneration. Swailem explained how they began the work:

The project was about how to uplift their living conditions. We started by helping them to move from being unconnected. We tried to make them understand the meaning of a family. I had a team to work with and we received money for

---

97. *Al-Hoda* (1965): 269.

98. Ibid., 224–226.

99. Hennein, interview.

the research. We started with a preliminary set of questionnaires and personal interviews. Every member of my workers
used the same set of questionnaires. Before starting they were
trained in how to use the questionnaires and make sure that
all of them make the same approaches. We surveyed 500–600
cases and it was supported by the head of the government
Social Work in Nairobi.[100]

Because of this survey project, the Kenyan government decided to rebuild Pumwani and help the people to develop their life. The government
recruited Swailem to take responsibility for supervizing the rebuilding
project. Swailem asked the government not to displace the residents, but to
first build their new homes before razing the old. Through this project and
his ministry in the Seminary, Swailem built deep relationships with many
officials, including President Jomo Kenyatta, his family, and a number of
government ministers.[101] Swailem then used this study and regeneration
project as his basis for writing a number of articles on social work. His doctoral degree dissertation for Northwest University in Evanston, Chicago
was also based on this highly significant venture.

The Evangelical Church in Egypt had commissioned Swailem for his
ministry in Kenya. The Egyptian Church paid his salary, and Swailem occasionally reported to the Synod about his work in Kenya. However, contact was much less than had been when Swailem served in Sudan. Swailem,
for his part, increasingly found it difficult to find the time to maintain connections and write reports. The Synod, for their part, were not as interested
in his work in Kenya because it was not one of their programmes or under
their direction. They had no vision or plan for his work there. Criticism
started to arise concerning the benefit of the Egyptian Church's involvement in Kenya, but the leaders of the Mission Council defended Swailem
and his mission.[102]

---

100. Ibid.

101. Ibid.

102. In an article in *Al-Hoda* (1965): 268–272. There was a defense of the missionary and
his mission in Kenya after a number of Synod members questioned it. The title of this
article was "What does our missionary do in Kenya?"

6.10 The End of an Era

After seven years of mission work in Kenya, and a total of seventeen years of missionary service, Swailem decided to return to Cairo in 1970. He had received a scholarship for one year of study in the United States and the Synod had granted him permission to travel, and made plans to appoint him to other projects when his studies were completed. The Synod hoped that Swailem would train laymen to do developmental and evangelistic work in their villages. It also asked him to organize conferences and meetings in order to raise the Church's awareness of modern social changes. They further proposed that he could lead ministries in new industrial areas and in poor districts and villages.[103] After his effective ministry elsewhere, the Church hoped to use his experience to develop new methods and understanding of ministry.

When the Swailem family returned from Kenya, they were unable to find placements for their children in either the government or private schools. After months of contacting officials in the Ministry of Education including the minister himself, they still had no guarantee of a place for their four children.[104] As a result, Swailem took his family with him when he went to study in the United States.

In 1971, Swailem asked to go back to Kenya but the Synod refused his request.[105] The Synod still proposed that Swailem should use his experience to help develop new ministries inside Egypt, but there was no actual plan and no finances to fulfil this proposal. Swailem therefore decided to remain in the United States where he continued his studies, finally receiving a PhD in public health.[106]

---

103. Synod of the Nile, *Minutes of the Year, 1970*, 162–163.

104. Hennein, interview.

105. Synod of the Nile, *Minutes of the Year, 1971*, 176.

106. When Swailem lived in the United States, he joined the faculty of Public Health at the University of Illinois in Chicago where he taught for several years. While in the Chicago area, Swailem worked among Christians from Arab countries and started an Arab Christian congregation. This congregation grew in number and ministry until it grew into 6 different congregations with Arab pastors. One of these churches became a member of the Chicago Presbytery. After conflict with the Presbytery concerning homosexuality the Arab congregation split and became independent. Pastors from different Arabic countries came and ministered in these churches serving the growing Arab Christian population in

When the Synod sent Swailem to Sudan and Kenya, it was the beginning of a unique era in the life of the Evangelical Church of Egypt. It united the efforts of the Church in both commissioning and fully supporting a missionary in a foreign field. The end of Swailem's mission to Southern Sudan and Kenya in 1970 was the end of the Synod's foreign mission work. Since then, there has been no organized mission effort to any country outside of Egypt.

In 2000, Swailem returned to Egypt in response to an invitation from the Evangelical Theological Seminary in Cairo to establish a new department for missions and evangelism.[107] The Seminary hoped to renew the missionary role of the Evangelical Church and looked to his involvement to sow the seeds for a future era of missionary activity.[108]

6.11 Conclusion

As we have looked at the history of the Evangelical Church's mission endeavours in Sudan, we have noted both its strengths and weaknesses. The

---

Chicago. Swailem worked as mentor and father for these Arabic churches and used his mission experiences in doing evangelistic work among the Arabs there.

Swailem also started a mission project in Malawi: "It was a combined work of spiritual as well as agricultural development, seeds, plants, nutrition, taking care of babies and of pregnant women, a combination of looking after the social, physical and spiritual life. We worked in 20 villages and we turned all the resources we have to a council we made in Malawi, we turned everything to them but we continued to be their advisers, until today I receive reports almost every day from them. The Committee itself in Chicago disintegrated, I think those of us who were interested continued, 2–3 continued, because now it is completely in the hands of the Malawians.' (Hennein, interview.)

The relationship between Swailem and Africa continued in different ways. Besides the work in Malawi, he worked at building reconciliation and peace in Rwanda. The minister of Health in Rwanda during the peace negotiations had been one of his students in Chicago. Swailem visited Rwanda and later told about his mission there:

"When I went during the war carrying medical relief, again we formed a committee in Chicago and we gathered aid, medicines, food and so on. We would carry the aid to them. One time I went alone and distributed it to the Christian hospitals. They showed me a church building and wanted to open it. I said no you can see the blood all over which until that moment had 500 dead bodies inside it, killed by spears, I did not know. They kept it closed as a witness for the evil of civil war." These missionary efforts which Swailem made during his stay in the United States were personal, and had no relationship with the Evangelical Church of Egypt. The Church and Swailem lost their contact on the official level after Swailem left the field in Kenya and could not find a place in Egypt [sic.]". (Hennein, interview.).

107. Lorimer, *Presbyterian*, 45.

108. Hennein, interview.

vision for ministry outside of Egypt did not arise from the Synod, instead being the result of pressures from the American Mission. However, as the Egyptian Church matured, it began to take more active steps. At the invitation of the American Mission in Southern Sudan, and through the vision of one Synod leader who visited the field, the Synod was finally convinced of the need to send a missionary to this needy and unevangelized area. Where before the Synod had focused solely on pastoring expatriate Egyptians, it now started to see that the Church had a wider mandate. The Synod took five years to decide to respond, only slowly coming to a realization of their mission responsibilities.

As the concept and vision of foreign mission work grew in the Evangelical Church, there was a corresponding growth in ministry within Egypt. Especially during the 1950s and 1960s, a variety of mission methods were employed to great effect, with programmes in social work, evangelism, youth work, and women's ministry beginning to take place.[109]

With the exciting mission work in Sudan and then Kenya, and the increase in ministries within Egypt, hopes were raised that they were at the cusp of a great revival. There was an anticipation that a new spirit of ministry was awakening, and that this reflected a deeper understanding of the role of the Church and its call to be a missionary church.

The financial support from the Evangelical Church was remarkable for a poorer Middle Eastern church that supported its own mission work in a foreign country. The members of the Church gave generously to the work in Sudan and proved that when a vision was well explained the response could be positive.[110] There was excitement about what Swailem was accomplishing, and many saw this as a proper extension of the Church's mission. On the other hand, the support for the mission work in Southern Sudan did not come entirely from the Synod budget. Only some individual churches, members, and leaders were fully committed to support

---

109. The minutes of the Synod during years 1960 to 1971 had a lot of plans for evangelism, internal mission work, youth ministry, and expanded theological training. *Al-Hoda* also included news of activities inside the Church which raised the expectations of a real revival but it ended by organizing few activities without continuation. (See chapter 7).

110. In the minutes of the Synod of the Nile and in *Al-Hoda*, there are lists of supporters to the mission work in Sudan. Many local churches and individuals gave regularly responding to the requests which the Chairman of the Mission Council made.

this mission involvement, while most of the Synod did not take ownership of this vision. Nor did the Synod continue supporting the mission but left this task to its Mission Council – a minority who loved mission work.

Swailem was the first and last missionary. He had asked the Synod several times to send someone else while he studied, but the Synod failed to do so. In part, this was because there were difficulties in acquiring a visa for the chosen replacement, but also because the Synod had no clear vision or plan for mission work.[111]

There were good beginnings, but the Synod did not continue in its interest, especially when Swailem moved from Sudan to Kenya, and contact lessened. It was proposed that an independent mission council should be created. After many years of negotiations in the Synod, this proposal was denied. In 1968, the Synod decided that there was no need to have a mission council since they believed that a committee was sufficient to handle the work.[112] Once Swailem had returned from Kenya, there was no longer any need for a mission council, as mission endeavours ceased.

The Synod as an institution lacked a vision and a formalized mandate for mission work. This repeatedly resulted in its inability to recognize its basic and foundational missionary role. This in turn has led to the Synod's repeated limitation to develop or officially support its own missional programmes. Instead, the development and evangelistic work both inside and outside Egypt have generally been left to parachurch organizations and mission groups. These organizations use the personnel of the Church and its best lay workers to impact society. The Church thus continues to depend on the money, strategies, and leadership of the West, while only supplying the workers from within Egypt.

---

111. Synod of the Nile, *Minutes of the Year, 1961*, 280.
112. Synod of the Nile, *Minutes of the Year, 1968*, 197–198.

CHAPTER 7

The Development of the Relationship between the American Mission and the Egyptian Evangelical Church 1958–1970

7.1 Introduction

The relationship between the Evangelical Church and the American Mission in Egypt went through major changes after the end of World War II. This period witnessed major changes in the political situation throughout the world, including the Middle East and Egypt. Moreover, within the world mission movement, dramatic shifts in the theology and practice of mission were occurring, especially with the flourishing of ecumenical movement. These changes directly influenced the work of both the Mission and the Synod.

This chapter will cover the period between 1958, when the Evangelical Church of Egypt became independent from the General Assembly of the United Presbyterian Church of North America, and 1970, when the Synod declared the end of its relationship with the American Mission. We will study the effect of the political changes on the mission work of both the Synod and the Mission, as well as the changes in their mission practices. Special focus will be given to exploring the new initiatives undertaken by the Synod because of its changing political and theological view of mission. The chapter will also examine the handing over of mission work to the

Synod both inside and outside Egypt, looking at the theological, financial, and ecclesiastical aspects of the situation.

7.2 The Influence of Political Developments upon the Relationship between the Evangelical Church and the American Mission

After World War II, many countries around the world were demanding independence from their colonial masters. The situation in Egypt was no different. The Egyptian Revolution of 1952 was a significant step in enabling Egypt and other African, Asian, and Arab countries to gain full independence. After the revolution, the Egyptian government began to initiate changes in Egyptian society, and in an attempt to address entrenched socio-economic problems, the government limited the amount of agricultural land that could be owned by any individual to approximately two hundred acres,[1] and initiated programs of village development, health services, and education for all Egyptians.

Under government pressure, the Mission and the Synod began addressing the issue of transferring properties and ministry to Egyptian control. In 1953, the Synod held an emergency meeting to discuss handing over the properties of the American Mission to the Synod,[2] and an Egyptian board of administration was established to manage these transfers.[3]

In 1956, Nasser nationalized the Suez Canal, which had been under British control, and Israel, France and Britain retaliated by launching a military attack. During this time, the American missionaries in Egypt fled to Cyprus until the situation settled down, while the American government voiced its disapproval of the threats to Egypt. Because of this, demonstrations against the British and foreigners in general did not greatly affect the work of the American Mission, and Americans were not viewed as negatively as other foreigners.[4]

---

1. Elder, *Vindicating a Vision,* 280.
2. Synod of the Nile, *Minutes of the Year, 1953,* 97.
3. See chapter 2.
4. Lorimer, *The Presbyterian Experience,* 160–167.

Jack Lorimer commented on the uncertainties that the missionaries faced during the 1956 crises and the future of the American Mission work in Egypt:

> Since the missionaries were not expelled, but evacuated at the advice of the US government and the Foreign Board, by the spring of 1957 a number had returned. The hospitals continued to function and the schools were back to normal. However the Suez War brought Mission and church face to face with the realization that this major event could easily disrupt the best laid plans. It undoubtedly added a sense of urgency to the integration process. If, for example, America had not opposed the invasion as it did, but instead took the side of the Tripartite powers, missionaries most likely could not have returned. The church would have been left with two hospitals, 12 schools, the literacy/ Bible Study program, not to mention any number of other programs, none of which were they prepared to manage at that time.[5]

The political developments did not leave many alternatives for the Mission. The Egyptian government issued many laws limiting foreign control over schools, hospitals, and properties. The American Mission responded by selling many of its properties or transferring them to the Synod. The Mission also began to integrate their ministries with the Synod, viewing them as partners. Where previously the Mission had recruited its missionaries and appointed them to different projects without any consultation with the Egyptian Church, the Synod was now allowed to share in decisions about their recruitment, appointment, and ministry. The Board of Foreign Mission in America and the Synod became directly connected without interference from the American Mission in Egypt.[6]

Although the Board of Foreign Mission in its report to the General Assembly of the UPCNA in 1956 stated its uncertainty about the future of its work in Egypt, there was a strong commitment to giving the Synod control and responsibility for the ministries. The Board said that "such

---

5. Ibid., 238–239.
6. Synod of the Nile, *Minutes of the Year, 1958*, 280.

revamping of the work is not withdrawal from ministry but the seizing of new opportunities and a real moving forward in missionary enterprise."[7]

Donald Black, the chairman of the Board of Foreign Mission, hoped that this development would help the Egyptian Church to have its own leadership and financial support. In a letter written in 1956, Black described the situation saying that,

> . . . it is well to recognize that mission work will not in the future be operating on the same basis it has in the past. With a strong and able Church leadership on the field it is no longer right that our American missionaries should operate as an independent autonomous mission group determining all their own policies. The Egyptian Church has reached a maturity which, with training, will enable it to direct the affairs of all mission institutions and activities. They can quickly learn to direct, they cannot yet support, but they will carry a share. The missionaries who go to Egypt in the days ahead will expect to work within the fellowship of the Evangelical Church and under the direction of its leadership. To make adjustments in program and organization to accomplish such a transfer of authority will take some time. We pray for time to do the task aright, but it is well to realize there is no time to waste.[8]

The new political climate changed the immediate goals of the missionaries. Negotiations between the Synod, the American Mission in Egypt and the Board of Foreign Mission in the UPCNA, took on a new urgency, as they worked to have all properties and ministry become fully directed by Egyptians.[9] After more than a century the American Mission finally realized that the work belonged to the Egyptian Church and that the Egyptians should be responsible for their ministry.[10]

---

7. UPCNA, *Minutes of Ninety-Eighth General Assembly of the United Presbyterian Church of North America: Part 1* (Pittsburgh: Board of Christian Education of the United Presbyterian Church of North America, 1956), 59.

8. PHS UPCNA RG 209-22-56: Missionary Horizons: Donald Black to Miss Elith L. McBane dated 21 December 1956.

9. American Mission in Egypt, *Minutes of the Year, 1956*, 21.

10. See chapter 2.

7.3 Changes in Theology and Relationships

The political changes, however, were not the only driving force behind the re-alignment of the relationship between the American Presbyterians and the Evangelical Church of Egypt. The changing theology of missions worldwide and in the American Presbyterian Church especially had a major impact, shaping a new era of mission work among the younger churches, including the Evangelical Church of Egypt.[11]

The 1950s saw a dramatic shift in the orientation and mission theology of the American Presbyterians. In 1958, after years of negotiations, the United Presbyterian Church of North America, UPCNA, and the Presbyterian Church in the United States of America, PCUSA, united together to form the United Presbyterian Church in the United States of America, UPCUSA. The new united church merged the Boards of Foreign Mission and Inter-Church Relation Committees together, forming the Commission on Ecumenical Mission and Relations, COEMAR.[12] This name change signalled a major shift in perspective with a total re-evaluation of the meaning of missions, especially as it pertained to relationships with the younger churches, and the significance of the ecumenical movement.

7.3.1 The Mohonk Consultation

The American Presbyterians gave the younger churches a growing role in discussing the future of mission and their relationships with each other. In 1956, a group of American Presbyterians, at Lake Mohonk, New York, met with consultants from younger churches, seeking together to discern procedures that would assist integration between the indigenous churches and the American Presbyterians.[13] Although the Egyptian Church was not represented at this consultation, the recommendations were helpful in

---

11. The terms "younger churches, daughter churches and related churches" were all used by the American Presbyterians to describe those churches which had been founded during the period of the modern missionary movement.

12. John Coventry Smith, *From Colonialism to World Community: The Church's Pilgrimage* (Philadelphia: Geneva Press, 1982), 157, 167; Rycroft, *The Ecumenical Witness*, 175; Skreslet, "American Presbyterians and the Middle East," 223.

13. Rycroft, *The Ecumenical Witness*, 230.

establishing the independence of the Egyptian Presbyterian Church from the General Assembly of the UPCNA.[14]

7.3.2 The Asmara Conference

In 1959, another conference was organized in Asmara, Ethiopia to discuss a Christian approach to Islam. Six Egyptian representatives attended the conference and participated in the discussions.[15] At this conference, a more open approach to Islam was adopted, which sought to avoid the confrontational, polemic approach of the earlier missionaries that had alienated many. There was a cautious optimism that new political and social currents might afford unique opportunities for evangelism, and that a shift in approach would be more effective. Further, it was felt that work among Muslims must now include an acknowledgment of the wrong done to Islamic nations by the West. The conference suggested that Christian workers should go to Muslims in a spirit of humility, respecting Islam as a sister faith.[16] The Asmara conference also highlighted the usefulness of both print and radio media, and the provision of social services as more suitable methods for reaching Muslims.[17]

The Egyptian Church welcomed these recommendations. The Synod adopted the new non-confrontational ministries, feeling released from a sense of guilt for past ineffectiveness in its traditional work among Muslims.[18] However, neither the confrontational nor the modest approach produced notable numbers of converts. Despite this, the Synod was not ready to discuss the issue of Muslim evangelism, or seek to create its own methodologies apart from American influence and "expertise." Two years after the Asmara conference, the Synod dissolved its Committee for the Work among Muslims and put most of its efforts into the social ministry and the pastoring of Christians in Egypt.[19]

---

14. Synod of the Nile, *Minutes of the Year, 1958*, 268–272.

15. Synod of the Nile, *Minutes of the Year, 1959*, 278.

16. Lorimer *The Presbyterian Experience*, 104.

17. For more details on this conference and its results see, *Report of the Study Conference on The Christian Faith and the Contemporary Middle Eastern World, Held at Asmara, Eritrea, Ethiopia April 1–9, 1959* (New York: Commission on Ecumenical Mission and Relations of the United Presbyterian Church in the U.S.A., 1959).

18. Synod of the Nile, *Minutes of the Year, 1961*, 279.

19. Synod of the Nile, *Minutes of the Year, 1963*, 234. See chapter 3.

7.3.3 An Advisory Study

In 1960, COEMAR invited representatives from both the younger and American churches to form a committee to decide "the policies which should determine the participation of the United Presbyterian Church in the USA, through its Commission on Ecumenical Mission and Relations, in ecumenical mission and relations during the years immediately ahead."[20] The committee met three times from January 1960 until September 1961, producing the document *An Advisory Study* that was translated and published in many countries all over the world.[21]

The study came in three sections. The first section addressed the theological principles of mission work. The second section emphasized the role of each church as a missionary community. Churches were to be indigenous, charismatic, evangelistic, and serving, as they worked together across denominational lines for the sake of mission in its broader meaning.[22] The third section emphasized the importance of integrating the mission of both the sending western organizations and the indigenous churches. It was further assumed that the number of missionaries serving in any one place would decrease, to prevent unintentional domination.[23] The study also stressed the increasingly important role of non-professional missionaries, citing a new shift from missionaries to lay people as the symbols and instruments of Jesus Christ in the world. Correspondingly, the study suggested appointing people for a specific number of years of service and only extending their term if they were found to have a "special gift" for lifetime service.[24] Inspired by an ecumenical perspective, Christians were called to unite in their efforts of ministry and service, arguing that "the Christian community must be a community welcoming all men as they are, giving them a place in the Christian family."[25]

---

20. COEMAR, Advisory Study Committee, *An Advisory Study: A Working Paper for Study* (New York: UPCUSA, 1961), 5.

21. Rev Fares and Rev Menes Abdel Noor translated this study into Arabic and published it in 1961.

22. COEMAR, *An Advisory Study*, 61–70.

23. Ibid., 76.

24. Ibid., 78.

25. Ibid., 92.

7.3.4 Egyptian Response to Theological Changes

The Egyptian participant in the Advisory Study was Rev Fayez Fares, pastor of the Second Evangelical Church in Minya and one of the primary theologians of the Egyptian Church. In March 1961, he shared the results of the study with the Synod, using it as a tool to evaluate the current situation within the Egyptian Church. He noted that the Evangelical Church in Egypt had begun with a strong desire to evangelize, having suffered under the poor spiritual climate and limited ministry of the Coptic Church. In those early years, the Evangelical Church had thought that its only role was to evangelize and win others to the Church. However, evangelistic efforts were addressed only among nominal Coptic Christians, with limited work among Muslims. He saw Christians as an isolated minority, who had limited their involvement in society to providing schools and hospitals. Fares opined that both inside and outside Egypt, the mission and evangelistic ministry of the Evangelical Church was insufficient, and he challenged the Church to change its view of ministry. He believed that the Church should seek to meet the needs of society even if this did not result in an increase in conversions. Viewing social ministry as part of the message of the Church, he encouraged the Church to change its methods to adjust to the changing society around them.[26]

Rev Fares challenged the Church to put aside the traditional methods of witnessing which were no longer sufficient. He said that the Church should encourage national goodwill efforts, since the good of the nation was the good of the Church's children and their future.[27] In his talk to the Synod, Fares described the church as a witnessing community in the world with both clergy and laymen responsible for carrying the Christian message. He saw the need for the Church to train laypeople, equipping them as Christian stewards to be witnesses for Christ in their community.[28]

Fares outlined the relationship that had developed between the foreign missions and the Church, stating that the time had come for the Church to have missionaries who could work side by side with nationals not only as evangelists but also as experts and specialists. He criticized the missionaries

---

26. Synod of the Nile, *Minutes of the Year, 1961*, 278–279.

27. Ibid., 279.

28. Ibid.

for their deep involvement in administrative matters and not the real field ministry. He encouraged the Church to have ecumenical relationships with other mission organizations that would allow for the exchange of missionaries from different denominations and nationalities. He envisioned a network of ecumenical organizations that would help the Church financially, providing structures of accountability while also giving freedom to spend the money as deemed best by the national church.[29]

Fares' address to the Synod made a significant impact, with the new viewpoints influencing many future ministry decisions. The leaders of the American Presbyterian Church fervently pursued an ecumenical approach, and many young Synod leaders took up this vision. In the 1950s, the Americans were involved in the establishment of ecumenical organizations, and with their strong connections within the Evangelical Church, they then facilitated Egyptian involvement in this growing movement and perspective.

The Advisory Study had discussed the relationship between the Evangelical Church and other regional and ecumenical organizations such as the Middle East Council of Churches, and the World Council of Churches. It advised the Church to seek out more information about these organizations, their teachings, and the member churches before joining them.[30] Despite this, the Synod quickly participated in regional and international ecumenical organizations such as the Middle East Council of Churches, the African Conference of Churches, and the World Council of Churches,[31] with the Synod sending representatives to attend their meetings and conferences.[32] The ecumenical discussions and recommendations that arose from these conferences created two different approaches among the Synod leaders. On the one hand were the conservatives who refused both the theology and the methodologies. They criticized the ecumenical approach, which in their opinion concentrated on a moral and social gospel while neglecting the cross and salvation.[33] They considered some

---

29. Ibid.
30. Ibid.
31. Salama, *Tarikh al-Kanysa al-Injilya*, 285–297.
32. Ibid., 287.
33. *Al-Hoda* (1965): 17–19.

theological teachings and moral practices to be in direct contradiction with biblical teaching.[34] More liberal-minded leaders on the other hand, believed that the Synod could benefit from these organizations by widening its relationships with other Christians around the world. These leaders asked the Synod to join the ecumenical organizations because of their call for unity and for the potential financial benefits.[35] They defended the changes, seeing them as necessary to expand the scope of ministry in keeping with the changing political and social direction within Egypt, but without neglecting evangelism. They hoped that the new programmes would expand the Church's connections within society, which would indirectly benefit future ministry.[36]

New ties with ecumenical organizations were a sign of other changes. The Synod began to develop new ministries, including new media and radio ministries, gave a new emphasis to social work and village development, and started a youth camp ministry.[37] This was not just a change in methodology, but reflected the view that the Christian message must address not only spiritual needs, but meet the needs of the whole person.

These more liberal approaches were supported by the American Mission that recruited young Egyptian leaders, facilitated their studies in the United States, and then worked closely with them in their ministries of social development. Samuel Habib, Menes Abdel Noor, and Fayez Fares were the most prominent of these, becoming highly influential Synod leaders, at the expense of more senior leaders who emphasized the traditional methods of direct evangelism.[38]

7.4 The Integration between the Synod and the Mission

The political situation and the theological developments affected the relationship between the Mission and the Synod, accelerating the process of

---

34. Synod of the Nile, *Minutes of the Year, 1970*, 315–317.

35. *Al-Hoda* (1964): 205–208.

36. Synod of the Nile, *Minutes of the Year, 1961*, 279.

37. Synod of the Nile, *Minutes of the Year, 1959*, 67.

38. Synod of the Nile, *Minutes of the Year, 1965*, 18–9.

independence and moulding their future interactions. However, both the Board of Foreign Mission and the American Mission in Egypt had their doubts about the Synod's ability to fulfil its responsibility for the propagation of the gospel in Egypt. The leaders of the Board and the Mission questioned "whether or not in turning everything over to the national church were we not placing burdens upon the church which it could not bear?"[39]

7.4.1 Steps towards Integration

Although there were hopes that the Egyptian Church would continue to mature and develop, some missionaries doubted the Synod's ability to manage the situation. The Egyptian Board of Administration was established in 1957, to represent the Synod in administering the ministry and properties of the American Mission and to oversee the whole work of both the Synod and the Mission.[40] The Board contained Egyptian leaders only and had no American missionaries.

Willis McGill, an American missionary in Egypt at the time, reported his impressions of the strengths and challenges facing the new Board of Administration of the Synod of the Nile:

> I wish I could adequately describe the impression I got that the new Board does not seem apprehensive about the ultimate ability of the local Church to grow into this suit of clothes which is at present too big for it. All the men present have seen synod assume increasing financial burdens every year until now it carries a load which would have seemed ridiculously visionary not so many years ago. After much discussion this new project now has some strong "converts." These men believe it will be a healthy development in the Church's life. They believe that, under God, it will be instrumental in raising the Church's level of giving as well as its effectiveness in carrying the Gospel of Christ into all of Egypt and beyond. And because they so believe they naturally do not want to ruin

---

39. Lorimer *The Presbyterian Experience*, 235.
40. See chapter 2.

the chances that synod will approve, by proposing that synod's share of the burden be out of line with proved capacity.[41]

McGill had the impression that the Egyptian Church was partly ready to manage the financial and administrative responsibilities and the mission and evangelism programs on its own. He was giving not only his own view but also reflecting the viewpoint of the majority of missionaries who had worked with the Egyptian church and knew its strengths and weaknesses. Primarily, they were concerned that the Synod would be unable to raise sufficient funds to finance its ministry and mission.[42]

The Mission gradually transferred responsibilities to the Synod, encouraging them to direct and oversee Mission personnel, ministry, and properties. In 1960, there was progress in integration with missionaries serving as active members on the Synod institutions such as the Board of Administration and the councils.[43] In 1961, the American Mission considered financial grants to the Synod to support specific projects such as evangelistic work in the presbyteries and village development projects.[44] In 1962, a new constitution for the Mission was proposed, which incorporated the principles of integration. Synod members were invited to attend the Mission administration meetings and to serve on committees with the right to vote.[45] In 1963, there was a call for greater inclusion of Synod members on the Mission Executive Committee with the right to vote; and a joint Synod-Mission committee was appointed to study the integration process.[46]

In March 1965, a major consultation was held between the Evangelical Church and COEMAR representatives to set up a plan for further integration. This group proposed that there should be a study of the situation of the Evangelical Church, including its spiritual, social, and financial aspects. Seeking to further the cooperation between the Synod and the Mission, the committee planned to work together to solve ministry problems and

---

41. PHS UPCNA RG 209-4-22: McGill, Willis A. and Anna S. Papers: from Willis McGill to Donald Black, dated 18 September 1957.

42. Ibid.

43. American Mission in Egypt, *Minutes of the Year, 1960*, 439–440.

44. American Mission in Egypt, *Minutes of the Year, 1961*, 198.

45. American Mission in Egypt, *Minutes of the Year, 1962*, 234.

46. American Mission in Egypt, *Minutes of the Year, 1963*, 266, 279.

to find ways for the Church to pursue revival and evangelism using new methods such as publications and radio with the help of the Mission.[47]

7.4.2 The Dissolution of the American Mission in 1966

In 1966, the Mission suggested that the terms under which its missionaries worked with the Evangelical Church should be changed.[48] It detailed that the new responsibilities of the Synod should include requesting missionaries; locating them in the Egyptian field; and participating in their orientation, including language study, field training and pastoral care. It also proposed that the Synod take the responsibility for transmitting the missionaries' salaries and pensions that came mainly from America. The missionaries would then continue as members of the American Mission in Egypt, which would be responsible for matters of maintenance, including residence and work permits, housing, medical care, and the education of missionary children. It was also decided that the Synod and Mission should be jointly responsible for missionaries' furloughs and vacations. The American Mission, however, would continue to be completely responsible for those missionaries who were working in administrative and missionary maintenance positions. At the time, the Mission retained a few institutions and ministries under its authority, including the Tanta and Assiut hospitals, the audio-visual service, and the school for the missionaries' children in Alexandria.[49]

As the final action of the meeting, the president of the American Mission in Egypt declared "the dissolution of the organization of Association of the American Mission."[50] The missionaries continued their work under the supervision of an administrative council that consisted of a small number of missionaries. Both the Synod and the Administrative Council supervised the missionaries.[51] From that date, there was no formal body called "the American Mission." Instead, the American missionaries were termed

---

47. Synod of the Nile, *Minutes of the Year, 1965*, 35.
48. See Appendix B.
49. American Mission in Egypt, *Minutes of the Year, 1966*, 9–10.
50. Ibid., 19.
51. Ibid., 40–41. See also Lorimer, *The Presbyterian Experience*, 243.

"ministry partners" by the Synod.[52] In later years, they were called experts to avoid the government pressures and its sensitivity of missionaries.

7.4.3 The American Mission Departure in 1967

In 1967, the American government supported Israel in the war between Egypt and Israel, and diplomatic relationships between Egypt and the United States were temporarily terminated. Although the American missionaries were not expelled, they all left the country. Most of them spent the summer at Rocky Point Camp at Troodos, Cyprus until they could be assigned elsewhere.[53]

The Egyptian Church found itself in a difficult situation. On the one hand, the Church faced severe government pressure to separate itself from its connections with the Americans. On the other hand, the Synod had a long history of ministry and relationship with the American Mission, and furthermore, was still financially dependent on American donations to the Synod general budget and ministry programs. Because of this, both the American Mission and the Synod maintained contact with each other through the World Council of Churches.[54]

In 1968, the Synod and the World Council of Churches jointly studied five different areas of Synod ministries: the Seminary, schools, hospitals, audio-visual ministry, and CEOSS.[55] They arrived at an interim agreement of shared participation between the Evangelical Church of Egypt and COEMAR in these ministries. Full responsibility for former Mission work was assumed by the Synod of the Nile.[56] This strategic move opened the door for the Synod to extend its international relationships to other denominations and countries through the World Council of Churches, which proved to be an enriching experience for the various Synod institutions.

---

52. Synod of the Nile, *Minutes of the Year, 1966*, 63.

53. Lorimer, *The Presbyterian Experience*, 243. For more details on the American Mission's actions during the War and the story of the missionaries' evacuation from Egypt see, PHS UPCUSA RG 151-1-56: Arab-Israeli conflict: Martha Roy and Willis McGill, Report on the Middle East Crisis and the Egyptian Mission, dated New York, 21 June 1967.

54. Lorimer, *The Presbyterian Experience*, 243–244.

55. CEOSS is the Coptic Evangelical Organization for Social Services. There will be more study about its establishment and work later in this chapter. See Synod of the Nile, *Minutes of the Year, 1968*, 151–152.

56. Lorimer, *The Presbyterian Experience*, 244.

For example, the Seminary was able to receive teachers from churches and organizations in the Netherlands, Germany, and England.[57]

Despite these international links, the Synod continued to be pressured by the government. The Synod was placed in an increasingly difficult position as hostility against Americans continued to grow. On one occasion Samuel Habib, director of CEOSS, publicly declared that there was no connection between the Egyptian Church and the American Mission.[58] In 1971, the Synod responded to a government request to explain its foreign relationships. In a long document, the Synod's history and administrative and ministry programs were detailed, and it was made clear that the American Mission had been dissolved after transferring its ministry and properties to the Synod. The document declared that any American representation in Egypt was now under the authority of the Synod. The document also justified the support that the Synod received from foreign resources, indicating that this support was only for certain projects and under certain conditions that were set by the Synod. The document demonstrated that the foreign missionaries were experts whom the Synod had requested. The Synod declared itself a national, indigenous church with national support and a leadership that worked for the highest benefit of the country and its national security.[59] This documentation helped ease the pressure from the Egyptian government, although specific issues continued to arise. On another occasion, the government wished to expropriate some Church properties for national use. The Synod justified its objection by writing to the government explaining the religious position of these properties.[60] This was a critical and transformative period for the Egyptian Church as it sought to establish and demonstrate its separate identity, apart from the direct influence of the American Mission.

This political climate also led to a sharp decline in the number of American missionaries serving in Egypt. In 1966, there had been sixty-seven missionaries, but by 1970, this number had dropped to twenty-five.

---

57. Ibid., 245.
58. Ibid., 244.
59. Synod of the Nile, *Minutes of the Year, 1971*, 50–72.
60. Ibid., 34–43.

The Synod invited specific missionaries to return and work in the Synod's schools, seminary, evangelistic projects, and CEOSS.[61]

7.5 The Characteristics of the Practice of Mission in the Evangelical Church of Egypt 1958–1970

As we have noted, the Evangelical Church of Egypt underwent many changes in its relationship with the American Mission, and in its theology of mission. The Church was searching for an identity after having been strongly linked with and influenced by the American Presbyterians for more than a century. The time between 1958 and 1970, was an important period in the formulation of the Synod's practice and understanding of mission.

7.5.1 Administration and Finances

During the 1950s and 1960s, the Synod leaders were overwhelmed with many new administrative tasks that distracted them from their primary ministry of evangelistic and spiritual work. Issues of the Egyptian Board of Administration became the focus of Synod leadership as can be seen in the Synod reports of 1958–1970 where little emphasis is given to matters of church ministry.[62] Concerns about the schools, property and buildings, village work, and writing the church's new constitution consumed Synod meetings. Some of the Mission institutions, and especially the schools were supervised successfully; however, this was at the expense of spiritual ministry and mission initiatives. During these years, the Synod gave little attention to needs for church planting, youth ministry, or expansion into new missionary fields.[63]

---

61. Lorimer, *The Presbyterian Experience*, 131; Stanley H. Skreslet "American Presbyterians and the Middle East," in *A History of Presbyterian Missions*, eds. Scott W. Sunquist and Caroline N. Long (Louisville: Geneva Press, 2008), 226.

62. Synod of the Nile, *Minutes of the Year, 1958*, 59; Synod of the Nile, *Minutes of the Year, 1959*, 81; Synod of the Nile, *Minutes of the Year, 1960*, 113.

63. For more details of the attempts to have Synod boards handle the Mission properties and ministry, see Iskander Abiskhairoun Aboklog, "A Profile of and Proposed Program for the Synod of the Nile" (A Master's thesis submitted to the faculty of the Pittsburgh-Xenia Theological Seminary, Pittsburgh, Pennsylvania, May 1957).

Finances played an important role in forming the Synod approaches towards mission and evangelism. The financial aid received from American sources decreased, although COEMAR helped the Synod by contributing funds to projects related to schools, CEOSS, village development, and the hospitals. The American Mission had been integrated into the Egyptian Church; but Americans retained a disproportionate power because they chose which Synod projects they would support financially. In Kenneth Bailey's opinion: "Mission giving creates missionary power, and that missionary power resides necessarily in the hands of the church from which mission giving generates."[64] Because of COEMAR's new theological approaches, money was given to projects that adhered to their own priorities, namely social ministries. In this way, while Synod was establishing its own separate identity, it was also being subtly reshaped according to Western priorities.

In 1965, the Synod Executive Committee suggested that every three years the Synod and the American Mission should review the work and budgets of the Synod organizations that the Mission supported.[65] However, it was the Mission in Egypt's final decision where the monies were allotted, and the missionaries had strong relational ties with the social work organizations and international ecumenical councils that they supported. Many of the Synod leaders associated their ministry initiatives such as social work, audio-visual, youth ministry, and women's ministry with the American Mission and the international ecumenical councils.[66] Thus, the Synod was not fully independent: policies, mission theology, and internal relationships were all affected by their financial dependence.

The evangelistic and mission work that the Mission had delegated to the Synod was neglected because the Synod had limited financial resources for these ministries. When no outside financial support was forthcoming, the

---

64. Bailey, "Cross-cultural," 15–16.

65. Synod of the Nile, *Minutes of the Year, 1965*, 14.

66. One of the senior Synod leaders, Rev Labib Mishrikey, was the Synod representative in many international councils including, the Near East Council of Churches, the World Council of Churches, and the Evangelical Alliance. He was followed by Samuel Habib who was an active member of these organizations and who used his international relationships to develop his ministry as a leader of CEOSS.

Synod closed the evangelistic projects or delegated them to the presbyteries and local churches.[67]

7.5.2 Ministry Approaches and Opportunities

Before World War II, the Church in Egypt concentrated on the spiritual aspects of pastoral and evangelistic ministry, with a minor emphasis on serving society through the schools and hospitals. Following the theological changes in global missions, which adopted the ecumenical focus on meeting the social needs of people, the Synod changed its approach to ministry. These changes dominated the emphases of the Church and took most of its budget and its best leaders. The work of CEOSS, youth work, audio-visual ministry, and women's ministry were given priority. Financial concerns, the theological emphasis on social work, missed evangelism opportunities and the coming of parachurch organizations all contributed to the changing approaches to ministry within the Synod.

7.5.2.1 Coptic Evangelical Organization of Social Services, CEOSS

The Coptic Evangelical Organization of Social Services was a result of this new approach to ministry. The vision for such a ministry arose in 1947 with Davida Finney, who sought to convince both the American Mission and the Synod of the Nile that they should address issues of village development.[68] Her plan was to help villages in agriculture, health, village industries, and literacy. The General Committee of the Synod persuaded the Synod to take on this village church ministry project as its own program and the Synod established Committee of the Work in Villages.[69] The American Mission recruited a number of young Egyptian leaders for this work, including Samuel Habib who joined this work in 1952 and played a key role in its development and growth. Habib was appointed by the

---

67. Synod of the Nile, *Minutes of the Year, 1965*, 14–16.

68. Lorimer, *The Presbyterian Experience*, 55. For more details about the vision of social work, which Davida Finny adopted in 1939 and worked hard to convince the Mission and the Synod to adopt see, Finny, *Tomorrow's Egypt*.

69. Synod of the Nile, *Minutes of the Year, 1949*, 81.

Synod to work in the Committee of the Work in Villages and later to be its head.[70]

After many years working in several villages this pioneer social work programme achieved widespread recognition both inside and outside Egypt. In 1959, the Committee of the Work in Villages reported to the Synod about its ministries, which included literacy campaigns in many villages in Upper Egypt, housekeeping training for women, agriculture projects, and leadership training conferences, for those who would be involved in their various initiatives. Because of the growing role of this Committee, the American Mission dissolved its equivalent committee and entrusted the whole work to the Synod.[71]

Prior to this new ministry in the villages, the major classical approach of both the Synod and the Mission was to focus on people's spiritual life while also providing education and medical services. The new holistic concept – the whole gospel for the whole person, which had begun through the development work in the villages – affected the Synod's view of all its church ministries. The Committee of the Work in Villages believed that the villagers should learn that the Church spoke not only to spiritual matters but was relevant for every aspect of their life. Further, the Committee declared that the time had come for the Church to change its strategy from being only a place for Bible study and preaching to being a place concerned about agriculture, social work, house keeping, and literacy. They believed that the time of evangelistic missionaries was now past, and that in this new era, the church must serve the needs of the whole person either social or spiritual.[72]

In 1960, the Synod established a Committee for Christian Publications and Literacy that was separate from the Committee of the Work in Villages. Samuel Habib headed this committee as well and was a key figure in developing its work.[73] Then, in 1961, both committees received notice from

---

70. David W. Virtue, *A Vision of Hope: The Story of Samuel Habib, One of the Arab World's Greatest Contemporary Leaders and His Plan for Peace in the Strife-torn Middle East Where the Cross and the Crescent Meet and Where Bible, Koran and Torah vie for Centre Stage* (Oxford: Regnum Books International, 1996), 20–21; Lorimer, *The Presbyterian Experience*, 64.

71. Synod of the Nile, *Minutes of the Year, 1960*, 143.

72. Ibid., 143–144.

73. Ibid., 190.

the government that they must close their work until they were registered as social organizations under the Ministry of Social Affairs. The Synod decided to combine the two committees, uniting them as the new organization Coptic Evangelical Organization for Social Services, (CEOSS), under the leadership of Samuel Habib.[74] This move met the government demands and opened the door for CEOSS to expand its work outside the church to the whole society.

During the first few years, the Committee of the Work in Villages depended on the financial support of the American Mission that was sent through the Synod and designated for the village work. In 1961, when according to the government directive the Committee became registered as CEOSS, it announced to the Synod that no financial commitment towards its work was required from the Synod because of its limited resources. However, it assured the Synod that despite its new status it would be under the Synod's authority and would continue to be active as a Synod organization.[75] In the Synod Minutes of 1961 and in its first meeting CEOSS re-iterated that its relationship with the Synod was vital. CEOSS wished to cooperate with the Evangelical Church in fulfilling its mission, and to submit its work to Synod authority. But this relationship was not without its problems. From its inception as a registered organization, CEOSS received a large sum from American sources through COEMAR out of the Synod general budget. In 1968 Willis McGill, COEMAR representative for Egypt, wrote to Samuel Habib about the growing budget of CEOSS:

> There is so much concern here over the fact that your *entire* budget is underwritten from the outside, with nothing going to it from Synod or other local sources, and with all of it coming from the UPUSA Church, and that it is so large as compared to other programs' share of Commission Assistance, that I seriously doubt that the Commission will ever agree to enlarge it.[76]

74. Synod of the Nile, *Minutes of the Year, 1961*, 216.

75. Ibid., 238.

76. PHS UPCUSA RG 151-1-58: COEMAR: Budget, from Willis McGill to Samuel Habib, dated 17 December 1968, 1.

In 1968, CEOSS received $42,675 from COEMAR, while the Synod ministry of evangelism received $866.[77]

The work of CEOSS was linked with the Church for a long time and the leaders of the organization were pastors and members of the Church. The American Mission supported CEOSS and found in it the channel for their new vision of mission work. Dr John Lorimer, who was a leader in the American Mission, worked with CEOSS for many years. He viewed CEOSS as independent from Synod control, not only financially but in vision, policy and ministry as well. In later years, he would recall: "CEOSS enjoyed a greater range of freedom as an independent organization than it ever would have under the Synod."[78] Gradually the new organization controlled many areas of ministry in the Evangelical Church that created problems in its relationship with the Synod in later years. Meanwhile, the Synod questioned its budget, ministry, and relationship with foreign organizations.[79]

The work of CEOSS opened many doors for the Evangelical Church to expand its ministry to the whole society. It broadened the Church's vision of ministry, served as a powerful model of administrative excellence, and gave an example of the possibility of raising financial support. It reflected the change in global missions, while also fitting the political and sociological climate in Egypt. Despite these strong positive aspects, CEOSS also revealed the lack of evangelistic and spiritual ministry in the Church. Previously, the Synod had largely depended on the American Mission to carry out needed "non-pastoral ministries" such as evangelism.[80] Lacking the finances, the Synod initiated very little evangelistic work in both villages and cities. Contributions for evangelism came from individuals rather than from the Church as an institution.

7.5.2.2 Evangelistic work

For almost a century, the Mission had undertaken evangelistic work in Egypt. During the 1950s and 1960s, there were calls in the Synod to also

---

77. PHS UPCUSA RG 151-1-58: COEMAR: Budget, from Fredrick Wilson to Willis McGill, dated 10 December 1968, 1.

78. Lorimer *The Presbyterian Experience*, 81.

79. Ibid., 80.

80. Synod of the Nile, *Minutes of the Year, 1958*, 57.

instigate its own evangelistic work. Throughout this time, there were several initiatives and activities which raised hopes of a spiritual revival in the Egyptian Church. Then, as the American Mission changed its focus, its evangelistic ministries waned. Likewise, the Synod focused on other areas. This decline led one Synod leader to criticize the Synod's lack of interest in evangelistic ministry, objecting that there were more evangelistic centres in the 1930s than in 1961.[81]

In 1961, the Mission wrote to the Synod asking it to fully oversee the evangelistic work. It would be the Synod's responsibility to appoint workers, follow their work and evaluate the strategy of placing missionaries as evangelists in the presbyteries.[82] This was a major step. Although the Mission had been involved in evangelism for over a century, with its reduced numbers of missionaries, and their change in focus they realized that this ministry now needed to be handed over to the Synod.

One of the evangelistic programmes that the Mission wanted to transfer to the Synod was that of the Bible Women ministry. The Bible Women work included Egyptian women whom the Mission hired to work as evangelists in presbyteries and local churches. They had played an important role in the history of the American Mission's work among women in Egypt and in Sudan. In transferring the evangelistic ministries to the Synod, this work came under discussion.[83] Many difficulties were raised. First, these women were not well educated and would not have been suitable for any other jobs in the Church. Second, the American Mission had supplied their salaries, and the Synod was unable to take over such a financial responsibility. Third, these women were loyal to the Mission, not to the Synod, and there had been complaints about their work from presbyteries. In the end, the Synod decided to end this work, quoting financial and legal reasons.[84] They allowed their work to continue in local churches if those churches would undertake sole responsibility for their ministry, financial support and legal issues.[85]

---

81. *Al-Hoda*, 1961, 38.
82. Synod of the Nile, *Minutes of the Year, 1962*, 131.
83. Ibid., 131–132.
84. Ibid., 161; 221.
85. Synod of the Nile, *Minutes of the Year, 1963*, 150; 161.

Although the Mission had wished to transfer the evangelistic ministries to Synod supervision, the Synod released itself from the burden of supporting any other evangelistic workers beyond its own pastors. There was little interest in opening new evangelistic centres or appointing evangelists to the existing work.[86] The Church began to focus more on its own pastors' benefits, rather than its evangelistic mission to Egyptian society. Their limited finances and the gradual withdrawal of American financial contributions for evangelistic work forced the issue. CEOSS operated as the social ministry arm of the Synod, but the Church did not create an equivalent evangelistic, mission arm. Instead, the Synod left its evangelistic ministry under the supervision of regular councils and committees that worked routinely and slowly. Evangelistic work became the responsibility of individuals, local churches, and parachurch organizations.[87]

7.5.3 Understanding and Practice of Evangelism

The Synod understood that the church's role of evangelism was merely to establish and organize churches. Thus, it took note of the small village churches with too few believers to pay the salaries and housing for pastors, and considered these as evangelistic targets. In 1964, the Synod suggested that every presbytery should identify a certain number of such locations that could be supported until they become financially independent. They proposed a study giving details about such churches, their buildings and potential for housing pastors, and their financial capabilities. Further, they wished for the study to develop a plan to help the local church become self-supporting in five years.[88] The Synod then appointed evangelistic district centres under the supervision of local pastors. Every pastor who lived close to an unorganized congregation was to recognize it as an evangelistic extension to his ministry.[89]

In 1958, the Synod had created a Committee for Spiritual Revival to hold evangelistic meetings and promote church growth. Pastor Tanyws Zakhary, the representative for the spiritual revival activities, made many

---

86. *Al-Hoda*, 1961, 38.
87. Synod of the Nile, *Minutes of the Year, 1971*, 151–152.
88. Synod of the Nile, *Minutes of the Year, 1964*, 267.
89. Synod of the Nile, *Minutes of the Year, 1965*, 13.

efforts in this direction, and initial reports were encouraging: 31,000 attendees, resulting in 234 new members. There had been hopes that these activities would revive the church.[90] Unfortunately, financial and administrative conflicts with Rev Zakhary led the Synod to end his work one year later.[91] The Synod refused to reconsider their decision, and the Committee of Spiritual Revival was dissolved.[92]

In 1960, the Board of Spiritual Affairs suggested that 1961 should be a year of evangelism. The Synod accepted the suggestion, but in actuality, only a small number of churches held evangelistic activities.[93] Minya Presbytery, for example, arranged for public evangelistic meetings, with elders, pastors, and laymen sharing the responsibility to preach the gospel.[94] These evangelistic events were held only occasionally and for a short period, and were limited to public preaching activities.

During the 1960s, the Synod received a number of ministry proposals from Church leaders or laymen who had a burden for evangelism. These proposals included ministry to factory workers,[95] youth evangelism,[96] and work among Sudanese in Egypt.[97] A pastor in the Assiut Presbytery, who wished to open a work in the New Valley, a newly developing district in the Egyptian West Desert, put one such proposal forth. The Synod and its various institutions had many ideas for evangelism and mission work but very few came to fruition, since the Synod lacked the funds. When the Synod did have resources, they were primarily spent to cover the needs of the pastors and some more popular organizations. When the Synod

---

90. Synod of the Nile, *Minutes of the Year, 1958*, 287.

91. Ibid., 16.

92. Synod of the Nile, *Minutes of the Year, 1959*, 62.

93. Synod of the Nile, *Minutes of the Year 1961*, 291.

94. Ibid., 290.

95. Synod of the Nile, *Minutes of the Year, 1962*, 128. The ministry among workers led the Synod to have a Japanese missionary who came to work among workers in Delta. The Synod cooperated with the Japanese Church for the first time because of their experience in ministering in industrial areas. Synod of the Nile, *Minutes of the Year, 1967*, 67.

96. Synod of the Nile, *Minutes of the Year, 1966*, 63.

97. Synod of the Nile, *Minutes of the Year, 1965*, 35.

decided to engage in any evangelistic programs, they merely asked the American Mission to fund the work without making any effort to secure the needed funds.[98]

In 1966, the Board of Spiritual Affairs proposed to the Synod that every presbytery should have a pastor for evangelism who would be located in its most successful evangelistic centre. They suggested that a committee of three members be appointed in every presbytery to plan and supervise the evangelistic ministry. They hoped that the initial funding would come from the American Mission, with the funding being reduced annually by 10 percent after the first ten years, with the presbyteries then paying the difference. Due to a lack of funds and personnel, the proposal was dropped.[99] Unfortunately, the Synod lost many such opportunities to extend its evangelistic ministry.

In 1970, the Synod Board of Spiritual Affairs proposed that 1971 should be the National Year of Evangelism. This time, they envisioned holding evangelistic activities in local churches, presbyteries, and in the Synod, and their plans involved a great number of churches and pastors, elders and women leaders.[100] The Synod passed the proposal, and 1971 saw many activities throughout the country. Preaching, singing teams, drama, audio-visual productions, conferences, caravans,[101] and Bible distribution were all employed.[102] Many Church members welcomed this effort, with some individuals contributing funds in the hopes that this would become a continuing movement. The Year of Evangelism proved a great success, with many activities and a large number of church members' involvement

---

98. The Synod used to ask the Americans to support any kind of evangelistic work. This happened occasionally in the 1960s and early 1970s. See Synod of the Nile, *Minutes of the Years: 1962; 1965; 1966; 1970.*

99. Synod of the Nile, *Minutes of the Year, 1966,* 68.

100. Synod of the Nile, *Minutes of the Year, 1970,* 227.

101. Caravans were one of the new methods which had been successfully used by a group of young men, starting in 1953. These men went on to become major leaders in the Synod. A group of young men would visit a village or city for 5–7 days, making home visitations, and holding Sunday schools, evening meetings, and social ministry including medicine services. This method developed over time and contributed greatly to the spiritual life of the visited churches and the participants.

102. Synod of the Nile, *Minutes of the Year, 1972,* 130–134.

in evangelism, Bible distribution, and training. The Synod, motivated by the response, designated 1972 as the year of follow up.[103]

Unfortunately, this work did not become a permanent programme, being too dependent on a few charismatic leaders who pushed the idea through Synod. In later years, such evangelistic endeavours were either local in nature, or were organized by such parachurch organizations as Campus Crusade for Christ, Youth with a Mission, World Vision, Operation Mobilization, and the Navigators, who came to Egypt in the 1970s.[104] Lorimer commented that these organizations often built their relationships with individual pastors and congregations, which again failed to ignite a national vision.[105] This was an era of individual efforts in evangelistic work since the Synod as an institution played a traditional, limited role in evangelism depending on short time activities.

7.5.4 Mission Opportunities

The years 1958–1970 also provided many opportunities for the Synod to explore new fields and to send ministers to regions other than Southern Sudan. Most openings came through the American Mission, while others came through the migration of Evangelical Egyptians to Arab counties. There were mission opportunities in Ethiopia, Iran and Kenya, and calls for pastoral work in Arab countries such as Kuwait and Syria.

7.5.4.1 Ethiopia

Originally, the American Mission and the Evangelical Church had sent missionaries to Sudan, hoping that it would also provide a door into Ethiopia. The American Mission believed that the Egyptian Church should be involved in Ethiopia because of the historical relationships between the Coptic Church and the Ethiopian Church.[106] In 1920, the Board of the Foreign Mission of the United Presbyterian Church in North America started mission work in Ethiopia through its missionaries in Southern

---

103. Ibid., 115.

104. Lorimer, *The Presbyterian Experience*, 250.

105. Ibid.

106. The Coptic Church was considered the reference for the Ethiopian Orthodox Church. Although the Ethiopian Orthodox Church started by the Assyrian Church, it came under the Egyptian Coptic Church from its early history until 1946.

Sudan.[107] This goal of sending Egyptian missionaries to Ethiopia remained in the background until 1958 when the Secretary of the Board of Foreign Mission in America announced to the Synod that Miss Hiyat Tawfik, an Egyptian, had volunteered herself to work as a secretary for the American Mission in Ethiopia. She had worked as an administrator with the American Mission in Cairo and had travelled to study administration for one year in the United States. An American missionary who had served in Egypt described her desire to undertake missionary work:

> Now I want to write you about Miss Hiyat Tewfik who had a conference with me here in Philadelphia before she left. Hiyat manifested the same vision and call to service, the same promptings of spirit and heart, which come to all of our young people when they go out to be a missionary. She signified her willingness to go anywhere, to India, to Ethiopia, or where ever the Lord might lead; but she wants to give her life completely to the Lord's service and will consider herself as a missionary wherever that service may be. She is highly qualified, I believe, to carry on the work of your office there.[108]

The American missionaries in Egypt, together with their Board, sought to convince the Synod to send her to work as a secretary for the American Mission in Ethiopia. A letter from Donald Black, chairman of the Board, to Willis McGill, chairman of the American Mission in Egypt says:

> As for her being a secretary, it will be good for them to understand the multitude of opportunities for Christian witness that come in any line of work. She will be in constant contact with Ethiopians through her work in the business office . . . Furthermore, it must be made clear that we are interested in helping the Coptic Evangelical Church with this

---

107. Rycroft, *The Ecumenical Witness*, 215.
108. PHS UPCNA RG 209-4-22: McGill, Willis A. and Anna S. Papers: from E. E. Grice to McGill dated 13 August 1957.

project because we are interested in the missionary outreach of that Church.[109]

This proposal was difficult for the Synod to accept. First, it would mean sending a woman as a missionary to a foreign country, and second, her missionary role would be as a secretary and not as a minister. The Board was ready to pay her salary for three years after which the Synod in Egypt should cover her costs.[110] Hiyat was never sent to Ethiopia as the Synod rejected the proposal.

In 1960, the Egyptian Mission Council received another request letter from the secretary of the American Mission in Egypt about the desire of COEMAR to have an Egyptian missionary in Ethiopia.[111] This request also found no response from the Synod and the idea of having the Synod support mission work in Ethiopia has never been achieved.

7.5.4.2 Iran

In 1960, the American Mission asked the Egyptian Board of Mission to send a doctor to work as a missionary with the American Mission in Iran. The American Mission in Iran would pay for this position. The Synod asked that the request be sent directly to them through the Board of Commission on Ecumenical Mission and Relation.[112] This request also was never fulfilled.

7.5.4.3 Kenya

In 1961, a conference in Nairobi, Kenya studied missional work among industrial communities. During the conference, it was suggested that two Egyptian missionaries, a doctor and an evangelist, be sent to the work in Kenya where there was an Arabic-speaking community. The World Council of Churches approved the project and was ready to fund it.[113] This project

---

109. PHS UPCNA RG 209-4-22: McGill, Willis A. and Anna S. Papers: Donald Black to Willis McGill dated 20 December 1957.

110. Synod of the Nile. *Minutes of the Year, 1958*, 279.

111. Synod of the Nile, *Minutes of the Year, 1960*, 167.

112. Synod of the Nile, *Minutes of the Year, 1959*, 59; The American Mission in Egypt, *Minutes of the Year, 1959*, 213.

113. Synod of the Nile, *Minutes of the Year, 1962*, 128.

also did not become a reality because the Synod was not ready to send or fund any missionaries to other countries for financial and political reasons.

The mission opportunities in Ethiopia, Iran and Kenya all originated from outside, and were not part of the Synod's vision. At this time, the Synod seemed determined not to involve itself in any kind of ministry that might cost it money in the present or future.

7.5.4.4 Arab countries

In 1950s and 1960s, the Synod received invitations to send pastors for other Arab countries either which have indigenous evangelical churches such as Syria and Lebanon, or which have Egyptian evangelicals who were living there for work such as Kuwait. In 1962, the World Council of Churches studied the Egyptian Church and noted that:

> One of the most striking features of this church is the number of pastors it has trained and sent to minister elsewhere. Of these 7 are in North Sudan, one in South Sudan, two in Syria, one in Lebanon, one in Iraq, and one in Kuwait.[114]

In 1960, the Synod's Board of Spiritual Affairs received a request through the Synod of Syria and Lebanon, with whom they had a strong relationship, asking that an Egyptian pastor be sent to serve at a church in Kamishley, Syria.[115] The Synod responded favourably, sending one of its pastors who later was followed by others.

One of the first countries to which the Synod had sent pastors was Kuwait, where Rev Yussef Abdel Noor went to serve the Evangelical Church in Kuwait in 1959, after being ordained as an evangelistic pastor for Kuwait by the Lower Egypt Presbytery.[116] He was ordained in an Egyptian Presbytery as a pastor and not as a missionary since all the pastors who worked outside Egypt were members of a presbytery. Throughout

---

114. Douglas Webster, *Survey of the Training of the Ministry in the Middle East* (London, World Council of Churches, Commission on World Mission and Evangelism, 1962), 35.
115. Synod of the Nile, *Minutes of the Year, 1960*, 164.
116. Ibid., 96; 169.

most of Synod history, ordination for mission work or any other ministry apart from pastoral ministry has not been recognized.[117]

Lewis Scudder III, a long-time missionary to Arabia and a friend of Yussef, described Yussef's ministry saying:

> Through the growth years, using remarkable pastoral skills, Yusuf welded together a single congregation from Arab Christians of extremely diverse ethnic and denominational backgrounds. His ecumenical vision was far sighted, his pastor's heart profound, and his plan for the new shape of the church's future in Kuwait passionately advocated . . . The English Language Congregation pastors who served with him sometimes grated upon him, not infrequently contended with him, but they always learned a great deal from him.[118]

In 1962, the Board of Spiritual Affairs received a request from the leaders of the church in Kuwait asking for a pastor to serve there during Rev Yussef Abdel Noor's study leave in the States. The church in Kuwait arranged to pay the salary, travel expenses, insurance, and other facilities for the appointed pastor. The Synod responded by sending one of its evangelists for a year and a half, thus indicating a growing spirit of cooperation between the Synod and churches in Arab countries[119]

In studying the ministry of its pastors abroad, the Synod discovered that these ministries were drawing the evangelical churches in Arab countries into unity.[120] They envisioned the day when these churches might establish a general assembly of the Arab countries. However, the connection between these other Arab congregations and the Synod of the Nile remained friendly, but never developed into any official relationship.[121]

---

117. In the 1950s the Synod ordained a number of pastors, through presbyteries, for specialized ministries including publication, development, and youth work.

118. Lewis R. Scudder III, *The Arabian Mission's Story: In Search of Abraham's Other Son* (Grand Rapids: Wm. B. Eerdmans Publishing Co., 1998), 237.

119. Synod of the Nile, *Minutes of the Year, 1962*, 93.

120. Synod of the Nile, *Minutes of the Year, 1960*, 164.

121. *Al-Hoda* reported on the growing ministry among Egyptians in other Arab and Western countries. The increase of the Egyptian emigrant to these countries helped in establishing congregations which were directed as the local churches in Egypt. A small

The vision of sending Egyptian missionaries abroad came from individual Synod leaders who still hoped that the Synod would not just send pastors, but would become a missionary-sending body as had happened in Sudan. However, this endeavour instead imitated the experience of Northern Sudan, which had begun with a missionary vision, but ended up with a pastoral focus. Most pastors who worked in Arab countries saw themselves strictly as pastors: a perspective shared by a majority of the Synod.

7.6 Conclusion

Although the Evangelical Church received its full independence from the General Assembly of the UPCNA in 1958, there were many connections with the Americans which continued to influence their practice of mission and evangelism. Although the changing political situation in the Middle East, and in Egypt specifically, dictated that properties and control be transferred to the indigenous church, the actual balance of power between the Synod and the Mission was not so clear-cut. Further, the Egyptian Church was faced with changing theological views of mission and a flourishing ecumenical movement that their American partners supported. The financial limitations of the Egyptian Church meant that it could learn from and interact with the new views but it was not free to determine its own way in mission and evangelism. The Church was subverted in its theology and missionary vision by the American influence, and by American money.

After the departure of the American Mission in 1967 and the transfer of properties and ministries to the Synod, the Synod found itself engulfed by many administrative and financial matters that distracted the leadership from their evangelistic ministry responsibility.

Although the Synod received many suggestions and opportunities for evangelistic work inside Egypt and missionary work outside, it did not develop its own national plan, preferring for the most part to depend on the evangelistic initiative of individuals and local churches. Although the Synod sent one missionary to Southern Sudan and to Kenya, every other

---

number of these pastors had a missionary attitude. For more details see, *Al-Hoda* in years from 1961 to 1972.

opportunity of becoming a missionary-sending church failed because of a lack of finances, a preoccupation with administrative matters, and a lack of vision on the part of the Synod as a whole. Furthermore, the Synod continued to view missionary service as a pastoral role, and within Egypt concentrated on social work and village development along with its pastoral ministry. The American Mission and the Synod both share responsibility for the formation of this limited perspective of mission and evangelism.

CHAPTER 8

Conclusions and Contributions

8.1 Conclusions

This study has examined the relationship between the American Presbyterian Mission and the Evangelical Church of Egypt from 1854 when the Mission explored Egypt, until 1970 when the Synod of the Nile declared an end to its official relationship with the Mission. The study focused on the effects of these interactions in the formation of an Egyptian understanding and practice of mission.

8.1.1 Politics

The study demonstrated that the political situation in Egypt had a major role in changing the interactions between the Mission and the Church. As was seen in chapter 1, the Ottoman Empire of the mid-nineteenth century allowed Christian denominations to have their own churches. This enabled the Evangelical Church in Egypt to gain official recognition. Mohamed 'Ali and his family showed tolerance towards Christians, and this together with the political climate with its emphasis on the development of Egyptian society, meant that the government and society were open to the Mission's establishment of Christian schools, hospitals and churches. The growing role and influence of Western powers in Egypt gave the American missionaries the opportunity to enjoy many privileges, including the Capitulations.[1] These privileges also indirectly helped the Evangelical Church to build its own role and ministry. Although the government and social norms

---

1. See chapter 2.

ultimately restricted the missionaries in their work among Muslims, they enjoyed great success in their ministry among Copts.

When the British occupied Egypt in 1882, Egyptians increasingly connected the missionaries' activities with colonialism, even though the American missionaries had no special privileges under the British occupation. The nationalistic movement, together with the Muslim Brotherhood, played an important role in solidifying opposition to evangelizing Muslims, which affected the Mission and Church work. The later restrictions against the Mission schools, visas, work permits, and changing taxation laws also forced the Mission to speed up the transference of its properties and ministry to the Egyptian Church. In the 1950s and 1960s, the change in American policies towards the Middle East in general, and Egypt in particular, placed both the American Mission and the Egyptian Church at a crossroads. In 1958 the Synod of the Nile declared its independence from the UPCNA General Assembly. Gradually, the Mission handed over its entire work to the Synod, with all official ties ending in 1970.

The political changes not only shaped the mission work inside Egypt but also influenced the mission work in Sudan. Egypt's involvement in the political, economic, and social situation in Sudan opened the door for both the Mission and the Church to explore the Sudanese mission field. The Egyptian Church ministered in Sudan for almost a century until 1956, when Sudan gained its independence. This and the resulting tensions in Southern Sudan played a major role in ending the official relationship between the Sudan Presbytery and the Synod of the Nile in 1964. This political situation also resulted in the termination of the ministry of Rev Swailem, Egypt's missionary to Southern Sudan.

There were two pressures on the Egyptian Evangelical Church throughout this era. The Church wanted to be faithful to its call to evangelize Egypt, as mandated by Christ and envisioned by the American Mission; however, the Church also felt the many political, religious, and social pressures that sought to limit its freedom and its mission and evangelistic endeavours. The Church barely resisted these pressures and limitations, instead seeking to prove itself a patriotic member of society. Ministry to Muslims, and relationships with the American Church were minimized.[2]

8.1.2 The Relationship between the Church and the Mission

This study examined the coming of the American Mission to the Egyptian field and the establishment of the Evangelical Church. As a Protestant organization, the American Mission had a particular Protestant understanding of the gospel that they wished to share. This led to a confrontation with the Orthodox Coptic Church, which did not accept certain doctrines. As a result, the Mission established the Evangelical Church of Egypt, which then became their main instrument for reaching out to the Egyptians. Both the Mission and the Evangelical Church worked together towards the eventual self-support, self-government, and self-propagation of the Evangelical Church. This process was affected by conflicting and changing political, ecclesiastical, and financial considerations, but eventually resulted in the full independence of the Evangelical Church in 1958.

The Mission and the Church experienced many difficulties in their relationship that hindered the transference of the whole Mission ministry to the Egyptians. The atmosphere of mistrust and tension between the Mission and the Synod slowed down the process and negatively affected the Church's sense of its missionary role. The Egyptian church had a limited missionary role, not only because of the socio-political situation, but also because it depended mainly on American money, ideas, initiatives, and workers. As we have seen in this study, the sending Western church made a great contribution to the Egyptian society through its missionary work; however, it failed to adequately transmit its vision to the daughter church. There was a gap between the theories of mission and the practice on the actual field.

During the 1950s and 1960s, there were major shifts in the theology of global missions and in the relationship between the Evangelical Church and the American Presbyterian Church. As discussed in chapter 7, these changes resulted in a reduction of American financial support, personnel and evangelistic ministries coming into Egypt. These developments,

---

2. See chapter 7; Synod of the Nile, *Minutes of the Year, 1961*, 279.

alongside the political changes, meant that the Egyptian Church lost its work in Sudan and Kenya. The Church also dissolved its Committee for the Work among Muslims. American perspectives directly influenced the Evangelical Church and formed its understanding and practice of mission and evangelism.

8.1.3 The American Mission and the Synod Interactions in Mission and Evangelism

This study looked at the interactions between the Mission and the Church in their mission work together. The American Mission hoped that the Evangelical Church would shoulder the responsibilities of the mission and evangelistic work both inside and outside the country. We examined two case studies: evangelism of Muslims within Egypt, and second, both the American Mission and the Church's mission to Sudan.

Both the Mission and the Church were involved in reaching Muslims in Egypt, but this resulted in very few converts. Both the Mission and Church seemed to limit their efforts due to their fear of reprisals. Egyptian Christians have inherited a fear of Muslims, which they have never overcome, and their desire to avoid suffering and persecution led them to limit their work among Muslims. Furthermore, the political, religious, and social situation in Egypt was not conducive to a productive ministry. Both the Mission and the Church made reasonable but sporadic efforts to find creative and effective methods for communicating the gospel to Muslims, but they failed to continue in their efforts.

When the American Mission began to explore the Sudan field, it believed that this work could become an extension of the Egyptian Church's ministry and foreign mission field. The American Mission did not consult with the Synod when opening the work in Sudan, nor did they start with any clear agenda, or agreement about collaboration. This led to two different approaches being employed. The American Mission considered Sudan a mission field, while the Synod handled the work as a pastoral ministry among Egyptian expatriates.

The difference in views produced tensions concerning the work in Sudan. Although the American Mission gradually made concrete progress in its mission in both Northern and Southern Sudan, there was little cooperation with the Evangelical Church. On many occasions, the American

Mission criticized the Evangelical Church for its lack of missionary vision, but gave no solid plans for working together. If there had been a clear vision and plan, the Mission and the Church might have created a unique mission programme in Sudan. The Egyptians could have provided the workers and used their influence as well as their ability to communicate with the Sudanese. If this had been combined with American planning capabilities and financial resources, the two bodies together could have developed a strong missionary team in Sudan. Unfortunately, they failed to see the possibilities, and continued on their separate paths.

The Mission had stated that its goal was to help the Egyptian Christians to become the evangelizers, and to form a missionary church.[3] However, in practice, the Mission did not make enough effort to achieve this goal in its teaching, example, administrative structures, or delegation of ministry responsibilities. For many years, the Mission excluded Egyptians from membership in its associations and did not involve them in making decisions about its evangelistic ministry. The Mission thus implied that evangelism and missionary work was only for Westerners. At the same time, the Egyptians were given a limited picture of evangelism, seeing it as confined to sending pastors or seminary graduates to pastor a group of evangelicals in a city or village.

When the American Mission established the Evangelical Theological Seminary, they hoped that it would produce leaders to evangelize Egypt. However, the Seminary only trained Egyptian leaders for pastoral ministry. This was the Mission's responsibility since at that time the Evangelical Church remained under American control and influence, and followed the path that the Mission indicated. The American Mission also underestimated the Evangelical Church, denying it self-government for a century and making the Church financially dependent on the American Church to cover the expenses of their evangelistic ministry. The Mission took a ruling role: directing the vision and planning, taking the initiative and dictating methodology and theology to the Church. This put the Church in the passive position, which did not allow it to set its own course, especially in mission and evangelistic work.

---

3. Watson, *Egypt*, 234–236. See also chapter 4.

8.1.4 Egyptian Understanding and Practice of Mission and Evangelism

The Egyptian Evangelical Church limited its understanding of mission and evangelism to pastoral ministry in new internal and external locations where there were evangelicals. This limitation raised questions about the Church's seriousness about having an effective missionary work and practice its self-propagation.

The leaders of the Evangelical Church were primarily involved in administration, finances and ecclesiastical matters rather than actual ministry. Although there were efforts by individuals and a small number of congregations to reach out to Muslims, regretfully, this did not develop into a significant mission movement by the Church as an institution. Muslim evangelism as a major focus remained a largely unfulfilled goal.

The Evangelical Church did not consider Sudan as a mission field. Instead, as the Mission had previously done in Egypt, the Synod established churches, a Sudanese Presbytery, and the Committee for the Work in Sudan. The work concentrated mainly on the Christian Egyptians who were living in Sudan, with limited vision to reach the Sudanese. A few individual Egyptian pastors and laymen and women had a vision for missionary work among the Sudanese, but were prevented from being fully effective by administrative, financial and ecclesiastical obstacles. As we saw in chapter 5, they had to find other channels for their ministry, working under the American Mission or other parachurch organizations in order to fulfil their evangelistic calling.

The sending of the first and only Egyptian missionary to Southern Sudan was a unique step in the practice of mission. Swailem's character, expertise, and ministry produced great results and raised the hope of both Egyptian and American churches that a new era of mission had dawned. The enthusiasm for supporting the work in Southern Sudan and the revival of other ministry methods raised hopes that the Egyptian Church would continue to make a major contribution to missions. However, the Synod did not continue its interest, especially when Swailem moved from Sudan to Kenya. Unfortunately, the vision for missions did not flourish since the Synod did not recognize missions as a basic and foundational ministry of the Church. The Synod was not ready to handle an independent mission work of its own without the supervision of the Americans.

The Egyptian Church missed a great opportunity to become a major player in the world mission movement within the Middle East. Egyptian culture, art and language are widely disseminated throughout Arabic countries, giving Egyptians considerable influence and opportunity. Egypt has also been a key player in Africa, especially in Sudanese political affairs. All of these factors could have enabled the Egyptian Evangelical Church to make a significant contribution to mission work in Africa and other Middle East countries. Unfortunately, the Evangelical Church was blinded by alternative theological ideas and limited by political and financial factors.

Egyptian Christians have suffered for many centuries under Islamic oppression and government pressures. This suffering has left a heritage of fear between both the Orthodox and Protestant Egyptian Christians that then prevented the Church from consistently initiating and developing missions and evangelism. Like the American missionaries before, the Evangelical Church found work among the Copts to be an easier task than reaching Muslims. The Church also had limited financial resources. The monies that they had were used to pay the salaries of its pastors and other essential expenses. Very little money was budgeted by the Church for evangelistic and missionary work – such projects instead being funded by individuals. Later, as mission theology changed, the Synod was largely controlled by the American designation of funds to social work, and influenced by the ecumenical and pluralistic theologies that prevailed during the 1950s and 1960s. This movement away from direct evangelism released the Church from a sense of guilt about its failure to evangelize Muslims or to send missionaries to other nearby countries.

The leaders of the Church played a limited role in opening opportunities for the Church to practice its mission. They limited their interests to local pastoral work, thus confining themselves and their people within this narrow view of ministry. Although there were laywomen and men who made great efforts towards mission work, their individual efforts never ignited a similar passion within the Church as an institution.

8.2 Contributions

As well as drawing the above conclusions, this thesis has contributed to the study of mission history and practice in the following areas:

8.2.1 Egyptian View of the Relationship between the American Mission and the Egyptian Church

Previous studies about mission work in Egypt either examined only the American Mission and its work, or utilized a church-growth approach in their reports.[4] These theses depended on available American sources but used limited Egyptian sources, whereas this thesis has utilized extensive American and Egyptian sources in its examination of the Evangelical Church interactions with the American Mission and the Egyptian contribution to the mission movement. Furthermore, this present study is unique in that the author has taken advantage of Synod of the Nile historical documents, including its annual minutes. Substantial use has been made of Egyptian books, newspapers and church papers, while interviews with Egyptian missionaries have also provided valuable first hand insight into the role of Egyptians in mission work in Sudan.[5]

The American Church has accused the Evangelical Church of not undertaking its missionary responsibilities, without considering the situation from the Egyptian perspective. This study has sought to explore the reasons, motivations, and circumstances that have resulted in the attitudes towards, and practices of, mission and evangelism within the Evangelical Church in Egypt.

8.2.2 Egyptian Contribution to Mission Work

This thesis explored the Egyptian contribution to mission work both inside and outside Egypt. Although the Church played a different function than that of the American Mission, the Evangelical Church was, in fact, one of

---

4. In his study "The Establishment of the American Presbyterian Mission in Egypt," Burke described the American Mission and its early ministry in Egypt. He relied primarily on American and British sources and focused on the Mission methodologies. In "The Growth of the Evangelical Church in Egypt," Ghabrial conducted a field study utilizing a church growth model to analyze his findings, but gave little attention to the historical background.

5. See Appendices C and D.

the first Majority World countries in modern mission history to send missionaries to a neighbouring country. As we have noted, when the Synod began its mission work in Sudan in 1900, the potential existed to form an enduring mission movement or board. Initially, the Synod of the Nile considered Sudan as a mission field. Some Evangelicals in Egypt responded to this initiative by contributing financially, and their example motivated other churches to do likewise. Although the focus in Sudan shifted to pastoral ministry, the work of individual pastors and laymen and women demonstrated the Egyptians' ability and willingness to be effective missionaries if given the opportunity.

The same potential was evident during the 1950s when the Synod sent Rev Swailem as a missionary to Southern Sudan. This opened the door once again for the Synod to create a mission movement and explore other fields. Rev Swailem demonstrated a high degree of accountability and commitment to the mission work and to the Synod as a sending body. His ministry serves as an example of the cooperation that was possible between the American Presbyterian Church which gave the invitation and administered the work, and the Egyptian Church which initially commissioned and fully supported him.

The Synod also recognized the needs of Egyptian communities in other nearby countries, sending pastors to meet the spiritual needs in these locations.[6] These ministries could also have become a missionary extension of the Church, but the opportunity was wasted, and the focus was limited to providing pastoral care. The Synod failed to broaden its vision, exporting the same limitations and fears as experienced at home.

8.2.3 The Influence of the American Church's Changing Mission Theology as Experienced in Egypt

In the early years of the work of the American Mission, the American missionaries were pietistic in life and ministry. As seen in chapter 1, the evangelization of Egypt was their priority, and the missionaries designed their programmes to serve this clear goal. They built schools and hospitals not

---

6. The Synod in 1970s and after sent many pastors to other countries such as Kuwait, Syria, Iraq, Oman, and United Arab Emirates. A number of pastors also went to western countries such as the United States, Canada, Australia, and Europe to pastor Arab and Egyptian Evangelicals. The work of these pastors exceed the time and focus of this study.

only to meet the needs of society, but also to use them for evangelism. When they established the Evangelical Church, they hoped that it would become the main instrument for evangelizing Egyptians. During the first hundred years, the evangelistic focus of the American Mission, which also reflected the theological views of the UPCNA sending body, was clearly embodied in their ministry practices. In the late 1940s and 1950s, major developments occurred in mission theology inside the American Presbyterian churches that then changed the focus on the mission field. Mission Boards were called to give indigenous churches their complete independence. At the same time, the new theologies of the social gospel, of ecumenism and later pluralism, were also gradually influencing the direction and practice of mission. This turned the focus from evangelism and spiritual ministry to a wider understanding of mission and Christian responsibility. This led to the establishment of the social services branch of CEOSS, which then became the main recipient of financial donations within the Synod. Later, CEOSS became independent from the Synod, but no equivalent organization for the work of evangelism and mission was established. As noted in chapter 4 and chapter 7, this shift away from evangelism was brought about not only by increasingly pluralistic beliefs, but by the political and social pressures which limited Church involvement in evangelism.

This study discovered that both the Western American Mission and the indigenous Evangelical Church achieved limited results as missionary agents. Both the Church and the Mission became church-centred, not mission-centred.[7] Both bodies channelled most of their financial, personnel and administrative resources towards the needs of the Church, rather than towards mission work. Their evolving relationship produced an organized, self-governing Church, but failed to imbue it with a strong missionary vision or programme. This study sought to analyze the reasons for this failure in the hopes that Western mission agencies and indigenous churches can work together to avoid such problems in the future, and instead create new cooperative approaches which will facilitate greater mission achievements.

---

7. Alexander, *Should the American Mission*, 12.

Constitution of the Egyptian Association of the Missionaries of the United Presbyterian Church of North America

Cairo, March 17, 1871

Art. 1. There shall be an Association of all the Missionaries in Egypt, both lay and clerical, of the United Presbyterian Church of North America.

Art. 2. This Association shall be known by the name and title of the Egyptian Association of the Missionaries of the United Presbyterian Church of North America.

Art. 3. This Association shall be amenable to the General Assembly through its Board of Foreign Missions or any other agency which the Assembly shall authorize to communicate with the Association.

Art. 4. This Association shall have the following officers: President, Secretary, and Treasurer, all of whom shall be elected at the annual meeting of the Association by a majority vote of members present at that meeting.

Art. 5. This Association shall have power to fill vacancies in these offices whenever they occur.

Art. 6. It shall be the duty of the President to preside at all the meetings of the Association and discharge all other duties usually incumbent upon such an officer.

Art. 7. It shall be the duty of the Secretary to keep a record of the transactions of the Association and conduct all its official correspondence except such as belongs to the Treasurer.

Art. 8. It shall be the duty of the Treasurer to hold, in the name of and in trust for, the Board of Foreign Missions aforementioned, all lands, tenements, permanent funds, libraries, printing press, and apparatus, and all property whatsoever pertaining to the Mission; and he shall give such legal security for said property as shall be demanded by the Board of Foreign Missions. It shall be his duty also to receive, hold, and, according to the direction of the Association, dispose of all moneys received for missionary purposes by the Association from the Board or from any other source whatsoever; and he shall render a full annual report to the Association.

Art. 9. In conducting its business the Association shall be governed by the general rules of similar bodies, and shall have power to enact such by laws as any peculiarities in its circumstances may demand.

Art. 10. The Association shall meet annually pursuant to its own adjournment, and shall besides meet as often as the circumstances of its work may require, and special meetings shall be called by the president when requested by two of the members of the Association.

Art. 11. A majority of the members of the Association present in Egypt shall constitute a quorum for the transaction of business.

Art. 12. It shall be the duty and exclusive right of the Association to dispose of all funds committed to its trust and to transact all missionary business arising out of the relations of its members to the home Church, and it shall report all of its proceedings to the Board of Foreign Missions for its consideration and approval.

Art. 13. This Association shall be organized and go into operation as soon as practice able after the authorization and approval of this constitution shall have been received from the General Assembly.

Art. 14. This constitution may be altered or amended by a majority of any future meeting of the Association with the concurrence of the General Assembly.

Constitution and By-laws of the American Mission in Egypt, UAR of the United Presbyterian Church in the USA, 1966

Constitution

Article I – Name: The name of this organization shall be the American Mission in Egypt, U.A.R. of the United Presbyterian Church in the USA.

Article II – Purpose: The purpose of the Mission, representing the United Presbyterian Church in the USA is to share with the Christian church in Egypt in fellowship, service, and witness in testimony to the unity and mission of the world wide church of the Lord Jesus Christ.

Article III – Membership: All missionaries and fraternal workers, career and special term, appointed to Egypt by the Commission on Ecumenical Mission and Relations of the United Presbyterian Church in the USA shall constitute the membership of the Mission. Their relations to the commission, as individuals and as a group, are defined in the Manual of the commission.

Article IV – Meetings: The business of the Mission shall be conducted at sessions of an Administrative council elected by the voting membership of the Mission. The administrative council shall meet at least three times a year. Regulations governing the procedures of the Mission and its Administrative council shall be defined in the by laws of the Mission.

Article V – Officers: The Mission shall have the following principal officers: president, secretary, and treasurer, other officers may be provided for in the by laws as needed. The selection of mission officers, their tenure and duties shall be as set forth in the by laws and in accordance with commission regulations.

Article VI – Amendments: This constitution may be amended by a two-thirds vote of the Mission, subject to the approval of the Commission on Ecumenical Mission and Relations of the United Presbyterian Church in the USA an amendment must be proposed in writing at a meeting of the administrative council and decision for its adoption taken at the next regular or called meeting.

Article VII – Authority: This constitution shall replace the constitution of the Egyptian Association of the Missionaries of the United Presbyterian Church of North America, which was adopted in Cairo on 17 March 1871 and amended in Assiut at the 1874 winter meeting of association, and it shall become effective when approved by the Commission on Ecumenical Mission and Relations of the United Presbyterian Church in the USA which is the mission's controlling body in the USA and the source of its support and authority.

By-laws: (Adopted February 1966)

I – The Mission

A – Voting Membership: All missionaries with one year or more of career service with the Mission in Egypt and who have completed the language requirements for the first year are entitled to vote. Exceptions to these qualifications for voting may be made by the mission upon recommendation of the Administrative council. (Ref. CM 1963, section 311-c).

II – Officers

A – President: The president shall be elected by the administrative council from its voting membership for one year at the fall business meeting. He shall preside at all meetings of the council and shall exercise the usual prerogatives of such an officer in all cases.

B – Executive secretary: Whenever a commission representative serves the field of the Egypt mission alone, he shall act as executive secretary of the mission. Otherwise he shall be nominated by the administrative council and elected by the voting members of the mission for a term of two years, subject to commission confirmation. The council may choose an acting executive secretary to serve during the absence or incapacity of the executive secretary. The executive secretary has both administrative and secretarial functions.

1) *Administrative Functions*

   a) In general, he is the agent of the mission and the administrative council to see that their actions are carried out.

   b) He shall sign on behalf of the mission all communications reporting mission decisions to all official agencies, whether government, ecclesiastical, or other.

   c) He shall be secretary of the administrative council, member of the nominating committee, and ex-officio member without vote on all other committees.

   d) If the president is absent or incapacitated, the executive secretary shall take the chair for the election of an acting president.

2) *Secretarial Functions*

   a) He shall keep the official mission records and files.

   b) He shall conduct the official mission correspondence.

   c) He shall forward to the commission through the regional secretary official minutes, estimates, and all requests requiring its action, together with covering explanations.

   d) He shall distribute all forms for reports and inquiries and arrange for their return to the collecting source.

   e) He shall report to mission members, committees, organizations and institutions, assignments of work or actions affecting their activities, both those arising from mission action and those arising from government or commission actions.

   f) He shall serve as an official channel of communication

between the Coptic Evangelical Church or other national ecclesiastical bodies and both the Egypt Mission and the Commission on Ecumenical Mission and Relations.

C – Assistant Secretary: An assistant secretary shall be nominated by the administrative council and elected by the voting members of the mission for a term of two years to assist the executive secretary in carrying out the secretarial functions of his office. The assistant secretary shall attend meetings of the council and serve as recording secretary.

D – Treasurer: The mission at a fall meeting of the administrative council shall nominate a mission Treasurer to be elected by the commission for the following calendar year. His duties shall be those specified in the commission manual. (Ref CM 1963, sections 339ff). He shall be a member of the administrative council.

E – Assistant Treasurer: The mission at a fall meeting of the administrative council shall nominate an assistant mission treasurer to be elected by the commission for the following calendar year. He shall assume the duty of the mission treasurer during the latter's absence or incapacity.

F – Other Treasurers: The mission at a fall meeting of the administrative council shall nominate to the commission for the following calendar year a treasurer for any group, unit of work, or institution that requires such an officer. The accounts of such treasurers shall be presented for audit as the mission may direct.

III – The Administrative Council

A – Membership: The mission members of the administrative council shall be twelve named by the nominating committee and elected by the voting members of the mission, for terms beginning with the fall business meeting of the council. They shall be chosen with a view to securing balanced representation of men and women, geographical areas, and major aspects of mission work and life. The executrices secretary, the assistant secretary, and the treasurer of the mission shall be ex-officio members but without vote. The Coptic Evangelical Church shall be invited to appoint five representatives, one of them from the women's Union.

B – Organization: The members of the administrative council shall be arranged in two classes serving terms of two years. Half the membership shall be elected each year according to class. After serving two terms consecutively, a member shall for one year be ineligible for re-election.

C – Meetings: The administrative council shall meet regularly at least three times a year, preferably in the fall, the winter, and the spring. Other meetings may be called by the executive secretary or by the president, with the concurrence of at least one other member of the council. When it is deemed necessary for reasons of expediency, the executive secretary may, in lieu of calling a meeting, submit a proposed action to the members of the administrative council by correspondence or by telephone for their decision.

D – Duties: The administrative council shall act for the mission in matters referred to it by the executive secretary, by any of its working groups or the mission's committees, or upon motion of any two members of the mission. Its work may be delineated as follows:

1) Actions that do not require approval by the entire Mission:
    a) Out of country travel.
    b) Emergency furlough (in consultation with the commission staff).
    c) Committee appointment changes.
    d) Implementation of decisions already made.
    e) Election of the president.
    f) Appointment and dissolution of working groups within the council's membership.
    g) Other matters deemed routine in the council's judgment.
2) Actions requiring approval by the voting membership of the mission:
    a) Decisions involving major policy.
    b) Appropriations and the expenditure of funds.
    c) Acquisition, disposition, and management of real estate.
    d) Location of missionaries in cases where this responsibility has not been delegated to an agency of the Coptic Evangelical Church.
    e) Appointment and dissolution of mission committees, and the appointment of their chairmen.

f) Nomination of executive secretary and assistant secretary.

g) Nomination of treasurers to the commission.

h) Nominating a new council member to complete an unexpired term.

i) Other matters deemed of major importance in the judgment of the council.

E – Working Groups: The administrative council may appoint working groups from within its membership, as needed to expedite preparation of work for meetings of the council, according to functions and areas of work concerning which matters are referred to the council for consideration. A convener shall be named for each working group. Other members of the mission may be co-opted and representatives of the Coptic Evangelical Church invited to assist and advise the working groups.

F – Mission Approval: Actions of the administrative council requiring approval by the entire mission shall become official mission decisions when approved by two-thirds of the voting membership on the field. Ballots shall be supplied to each voting member by the executive secretary and shall be inscribed with three squares to provide for votes of yes, no, and abstain. Voting shall be by signed, secret ballot, the votes being sent to the executive secretary. Any votes not returned within two weeks shall be considered as approving the action proposed.

G – Parliamentary Authority: The rules contained in Robert's rules of order Revised shall govern the mission and its administrative council in all cases to which they are applicable and in which they are not inconsistent with the constitution and by laws of the mission.

IV – Committees

In addition to the administrative council there shall be committees as provided below:

A – Nominating: This committee shall be appointed by the administrative council at its spring meeting from outside the membership of the council, with the exception of the president, the executive secretary, and those members not eligible for re-election. This committee shall consist of the president, the executive secretary, and five members representing as far as possible all areas of concern. The committee shall propose nominations for the class of administrative council members whose term shall start at the fall meeting of the council. After submitting this list to the voting membership of the mission for consideration, the executive secretary shall allow two weeks to elapse for further nominations. Additional nominations may be made to the list by proposal in writing to the executive secretary by any two voting members of the mission. After two weeks the executive secretary shall supply to each voting member a ballot on which all nominees are listed with instruction to vote for as many as are needed to fill the new class.

B – Other committees: The administrative committee may appoint other committees as needed for continuing administration of mission responsibilities, for special projects and assignments, and for compliance with commission regulations and directives. The Coptic Evangelical Church shall be invited and urged to appoint representatives to serve with committees whose responsibilities are concerned with or directly affect the work and life of the church.

1) **Standing committees:** These committees deal primarily with oversight of activities and areas of work for which the mission has a continuing responsibility between meetings of the council. They shall be appointed annually by the council at its fall meeting, subject to mission approval, at which time reports shall be received of their work and justification for their continuance in present or revised form shall be reviewed.

2) **Temporary committees:** These committees deal primarily with special projects, assignments, and requirements of limited duration. They shall be appointed by the council as needed, subject to mission approval and annual reappointment, and shall be dissolved upon completion of their particular work.

V – Amendment

These by laws may be amended by two-thirds vote of the membership of the mission on the field, subject to approval of the commission. An amendment must be proposed in writing at a meeting of the administrative council at least one day before the meeting at which action is taken on it.

An Interview with Swailem Sedhom Hennein Cairo, 5 March 2004

By Tharwat Wahba

Tharwat: Let us start from the very beginning.

Swailem: Swailem Sedhom Hennein, born in Garf Sarhan, which is a small village, belonging to Dirrot in the government of Assiut. It is a small place with a majority of non-Christians. My father was a cotton trader and other agricultural products like wheat. My parents were keen Christians. My father was a lay leader in the church and I grew up in an atmosphere full of Bible study and prayers every day. After primary school which was mostly in Dair Mawass.

Tharwat: When were you born?

Swailem: October 5, 1927. Before I was born my parents wanted a son because they lost two sons before I was born. They gave me a [strange] name (Swailem), because at that time, there was a myth or a connection between a [strange] name and survival – and it worked and I survived! I went to a Christian primary school (Assaad Abd El Motagly primary school) in Dair Mawass, which was quite a distance from home.

Tharwat: I think it was built by the American mission.

Swailem: I think the American Mission had a hand in building it, but Assaad Abd El Motagly's family was a rich family and very keen about education and church. They belonged to the Evangelical Church, actually leaders in the Evangelical Church. Then following Dair Mawass I went for one year to Assiout College and the second year was in another evangelical school in Sanaboo. I went back to Assiout College the following year and stayed there till I finished my secondary school.

It was in my fifth year of secondary through the influence of the "Soul Salvation Organization" and Joseph Zaki who was a student in the college that I made a decision for Christ in November 1945. As a result of that I started to be interested in the Christian work and we started as a group, Josef Saber, Menes Abdel Noor, and Fayez Fares, were there and we started a village work. We went on bicycles from Assiut College to various villages. It was there that I got the vision of coming to the Seminary.

Tharwat: Tell me more about your time in Assiut College and the role of the American Mission there and the Christian education.

Swailem: As a matter of fact, I was really influenced by two, three or four devoted missionaries: Neil McLaughlin, and John Thompson who was there for a short term, and I stayed with him for one year. The one who influenced all of us a lot was Davida Finney who was interested in rural development. She was really the primary influence in our lives.

Tharwat: Was she in Assiut College?

Swailem: Yes, she was residing there, living not teaching. As a result of that, in Assiut College, I made a decision to come to this Seminary of course.

Tharwat: Before that, tell me more about your visits to various villages, not just you but most of the students. Why was that? Was it part of the program there?

Swailem: No, not at all, actually, it was a voluntary work. A program we, the students, thought of ourselves and we knew that there are villages around Assiut which were not far away, 5–6 miles away, without ministry. So we decided that every Sunday each of us would go to a village and then come back in the afternoon, meet and share with each other what had happened. Our stay in Assiut was helped by the fact that it was a boarding school so we were not worried about preparing the food and other things and that gave us time.

Tharwat: Was there any supervision from anybody?

Swailem: No, not at all. It was the group work that gave us a push, not just me, but Menes and Fayez, a direct push to come to the Seminary. So we applied to Mallawy Presbytery and in the following year, which was 1947, we came to the Seminary and we graduated, me and Menes, in 1949. We were in the same class. During that period, some of us got the idea of getting more education while we were here, so we approached the AUC (American University in Cairo). Fayez, Samuel Habib, Abd El Messiah Stefanoos and I went.

Tharwat: Did Menes go?

Swailem: No, he did not go to that program.

Tharwat: Tell me more about that program. Was it permitted to you to go there or free to go?

Swailem: I think there were a lot of doubts about our going. Some wonderful leaders like Gobrial Rizk Alla and Labib Mishreky, whom we loved, were objecting to it. They thought we were departing from the ministry, so there was resistance.

Tharwat: So, was there any relationship between the Seminary and the AUC?

Swailem: I think that originally, the AUC was Presbyterian but at that time, there was no link at all between the missionaries and the AUC

Tharwat: You went there on your own?

Swailem: Yes, as individuals really. Samuel Habib joined the journalism. I, Fayez, and Abd El Messiah joined the social science and I worked on BA of Social Science.

My class was very small, I think only seven of us; two or three belonged to ministers in the Egyptian government, very important people really, so it was satisfying. It was at that time that I was exposed to the idea of research, exploring libraries and doing subject base research and I chose a rural uplift as my area.

At that time also, I had been serving Qalandul during the summer months and they asked me to serve there. Then later I became their minister and that encouraged me to concentrate my research on rural development. My area of research was Qalandul. So I concentrated my work on village life, their agriculture, their industries, and their family life. It was a variety of aspects of rural life and then my project dealt with how to improve life in the village.

At that time, it was clear to me that sanitation was very important and hygiene and nutrition. I focused on those areas: it was not basically medical but it was rather about improving their own physical condition and helping it. I thought little bit about income and how to improve that, but that wasn't the main focus of my thinking at the time.

Tharwat: Was the Church involved when you were working in that project?

Swailem: The real help I got was from Qalandul church where I was a pastor and they were wonderful really. They allowed me to come here [to the Seminary] from Monday to Wednesday and then go there Thursday or Friday, work and visit the people Thursday, Friday and Saturday. I used to lead the services on Sunday. Sometimes they went morning and afternoon, and then I left by train.

Usually, I spent most of the night coming by train to Cairo. I think the help I received from the church was by allowing me to continue living here in the Seminary. So I kept my room with a very little cost and that was a big service because without that, where would I have lived in Cairo? I think this was little unusual – through the AUC and the aid of the missionaries who were here, Elder and McGill, I'm sure they had a hand in that. I received a grant to go to India, because India at the time was the model for rural development in poor countries. It was known and read about and there was a centre in India called Mortandant, run by the YMCA, a centre of rural development.

Therefore, the grant allowed me to go to India, again thanks to the local church. They kept me as their pastor in spite of my leaving to India. So I went to India and through that centre I learned a lot about rural improvement in many parts of India. I started to go from one place to the other in India. I spent time with followers of Gandhi and I held many services in rural areas run by Gandhi's followers. Then the Reformed Church Mission in India had a rural project where I spent time with them also, and I was very fortunate. The Indian Government was running a project and they welcomed me. I went to their centres and in most cases the government did not charge me for anything except I paid for transportation to go there. So it was a worthwhile kind of project. I wrote my report on that and it was published here locally in Arabic and in a small part in one of the Christian magazines run by Moody Bible Institute in Chicago. I sent them the article and they published it. The amazing thing that when I was in India a team of missionaries from Southern Sudan, headed by Lawry Anderson, came to Egypt.

Tharwat: Were they from the American Mission?

Swailem: Yes. Anderson was a missionary of the American Presbyterian Mission in Sudan. He came to the Synod and I think he was accompanied by one or two of the missionaries from Sudan. He himself had been born in Egypt, and his father was a missionary in Egypt. Anderson recommended that the Synod should send a missionary to Sudan, which was a crazy idea at the time. The Synod accepted it and before I returned from India they had a committee formed and it was collecting support.

The people who were excited about this were Rev Iskander Abaskharion, Rev Farid Manqarious, Rev Tawfik Gaid, Rev Ebraheem Abd Allah, and others. So when I returned they told me: "Look, may be you shouldn't unpack. We are sending you or Menes to the south of Sudan, but the thing is between you and Menes."

So when I came back from India, I found that Menes had been married already for two years and had a child and the talk was between the two of us. So we agreed, Menes and I, that I should go since I was still single. Not only that, he told me that if I went and a lion ate me up I should come back and tell him! So I did really unpack, and I told them that I had only one condition: I would go to the Southern Sudan the slow way because I had had a lot of work in India and I need to go in a longer way. So they sent me by a steamer which took 7 or 8 days, instead of airplane.

Tharwat: When was that exactly, 1952–1953?

Swailem: In 1953, by train then by ship. I stopped in Malakal. Dr Anderson was there in the centre of the American Presbyterian Mission which was in Malakal in the Upper Nile.

Tharwat: Will you tell more about the American Mission before you went? Did you know anything about its history in Southern Sudan before you went?

Swailem: I had some idea and they told me that there were about 10–12 stations – that most likely I would have to spend a year in one of them to learn a language. There were Dinka, Shilluk, and Nouir tribes, and I would have to spend most of the time learning a language, most probably the language of the Shilluk because they had more districts without missionaries. So I was preparing myself for that because I did not know the language at all.

So I arrived in Malakal and Dr Anderson and his wife welcomed me. Both of them received me at the boat station because the boat went from Malakal to Joppa every two weeks and it carried mail. The missionaries in that station received and sent out mail every two weeks so they were there when the boat arrived.

Tharwat: Were you married then?

Swailem: No, I was engaged officially to Samira before I left. Actually, she was agreeing to the idea [of mission work]. Her mother was so happy with the idea, but her father was not at all happy with the idea although he was a Presbyterian elder in Heliopolis Evangelical Church in Cairo. He thought that it is a crazy idea to do that because at the time to go to Upper Egypt was thought of as a kind of punishment and to go to Sudan was an even greater punishment, and to go to the south of Sudan was very risky. I spent that year there learning Shilluk and Dinka in Dolieb Hill.

Tharwat: So Dolieb Hill was the centre of the American Mission in Southern Sudan?

Swailem: One of the main centres. Malakal was the administrative centre while Dolieb Hill was actually the centre of the Shilluk area, which had education, a school, and a large clinic. I started going to the villages and I was assigned a tutor to teach me Shilluk and Dinka. He was a Shilluk and continued with me till I left in 1964.

Tharwat: Was he a Shilluk?

Swailem: Yes, he was a Shilluk, but I think his mother was a Dinka and his father was a Shilluk, so he knew more than one language.

Tharwat: Was he working with the American Mission?

Swailem: I think he might have been related to the American Mission but not really because he was recruited to work with me full time. So he and I started to do evangelistic work and he was teaching me the language through quite a few books around.

Tharwat: What was his name?

Swailem: Paul Adina Adeljok. He is very old now and he became a minister. So we started to go to the villages because this was the way to practice the language. We carried with us machines, including a recorder with those large discs. Also I had managed to get a slide projector, 4 inch by 4 inch each slide and it was run by kerosene. So we used to carry those to the villages to attract people. We had a slide projector at night and a recorder player playing music and then there were already hymnal productions and the Bible translation which was not yet complete. So we had only one Gospel, parts of the Book of Acts, and parts of various Epistles. So I adopted the idea of engaging myself in translating the first letter to Timothy.

Tharwat: Was that in your first year there?

Swailem: Yes. I did the first letter to Timothy and I was hoping to finish Second Timothy and Titus but in the ten years I finished the first letter to Timothy then I went directly to Titus because of the great difference in focus between the two letters: the letters to Timothy and the letter to Titus. I was hoping to get back to second Timothy.

After that one year I came back to get married and two days after we got married we got on the boat.

Tharwat: When you came back here, what was the reaction of the Church?

Swailem: There was a lot of enthusiasm though I did not stay enough to enjoy it because I was keen to go back to work. So, as soon as we reached there, my wife and I, we were assigned to go to a station which had no missionary in Attar. We stayed for a little while in Malakal and from there directly to Attar.

The American Mission there was very helpful in certain things that we wouldn't have had without them, like a boat with an engine because that was the only transportation to Attar, which was in the White Nile next to the branch called Attar Branch. No one can go there, we had to depend 100 percent on a boat. I had to learn how to drive a boat, for one year before she arrived, and the American Mission helped me to have a boat with an engine.

Tharwat: For your own or for the station and did they pay for that?

Swailem: Yes, it was for the station. So in a sense without the American Mission it would have been much harder.

Tharwat: Were you working under the supervision of the American Mission?

Swailem: Actually, they did not call it supervision. They called it partnership because my salary came from Egypt, and the expenses of my missionary work was mostly paid by the American Mission. Buying the boat for example, I do not remember if we bought it. I think the American Mission did because they could import such things but we could not.

So my salary came from Egypt to the American Mission in Malakal and then they gave it to me. Actually the American Mission was very helpful because even if Egypt was delayed in sending this it did not matter at all. I received it anyway. They were really good and then every year when all the missionaries gathered in their annual administration meeting, we were part of that and I did have the honour to be assigned to certain administrative tasks.

Then at that time, the Upper Nile Presbytery was formed and I was in charge of it for two years in succession.

Tharwat: I will come back to that, but before that you said that your salary came from Egypt.

Swailem: Yes, and the cost of the work and paying for Adeljok.

Tharwat: Did they agree to that, the Egyptian Church here?

Swailem: Yes, the amazing thing is that they were generous, as far as I remember; they had no problem finding the money.

Tharwat: Egyptian money?

Swailem: Yes, 100 percent Egyptian money and it was sent through the America Mission in Southern Sudan. They were really helpful by partnership and being a colleague to all these stations. We had ten to fifteen stations with probably thirty missionaries, single or married, in all the Upper Nile – which was huge. It is like two to three times the distance from Alexandria to Aswan. It was huge, but my station was south of Malakal, at Lake Noo, a little tiny lake near Bahr El-Ghazal.

Tharwat: At the very south of Sudan?

Swailem: At the south of the White Nile, there were others in Sobat and in other villages.

Tharwat: Will you tell me more about your time there? First of all, what was your first impression when you were there with Samira?

Swailem: The real challenge was mastering the language and being able to move by ourselves into the villages. So I think we found wonderful acceptance with the people on the station. Once a year we had a gathering among the heads of the villages, and that was usually at Christmas. And many times we had a 1,000 people in the station who were the heads of the villages and the heads of the tribes too. We became such good friends with many society leaders including the king of the Shilluk, King Koor, who came to our station and we became very good friends. One time, he asked me to take him to Khartoum for treatment and I did.

Tharwat: Were the Shilluk Christians?

Swailem: No, the great majority were non-Christians, and they did not work. When they accepted Christ and converted, we usually had classes in the village, which [were] run the whole year, and here the work of Paul Adina became very important. We had some kind of curriculum to teach them before their baptism. All baptism was in the river by immersion.

Tharwat: So your first and primary work was evangelism?

Swailem: Yes, the primary work was evangelism and Bible translation.

Tharwat: Tell me more about evangelism among those people.

Swailem: We went to villages carrying those machines which interested and attracted the people. We would have a crowd of 200 to 300, then we would run those machines and they listened and at night, they would see the pictures. Then we invited them to accept the Lord and if they were willing and raised their hands, we would meet those who made the decision and make classes for them.

Tharwat: Was there any religious resistance to your work among them?

Swailem: No, no religious resistance from among them, there was nothing. The only resistance that we would talk about is that they did not accept. In addition, there were questions raised, about for instance, they were polygamist, and they thought that the richer you became the wiser you got. Polygamy was a hindrance to them, because what if he wanted to marry a second or a third wife. What if it had already happened and he had two wives? This happened several times. If the three of them accepted the Lord and were educated in Christian education, I baptized all the three and I never accepted the idea of keeping one and sending the other away. I thought it was a cruel thing to do. And what if he married the second wife shortly before accepting faith in Christ?

Tharwat: After accepting faith in Christ?

Swailem: It happened yes, but what if he was wise enough to marry the second wife shortly before being baptized. How would I know? So they declared their faith and took a period of one year in education, then they were baptized. I did baptize several cases of more than one wife and we instructed them to keep the two wives, being equally fair to them and their children and so on.

There were cases where the whole family was baptized, grown-ups and children at the same day. I enjoyed this because when the whole family is a Christian family then usually we had a group of Christians in a place and they could build a house for the Lord or a build a place, which usually would be used as a school.

We always had a school starting along with the building of the church. We assisted in that too. Gifts were given and we would celebrate the new building usually by making a party for the whole group with a lot of fun.

Tharwat: What was the other means you used for your mission? You mentioned translation, evangelism, and schools.

Swailem: Yes, schools in the Upper Nile and in the Catholic area where they worked. The schools were very important and there was no missionary school so when we had a school we tried to work with the Mission to see that the kids would have a proper place. In most cases, they would go to good primary school and we had to seek the permission of the parents and the elders of the village; and then almost invariably we provided transportation, clothing, food, education and also took them back home for holidays and so on. So it was a big job. We had a large work to start a school and maintain it, and also it was good working with the Mission.

Tharwat: So, the schools were owned by the American Mission and not the Egyptians.

Swailem: Yes, the local ones belonged to the American Mission. The one we started with was Egyptian, with 20 to 25 students and after that a selection of people continued their education. Not everybody continued their education because the children were valuable to them. The girls were more valuable than boys because they brought in a dowry and got married early, so they did not stay in school. The boys who continued with us, would be sent to a higher preparatory school. Ours was the best one can have.

Tharwat: Who paid for them? The mission?

Swailem: You mean in Dolieb Hill?

Tharwat: No.

Swailem: We paid the cost of the teacher.

Tharwat: Were there any other kinds of ministries beside that?

Swailem: Nothing at that time, no agricultural work or such. It was all an informal thing; they came to our station, saw something growing and we helped them to grow things in their own village. But it wasn't like a project; it was person to person help. We gave them the seeds and also helped them to water it and look after it and instructed them.

Actually, this was resisted at the beginning of the work. But after some people accepted Christ and were baptized and built a church and we went to them, then they started to come and garden for everybody. That was the custom, if you are growing something; it is for everybody not just your family. So it happened many times that after we grew it and the plants flourished, some one might come at night and destroy it, because in the tribal way, they depended on the forest and on the bushes, not on growing things. I said to them at the beginning that they must grow things, but they were afraid of their gods, so they destroyed the plants.

Tharwat: You mentioned that there was also a Catholic missionary work.

Swailem: No, not in the Upper Nile. It was our own Presbytery except in the school, in my station, where we had a middle school after the primary. They went on to middle school which belonged to the government and we did not contribute in that middle school except by offering to teach and providing daily (morning and evening) prayers, Bible study at school, and pastoral care – that was our job.

So in the school, there were Catholics and evangelicals. The evangelicals were represented and also the Anglicans. It was a boys' school – the majority were boys – so the boys I was serving were either Anglicans or Presbyterians. There was a Catholic priest who was my neighbour and we had good times together because he had an open heart, too.

Tharwat: So, there were Catholics?

Swailem: In the middle school.

Tharwat: Only in the school?

Swailem: Yes, only in the school. He did nothing else.

Tharwat: How did that happen? Why did not they do missionary work besides the school work?

Swailem: Because the missionary work was divided under the British. The people in the Upper Nile were Presbyterians; in the Equatorial, they were

Anglicans; and the people in Bahr El Gazal were Catholics. We had a meeting every year or so between all the three groups. Every group was keen not to step on the others field and not to offend them. So that division was before I went there and this was important because the school was built, run and cared for by the missions, except for that middle school which was owned by the government. Before Sudan became independent, the British used to pay for those middle schools. There was only one secondary school for the whole Southern Sudan, but for every province, there was a middle school: the Upper Nile, Equatorial, and Bahr El Gazal each was a province with a middle school. Ours was the largest because it had children from the other provinces.

Tharwat: Tell me more about your time in this area.

Swailem: Another service we used to have, almost once every two or three years – they had bad rains and a dry season and they did not irrigate. So when this happened there was starvation and hunger. We received a lot of help, money to buy grain, and we gave it to the hungry village. The beauty of it was that when there was a hungry family that meant that everyone should help. Something happened concerning that which greatly influenced my life. There was a dry time in a village where we used to preach. This dryness caused a famine. I was teaching the people outside the hut when a girl came from outside carrying a basket and she put it under the pole. Every village has a pole at which they gather and make a festival. It is like a social centre: we preached there, and people would gather there and we could talk to them. She put the empty basket and left. We were there preaching for two to three hours. Gradually the basket began to fill up as they brought grain and things from their huts and filled the basket. The girl came back and put the full basket on her head. Nobody asked: Who is this girl? They did not know. All they knew was that there was somebody in need of food. This really influenced my life a lot.

Tharwat: I know there are many good things in those people, more than we can imagine.

Swailem: Yes, no selfishness. They really practised socialism. King Koor and the chiefs, after two years, came to me at the centre of Attar and gave me a Shilluk name, and that was a real honour. *Shatakosh*, that was the name the whole village knew me by.

Tharwat: Which means?

Swailem: It means some one like a leper, neither black nor white.

Tharwat: Was that common among missionaries?

Swailem: No, no, they would select and when they gave you a name this meant that you are one of them; you are then a Shilluk in a sense, and so I was. We never at any time or any moment, even when we come here for a holiday, locked the door. The whole house was open and they could come for a drink or whatever we had left in the house: it is for everybody. Although it did happen that when there is a starvation not far away, if you had a meal at home you couldn't eat it as you felt guilty if you did. There was a great human touch which is true to the gospel.

By the end of my stay there, when I finished first Timothy and Titus, I sent it to Ann Doudilan, a good friend and a missionary. She was excellent in Shilluk and she was in charge of translating the whole New Testament. It was three years later after we were kicked out (she was kicked out too, everybody was), that she went to Uganda, there she managed to print the New Testament, and she sent me my copy.

Tharwat: You said you baptized a large number of people.

Swailem: There were 3,000 including the children.

Tharwat: How many were converted?

Swailem: The majority were converted to Christianity from spiritualism – you can call it that because it was a spiritual religion. If we add to that the fruit of the work in Dolieb Hills station which had no male missionary . . . It was not far from Attar, two hours by boat and we had three women working as missionaries. Ann Doudilan was one of them and when they needed someone to be baptized; I would go and baptize him.

Tharwat: At that time, many Egyptian pastors went to Northern Sudan, to Khartoum and so on.

Swailem: There were pastors but the local congregation paid them.

Tharwat: What was the difference between your work as a missionary and theirs as pastors?

Swailem: They worked as pastors, usually among Christian immigrants to Sudan who spoke Arabic. Therefore, they had congregations and did all what was needed including communion, baptism, teaching, preaching, pastoral care, and so on. Nevertheless, in our case we did not do that. Our task was evangelism, preaching, taking care of the people physically, and teaching them.

Tharwat: Did you start a church in Attar?

Swailem: Yes, of course, the Church of Attar was mostly composed of students in the school. The only time when we had people coming from the area around was for special celebrations, because the villages around had churches. We had six sizable congregations and several small ones. Several young ones were very small, but they all came once a year at Christmas time to celebrate at the station. They would come early in the morning, some of them would spend the night, and we celebrated by singing, praying, and hearing once again the story of the Bible. Sometimes we showed slides at night. It was a time of celebration.

Tharwat: You were preaching in Shilluk at the time.

Swailem: Yes, I think they were good, but I am sure I made many mistakes. In Shilluk you can make mistakes just by the tone of the word. It could be "my eye" and it would mean "my grandmother" or "something out in the field." The difference is in the tone, so you have to remember what tone to use and I am sure they were very patient with me. There were many times when they would laugh. They knew what I meant and that I was saying it wrong but they were very polite. They hardly ever mentioned that you made a mistake, but Paul would tell me if he was with me and I did not use the correct tone.

Tharwat: Were they accepting of an Egyptian at the beginning?

Swailem: I think they did not hear anything about an Egyptian or non-Egyptian. For them I was somebody with a different colour or clothes. Of course we did not use trousers there. The Dinka used to shave all their bodies. It happened many times that when I would go to the village, the kids would come around me to put their hands on my legs saying, "Ghost, ghost!" To them I was a ghost with all that hair on my legs. They only noticed my colour and they knew nothing about Egyptian. In school, of course, when we taught history and geography, they learned about it.

Tharwat: Someone told me about the shock you had when the first woman came to your church.

Swailem: The majority of people were naked: men, women, and the young people. They only dress when they feel they have something ugly that needs to be hidden.

Tharwat: How did you face that?

Swailem: After one month, you forget it. I remember a case that stayed in my mind. There was a girl and I remember her features when she came to Attar, (not our church), and Paul and I were walking near her village. She came to greet us, and Paul looked at her and said, "Ahhhhh," but I did not notice anything. Therefore, I asked what was wrong and he said that she had nothing on, and she was looking at us, wondering what was wrong. For to her there was nothing wrong with her body, so why would she cover it? They covered in the church, but not outside. That is why when they come to school we had to pay for their clothes. To them nakedness had nothing to do with immorality.

Tharwat: So you could manage that.

Swailem: Yes, yes I could, it was not really a problem at all.

Tharwat: What were the difficulties you faced, especially in culture and life?

Swailem: We had almost no resources. I had someone who could plant some crops in the ranch between the branch and the Nile. We had a huge area which was excellent for gardening, so we had somebody to plant it for us with vegetables and so on. We had fruit trees – mangos grow there wild. Of course there were things hurt during the dry season and if it went longer than usual, someone might die.

We used to receive mail every two weeks. If you missed it, your mail would stay for two more weeks. They brought the mail on the beach, so we did not lose it. They passed it onto the shore and bundled it together. Then you could pass by and pick it up. They put your name in big letters but if you do not catch it, then you would not send mail. And we had no telephones at all.

Tharwat: Did you have electricity?

Swailem: We had no electricity and no running water. We had a tank at the top of the house with pipes going to the bathroom and we had another person working, who brought the clean water from the depths of the Nile, and he carried all that up the ladder to the tank. We also had 3–4 pottery jars to put the drinking water for the villagers who were passing by.

My house was a place for the workers who left their work in the river; for those who were not hunting or preparing for a dance. Somehow, each one knew his own spear or his own shed! The pottery jars were at the house but in an easily accessible place. They used to leave their things in the house and come back later to take them.

Tharwat: So you lived your life exactly like a Shilluk.

Swailem: As closely as I could.

Tharwat: What about your children?

Swailem: They were born there.

Tharwat: Was it not uncomfortable for them there?

Swailem: No, not at all. The kids went to play with the nearby kids and they used to come and play with them. They adjusted easily but they were in preschool. Samira taught them how to read and write at home and told them stories.

Tharwat: But they did not go to schools?

Swailem: No, there were no schools and they were not old enough to go anywhere.

Tharwat: Tell me more about the political situation that led you to leave.

Swailem: Of course, that was in 1960. About 1958 or 1959, the British gave Northern Sudan its independence, but we still had a British government in the South. Northern Sudan managed somehow to embarrass Britain in front of the United Nations, so Britain made Northern Sudan responsible for the South.

Tharwat: Before that, was it Egypt and Britain?

Swailem: Not in the South.

Tharwat: Did Egypt have authority in the North only?

Swailem: The only authority Egypt had in the South was the inspection of the sources of the Nile. They inspected by boat and they never left the boat. Actually, they were scared to death to leave the boat. So the only Egyptian presence in the South concerned the water of the Nile. Nevertheless, they had political power only in the North, but nothing with the South. I think that is why Islam was not there and it was blessing.

Tharwat: So, Britain gave the authority to the North.

Swailem: Yes, Britain gave the authority to the North, but I think that after independence Britain was reluctant to give the authority to the North.

They started sending people to hospitals, and schools, headmasters and teachers. A small number of Northerners began to appear in the South but that was gradually and very slowly. Most of the government of Malakal, for instance, became Northern and as soon as the governor came. He stayed in Malakal and we became very good friends.

Tharwat: Was he a Sudanese?

Swailem: Yes, and he and his wife became our friends. They came to our station, and they used to come by boat and invited us to dinner, travel, eat and stay with them in the American Mission station and this continued until I think 1962.

Because of the exploration by American oil companies, petroleum was found in the South. That was when the North became very keen about possessing the South, since petroleum is a moneymaker. In 1961–1962, they started to have a military presence in the South through military ships in the Nile. We began seeing military things at various stations. Actually, my station became a camp full of the military. Then the South felt that and they did not actually have an army, but just a group of policemen, so they started to secretly train so that they could fight the Northerners.

Tharwat: Before that, was the government present in the South?

Swailem: No, each province has its own, Upper Nile in Malakal, Equatorial in Joppa and Bahr El Gazal in the Waw.

Tharwat: Was this under the British?

Swailem: Yes, but it was ruled by the tribal leaders, so the South decided to resist the presence of the Northern. In secret, they began with very weak military power: they had very few military weapons, and very little equipment which they got from Ethiopia, Somalia, and so on. The missionaries were never involved in that. Moreover, with these simple weapons they thought they could fight or at least frighten the Northerners.

Therefore, they started to attack, but the North was ready, so they counter-attacked and re-attacked to suppress the uprising in the South which was like an underground uprising. The Northerners were vicious and won easily in the beginning of 1962. They started to kick out the missionaries, thinking that they were helping the uprising, which was not true.

The head of the uprising in the South was John Garang, whom I knew, and he came to Attar later. I loved him and of course, it was stupid to link him to me. We were far away and we just wanted the South to enjoy their freedom. We had nothing to do with the oil. If they are going to explore it and drill it, for whomever, it was not our concern and we did not care about it.

So the North kicked us out using persuasion not force. The governor of Malakal was my friend and he called me saying, "Swailem you are tired." I told him "I'm not." Then he said, "No, you are tired and you need a vacation." I told him, "I really do not need a vacation." Anyway, at the end he said, "I will tell you the truth. I have orders that you must leave and I do not want to force you to leave. Do not take anything but leave everything and I promise you . . . " and he swore twenty-five times that we would be back and he would send me the visa for my family to go to Egypt. Moreover, at the end he said, "These are the orders. I'm sorry, you have to obey." After two week we came back to Egypt.

Tharwat: After ten years of being there?

Swailem: Yes, after ten years of being there.

Tharwat: How difficult was it to leave?

Swailem: It was a trauma, not just for us, but for all the missionaries. We did not want to leave because we all thought that if we left, the church would be dead. We knew how vicious the North could be and they could destroy all the churches, and that the Southerners had no weapons at all. How could they resist such stupid power? So we were very sad. I held a meeting before we left and all the missionaries were really crying.

Tharwat: So, they kicked out all the missionaries.

Swailem: Yes, they kicked us out in three groups. I was in the middle group.

Tharwat: Then you came back to Egypt?

Swailem: Yes, directly to Egypt. I was distressed and I told them that he had promised that I would go back. But Farid Manqarious and the rest of the Mission committee told me, "Do not expect it, be realistic, it will never happen."

Tharwat: And you left everything there?

Swailem: Yes, I came with only two or three suitcases.

Tharwat: What happened there?

Swailem: Because of that, Attar was destroyed and when I went back after 5–6 years, I found it all destroyed. We had had lovely buildings there in the station, but they were all destroyed. We had had one of the best school labs and for sure, and I mean this, it had been the best school in the whole of Sudan. We had received contributions for the lab from all over the world and we had very good and comfortable clinic: the only one in the South.

Tharwat: You did not tell me about the clinic.

Swailem: The guy who was working in the clinic was paid by the American Mission, I did not pay him.

Tharwat: What else was there beside that?

Swailem: There were houses, and the school which had many buildings. It was really a thing of pride, very well built, and when I went back later, I found out that the Northerners had destroyed everything. Why, I do not know.

Tharwat: When you came back, Farid Manqarious and the rest of the committee told you, "Do not expect to go back."

Swailem: The amazing thing was that, at that time Kenya had been in touch with the Synod. One of the heads of the Presbyterian Church in Kenya, John Gatu, came and told our committee, or I'm not sure, maybe he went to the Synod. He told them that there was a great need for a missionary to go to Kenya. I think they were thinking of sending Mishreky to Kenya but I returned. So they said that God was preparing things, and told me to leave my family and go to explore Kenya. So I went and John Gatu was a good man and we became friends. I told them, "I'm tired, send me by boat," which they did, and I went by boat through the Suez Canal to Mombassa.

Tharwat: When was that?

Swailem: In 1963, and in the boat I met a missionary from the American Mission who told me that they were amazed to know that Egypt was sending a missionary and he made contact by phone or telegram from the boat and took me to the director's house.

Tharwat: Was he already a missionary there?

Swailem: Yes, he was and he was coming from England, working for the American Mission. The American Mission in Kenya had English and Germans. Actually, in my station later on there were two Germans.

So I went to Mombassa and from there to Nairobi, and that missionary helped me find transportation from Mombassa to Nairobi. There I went

to John Gatu who met me like a brother and we continued being brothers. He told me that there was a Theological Seminary in Limuru and he
wanted an Egyptian to work in that Seminary.

Tharwat: In Nairobi?

Swailem: It's outside of Nairobi. It was a mission station outside of Nairobi,
about 40 miles away.

Tharwat: Was it different?

Swailem: Absolutely. Kenya had lovely buildings, good transportation,
electricity, telephones, and everything. It was a civilized country. When I
got there, they asked me to be the head of a department in the Seminary,
which was run by the Anglicans, Presbyterians and Methodists.

At that time there were no Kenyans – Sam Kaptichia came later – and
they were all foreigners. Kenyans came later to teach and they asked me
to be the head because of my background. They asked me to establish a
department called "The Missionary Work of the Church in a Temporarily
Society." I worked at that and started to teach in that department. Later
on, I developed a lay training program and later I built a centre. I received
gifts for that from America, England and we had a first-class centre and
residence for students.

Tharwat: When you went to Kenya, you were still a missionary sent from
Egypt. Did they pay your salary?

Swailem: Yes, I was a missionary from Egypt, but I do not know how
they made the arrangements. When the war broke out between Egypt and
Israel in 1967 it was difficult for Egypt to send money. I think they sent it
through the American Mission because there was a strong presence of the
American Mission in Nairobi.

I went and told John Gatu that my wife and I were going back home. He
asked why and I said, "Because it is impossible to send money from Egypt."

He said "Why? Did not you receive your salary?"

I told him "Yes, and I'm not here to complain. I'm coming here to tell
you that I do not want to take money from the Kenyan Church or from
the Presbyterian Church of East Africa."

He was a funny guy, so he said, "Is that your problem?"

I said "No, not my problem!"

Then he said, "There is a car waiting for you in the agency. Go, pick up your car."

I said, "What?!! What are you talking about?"

"Yes," he said, "I chose a French car (Peugeot). It is ready for you, go pick it up."

I asked who paid for it. Moreover, he told me that it was none of my business. He was very funny.

Samira and I were getting ready to go home, but at that time I was assigned officially to be a lay trainer, not in the Seminary, and not only for the Presbyterian Church, but for everybody.

Tharwat: So, at that time you left the Seminary.

Swailem: No, not at all. The centre for lay training was next to the Seminary building, an extension of it. John Gatu told me, "Now recruit people to work with you." That happened while I was going to leave. Really, the Kenyans were wonderful people.

It was through him and of course through the East African Conference of Churches that I received money. It was then the Kenyan people, John Gatu and John Camo who introduced me to Jomoo Kenyata, his wife Margaret, and his daughter. His daughter worked with me. They introduced me to the ministers of health, and finances. Mooy was vice president of the government and this gave me many open doors and soon we became like friends who had known each other for fifty years.

They had already earned their independence and there I was an Egyptian. I'm not a German or a foreigner but an African. They were proud of that. I did a new job and opened new buildings and when we inaugurated it, I invited Jomoo Kenyata and Mooy. Before he came the road between us and the city was painted. He and his wife came, and it was a great celebration. He gave the main address, he ate at my house, and he made Samira so upset. He wanted lemon juice and there was no lemon in the fridge, so we searched among our friends in the station till we found lemon at last.

After that, the doors of the government were wide open to us. I would go to Mooy for anything and he used to come and teach in my classes when I invited him, especially in the conferences.

Part of the lay training received support from the World Council of Churches, and sometimes we held international conferences. I'm not sure if there were Egyptians at them, because this was for all of Africa, and sometimes some Europeans also came.

Tharwat: This was besides your teaching in the Seminary?

Swailem: I was in the lay training centre.

Tharwat: What was the ministry of that lay training centre?

Swailem: It was training for the church.

Tharwat: What was it?

Swailem: A great range and variety: pastors would return for refresher courses; and the laity would come to be prepared for youth work in particular. We also had Christian nurses, many, many times, to learn what it means to be a Christian nurse working in a hospital or a clinic. Teachers came from schools to learn what it means to be a Christian teacher in a school. This included teaching the Bible as a subject in schools.

It was a very busy place, but I did not do the work alone but recruited people to do it with me. At one time, I had 15 to 17 people working under my leadership; among them were two Germans, two or three Americans, three or four British, and I had enough houses for all of them.

Tharwat: These houses were owned by the Seminary?

Swailem: Yes, and the centre. The support for the centre came from Britain and Scotland, which donated a lot of money and from America as well. After 1967, God knows from where my salary came, I do not know! Of course, they continued to pay my salary and even increased it. I had 5–6 cars that belonged to the centre and I had my own driver. It was a big business. I had a cook, a personal secretary, gardener, and someone to bring me the mail. I did not go to bring it, which is impossible really to believe it. Until now, I honestly and logically do not understand how I was raised to such a position.

Then I had guests from Egypt, too, such as Fayez Fares.

Tharwat: Did they come as personal guests, not in an official way?

Swailem: Yes, and my very good friend Labib Kaldass also came.

Tharwat: Did you need to write reports to the church here in Egypt?

Swailem: I confess, no, there was no time because I was so busy. I would work 14 to 15 hours a day in Kenya, and that's the truth. At the end of the day I couldn't do anything, all I wanted was to go and rest for 3 or 4 hours. But it was all enjoyable. During that time God gave us new work and we started to work among the Maasai people. They had no church and we had to go first to the chief and we started in the open air as we had in Southern Sudan. We also had another Christian presence in the slums of Nairobi, in Pumwani and Massai where there was already a Christian presence: many were already baptized.

Tharwat: What did you do in that area? Was it a kind of evangelism?

Swailem: In the Church of Nairobi, students came with me to preach. Usually in Kenya we had the advantage of using Swahili, which was the language everyone knew.

Tharwat: I heard that during your time there, you made your research in the slum area and developed it.

Swailem: Yes, Pumwani was an area for the poor people. It was a slum and it was as if the British, when they ruled, had pushed that area away from the city. The main city was beautiful but outside the city, it was for the trash of Kenya: a place of prostitution, drug addiction, and people in sin. Therefore, when I took my students to work there, I worked with them the first time and I used the old methods of having a tape player, and a table. We could carry things because we had cars, and we could carry it on, and we had books, etc. We invited people to come and listen on Sundays and later we went during the week. We offered them the gospel, asking them to accept Christ and to be baptized. Then they built a church, their own church, and so we sent them a pastor.

Tharwat: Did they come from a Christian background?

Swailem: Yes, Maasai was another slum area, but there was depletion in the ground. It was because when you were driving you could see it from the road. We could not go by car but we used to leave it on the road and go by foot to reach it. They call it Maasai valley. They were very poor but they were not immoral. In Pumwani there were prostitutes, but not in Maasai. They were from numerous tribes and very poor. They worked as daily labourers in the city and came back to their shantytown. This was where I did the first development work among the Berber. I had never done that before.

Our work in Maasai was to improve their living conditions. They were living in slums, very poor people, labourers, at the very bottom of the ladder. We started a church there very quickly, actually, we used one of their very old residential places, and the congregation started right away. We had a Kenyan Church, in Swahili. These were the two places in Nairobi where we worked among the tribes. We started among the Maasai who were non-Christians.

Tharwat: Was it outside of Nairobi?

Swailem: Yes, quite a distance from Nairobi. It used to take one and half to two hours from my station to get to Olasiuos, next to Maasai Hill. The people there had never heard of Christ and they had their own worship on that hill and all over the place. When I went there, I used the same methods I had used in Southern Sudan. It was a real privilege that the chief assigned by the government had been educated somehow and exposed to the gospel. He was very happy to receive us and so we started as we had in Sudan. We started a congregation and a school at the same time.

Tharwat: Under your supervision, through that centre?

Swailem: Yes.

Tharwat: From where did you get your support?

Swailem: After 1967, the support from Egypt stopped, so again I went to John Gatu, and as I told you I do not know from where.

Tharwat: Was your work supported from the centre?

Swailem: Yes, I had a large and generous budget for the centre and I could use the money. I told you we could have 16 or 17 people working full time in the centre. It was really a privilege to work there.

Tharwat: What about your research?

Swailem: My research started first through a connection with Pittsburgh in the United States, and then later on, it was shifted to Northwestern University in Chicago. I was working at the centre and because of that my main work was among Pumwani and Maasai. I did not get cases from Maasai, all my cases were from Pumwani. The entire project was about how to help them and improve the conditions they were living in. We first looked at how to help them by addressing their disconnectedness. They did not really have family relationships, as a woman had a man living with her, or 2–3 men, and that was not a family. We tried to make them understand the meaning of a family and tried to interview them. I had a team to work with and we received money for the research. We had the same set of interview questions. We started with a preliminary set of questions using personal interviews. All of my workers used the same questionnaire, but before they went, we would train them in how to use the questionnaire, and to ensure that all of them used the same approach. At the end of a free conversation, which they recorded but most of them had that from the questionnaire. We sent that and we surveyed 500–600 cases. The project was supported by the head of the Social Work in Nairobi, a friend of mine, he was a Christian, and we became friends. His office paid for it, hiring people, and overseeing the cost which his office paid for. We agreed from the very beginning that I would submit the reports to them because they were going to rebuild Pumwani and remove all the huts. I went and met the minister of social services and we agreed that we they would not move the people. I told them that if they did this, I would not do the research. I really refused until they wrote down that they would not move the people until after they had built new houses and then they would move the people gradually. After the people were relocated, they would bulldoze the old houses and build new ones. That was the way it was done, and I think we interviewed more than 500 people.

Tharwat: Did you get a degree based on that [research]?

Swailem: No, no degrees. It was only research and for my own satisfaction as a Christian and worker under the instruction of the Ministry of Social Work. It was agreed with them that I was free to keep a copy of the original and to do whatever I wanted with that.

Tharwat: Tell me more about the aspects of your work in Kenya, for example, how all the denominations worked together. Can you tell me more about that?

Swailem: One of them was through the Seminary. The Anglicans, Presbyterians, and Methodists ran it. It was run beautifully in a lovely, beautiful place that was 7,500 feet high above the sea level.

Tharwat: Could you breathe there?

Swailem: It was at the equator and it was cold all the year. We had no summer at all, and even the rain came at night. It was quite lovely, and the whole place had lovely green hills, simply majestic. Through my department, I introduced the idea that after everybody in the Seminary on Sunday went and preached in or outside of Nairobi, that when we returned for the evening service to have communion, we would alternate service styles. I introduced the idea that, an Anglican would serve the communion as the Presbyterians did, and I would serve it as the Anglicans do, and so on, with the others. We took turns in that and it was delightful. The Methodists initiate but the Anglicans use the Presbyterian form and in this way, the students who came from different parts of Kenya, Tanzania, and Uganda of course engaged with us.

Tharwat: Did the work include other denominations in the centre?

Swailem: Yes, all of them. I think all the denominations were represented and I think that this was one of the things in Kenya that I enjoyed very much. Although I was a Presbyterian and a member in the Presbytery of Nairobi all the time, they knew what I was doing and I had their blessings.

Tharwat: When did the Mission Committee in Egypt stop?

Swailem: I think with the war in 1967, the relationship was broken for good. Most likely John Gatu continued corresponding with Egypt but he was able to get resources from other parts of the world.

Tharwat: Tell me more about your role as a peacemaker in Sudan and in Palestine.

Swailem: While I was in Kenya, the Government of Sudan in the North led by Sadek El-Mahdi as prime minister and Ishmael Azhary as president, they went to the Pan-Africa Council of Churches in which I was an active member. The government asked them to send a member to be a mediator between the North and the South. Remember, this was Muslims asking the Christians to do that. The Pan-Africa Council of Churches had been formed years before, and actually, I was one of its founders.

Somehow, by the grace of God, this happened and the head of the council was a friend of mine, Sam Mitha from Ghana. He started to be the main worker in that, and he got in contact with John Gatu and together they formed a committee to spend time trying to negotiate this. They chose the Governor of East Nigeria (Frances Cilia), who with his family later became our good friends. There were Sam Mitha, John Gatu, San Francine and then they chose me to work with them. I was number four in that committee and we first went to various countries.

Tharwat: All the four of you?

Swailem: Yes, we met the Ministers of Interior and Exterior Foreign Affairs in Moscow, and Geneva, France, England, asking them to support our efforts, and asking if they would support us if we reached an agreement. They were happy to see us doing that and we went to Sudan and were treated like big shots that I felt very uncomfortable with.

Tharwat: When was that?

Swailem: Actually, I made a report about that and I have it and the appreciations we got. It was in 1967 also – I think it was around that time. I have the originals.

Tharwat: Is it here?

Swailem: Maybe, we taped everything and I have records of everything. When we went to Russia, Geneva, Sudan, I would get permission to record. So I recorded everything and had a transcript made later, or I gave it to a secretary and had a transcription later.

Tharwat: Did you visit Khartoum after that?

Swailem: Yes, Khartoum and the Southern Sudan and I met with John Garang who was my student and we agreed on a peace agreement. It was written, that the South would be autonomous but not independent; it would have its own autonomous government. They would share the police force, the army and any economic income would be to the South. The Southerners would have their own parliament and government and there would be representation from the North in the South and southern representation in the North. There was a great celebration and the embassies were involved.

Tharwat: All that was in Khartoum?

Swailem: Yes, and then they respected the agreement. The war stopped completely and there was peace until 1970. When Ja'far Al-Numerry came to power, he destroyed it all.

Tharwat: . . . and the war started again until now.

Swailem: Yes, till three years ago. They almost stopped. You know they almost reached Khartoum, amazing how a small army like that could do this. They threatened Khartoum. I think it was a great honour to have been selected to be part of that group. Until today, I have the whole documents and no one has asked to take them away.

Tharwat: I also know that you had a role in Palestine. Did you do anything else concerning peace making in Africa?

Swailem: No, in Palestine only, I cannot remember anything else. In Palestine, the World Council of Churches asked us; because of the experience we had in Sudan, to start peace efforts. They had a group of us go and meet the leaders in Palestine and Israel. But I'm sorry to say we got nowhere.

Tharwat: When was that?

Swailem: After the peace agreement between Egypt and Israel, from there we went to the United States, but we accomplished nothing.

Tharwat: Let us go back to Kenya; tell me more about your work there.

Swailem: I think that was all I did there. Then in 1970, the Synod invited us to come back and take an administrative position at the Seminary in Cairo. By that time, I was ready to move from Kenya, I was very tired.

Tharwat: So, you spent seven years in Kenya and ten in Sudan.

Swailem: Yes, we did not observe taking vacations and that was a mistake, so I came here. We felt it was a real honour to come to the Seminary. Although we could have been citizens of Kenya. We were invited to take Kenyan citizenship but we told them we will wait and think about that, and it was a real honour.

Because our children went to English schools around Nairobi, we accepted the invitation to come back and right away looked for schools for our children. Samira's sister was working with the Ministry of Education and she knew high officials, including the minister Yousef El Taweel, himself. We thought that the American Mission school here would accept our kids. We were told yes, but that they must meet the requirements of the government, one of which was the Arabic language. The kids failed written Arabic.

So we went to the Minister of Education who received us very well and offered us tea. Samira's sister knew him very well and I told him that I was a minister. He welcomed us, we told him about our problem, and we promised that in one year the kids would be able to pass the Arabic exam. We asked him to admit them to school, and I think I told him that I was a pastor. He said, "No, I do not make exceptions. Not even to our own ambassadors."

So we immediately packed up and went to America.

Tharwat: What was the situation of the church here or what did the church or the Synod here do with that decision?

Swailem: Nothing really. Maybe there was a grudge or anger with us somehow, once we were rejected, we announced it and left. Some of our friends said that we could stay anyway. The American Mission here I think, McGill and Lorimer, told us that they could communicate with America and raise funds for the kids to go to schools in London and we could stay in Egypt. Samira refused, saying, "How could you put four kids in London and you stay here in Cairo?" Therefore, we packed up and left.

Tharwat: Was there any arrangement for you to go to in the States, or friends?

Swailem: No, there were no arrangements but we had some friends who had come to us in Kenya when I was working there. They helped us in our move to the United States. One of them in particular, McCormack, was at a Seminary in Chicago, and we ended up staying in Chicago. What was strange really that when he and his wife heard that we were going to America, they became very excited and came to visit us at our house. Before we went, they rented an apartment for us and I remember that it was in winter, January, when we left here. We went to their house and they showed us our apartment, and we spent a week at their house.

Tharwat: When was that?

Swailem: January 1972, so we started to settle there because Northwestern had published my research and had a place for me.

Tharwat: Before we start that trip to the States, let us briefly go back to the situation in Sudan. I know that when you left you were very upset because the church in Sudan might die, but was there another plan from the Lord about that?

Swailem: The amazing thing was that after all the missionaries had left, suddenly the Church, with the usual Christians, started to carry the gospel. There were no pay arrangements, nothing at all and of course, the war made them very definite and stubborn. Many villages endorsed the religion immediately and they became Christians. The majority now in Southern Sudan are Christians.

Tharwat: That was because of the seeds you and the other missionaries planted.

Swailem: The Lord used that, and I'm sorry to say that it is one of the things that illustrates that the Lord can work without us.

Tharwat: Tell me more about your visit after that.

Swailem: Yes, when I joined the peace-making committee I visited Malakal. We had several long meetings, for example, for the Moro we met for 6 hours, and with the Shilluk 8 hours, the Dinka 9 hours and so on. We had an English service in the evening. While we were there, the Church could not hold all the people. They were standing in the back yard; 8 acres of grass, 3 to 4,000 people were there. How and from where did they come?

Tharwat: Where was that?

Swailem: We found it to be true in Malakal, Joppa, and Waw.

Tharwat: And that was after you had left for many years?

Swailem: Yes, we left there in 1963, and returned in 1967. That was really a miracle; I could not believe my eyes in Malakal. That large crowed, when and how.

Tharwat: And the local people carried the entire ministry there?

Swailem: Yes, there were no missionaries at all. Our visit was for peace and we were the first foreigners to go there. I hope that it can be written someday, about the miracles of the 20th century, in spite of the changes.

Tharwat: Did you organize the church before you left?

Swailem: Yes, we did, we selected people and had elders.

Tharwat: What about the theological training, did you start any?

Swailem: Not in the Upper Nile. That work was mostly done by the Anglicans and Presbyterians.

Tharwat: Where was the Seminary?

Swailem: In Equatorial Sudan and later on it moved to Khartoum because of the war.

Tharwat: Let us get back to the States and your journey there.

Swailem: So, we went to Chicago, settled there, the six of us were at schools. I was very fortunate because in the Northwestern College, I paid only one term, and then I was invited to lecture.

Tharwat: You only had your master's degree from the AUC here.

Swailem: No, I also had my master's degree from Pittsburgh.

Tharwat: You got this by correspondence.

Swailem: Mostly.

Tharwat: Was this your first visit to the States?

Swailem: No, I went for my master's degree, the time between Sudan and here.

Tharwat: What was your degree?

Swailem: Master in Education.

Tharwat: All general?

Swailem: Yes, so I started to teach and they started to pay me.

Tharwat: Which field?

Swailem: Applied Social Sciences and then the head of the department invited me to teach a course. I made a syllabus, gave it to him and he was happy. From then on I was receiving a large salary, which at the time I couldn't believe. I continued my study and had my PhD in 1972.

Tharwat: Just after two years of your arrival?

Swailem: Yes, I think that master's degree from Pittsburgh helped, and then my research in Pumwani was a real blessing. It was already done and accepted by the doctoral committee. They were thrilled about it and I had already published a book and written a few things. I had written four chapters about the Meaning of Man and World, and for the Pan-Africa Council of Churches.

Tharwat: Were these chapters a summary of your research?

Swailem: No, my research was not published, I forget the name of the book but I have it and it is in my CV. All of that helped.

So as soon as I graduated, I received an invitation by the college of Kentucky, a Baptist Church College. The Dean met me in Chicago and he invited me to go and head up their Social Department. This was really one of the great things, when he heard of me and came, he had lunch with me and over lunch, he said to me, "Would you accept to be the head of the department?" And I exclaimed, "What!!?"

So as soon as I had finished my degree, we all moved. He also gave Samira a teaching position there, for she had her masters in counselling.

While I was in Chicago, the University of Illinois invited me to lecture there and again I was getting a little money from Chicago and Illinois. In both cases, I was lecturing about my experience in Africa and about Applied Sociology from a Christian perspective. When I went to Kentucky, they used to invite me to go and even paid my ticket, whether I went for a day or a week, they would pay my ticket.

Tharwat: What was your PhD research about?

Swailem: The Limuru.

Tharwat: So, you went to Chicago. I know there were two major things happened in Chicago; I need to know more about them, first starting with the Arabic meetings.

Swailem: OK. Well, right away after I went there, we held a meeting in our house, with the Egyptians and their families. When the other Egyptians heard that, we had a meeting at our house they started to come too. After a while they said, "We thank God for the house, but this isn't working. We need to rent a larger place." So, we rented a place from the Lutherans, and it was announced among the Arabs. They came and joined us, some from Syria, Lebanon, and Jordan.

We started in the house, and then at the Lutheran's place which had an advantage because it had a chapel outside the church. This meant we could meet Sunday morning and evening. We started some activities and bit-by-bit we began thinking of building our church. At the time, Rafaat Shehatta and Wafik worked with me and gradually the work expanded until the building was built. It cost half a million dollars and we did not receive any donations from anybody. I'm also proud to say that since my time in Kenya I have had no financial support from any church. All the money we had we used for the ministry. We even gave away money to Egypt and Jordan, but I received no money from the church.

Tharwat: You were their pastor.

Swailem: Sort of a pastor, but not officially. I joined the Presbytery as soon as I reached Chicago and I was accepted as a full member of the Presbytery, but without pay. I have all the rights as a member, and after two years the Presbytery was proud of our wonderful work, and that we had done it without taking one penny from them. They were not contributing.

Then the big discussions started about homosexuality. Our leaders were ordained by our Presbytery and one of the elders was a woman. When the Presbytery began discussing this issue of homosexuality, the leaders of my church rejected it and they came to me saying, "What is this? It is clear in the Bible that it is a sin. Are they denying the Bible? We are going to leave. The whole church is going to leave."

So I called a committee to come and listen. They came and then we decided that we had to leave the Presbytery.

I went to the Presbytery in a general meeting with 2 or 3 elders of my church and I told that we were sorry but we had to leave and become an independent church. This is what happened: we became registered as an independent church under the United Evangelical Arabic churches.

Tharwat: This was your church.

Swailem: The Presbytery was so sweet. In my speech I told them that we hadn't received any aid. They said that they appreciated that and that the money we had in the bank was ours. It was $120,000. I was surprised that there was no argument about it and that the money went to us.

Tharwat: It was from the church.

Swailem: The work of the church spread. It was a huge church that sprung up and it did not have to be Presbyterian. Some members joined the Baptist, some Nazarene and I did not object to that because we were recruiting pastors from all over and those pastors had families. These congregations sometimes received financial aid from different denominations. Moreover, all this grew from a small house meeting.

Tharwat: How many churches are there?

Swailem: Six, five with pastors and the one where I was helping which is a Nazarene Church. Our own has a pastor and it is an independent church.

Tharwat: I have two major questions about the role of the Egyptian pastors in the West, either in the States or other countries, – Is it missionary work or what?

Swailem: I think it depends on the minister himself. My own role developed because of my background as a missionary. Although even then, I couldn't totally ignore the pastoral work – in times of need, sickness, baptism, weddings, funerals and so on, there is no way you can avoid it. Most of the ministers who came from outside were pastors first. It is not easy because the immigrants might have very special kind of needs that we do not need here such as adjusting to a new culture, finding schools for children, dealing with insurance and hospitalization, establishing friendships, and becoming a part of the society. Therefore, the pastoral role is many-sided in a place like Chicago and the surrounding area. If somebody wants to be involved as a missionary, they can, but I do not remember any who did.

Tharwat: The other thing, when you were in the States you did not forget about Africa but continued to serve it. Tell me more about that.

Swailem: Actually, this is church-related as well as related to the past. We started to work in Malawi when we heard about a need there. Christians there live below the average income. So a group of Christians in all of Chicago formed a committee. We called it: Village Committee Enterprise Zone Association International. Then we recruited an agricultural engineer who was instrumental in all of this. He had served with the Peace Corp in Malawi. The Peace Corp is a group of volunteers who work under the American government, under the Branch of Development. They were students who were about to graduate from university. They would receive a small salary, but really, they go to help. They served in Malawi for six months and then came back. We heard from this man about the needs and the work in Malawi.

Tharwat: Is he an American?

Swailem: Yes, and he told us about the need there and he was willing to go back and work there, even without any support. We formed a committee and we supported him. We did all the work among ourselves. We were six or seven of us on the board and I was in charge of the curriculum for education, and the other six had other things to do. We supported him from our pockets or by receiving gifts. He was not married and that made things easier. We also started to go with him and spend time with him in Malawi. The work continues until today. He developed cancer and died five years ago. However, while he was there, he trained the Malawian people to work with him. The work reached twenty villages.

Tharwat: What kind of work?

Swailem: It included spiritual service as well as agricultural development, seeds, plants, nutrition, taking care of babies and pregnant women. It is a combination of social, physical and spiritual life. We worked in twenty villages and we turned over all our resources to a council that we established in Malawi. We continue to be their advisers, until today. I receive reports from them almost everyday.

The committee in Chicago disbanded, but those of us who were interested continued. Now it is completely in the hands of the Malawians.

Tharwat: How did your experience as a missionary in Africa affect this project?

Swailem: Of course, it was not a foreign land for me. I am used to working with the Africans and I think they have a common understanding about life as you may call it and we have common culture.

Because of the war in Rwanda I had been involved in another project there. The Minister of Health of Rwanda was a student of mine during his doctoral study. He was a physician and he and his wife became very close friends to us. He used to come to our house anytime. They have a little daughter, and I visited him when he was a Minister of Health in Rwanda. Nobody was expecting the war between the two tribes, the Hutu and the Tutsi.

I think the war started by the Tutsi wanting to be the rulers of the country and they secretly formed and trained an army in Uganda. They invaded Rwanda and the war began. There was so much pain and suffering. The reports say that one million human beings were killed.

I went to Rwanda after the war. Our friend and his wife fled and we helped them to run away. It is amazing that in all that country there are very few Anglicans, almost all are Catholics, and the whole nation is Christian. When I went during the war I carried relief. We had formed a committee in Chicago and gathered aid, medicine, food and so forth. We would bring the aid to them. Sometimes I went alone and distributed it to the Christian hospitals. They showed me a church and wanted to open it. I said no, that you could see the blood all over. Until that moment there were 500 dead bodies outside it. They had been killed by spears and I did not know. They kept it closed as a witness to the evil of civil war. I went to Rwanda 2 or 3 times carrying aid and I know some people in the government.

Tharwat: You were the only one that the Church in Egypt officially sent as a missionary, but this vision of mission did not continue. How do you evaluate this? And how can the church of Egypt regain this vision?

Swailem: The meaning of mission has changed over time. I think the main positive thing today which is possible now, is building mission partnerships between people from various backgrounds including denominations, various skills, nations, and not just involving evangelism, but also medical, agricultural and social services. The meaning of mission is through those partners doing it together. Again it is not money or resources which make mission right now – those do not really matter. The Church could give the people with a skill, like a doctor, the other can pay the cost and so on. We are at a stage in the world today which I think is very positive.

Another aspect of mission is that it does not have to be overseas. It is wonderful to do it overseas but it can be the next-door neighbour, reaching out from Jerusalem to Judea to Samaria. The church of Egypt is challenged today and I think we are in a state of slumber. I hope I'm mistaken but from what I heard yesterday and what I have seen, I think we are in a state of slumber. We have to wake up and get out of this, of being centred on ourselves, and reaching out in missions.

I think that mission would be the best means to wake up the Church and to increase its focus on others. I think that during the 1950s the Church was at its height because she was thinking of others and sending somebody. I think any church or congregation can do that and should be engaged in missions, no matter how small or weak. She will grow beyond her weakness when she gets out of herself and thinks of others.

When you think of all the negative issues we face in our country – how we can respond to that, and fight it? No, it is not by fighting, it is by giving positive input to young people, to the new generation, to overcome this negativity. These violent things that make people frustrated, do we have a role? Yes, if we adopt that vision we would have a very positive and constructive role in our country and beyond. So I hope through our [mission] department we can motivate the church to reach beyond herself and motivate her to get out of herself and forget her own interests.

Tharwat: You are a great example. Do you have anything else to say?

Swailem: No, when you think of something, come and let us talk about it and thank you.

Tharwat: Thank you very much.

Interview with Bakheet Matta Alexandria, 3 March 2004

By Tharwat Wahba

Tharwat: It is great to talk to you Pastor Bakheet about your ministry in Sudan. But why was it Sudan in particular?

Bakheet: It began when I was a student in the Evangelical Theological Seminary in Cairo. At that time Pastor Swailem Sedhom went to be a missionary in Southern Sudan. This made me feel that God was calling me to be a missionary there as well.

Tharwat: Do you mean that Dr Swailem Sedhom's mission inspired you?

Bakheet: No, my motive was primarily a missionary idea, but I had it from the very beginning and when Pastor Swailem went, I felt that the door was now open. So I wrote to Pastor Swailem who rejoiced at this news, because he knew me beforehand.

Tharwat: Can you remember when this was?

Bakheet: It was between the years 1952–1953 and after. The letters kept going and coming between us. Pastor Swailem was a friend of mine since I was a student at the Evangelical Theological Seminary in Cairo when he was studying his BA in the American University in Cairo. We lived together in the seminary hostel because, at that time, they had a vacancy.

When he went to Sudan, I kept in contact with him, and he used to send me news that no one else knew about except the Egyptian Mission Council.

Tharwat: Was there something called the Mission Committee?

Bakheet: Yes there was, its chairman was Pastor Faried Manqarious and its secretary was Pastor Onssy Abd Elmalek. Both worked in Sudan.

Tharwat: What was its assignment?

Bakheet: To collect and supervise the funds, and send it to Pastor Swailem. They were to receive his reports and know everything about his ministry, to encourage and counsel him.

Tharwat: Do you mean that this council did not supervise anybody but Pastor Swailem?

Bakheet: Yes, only him at that time.

Bakheet: Then the Sudanese government was angry with all the missionaries including Pastor Swailem and threw him out of Sudan.

Tharwat: Was it because of the civil war?

Bakheet: I will tell you all about it. At that time, the Synod did not approve my request to go to Southern Sudan for two reasons. First was the political situation in Sudan, and second were the Synod's financial needs. The Synod said, "We aren't able to sustain the one already there, shall we send another one? We're sorry, but we have no finances."

Tharwat: What was the political reason then?

Bakheet: Two governments, the British and the Egyptian, governed Sudan. There was an agreement between the two that if either left Sudan the other would also leave immediately. Thus, they continued to rule Sudan together until the days of Nasser. On 1 January 1956, Egypt and the British gave Sudan its independency.

Tharwat: Was there any revolution in Sudan?

Bakheet: No, not yet. When Sudan gained its independence, there a relapse occurred. This prevented me from entering Sudan.

Tharwat: Do you mean in interrelations?

Bakheet: Yes, someone called Ali Baldo, from El-Mahdi family, a police officer from Obiadd, West of Sudan, who was a representative of the internal ministry in the South, swore to invade the South with Islam. So he trapped twenty black Southerners, who were ignorant and from different tribes. He told them, "I want to do you a favour. What are you doing here?"

They replied, "We are shepherds, tending our sheep."

"What do you eat?" he asked.

They answered, "We eat from the corn that we plant."

He continued: "You are poor and anomic and I want to help you out. Just say one sentence: 'There is no God but Allah and Mohammed is the prophet of Allah.' Then we will consider you to be Muslims and send you to Egypt. There you will study from the beginning until you finish the Allamia (the PhD in Islamic Studies), and we will appoint you as callers for Islam. Your salary will be 200 Sudanese Pounds."

This was considered a fortune at the time. My salary was only 35 Sudanese Pounds. Thus, anyone can easily be tempted by such an amount of money. Furthermore, he told them, "We will build you houses, furnish it for you, we'll allow you to marry four wives (you'll have the right to do so, if you want), and we will educate your children. All this will be yours, if you just say this little sentence." Immediately the twenty recited it.

I met one of them in the students' youth club in Cairo who told me in English, "They brought me here to become a caller of Islam, which I myself do not know anything about. Moreover, when I came, I could not understand it and thus I cannot accept it. How then can I be a caller of something I am not convinced of? Here is what I am going to do, I will flee to any African country, and there I will declare my Christianity."

This was one of the twenty, and obviously, he was the only one, because all the rest returned to Sudan as Muslim callers, and they worked among the Southerners. This was when Pastor Swailem was there. At that time, the Muslims failed with the evangelicals and the non-Christians, but succeeded among the Catholics.

Do you have any idea how they got rid of the evangelicals? They caught all the evangelical church pastors. Meanwhile, all the other evangelical churches in the South were out of work (the Anglican, the Dutch Reformed, and all the rest). As a result, Bishop Gwynne suggested that they could unite them all into one presbytery called The United Church of Christ in Southern Sudan. That was a cunning idea from the bishop, to make them all Anglicans and under his supervision. But he failed in his attempt. They all became Presbyterians, and formed one Presbytery in the South which was independent from the North.

Tharwat: Is it still there until now?

Bakheet: Yes, but let me point out an important thing. They caught all the evangelical pastors, bishops, deacons, and all types of church leaders.

Tharwat: Did they cast them out of the country?

Bakheet: No, they beheaded them.

Tharwat: Oh Lord, were all of them Sudanese?

Bakheet: Yes. In this way, the Southern churches lost all their leaders.

Tharwat: Was this in the 1950s?

Bakheet: Yes. The Catholics realized what the Muslims were up to, their priests began warning their children, and indeed you know the authority of the Catholic Church.

Tharwat: Yes, of course.

Bakheet: So in this way, the door was closed for the Catholics, and as a result, they threw all the Catholic priests out of the country and considered them "unwanted or undesirable persons." These priests were Italians and if they had harmed them, there would have been political conflict between the government of Italy and the government of Sudan. So they sent all the Catholic priests out of the country. In this way, the Christians in Southern Sudan lost all their leaders.

After thirteen years of hurting, exiling, killing and harming the church leaders, relief finally came. In the meeting of the council of the Sudanese churches which was held in Addis Ababa, and headed by the Emperor Haile Selassie, there came [Sudanese] President Numeiry, telling the Emperor that he was the only one who could solve this problem. That is what happened. The World Council of Churches solved it by enacting certain decrees, as follows:

1) Religious freedom is a right for all Sudanese.
2) No one is to be forced to follow any religion.
3) All the churches which were destroyed, harmed or burned, will be rebuilt at the expense of the Sudanese government, and that which was built in hay will be built in concrete.
4) The Sudanese constitution will guarantee their religious freedom.

Moreover, this is exactly what was written into the Sudanese constitution enacted in 1974: "Islam is the religion of the country and Christianity is a divine religion to be guided by." An item which is not in the Egyptian constitution. By this we came to have the freedom and the ability to preach and fulfil our vision as we wished.

Let us go back to 1956, before Sudan gained its independence. At that time, the Southern part was called the British Closed Area, which no one could enter but the English people, the Sudanese from the South, or Sudanese officials from the North. At that time Pastor Swailem was there, but he was permitted to enter only as a member of the American Mission, not as an Egyptian. However, later he was forbidden, because of what Ali Baldo did to the pastors there.

In the year 1956 when Sudan was liberated, they announced in the North that any foreign resident working in Sudan as an official worker or trader or whatever, had two options. Either they could become Sudanese and take Sudanese nationality, or they had to leave the country. Because of that, 75 percent of the Egyptians living in Atbara left the country. The rest, around 25 percent, accepted to become Sudanese. Those either went to heaven, or were transferred by the government to other places, so when I reached Atbara in 26 of December 1966.

Tharwat: Was this the time of your beginning there?

Bakheet: No, it was earlier than that. I was in Obiadd for one and half years, at what was then called the American Mission station, from which the missionaries and the leaders came.

In 26 December 1966, the second day of Christmas, I reached Atbara. On my first Sunday there, in 1 January 1967, the only attendees were a white Egyptian widow who remained with those who did not leave Sudan, her daughter, one black man from the South, one black man from the West, and my family.

Tharwat: When was your first arrival at Sudan?

Bakheet: On 31 July 1965, I stayed as a guest at Pastor Raddy Illias's house in Khartoum, until I took the train to go to Obiadd, which I reached on 24 August 1965.

Tharwat: Depending on what?

Bakheet: It depended on the decision of the Mission Council in Egypt who permitted me to go to the church in Obiadd, as a pastor by name, but also as a missionary. Consequently, after my mission work there for one and half years, it gradually became a church.

Tharwat: What was the nature of your mission work?

Bakheet: First, I began teaching catechisms, and then leading people into Christian life. Consequently, those who had accepted the Lord Jesus Christ as their Saviour were baptized, and added to the group of believers in the church. It was a newly organized church but still considered the American Mission station.

Tharwat: Did you belong to the American Mission station, and were funded by it?

Bakheet: No, we did not belong to it, and it only funded us in a minor way. They used to send money to the Synod in Egypt and the Synod sent us some of it.

Tharwat: Was the American Mission in Egypt funding you or the Sudanese?

Bakheet: No, Sudan had its independent presbytery. Before that, I had gone in 1963, and they had two presbyteries, one in the North, and another in the South. The Southern one was very independent and had been independent a long time before, but the North got its independence in 1963, for political reasons in Sudan. When I reached there, I had to take permission from the National General Security as a foreign pastor, even though the church was ours.

Tharwat: Sir, before that, about the church in Obiadd. Who founded it, the Egyptians or the Americans?

Bakheet: The Americans founded it.

Tharwat: Was there any Egyptian serving in it before you?

Bakheet: There was an evangelist whom I knew, called Yoakim Abd Elmalek. He had graduated from the evangelist-training program. He was there temporarily until I finished the embassy procedures and legal papers.

Tharwat: So you were the first Egyptian pastor in that church?

Bakheet: And the first pastor to serve there after the Americans had left. From there I went to Atbara. When I went to Atbara, I worked among the Westerners and Southerners who had run away from civil war, hunger, persecutions, humiliation, and murder. They were ignorant, illiterate, and unskilled. They began learning skills while they were serving in houses. As the Evangelical Church, we helped them, teaching them how to read and write, arranging Bible study classes and catechism for them, and whoever accepted the Lord Jesus Christ as his Saviour, was baptized.

Tharwat: What were their backgrounds?

Bakheet: Yes, all those whom I worked among were non-Christians but of course I worked also between the two other churches present there, the Catholic and the Orthodox. I will tell you also about our relationship. Those we were working among, did not know Arabic or English, they had their own languages.

Tharwat: Did not they speak Arabic in their tribes?

Bakheet: No, they spoke with me in Arabic and in their own languages with their tribes. In Sunday morning services, I used to serve in Arabic and write notes in English for the foreigners who were attending and did not understand Arabic. During certain periods, we had four couples: two left and two others came instead. There were two German, and six British couples in all.

Tharwat: Were they working there?

Bakheet: The American Mission and the Mennonites had sent them to work with the Sudanese government in developing the education system. Some of them worked in teaching English, and French, and mechanical engineering. We in turn embraced them as a church.

The first couple I met surprised me. One day they came knocking at my door. When I opened it, I found a black man and a white woman in front of me. She did the talking, "This is Mr George Thompson, and I am Karri Thompson. May we come in?" I said, "With pleasure."

She went on speaking, "We asked in Khartoum about a church here, and they told us about you and your church, and we'd like to attend your church." Therefore, I told them that they were certainly welcome.

Tharwat: Tell me more about the missionary work.

Bakheet: Each group that finished the catechism classes and passed the exam, was asked individually about his salvation. Those who had gained the grace of salvation, we left for a month to verify it, to see if what they had gained was real or not. Then we baptized them.

During twenty-one and a half years, about 2,500 people were converted from their traditional religions to Christianity; all of them were Sudanese from either the South or the West. Some of them became pastors, deacons, and even missionaries.

The two pastors ministering in the church of Atbara, were baptized in it, its three elders, and three deacons (including the white Egyptian widow who was there when I first arrived) were all baptized in it as well. All of them began with a class in reading and writing, studying catechism, and attending Sunday services in Arabic with notes in English.

During the week, each tribe or group met to pray, worship and build up fellowship. They listened to their leader telling them the Sunday sermon in their own language or dialect. So they grew quickly and became spiritually strong. After a while, they planted two other churches in Atbara. One was in the suburbs, for, as you know the poor live in suburbs, because it is cheap to rent houses there. However, because of this our church was too far for them. So having a nearby church facilitated things for them. The government, who gave it to them in place of the church that had been destroyed when the whole district had been evacuated and demolished by the government, donated that church's land. The third church was founded because its people refused to elect one of its leaders as an elder, so he left and founded a church which he called the Church of Christ.

Our church was a Presbyterian Evangelical church. That is how there were three churches in Atbara. We also founded another church in Shinday, 130 km from Atbara, and we ordained a pastor.

Tharwat: How did you manage to serve and pastor these churches?

Bakheet: In Sudan, there was a school called the School of Evangelists. These evangelists were very well equipped and trained to do their work efficiently and to lead groups.

Tharwat: Who trained them and was responsible for them?

Bakheet: The Sudan Presbytery and all of its members were either Egyptians, or those having the Sudanese nationality. One of them was Pastor Helmy Hennein, who can tell you more about it.

In Khartoum there was something called the Sudanese Evangelical Council. It owned the properties of the American mission, and all its members had to be Sudanese. But Pastor Helmy Hennein was not – he was an Egyptian. Moreover, I was one of its leaders. That was at the end of my service there.

I went to Sudan in 1965, took Sudanese nationality in 1978, and left in 1988, thus holding citizenship for ten years. Atbara's church was at peace, because most of its members were Sudanese. However, this wasn't the case with the church in Khartoum or Umdorman. They were comprised of both the Egyptians and the Sudanese.

All of the schools in Sudan follow the Sudanese educational programs, except the Evangelical School in Khartoum, which followed the Egyptian system. When the relationship between the government of Sudan and the government of Egypt deteriorated, they closed the Egyptian University in Khartoum, as well as all the Egyptian schools. I am not aware of all of that because it happened after my leaving. But at the time of the British reign, the evangelical schools had great impact, primarily teaching of the Christian religion without any mention of the Islamic religion. Now since Sudan has gained its independence, the two religions are taught in schools. The Christians were very limited in number in both the governmental and private schools, so they made a special system for them. They had to learn religion in classes held in churches outside of school hours. Then they had to pass an exam. The marks they earned were then added to their total grades because religion was considered a major subject.

Tharwat: Pastor Bakheet, let me go back to the mission.

Bakheet: OK.

Tharwat: I would like to ask you two important things. First, who funded the mission there? Was it the American Mission, without any role from the Egyptian Mission?

Bakheet: No, nothing from Egypt. The American Mission was generally supplying the Egyptian committee with aid, but Atbara was supporting itself. At first, it was totally dependent on the Synod's support, a mere twelve pounds. Just renting the two houses, which belonged to the church, cost twelve pounds, so this meant almost nothing.

Tharwat: So, the local church covered the expenses of the work.

Bakheet: Yes, it came this way. There were empty houses around the church ready to be rented. Therefore, I invented a system for renting them, and raised money from this. Second, I made a system of pledges, which they had no idea about it. Third, I gave them a course in Christian stewardship, for, as you know they were a little group of people. However, the foreigners among them were rich, and had high salaries. So even though we were a little church we were able to collect much money. This is how the church was self-supporting.

Tharwat: What were the other activities in the missionary work? You said you had literacy and catechism classes. What else?

Bakheet: We opened a preschool, which opened its doors to everyone, (except the children of the church since most of them were older than that, and besides, there were very few married members. I can remember performing only four marriage services all my time at Atbara. Of course, some were already married when they came, but generally, there were not many families in the church.) The preschool was for all, because Atbara, if you do not know, is the capital of transportation in Sudan. The Ministry of Transportation and Sudan's railroad base was there. Moreover, the supervisor of the railroad was there, with all its administration, factories and stores located in Atbara.

Atbara was built mainly as a city for the railroad. The railroad owned half of it, which is the most beautiful part in the west. The people or the city owns the other half. All the people in Atbara were working in the railroad except those working in the health department, in banks, or in post offices, with very few traders, carpenters, and so forth.

These people came to my wife asking her about a preschool, because the government's preschool did not accept babies under 4 years old. They told her, "Our babies are really in need of true care. We brought nannies, but they drank all the children's milk, and beat them until they will die. Please help."

Ester, my wife, and I were still Egyptians and it was written in her passport that she was not permitted to either work for pay, or free. What should we do? She said, "If you can help me find a way to get permission, then I can help."

I told her, "Darling, you can't do it; it is very hard work on you."

She said, "If you are not willing to help me with this, I will deal with it by myself."

Tharwat: What did you do then? Did you succeed in opening it?

Bakheet: Yes, we did, and that preschool gave us the chance to enter Muslims' homes and pray for them. Even the Coptic Orthodox who were so fanatic, and never attended any evangelical church or met any evangelical pastor, welcomed us claiming that our sermons affected and comforted them so much.

As for the Catholics, things were different. They were open to us. I used to do our Christmas service in our church, and then, wearing my robe, I would attend their Christmas celebration, for we were neighbours. One year, the priest surprised me by telling the congregation that they would be listening that night to the Christmas message from Pastor Bakheet. I told him, "This is your church. Delight them by your words and be delighted by them." However, he insisted saying, "It is finished. I have said that you will do it."

Tharwat: Was he an Egyptian?

Bakheet: No, he was Italian, and the Catholic bishop was accustomed that whenever he came to visit Atbara, one part of his program was to come visit me at my office. When I went to Khartoum, I was to go visit him.

Tharwat: Beside the preschool, was there any clinic or school?

Bakheet: No clinic, but there was an evangelical school, and I was its director. Occasionally, I taught when any teacher was absent for any reason.

Tharwat: How was the relationship between you and the church of Egypt during your ministry time?

Bakheet: Like today, though maybe today it is deeper.

Tharwat: Do you mean that there was no support or follow up?

Bakheet: Not at all. Before 1963, a Sudanese Church representative used to attend the Synod, bringing a report about the churches there, but after 1963, this sort of relationship ceased.

Tharwat: Do you mean that anyone who served in Sudan then went on his own?

Bakheet: Yes, except for Pastor Bakheet, who was sent with the blessings of the Mission committee?

Tharwat: And did this committee stop its activity after Pastor Swailem Sidhom left?

Bakheet: I think so. Pastor Swailem Sidhom was kicked out of Sudan, went to Kenya, then returned to Sudan for a short period, and was kicked out again, and from there he went to America as immigrant. In my year of graduation, I spoke to Pastor Tawfik Saleh suggesting that we should add a subject concerning the church and mission awareness. He replied, "You are suggesting something that no one is concern about. Are you interested in that? Are you really ready to go to Southern Sudan?"

I told him, "There are letters between me and Pastor Swailem, and I am not the only one who is ready to go."

He said, "If this is the case, I will take your suggestion to the Seminary board." When he did, the board agreed and gave me the chance to offer a message which I concluded with a prayer: "My Lord, I am not worthy, but if this is your will let it be. My Lord here I am, send me," and I prepared myself to go.

Tharwat: So you had a missionary vision right from the very beginning.

Bakheet: Yes, very much so.

Tharwat: How can the Egyptian church restore its role in mission work?

Bakheet: It is very important for the missionary to have a motive of self-denial, and to be an adventurer.

Tharwat: That is as person, but I am speaking as institution.

Bakheet: I think by re-establishing a committee for missionaries, just as we have for pastoral and financial concerns.

Tharwat: You are right. We have committees for everything, except for missionaries. However, what activities would it have?

Bakheet: It would have plans and visions, and suggest things like, choosing students from the Seminary who shared this desire: taking them and training them for mission. I hope that finances would not stand in the way of the council because we have bountiful resources. We have enough resources that they quarrel about it. Therefore, I think it is very important to establish a committee or a council to gather funds, bring leaders able to train others, and gather students and missionaries.

In addition, missionary work comes only because of revival. They always say that revival begins with prayers and then repentance, but I say that repentance precedes prayers, and these two bring the revival.

Tharwat: And that is what we need in our church.

Bakheet: It is very simple. In the Synod of the Nile, we are facing a very dangerous situation: the same dangerous situation as the church of Ephesus who left her first love.

Tharwat: Her missionary work?

Bakheet: No, love for each other. We struggle and exploit, crushing each other's hearts. We slander, mock, and curse each other. We dig holes for others to bury them in, and in this way become honoured and extolled.

The church of Ephesus is present in the church of Egypt. The Lord removed her lampstand from its place and what a grief to me if the Lord should remove the lampstand of the church of Egypt as well. I wish, and this is my heart's desire, for repentance and prayer to take place, bringing revival, and accordingly the missionary work. May God bless our love.

Tharwat: Thank you very much. God bless you.

Bibliography

I. Primary Sources

A. Evangelical Theological Seminary in Cairo Archive

Al-Hoda, From 1911 to 1981.

Al-Murshed, from 1901 to 1911.

American Mission in Egypt, *Minutes of the American Mission in Egypt from 1885 to 1966.*[1]

"Extension of Mission Work on the Nile." In UPCNA, *The 45ᵗʰ Annual Report of the American United Presbyterian Mission in Egypt for the Year 1899.*

Giffen, J. K. *The Fifth Report of the Sudan Mission of the year 1905.*

Hanna, Gabra. "Second Annual Report of the Work in the Soudan in the Report of the Soudan Mission for 1901." In *The 47ᵗʰ Annual Report of the Mission in Egypt.*

"Report of the Soudan Mission to the Board of Foreign Missions, January to June, 1901." In UPCNA, *The Forty-Seventh Annual Report of the American United Presbyterian Mission in Egypt for the year 1901.*

"Report of the Sudan." In *The 49ᵗʰ Annual Report of the American United Presbyterian Mission in Egypt and the Sudan for the Year 1903.*

"The Second Annual Report of the Sudan Mission, 1902." In *The Annual Report of the American United Presbyterian Mission in Egypt and the Sudan for the year 1902.*

Synod of the Nile, *Minutes of the Synod of the Nile from 1899 to 1981.*[2]

---

1. The American Mission had two semi-annual meetings one in summer and the other in winter. From the beginning of its establishment the American Mission used the name Egyptian Missionary Association which was changed in the 1930s to the American Mission in Egypt and remained until the dissolution of the Mission in its last annual meeting in 1966.

2. The Synod of the Nile used hand written Arabic in its minutes. It started to print them beginning from 1969. The Synod used to have an annual meeting unless there was an

Synod of the Nile, *Minutes of the Year, 1901.*

UPCNA, Board of Foreign Mission of the United Presbyterian Church of North America, *Eleventh Annual Report of the Board of Foreign Mission of the United Presbyterian Church of North America: Presented to the General Assembly in May, 1870.* Philadelphia: Young & Ferguson, Printers, 1870.

UPCNA, Board of Foreign Mission of the United Presbyterian Church of North America, *annual Reports of the Board of Foreign Mission of the United Presbyterian Church of North America from 1870-1958.*

UPCNA, Board of Foreign Missions, *The 43rd Annual Report by the Board of Foreign Missions of the United Presbyterian Church.* Philadelphia: Board of Foreign Missions, 1897.

UPCNA, Board of Foreign Missions, *The 50th Annual Report of the American United Presbyterian Mission in Egypt for the Year 1904.* Philadelphia: Board of Foreign Missions, 1904.

UPCNA, *Minutes of Ninety-Eighth General Assembly of the United Presbyterian Church of North America: Part 1.* Pittsburgh: Board of Christian Education of the United Presbyterian Church of North America, 1956.

UPCNA, *Minutes of the Fiftieth General Assembly of the United Presbyterian Church of North America, Pittsburgh, PA, May 27 to June 1908*, vol. 12, no. 1. Pittsburgh: United Presbyterian Board of Publication, 1908.

UPCNA, *Minutes of the Fifty-Fourth General Assembly of the United Presbyterian Church of North America, Seattle Wash. May 22 to 29, 1912*, vol. 13, no. 1. Pittsburgh: United Presbyterian Board of Publication, 1912.

UPCNA, *Minutes of the Fifty-Second General Assembly of the United Presbyterian Church of North America, Philadelphia, Penna. May 25 June 1, 1910*, vol. 12, no. 3. Pittsburgh: United Presbyterian Board of Publication, 1910.

UPCNA, *Minutes of the Forty-Eighth General Assembly of the United Presbyterian Church of North America, Richmond, Indiana, May 23rd to May 30th 1906*, vol. 11, no. 3. Pittsburgh: United Presbyterian Board of Publication, 1906.

UPCNA, *Minutes of the Forty-Sixth General Assembly of the United Presbyterian Church of North America, Greenville, PA. May 25th to June 1st 1904*, vol. 11, no. 1. Pittsburgh: United Presbyterian Board of Publication, 1904.

UPCNA, *Minutes of the General Assembly of the United Presbyterian Church of North America, from 1860-1957.*

UPCNA, *The Forty-First Annual Report of the United Presbyterian Church of North America 1899–1900.* Philadelphia: Patterson Printing House, 1900.

UPCNA, *United Presbyterian Mission in Egypt for Year Ending Dec. 31, 1881.* Philadelphia: Edward Patteson, 1882.

emergency matter. This thesis used the original minutes which are now located in the ETSC Archive.

UPCUSA, *Minutes of the General Assembly of the United Presbyterian Church of the USA from 1958 to 1968.*

B. Presbyterian Historical Society, Philadelphia

PHS UPCNA RG 209-14-29: Alex C. Wilson Papers: Wilson to Donald Black dated October 18, 1954.

PHS UPCNA RG 209-14-5: Shields, Ried F. Papers: Reed to Mr Shields, dated 7 July 1931.

PHS UPCNA RG 209-14-5: Shields, Ried F. Papers: Reid F. Shields to Milligan dated November 7, 1931.

PHS UPCNA RG 209-14-9: Shields, Ried F. Papers: Reid F. Shields to Rev. Glenn Reed, dated March 14, 1950.

PHS UPCNA RG 209-21-53: Field Committee Handbook: Young Church comes forward: Foreign Missions Handbook 1947.

PHS UPCNA RG 209-22-56: Missionary Horizons: Donald Black to Miss Elith L. McBane dated December 21, 1956.

PHS UPCNA RG 209-2-54: Finney, Davida, Papers: Sawilem Sidhom to Davida Finney dated November 20, 1952.

PHS UPCNA RG 209-26-34: Historical Background, Egypt Mission: McGill, *the American Mission in Egyptian: Its Educational work*, 1957.

PHS UPCNA RG 209-27-5: Religious Situation in Egypt: 'Christian minorities in Egypt,' unpublished report: dated 1944.

PHS UPCNA RG 209-27-5: Religious Situation in Egypt: Christian minorities in Egypt, unpublished report, 1944.

PHS UPCNA RG 209-4-22: McGill, Willis A. and Anna S. Papers: Donald Black to Willis McGill dated December 20, 1957.

PHS UPCNA RG 209-4-22: McGill, Willis A. and Anna S. Papers: from E. E. Grice to McGill dated August 13, 1957.

PHS UPCNA RG 209-4-22: McGill, Willis A. and Anna S. Papers: from Willis McGill to Donald Black, dated September 18, 1957.

PHS UPCNA RG 209-6-22: Watkins, Bradley Papers: Important Event in the Nile Valley' dated 1953.

PHS UPCUSA COEMAR RG 151-1-58: Budget: from Willis McGill to Samuel Habib, dated December 17, 1968.

PHS UPCUSA RG 151-1-56: Arab-Israeli conflict: Martha Roy and Willis McGill, Report on the Middle East Crisis and the Egyptian Mission, dated New York, June 21, 1967.

PHS UPCUSA RG 151-1-58: COEMAR: Budget, from Fredrick Wilson to Willis McGill, dated December 10, 1968.

PHS, UPCNA RG 209-26-12; 209-26-13: Anti-Missionary Campaign, Summaries from Egyptian Newspapers: Dated 1933.

Sudan Mission Association, *Minutes of the Years 1905-1963.*

Sudan Mission Association. *The American United Presbyterian Mission in the Sudan, the 5th Annual Report, 1905.*

Sudan Mission Association. *The Sixth Annual Report of the American United Presbyterian Mission in the Sudan, for the Year 1906.*

C. Newspapers and Magazines
The United Presbyterian.

Times of Blessing. Sept. 14, 1876.

Kawkab Al-Shark, August 12, 1933; August 14, 1933.

D. Interviews
Hennine, Swailem, Interview by the researcher, March 5, 2004, Cairo.

Matta, Bakheet, Interview by the researcher, March 4, 2004, Alexandria.

II. Secondary Sources

Aboklog, Iskander Abiskhairoun. "A Profile of and Proposed Program for the Synod of the Nile." A Master's Thesis submitted to the faculty of the Pittsburgh-Xenia Theological Seminary, Pittsburgh, Pennsylvania, May, 1957.

Addison, James Thayer. *The Christian Approach to the Muslim: A Historical Study.* New York: Columbia University Press, 1942.

Ahmed, Hassan Makki Mohamed. *Sudan: The Christian Design: A Study of the Missionary Factor in Sudan's Cultural and Political Integration, 1843-1986.* Leicester: Islamic Foundation, 1989.

Alexander, D. J. *Should the American Mission Dissolve its Organization and Merge Itself into the Evangelistic Church of Egypt and its Organizations?* Assiut: Non-published document, 1939.

Alexander, J. R. *A Sketch of the Story of the Evangelical Church of Egypt: Founded by the American Mission 1854–1930.* Alexandria: Whitehead Morris Limited, 1930.

———. "A Historical Word." In *Kitab al-Yubil al-Almasi lil-Kinisa al-Injilia bi Misr wal-Sudan* (The Book of the Diamond Anniversary of the Evangelical Church in Egypt and the Sudan). Cairo: Matba'at al-Muhit, 1937.

Anawati, G. C. "The Roman Catholic Church and Churches in Communion with Rome." In *Religion in the Middle East: Three Religions in Concord and Conflict*, Vol. 1, edited by A. J. Arberry, chapter 7. Cambridge: Cambridge University Press, 1969.

Anderson, W. B. *Deputation Tour of Egypt: 1923-1924* n.p. report in PHS UPCNA RG 209-21-16.

Anderson, Rufus. *Foreign Missions: Their Relations and Claims.* New York: Charles Scribner and Company, 1869.

Annesley, George. *The Rise of Modern Egypt: A Century and a Half of Egyptian History 1798-1957.* Edinburgh: The Pentland Press Limited, 1994.

Anonymous. *Haya Lelmal: kholasset mobahs wa mohadrat fy nassb al-kanaes al-watanyea men altabisheer* (Come to the Work: Summary of Discussions and Lectures in the Role of theIndigenous Churches in Evangelism). Cairo: Matb'at Al-Neel Al-Masseheya, 1930.

Assad, Maurice. "Mission in the Coptic Church: Perspective, Doctrine and Practice." *Mission Studies* 4, no. 1 (1987): 21–34.

Atiya, Aziz S. *A History of Eastern Christianity.* London: Methuen and Co Ltd, 1968.

Awad, Jirjis Philotheos. *Tarikh al-Highumanus Philotheos* (The History of Hegomenos Philotheos). Cairo: Matba'at al-Tawfiq, 1906.

Badr, Habib. "Mission to 'Nominal Christians': The Policy and Practice of the American Board of Commissionaires for Foreign Missions and Its Missionaries Concerning Eastern Churches, Which Led to the Organization of a Protestant Church in Beirut, 1819-1848," PhD diss., Princeton Theological Seminary, 1992.

Bailey, Kenneth E. "Cross-cultural Mission: A Tale of Three Cities." W. Don McClure lectureship in world missions and evangelism. Three lectures presented at Pittsburgh Theological Seminary, 23–25 September, 1984. Audiobook.

Baring, Evelyn. *Modern Egypt: by the Earl of Cromer.* Vol. 2. London: Macmillan, 1908.

Barton, James L. *Daybreak in Turkey.* Boston: The Pilgrim Press, 1908.

Beaver, R. Pierce, ed. *To Advance the Gospel: Selections from the Writings of Rufus Anderson.* Grand Rapids: William B. Eerdmans Publishing Company, 1967.

———. "The Legacy of Rufus Anderson." *Occasional Bulletin of Missionary Research* 3, Jl (1979): 94–97.

Bosch, David J. *Transforming Mission: Paradigm Shifts in Theology of Mission.* Maryknoll: Orbis Books, 1991.

Burke, Jeffrey Charles. "The Establishment of the American Presbyterian Mission in Egypt, 1854-1940: An Overview." PhD diss., McGill University, 2000.

Butcher, E. L., *The Story of the Church of Egypt: Being an Outline of the History of the Egyptians Under Their Successive Masters from the Roman Conquest Until Now.* London: Smith, Elder, & Co., 1897.

Cameron, D. A. *Egypt in the Nineteenth Century or Mehemet Ali and his Successors until the British Occupation in 1882.* London: Smith, Elder &Co., 1898.

Carter, B. L. "On Spreading of the Gospel to Egyptians Sitting in Darkness: The Political Problem of Missionaries in Egypt in the 1930s." *Middle Eastern Studies* 20, no. 4 (October 1984): 18–36.

Chapman, Colin. "Rethinking the Gospel for Moslems." In *Muslims and Christians on the Emmaus Road,* edited by J. Dudley Woodberry, chapter 6. Monrovia: MARC, 1989.

Church Missionary Society. *Outline Histories of C. M. S. Missions.* Vol. 1. London: Church Missionary Society, 1905.

COEMAR, Advisory Study Committee. *An Advisory Study: A Working Paper for Study.* New York: UPCUSA, 1961.

Cragg, Kenneth. *The Arab Christian: a History in the Middle East.* London: Mowbray, 1992.

Dewairy, Metry S. "The contribution of the Western Church." In *Voices from the Near East: Chapters by a Group of Nationals Interpreting the Christian Movement,* edited by Milton Stauffer. New York: Missionary Education Movement of the United States and Canada, 1927.

Eccel A. Chris. *Egypt, Islam and Social Change: Al-Azhar in Conflict and Accommodation.* Berlin: Klaus Schwarz, 1984.

Elder, Earl E. *Vindicating a Vision: The Story of the American Mission in Egypt 1854 -1954.* Philadelphia: The United Presbyterian Board of Foreign Missions, 1958.

Elsbree, Oliver Wendell. "The Rise of the Missionary Spirit in America, 1790-1815." *The New England Quarterly* 1, no. 3 (July 1928): 295–322.

El-Masry, Iris Habib. *The Story of the Copts.* Cairo: The Middle East Council of Churches, 1978.

Etteldorf, Raymond. *The Catholic Church in the Middle East.* New York: The Macmillan Company, 1959.

Ferris, Elizabeth. *Churches Reach Out to Refugees in Egypt,* World Council of Churches Office of Communication. http://www.wcc-coe.org/wcc/news/press/00/18feat-e.html (accessed on 2 April 2007).

Finney, Davida. *Tomorrow's Egypt.* Pittsburgh: Women's General Missionary Society, 1939.

Fowler, Montague. *Christian Egypt: Past, Present, and Future.* London: Church Newspaper Company Limited, 1901.

Gairdner, W. H. T. *The Reproach of Islam.* London: Church Missionary Society, 1909.

Ghabrial, Samy Hanna. "The Growth of the Evangelical Church in Egypt, with Reference to Leadership." PhD diss., Fuller Theological Seminary, 1997.

Giffen, J. Kelly. *The Egyptian Sudan.* 2nd ed. New York: Fleming H. Revell Company, 1905.

———. "Letter from the Soudan." *Blessed be Egypt* (April 1902).

Goddard, Hugh. *A History of Christian-Muslim Relations*. Chicago: New Amsterdam Books, 2000.

Goodall, Norman. *A History of the London Missionary Society, 1895–1945*. London: Oxford University Press, 1954.

Gordon, Lucie Duff. *Letters from Egypt 1862–1869: Enlarged Centenary Edition*. London: Routledge & Kegan Paul, 1969.

Hanalla, Salih. *Hayat al-Qis Shenuda Hana* (The life of Rev. Shenuda Hana). Cairo: Matba'at al-Muhit, 1922.

Hewitt, Gordon. *The Problem of Success: A History of the Church Missionary Society 1910-1942*. Vol. I. London: SCM Press Ltd, 1971.

Hitti, Philip K. *History of the Arabs: From the Earlier Times to the Present*. 10th ed. London: The Macmillan Press Ltd, 1970.

Hogg, Rena L. *A Master-Builder on the Nile: Being a Record of the Life and Aims of John Hogg*. New York: Fleming H. Revell Company, 1914.

Hourani, Albert. *A History of the Arab Peoples*. London: Faber and Faber, 1991.

Hutton, J. E. *A History of Moravian Missions*. London: Moravian Publication Office, 1923.

Jindy, Hoda. "The Copts of Egypt: Neither Christian nor Egyptian." In *Interpreting the Orient: Travellers in Egypt and the Near East*, edited by Paul and Janet Starkey, 97–110. Reading: Ithaca Press, 2001.

Jowett, William. *Christian Researches on the Mediterranean, from 1815 to 1820, in Furtherance of the Objects of the Church Missionary Society / . . . with an Appendix Containing the Journal of the Rev James Connor Chiefly in Syria and Palestine*. London: published for the Society by L. B. Seeley and J. Hatchard, 1822.

Khan, Muhammad Muhsin. *The Translation of the Meanings of Sahih Al-Bukhari: Arabic-English*. Vol. 9. Medina Al-Munawwara: Dar Ahya Us-Sunnah, 1997.

Lansing, Gulian. *Egypt's Princes: Missionary Labor in the Valley of the Nile*. Philadelphia: William S. Rentoul, 1864.

———. *Religious Toleration in Egypt: Official Correspondence Relating to the Indemnity Obtained for the Maltreatment of Faris El-Hakim, An Agent of the American Missionaries in Egypt*. London: Privately printed, 1862.

Lewis I. M., ed. *Islam in Tropical Africa*. London: Oxford University Press, 1966.

Lorimer, Jack. *The Presbyterian Experience in Egypt: 1950-2000*. Denver: Outskirts Press, 2007.

Lorimer, J. "Presbyterians in the Middle East: A Retrospective." W. Don McClure lectureship in world missions and evangelism. Pittsburgh Theological Seminary, 1994.

Macmichael, Harold. *The Sudan*. London: Ernest Benn Limited, 1954.

Mansfield, Peter. *A History of the Middle East*. New York: Viking, 1991.

Mansour, Kamiel. *Elsheikh Mikha'il Mansour* (The Sheikh Mikha'il Mansour). Cairo: Matbaat Al-Moheet, 1929.

———. "The Status of Islam." In *Voices from the Near East: Chapters by a Group of Nationals Interpreting the Christian Movement,* edited by Milton Stauffer. New York: Missionary Education Movement of the United States and Canada, 1927.

Markos, Antonius. *Come Across and Help Us: The Story of the Coptic Orthodox Church in Africa in Our Present Time, Book One in Ethiopia and East Africa.* Cairo: Coptic Bishopric of African Affairs, 1993.

McLaughlin, Ralph. "Important Event in the Nile Valley." *The United Presbyterian,* (30 November 1953).

Meinardus, Otto F. A. *Christian Egypt Faith and Life.* Cairo: The American University in Cairo Press, 1970.

———. "The Coptic Church in Egypt." In *Religion in the Middle East: Three Religions in Concord and Conflict,* Vol. 1, edited by A. J. Arberry. Cambridge: Cambridge University Press, 1969, chapter 8.

Milligan, Anna A. *Dr. Henry of Assiut: Pioneer Medical Missionary in Egypt.* Part 1. Philadelphia: The United Presbyterian Board of Foreign Mission, 1945.

Moravian Church in America. http://www.mcsp.org/who_history.htm. Accessed 8 March 2004.

Murphy, Lawrence R. *The American University in Cairo 1919-1987.* Cairo: The American University in Cairo Press, 1987.

Nazir-Ali, Michael. *From Everywhere to Everywhere: A World View of Christian Mission.* London: Harper Collins, 1991.

Neill, Stephen. *Christian Mission: A History.* Harmondsworth: Penguin, 1964.

Padwick, Constance E. *Temple Gairdner of Cairo.* London: Society for Promoting Christian Knowledge, 1929.

Partee, Charles. *Adventure in Africa: The Story of Don McClure.* Grand Rapids: Ministry Resources Library, Zondervan Publishing House, 1990.

Parker, Michael and J. Kelly Giffen. "Launching the American Mission to Sudan 1898–1903." In *Gateway to the Heart of Africa: Missionary Pioneers in Sudan,* edited by Francesco Pierli, Maria Teresa Ratti, and Andrew C. Wheeler. Nairobi: Paulines Publication Africa, 1998.

Paton, Andrew. *A History of the Egyptian Revolution, from the Period of the Mamelukes to the Death of Mohammed Ali: From Arab and European Memoirs, Oral Tradition, and Local Research,* vol. II. London: Trubner, 1870.

Persson Janet. *In our Own Languages: The Story of Bible Translation in Sudan.* Faith in Sudan. Nairobi: Paulines Publications Africa, 1997.

Philips, H. E. *Blessed Be Egypt My People: Life Studies from the Land of the Nile.* Philadelphia: Judson Press, 1953.

Pierli, Francesco, ed. *Gateway to the Heart of Africa: Missionary Pioneers in Sudan*. Nairobi: Paulines Publication Africa, 1998.

Platt, Miss. *Journal of a Tour Through Egypt, the Peninsula of Sinai, and the Holy Land in 1838–1839*, vol I. London: Richard Watts, 1841.

UPCUSA, COMEAR. *Report of the Study Conference on The Christian Faith and the Contemporary Middle Eastern World, Held at Asmara, Eritrea, Ethiopia, April 1-9, 1959*.

Report of the Study Conference on The Christian Faith and the Contemporary Middle Eastern World, Held at Asmara, Eritrea, Ethiopia April 1–9, 1959. New York: Commission on Ecumenical Mission and Relations of the United Presbyterian Church in the U.S.A., 1959.

Richter, Julius. *A History of the Protestant Missions in the Near East*. Edinburgh: Oliphant, Anderson and Ferrier, 1910.

Roberts, Colin H. *Manuscript, Society and Belief in Early Christian Egypt*. London: The British Academy, 1979.

Ryad, Umar. "Muslim Response to Missionary Activities in Egypt: With a Special Reference to the Al-Azhar High Corps of ʿUlama (1925-1935)." In *New Faith in Ancient Lands: Western Mission in the Middle East in the Nineteenth and early Twentieth Centuries,* Studies in Christian Mission no. 32, edited by Helen Murre-van den Berg, 281–307. Leiden: Brill, 2006,.

Rycroft, Stanley. *The Ecumenical Witness of the United Presbyterian Church in the U.S.A*. New York: Board of Christian Education of the United Presbyterian Church in the USA, 1968.

Salama, Adib Najib. *Alengelioon wal ʿmal Alkawmy* (The Evangelicals and the National Work). Cairo: Dar El-thaqafa, 1993.

———. *Tarikh al-Kanysa al-Injilya f y Misr 1854-1980* (The History of the Evangelical Church in Egypt 1854-1980). Cairo: Dar al-Thaqafa, 1982.

Sanderson, Lilian Passmore and Neville Sanderson. *Education, Religion & Politics in Southern Sudan 1899-1964*. London: Ithaca Press, 1981.

Saram, Brian de. *Nile Harvest: The Anglican Church in Egypt and the Sudan*. Marlborough: The author, 1992.

Scudder, Lewis R. III. *The Arabian Mission's Story: In Search of Abraham's Other Son*. Grand Rapids: Wm. B. Eerdmans Publishing Co., 1998.

Sedra, Paul. "Ecclesiastical Warfare: Patriarch, Presbyterian, and Peasant in Nineteenth-Century Asyut." Yale Center for International and Area Studies, research.yale.edu/ycias/database/files/MESV5-10.pdf. (accessed on 16 September 2007).

Sharkey, Heather J. "Empire and Muslim Conversion: Historical Reflections on Christian Mission in Egypt." *Islam and Christian-Muslim Relations* 16, no. 1 (January 2005): 43–60.

Shelley, Michael Thomas. "The Life of W. H. T. Gairdner, 1973–1928: A Critical Evaluation of a Scholar-Missionary to Islam." PhD diss., University of Birmingham, 1988.

Shenk, Wilbert R. "Rufus Anderson and Henry Venn: a special relationship?" *International Bulletin of Missionary Research* 5 (October 1981): 168–172.

Shields, Ried F. *Behind the Garden of Allah*. Philadelphia: United Presbyterian Board of Foreign Missions, 1937.

Skreslet, Stanley H. "American Presbyterians and the Middle East." In *A History of Presbyterian Missions, 1944-2007*, edited by Scott W. Sunquist and Caroline N. Becker, 215–233. Louisville: Geneva Press, 2008.

———. "The American Presbyterian Mission in Egypt." *American Presbyterians Journal of Presbyterian History* 64, no. 2 (Summer 1986): 83–95.

Smith, John Coventry. *From Colonialism to World Community: The Church's Pilgrimage*. Philadelphia: Geneva Press, 1982.

Solihin, Sohirin Mohammad. *Copts and Muslims in Egypt: A Study on Harmony and Hostility*. Leicester: The Islamic Foundation, 1991.

Stephens, John Vant. *The Presbyterian Dhurches: Divisions and Unions, in Scotland, Ireland, Canada and America*. Philadelphia: Presbyterian Board of Publication, 1910.

Stock, Eugene, ed. *The History of the Church Missionary Society: Its Environment, Its Men and Its Work*. Vol. 1. London: Church Missionary Society, 1899.

Sunquist, Scott W. and Caroline N. Long, eds. *A History of Presbyterian Missions, 1944-2007*. Louisville: Geneva Press, 2008.

Swryal, Ryad. *Al-Mujtam' al-Qibti fil-Qarn al-Tasi 'ashr* (Coptic society in the Nineteenth Century). Cairo: Maktabat al-Mahaba, 1984.

Thompson, Robert A. *History of the Presbyterian Churches in the U.S.*, American Church History Series. New York: Lenox Hill Pub., 1995.

Tibawi, A. L. *American Interests in Syria 1800–1901: A Study of Educational Literary and Religious Work*. Oxford: Clarendon Press, 1966.

Toledano, Ehud R. *State and Society in Mid-nineteenth Century Egypt*. Cambridge: Cambridge University Press, 1990.

Trimingham, J. Spencer. *Islam in the Sudan*. London: Frank Cass & Co. Ltd., 1965.

Vander Werff, Lyle L. *Christian Mission to Muslims: The Record, Anglican and Reformed Approaches in India and the Near East, 1800–1938*. South Pasadena: The William Carey Library, 1977.

Vantini, Giovanni. *Christianity in the Sudan*. Bologna: EMI, 1981.

Virtue, David W. *A Vision of Hope: The Story of Samuel Habib, One of the Arab World's Greatest Contemporary Leaders and his Plan for Peace in the Strife-torn Middle East where the Cross and the Crescent Meet and where Bible, Koran and Torah vie Centre Stage*. Oxford: Regnum Books International, 1996.

Wahba, Tharwat. "The American Presbyterian Mission: Its Reception by the Egyptians." Unpublished MA thesis, The Evangelical Theological Seminary in Cairo, 2003.

Warner, Roland. *Day of Devastation Day of Contentment: The History of the Sudanese Church Across 2000 Years.* Faith in Sudan no. 10. Nairobi: Paulines, 2000.

Watson, Andrew *The American Mission in Egypt 1854 to 1896*, 2nd ed. Pittsburgh: United Presbyterian Board of Publication, 1904.

———. "Islam in Egypt." In *The Mohammedan World of To-day: Being Papers Read at the First Missionary Conference on behalf of the Mohammedan World Held at Cairo April 4th-9th, 1906*, edited by S. M. Zwemer, E. M. Wherry and James L. Barton, chapter 2. New York: Fleming H. Revell Company, 1906.

Watson, Charles. "Fifty Years of Foreign Missions in Egypt." In *Foreign Missionary Jubilee Convention: of the United Presbyterian Church of N.A. Celebrating the Fiftieth Anniversary of the Founding of Missions in Egypt and India, December 6-8, 1904, Pittsburg, PA.* Philadelphia: the Board of Foreign Missions of the United Presbyterian Church of N. A., 1905.

———. *In the Valley of the Nile: A Survey of the Missionary Movement in Egypt*, 2nd ed. New York: Fleming H. Revell Company, 1908.

———. *Report of the Visit of the Corresponding Secretary to Egypt and the Levant: With a Discussion of the Missionary Situation and its Problems.* Philadelphia: The Board of Foreign Missions of the United Presbyterian Church of North America, 1912.

———. *The Sorrow and Hope of the Egyptian Sudan: A Survey of Missionary Conditions and Methods of Work in the Egyptian Sudan.* Philadelphia: The Board of Foreign Mission of the United Presbyterian Church of North America, 1913.

———. *What is this Muslim World.* London: Student Christian Movement Press, 1937.

Watson, John H. *Among the Copts.* Brighton: Sussex Academic Press, 2000.

Watterson, Barbara. *Coptic Egypt.* Edinburgh: Scottish Academic Press, 1988.

Webster, Douglas. *Survey of the Training of the Ministry in the Middle East.* London: World Council of Churches, Commission on World Mission and Evangelism, 1962.

Wessels, Antonie. *Arab and Christian: Christians in the Middle East.* Kampen: Kok Pharos Publishing House, 1995.

Whately, M. L. *Among the Huts in Egypt: Scenes from Real Life.* London: Seeley, Jackson, & Halliday, 1871.

Wheeler, Andrew. "Gateway to the Heart of African: Sudan's Missionary Story." In *Gateway to the Heart of Africa: Missionary Pioneers in Sudan*, edited by

Francesco Pierli, Maria Teresa Ratti, and Andrew C. Wheeler. Nairobi: Paulines Publication Africa, 1998.

Wilson, J. Christy. *Apostle to Islam: A Biography of Samuel M. Zwemer*. Grand Rapids: Baker Book House, 1952.

Wissa, Hanna F. *Assiut: The Saga of an Egyptian Family*. Sussex: The Book Guild, 1994.

Woodberry, J. Dudley, ed. *Muslims and Christians on the Emmaus Road*. Monrovia: MARC, 1989.

Young, John M. L. *By Foot to China: Mission of The Church of the East, to 1400*. Assyrian International News Agency, Books Online, 1984.

Zablon, Nthamburi. "The Beginning and Development of Christianity in Kenya." In *From Mission to Church: A Handbook of Christianity in East Africa*, edited by Nthamburi Zablon, 1–36. Nairobi: Uzima Press, 1991.

Zwemer, Samuel M. *The Moslem World*. New York: Eaton and Mains, 1907.

———. *The Law of Apostasy in Islam: Answering the Question Why There Are So Few Muslim Converts, And Giving Examples of Their Moral Courage And Martyrdom*. London: Marshall Brothers Ltd., 1924.

Langham Literature and its imprints are a ministry of Langham Partnership.

Langham Partnership is a global fellowship working in pursuit of the vision God entrusted to its founder John Stott –

> *to facilitate the growth of the church in maturity and Christ-likeness through raising the standards of biblical preaching and teaching.*

Our vision is to see churches in the majority world equipped for mission and growing to maturity in Christ through the ministry of pastors and leaders who believe, teach and live by the Word of God.

Our mission is to strengthen the ministry of the Word of God through:
- nurturing national movements for biblical preaching
- fostering the creation and distribution of evangelical literature
- enhancing evangelical theological education

especially in countries where churches are under-resourced.

Our ministry

Langham Preaching partners with national leaders to nurture indigenous biblical preaching movements for pastors and lay preachers all around the world. With the support of a team of trainers from many countries, a multi-level programme of seminars provides practical training, and is followed by a programme for training local facilitators. Local preachers' groups and national and regional networks ensure continuity and ongoing development, seeking to build vigorous movements committed to Bible exposition.

Langham Literature provides majority world preachers, scholars and seminary libraries with evangelical books and electronic resources through publishing and distribution, grants and discounts. The programme also fosters the creation of indigenous evangelical books in many languages, through writer's grants, strengthening local evangelical publishing houses, and investment in major regional literature projects, such as one volume Bible commentaries like *The Africa Bible Commentary* and *The South Asia Bible Commentary*.

Langham Scholars provides financial support for evangelical doctoral students from the majority world so that, when they return home, they may train pastors and other Christian leaders with sound, biblical and theological teaching. This programme equips those who equip others. Langham Scholars also works in partnership with majority world seminaries in strengthening evangelical theological education. A growing number of Langham Scholars study in high quality doctoral programmes in the majority world itself. As well as teaching the next generation of pastors, graduated Langham Scholars exercise significant influence through their writing and leadership.

To learn more about Langham Partnership and the work we do visit **langham.org**

Lightning Source UK Ltd.
Milton Keynes UK
UKOW05f1436180616

276363UK00016B/179/P

9 781783 681037